The Leader's Handbook

Making Things Happen, Getting Things Done

Peter R. Scholtes

McGraw-Hill

New York San Francisco Washington, D.C. Auckland Bogotá
Caracas Lisbon London Madrid Mexico City Milan
Montreal New Delhi San Juan Singapore
Sydney Tokyo Toronto

Library of Congress Cataloging-in-Publication Data

Scholtes, Peter R.
The leader's handbook : making things happen, getting things done / Peter Scholtes.
p. cm.
Includes bibliographical references and index.
ISBN 0-07-058028-6 (pbk.)
1. Leadership. 2. Management. I. Title.
HD57.7.S357 1998
658.4'092—dc21 97-51902
CIP

McGraw-Hill
A Division of The ***McGraw-Hill*** *Companies*

5 6 7 8 9 0 KGP/KGP 9 0 2 1 0 9 8

ISBN 0-07-058028-6

The sponsoring editor for this book was Richard Narramore, the editing supervisor was Fred Dahl, and the production supervisor was Claire Stanley. It was set in Stone Serif by Inkwell Publishing Services.

Printed and bound by Quebecor Printing.

This book is printed on recycled, acid-free paper containing a minimum of 50% recycled, de-inked fiber.

I dedicate this book to the people who have given me a life full of love and support beyond measure or remembrance.

My mother (Mary), father (Peter), and sisters (Carol and Mary K.).

My children: Peter, Matthew, Jenna, and her husband Paul, and Ben. They have, each in a unique way, given wisdom, challenge, fun, and support to me and helped me to give back to them.

Peg, my wife and best friend, who is herself a leader and manager. Peg teaches me and helps me to be more practical and realistic. Along with all this, she laughs at most of my jokes.

Contents

Foreword

Russell L. Ackoff

Peter Scholtes is an educator, not a guru. A guru is one who develops a doctrine and seeks disciples who accept and transmit it without modification. No deviation is acceptable. Any modification is a sign of disloyalty, in fact, heresy. Its consequence is excommunication.

Educators, on the other hand, encourage and even try to inspire progressive deviations from what they have said. Their objective is not to remove the need for further learning, as is the guru's, but to initiate it—to provide a springboard from which their students can dive into their own minds, discover what is there, and develop it.

The number of management gurus is increasing at an alarming rate. We do not yet have one guru per manager but we are rapidly approaching that number. The ultimate success of a guru is to produce the fad of the week, becoming number one on the managerial hit parade. Successful or not, gurus preach panaceas the validity of which they pretend to have received directly from the Great Manager in the Sky, who actually resides in the mind of the gurus.

What educators teach comes from experience, their own and that of others, not from revelation. This book is a distillation and condensation of years of rich experience of one who has the gift of learning from it. Unlike most books that deal with management, this one is relevant to managers at every level, from bottom to top, top to bottom, and sideways. It deals with the interactions of managers at different and the same levels and their interactions with others. It takes a systemic view of management and focuses on interactions, not actions. It deals with almost every aspect of management at every level of an organization. As a result, the book is firm and very tightly packed. Therefore, a complete reading should not be attempted at one sitting. Time to absorb and reflect on the material presented is essential.

I suggest a small group of managers or students of management read each chapter separately but simultaneously, and then gather to discuss what they have read. They should discuss what they agree with, what they disagree with, and, most important, how what they

---

Dr. Ackoff is Chairman of Interact, the Institute for Interactive Management, and Professor Emeritus of the Wharton School. He has written 19 books.

have read will affect their behavior. Discussion should also follow up on previous statements about what will be done differently as a result of reading the book. The format and the clarity of the presentation encourage such discussions.

The book is about the need to transform management from the old style, command and control, to the new style, inspiring leadership. It identifies the many changes that give rise to this need including the increasing educational level of the workforce, the increasing technological content of work, the ability of most subordinates to do their jobs better than their bosses can (thus obsoleting supervision), the currently imposed constraints that preclude subordinates from using all they know that is relevant to their jobs, and the failure of managers to recognize the need for enabling their subordinates to do better tomorrow than the best they can do today—that is, to enable them to *develop*. The proper objective of a social system is not growth but the development of all its stakeholders. Growth, at best, is a means, not an end. (Preoccupation with it is pathological.) Development means an increase in one's desire and ability to fulfill one's needs and desires and those of others. It is only through simultaneous contributions to the development of all of an organization's stakeholders that the organization itself can develop. A wagon pulled by a team of horses can move no faster than the slowest horse.

Preface

In October 1992, I was in São Paulo, Brazil, presenting a two-day workshop for a large corporation with a deserved reputation for being well advanced in the application of the philosophy and methods of quality. At the end of the second day, I was approached by a vice president who was regarded as their leading teacher and promoter of Dr. Deming's philosophy. The gentleman looked me in the eye and with great earnestness said, "You shook my brains!"

At first I wasn't sure whether this was a compliment or a criticism. Then I saw the smile forming in the corners of his eyes. He was pleased that I shook his brains.

I will be forever grateful to that gentleman. He provided, in one short statement, a description of what I think a major part of my purpose is. I know that what I teach is often unconventional and sometimes controversial. I cannot realistically expect everyone who reads this book to accept my message.

In the end, however, I will have done my job if you emerge from reading this book with at least a troubled mind and shaken brains. At best, of course, I hope this book provides some useful guidance and insights into developing a better approach to leadership for all those organizations—workplace and others—with which you are associated.

These are some of what I propose to be the "brain-shakers," the unconventional teachings of this book:

> More than 95 percent of your organization's problems derive from your systems, processes, and methods, not from your individual workers. Your people are doing their best, but their best efforts cannot compensate for your inadequate and dysfunctional systems.
>
> We look to the heroic efforts of outstanding individuals for our successful work. Instead we must create systems that routinely allow excellent work to result from the ordinary efforts of ordinary people.
>
> Changing the *system* will change what people do. Changing what people do will not change the system.
>
> Certain common management approaches—management by objectives, performance appraisal, merit pay, pay for performance, and ISO 9000—represent not leadership but the abdication of leadership.

> Current buzzwords like empowerment, accountability, and high performance are meaningless, empty babble.
>
> Ninety-five percent of the changes undertaken in organizations have nothing to do with improvement.
>
> The greatest conceit of managers is that they can motivate people. Managers' attempts to motivate people will only make things worse.
>
> Behind incentive programs lies management's patronizing and cynical set of assumptions about workers. Managers implicitly say to workers, "I'm okay, you need incentives." Managers imply that their workers are withholding a certain amount of effort, waiting for it to be bribed out of them.

The history of the human race is also the history of human leadership. For thousands of years, leadership has been hierarchical in its structure. In the Book of Exodus, Moses' father-in-law, Jethro, advises Moses to do the following:

> Select out of all the people some capable, God-fearing, honest men with an aversion to improper gain, and set them over the people as captains of divisions of a thousand, of a hundred, of fifty, and of ten; let them act as judges for the people on all ordinary occasions; all important cases they shall bring to you (18:21-22)

This, by the way, makes Jethro the world's first management consultant. (Perhaps this explains why soon after, in verse 27, "Moses saw his father-in-law off" and Jethro was never heard from again.) This incident also establishes management consulting as the world's second oldest profession.

The point is that for millennia we humans have learned to expect hierarchy. This view was illustrated by the Prussian Army in the 1700s, using what is now the traditional organizational chart (see Figure 1-1, page 3). As we shall see, it wasn't until the mid-1900s that this hierarchical view was challenged.

A new approach to leadership began in Japan in 1950. At that time there occurred a convergence of needs, opportunities, and resources—the right people with the right stuff in the right place at the right time. People like Dr. Deming, Homer Sarasohn, Charles Protzman, Frank Polkinghorn, Dr. Juran, Ichiro and Kaoru Ishikawa, and others then and since are credited with starting a new industrial revolution. Indeed, because of them, the world of work will never be the same. This book represents a modest contribution to the continuation of a leadership philosophy that began with those who preceded Deming and the Ishikawas (Shewart and others) and has been advanced many who have succeeded them.

The theme of this book, therefore, is this: There is a new way to do business, a new philosophy of leadership, a new way to get work done. This new way is enormously more effective than the old way, and it is a whole lot more fun.

This new way, however, is profoundly different from what has existed since before Moses and what we have learned since our childhood. Our instincts and reflexes as managers are shaped by our experiences and past associations—our parents and families, the principals, teachers, coaches, supervisors, and managers of our younger years. Our instincts as managers are elastic. They have "memory." We can stretch memories and reshape them, but there is a great likelihood that they will revert to their previous form. Change for leaders is usually hard, even when that change is sincerely desired and earnestly pursued.

Sometimes the difference between the new way and the old way is subtle as well as profound. Here is an analogy:

> One Christmas my wife and I received two books of Magic Eye™ art. When you look at Magic Eye™ art, you see an array of colors and figures. You can, however, learn to focus your eyes in such a way that a three-dimensional image will emerge from the array of colors and figures. ("Look, it's a giraffe!") But you must learn to look differently. Two people can look at the same picture. One will see only the colors and figures, and the other will see something entirely different. (I have been told that people with an astigmatism cannot see the hidden three-dimensional image.)

The same is true of management. Let us take two people, one firmly entrenched in the old set of premises (behind every problem there is someone who screwed up) and one who has developed a systems view (behind every problem there is an inadequacy in the system). Both will look at the same organization, the same event, and the same results, and each will see something very different. After the disastrous oil spill in Alaska's Prince William sound, one will see Exxon's systems working dysfunctionally, while the other will see the designated culprit, Captain Hazelwood of the *Exxon Valdez*.

THE LEADER'S HANDBOOK AND *THE TEAM HANDBOOK*

The only other book I have written is *The Team Handbook,* published by Joiner Associates in 1988. To be presented in a sensible chronology, *The Leader's Handbook* would have come out *before The Team Hand-*

book. Leaders need to know *their* roles before they start establishing teams. But I didn't know then what to tell the leaders. Finally knowledge and experience have caught up to me, and I became ready to write this book.

The two books have much in common: the same basic philosophy behind them, the same values attached to systems, statistical thinking, relations with people, and learning to master improvement. The direction-setting activities described in Chapters 5 and 6 are what ideally precede the establishment of project teams. Teams will be far more effective when the larger context and purpose have been carefully planned.

I see the two books, therefore, as companion pieces. The similarities in title and appearance are intended to convey the compatibility of the books.

My hope is that those who over the past ten years have learned from *The Team Handbook* and who have taken on leadership roles will find this book equally useful.

A NOTE ON THE STRUCTURE OF THIS BOOK

Chapter 1 offers a short history of management philosophy. There are two reasons for beginning with some history. One is that I love history and find that I can personally learn better by understanding the historic context in which philosophies were developed. The other is that I believe history allows us to understand why certain beliefs have existed and why we may now be able to discard them. Understanding history becomes a prelude to change. Understanding history well is a prerequisite to improvement.

I acknowledge that Chapter 1's history is centered on U.S. management history. The management history of the United States is what I understand best, though I am also fascinated by the long history of management in Europe and Asia. The Industrial Revolution started in England nearly 100 years before it reached America. Nevertheless there are many parallels between what is described in Chapter 1 about the United States and what was occurring in all of Europe at the same time. The central influence of the military and the railroads and their shaping of approaches to management were factors in European countries as well as in the United States.

If you don't share my fondness for history and choose to skip directly to the following chapters, by all means do so.

Chapters 2 and 3 explain the heart of the new philosophy.

Chapters 4, 5, 6, 7, and 8 describe various practical applications.

Chapter 9 confronts the most harmful managerial assumptions and practices (performance appraisal and merit pay, etc.) and offers alternative approaches.

Chapter 10 offers a summary of what it means to lead and to be a leader in today's world.

At the end of each chapter are questions and activities intended to stimulate more thinking and help with the applications of these approaches to your own situation. With regard to these questions and activities, *there are no right answers* (though there might be many wrong answers). The questions are not meant to be tests. Their value should be in the self-searching they inspire and the discussions they provoke.

A FINAL THOUGHT

My good friend Bill Hunter and I used to talk about such esoteric things as the relationship between Dr. Deming's philosophy and the teachings of Teilhard de Chardin. (Since Bill died Clare Crawford-Mason is about the only person I know who understands both Deming and Teilhard de Chardin.) Pierre Teilhard de Chardin was a French priest, paleontologist/geologist, philosopher/theologian, and mystic. He worked in China for over 20 years in the early part of the twentieth century. He was a major contributor to the discovery of the Peking man.

Teilhard de Chardin wrote eloquently about the future of evolution until his death in New York City in 1955. He proposed that humankind is evolving toward greater consciousness and that love will lead humans to a new unity and an end-state that he calls the "Omega Point."

> The day will come when, after harnessing the ether, the winds, the tides, and gravitation—after all the scientific and technical achievements, we shall harness for God the energies of love. And then, on that day, for the second time in the history of the world, man will have discovered fire!
>
> —Pierre Teilhard de Chardin
> *The End of the World*

Intrigued by the optimism of Teilhard de Chardin, Bill Hunter and I would explore how Deming's philosophy can help humankind evolve into systems that create better places to work and learn, better government, better institutions of health care, and improved organizational pursuits of every kind. Deming's philosophy, we concluded, represents a means by which people can contribute to the evolution of the human spirit. Therefore, as you engage in improving your workplace and pleasing your customers, you may consciously be attending to the immediate benefits of improvement occurring at *this* time and in *this* place. But your efforts may be part of something far greater.

If this is true, then what was begun by Shewhart, Sarasohn, Deming, the Ishikawas, and Juran, and what is continued by the many of us who follow in their footsteps—including Bill Hunter and the gentleman from São Paulo—is more than a new industrial revolution. It is part of a new renaissance.

Peter R. Scholtes
Madison, Wisconsin

RESOURCES

Juran, J. M., Ed. 1995. *A history of managing for quality.* Milwaukee: ASQC Press.

Teilhard de Chardin, Pierre. 1959. *The phenomenon of man.* New York: Harper Brothers.

I welcome your comments, feedback, and inquiries. To get in touch by:

Mail: Scholtes Seminars and Consulting, PO Box 259327, Madison, WI 53725-9327

E-mail: Peter@pscholtes.com

Fax: (608) 221-4935

You may also visit my web page: www.pscholtes.com

Acknowledgments

It was Isaac Newton who said, "If I have seen further than others, it is by standing on the shoulders of giants." I give credit to the giants for my being able to see at all:

> Dr. W. Edwards Deming, from whom I learned so much and whose teachings changed my life.
>
> Dr. Kaoru Ishikawa and his father Ichiro, who were pioneers in the new approaches of leadership in Japan.
>
> Dr. Malcolm Knowles, the pioneer in the field of adult learning, who was my teacher and friend at Boston University.
>
> Dr. Myron Tribus, from whose writings I first became acquainted with Dr. Deming and the new approach to leadership and who has been a source of learning, friendship, and support for over fifteen years.

There are several others from whom I have learned and whose wisdom and insights are in my work:

> Dr. Brian Joiner, with whom I worked for ten years and from whom I learned immeasurably. If it were not for Brian, I would not be doing what I am doing today.
>
> Dr. Bill Hunter, my good friend whom I have missed since his death in 1986. My first effort to apply the philosophy described in this book was done with Bill at my side, teaching me, learning from me, and learning with me.
>
> Dr. Henry Neave, an author, researcher, professor, and one of the founders of the British Deming Association—and a good friend.

There are many others from whom I have learned who deserve more than the mere mention of their names. But at least I can do that:

Dr. Russell Ackoff
Tony Alderidge
Yukihiro Ando
Dr. Nida Backaitis
Dr. Edward Baker
Tim Ball
Joop Bokern
Dr. George Box
Bill Braswell
Roland Coates
Clare Crawford-Mason
John Criqui
Lloyd Dobyns
Lynda Finn
Maurice Fletcher
Liz Freeman
Tim Fuller

Conrad Fung
Dorothy Gill
Spencer Graves
Heero Hacquebord
Britt Hall
Knapp Hudson
Barbara Hummel
Masaki Imai
Mary Jenkins
Nye John
Noriaki Kano
David Kerridge
Alfie Kohn
Phil Landesberg
David Langford
Barbara Lawton
Bill Lawton
Kevin Little
Dawna Markova
Kathryn Metzger
Ron Moen
Tom Mosgaller
Tom Nolan
Daniel Oestreich
Joyce Orsini
Chris Oster
Frank Pilecki
Gipsie Ranney
Debbie Ray
Virginia Satir
Bill Scherkenbach
David Schwinn
Carol Schwinn
Ronald Snee
Rob Stiratelli
Mike Tveite
Lonnie Weiss
Donald Wheeler

Many people helped in the processes that begot this book.

Jenna Casbarro Hansen acted as the project manager and contact person in my office.

Bj Dillon-Rauen did the desktop publishing work for each of the many drafts of this book.

Jack Covert, of Schwartz Book Store in Milwaukee, encouraged me and helped at some critical moments.

Dale Mann, a cartoonist philosopher, who illustrated *The Team Handbook,* now has shared his talent in this book.

Matthew Scholtes took on several research projects for his dad. ("Where exactly does the Oliver Wendell Holmes quote come from?")

Peter S. Scholtes is one of the best copy editors I have ever had nudge and tweak my writing.

Others who helped with the manuscript:

Tony Aldridge
Edward Baker
Jim Chandler
Patricia Clark
Maury Cotter
John Criqui
Liane Dolezar
Lynda Finn
Spencer Graves
Barbara Hummel
March Jaques
Phil Landesberg
Madison Public Library Reference Desk
Dave Nave
Lisa Nave
Kathleen Paris
Judy Schector
Myron Tribus
Al Viswanathan
Bill Warner

1 TRAIN WRECKS AND BAD RADIOS: HOW WE GOT WHERE WE ARE

TRAIN-WRECK MANAGEMENT

On October 5, 1841, two Western Railroad passenger trains collided head-on somewhere between Worcester, Massachusetts and Albany, New York, killing a conductor and a passenger and injuring seventeen passengers. That disaster marked the beginning of a new management era (Chandler, 1977).

Prior to the early 1800s in the United States (and the early 1700s in Europe), business was much the same as it had been since the Middle Ages: operating as cottage industries, tradespeople made their wares one item at a time and sold them to their neighbors. There was no "manager." The owners of the enterprises did the work themselves or coached apprentices and assistants who did the work alongside them. In Europe, quality was assured by guilds and their marks of approval.

Then came the development of coke as a fuel in England and the discovery of anthracite coal in Western Pennsylvania, both leading to the possibility of mass production and mass distribution. The owner of a cottage shop could choose to hire engineers to build machines of mass production and by 1830 begin to use the burgeoning rail systems for mass distribution. Or the shop owner could stay in the "cottage," continuously worrying about competition from those on the rail system who had entered the new industrial age.

It was the time of a great paradigm shift in managerial thinking, the equivalent of letting go of a managerial flat-earth perspective. For the owners of businesses, these were truly traumatic times, requiring them to rethink the premises and practices of their work: How, they asked, will we run a large, geographically dispersed organization?

Other than the army and the church, there were few models for such a management practice in the 1800s. The railroads were the first industry to come to grips with how to manage in the new era. In the United States the Western Railroad was the first to extend itself beyond ordinary regional boundaries, the first with complex schedules and multiple trains on the same track. It was also the first with a disastrous train wreck, a harbinger of worse tragedies to come.

The Massachusetts legislature launched an investigation into the causes of the train wreck and the directors of the Western Railroad appointed a committee headed by Major George W. Whistler to find a remedy. Their recommendations had major immediate impact on the railroads and, over the next decades, helped shape all of U.S. managerial practice.

Part of the recommendations for the railroads was an organizational structure that looked like the "train wreck" chart in Figure 1-1. While the standard organizational chart may seem ageless, it was, in fact, adapted from the Prussian Army and introduced to American

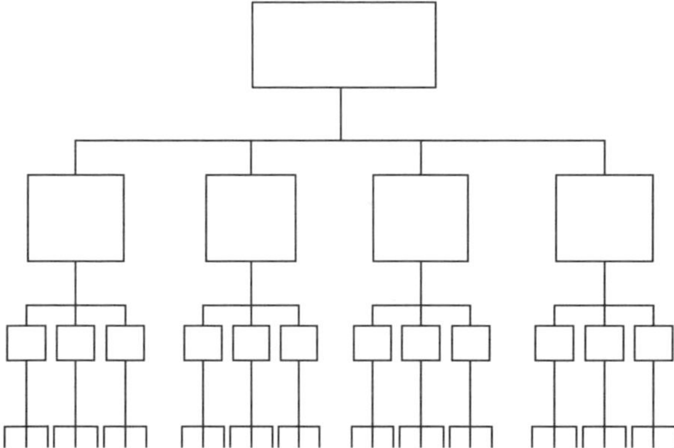

Figure 1-1. The "train wreck" chart.

business practice as a way to prevent train wrecks! In its time, it was revolutionary. Its unique features:

- Central offices run by people called "managers" (a new term)
- Distinct functional divisions
- A "chain of command," clear lines of authority
- Clear lines of communication and reporting
- Clear descriptions of responsibility for each individual from top to bottom

Daniel McCallum, President of the Erie Railroad, later elaborated on the Western Railroad's chart with his *Six Principles of Administration:*

1. A proper division of responsibilities.
2. Sufficient power conferred to enable the same to be fully carried out, that such responsibilities may be real in their character (that is, authority to be commensurate with responsibility).
3. The means of knowing whether such responsibilities are faithfully executed.
4. Great promptness in the report of all derelictions of duty, that evils may be at once corrected.
5. Such information, to be obtained through a system of daily reports and checks, that will not embarrass principal officers nor lessen their influence with their subordinates.
6. The adoption of a system, as a whole, which will not only enable the General Superintendent to detect errors immediately, but will also point out the delinquent. (See Chandler, 1977.)

A fundamental premise of the "train-wreck" approach to management is that the primary cause of problems is "dereliction of duty." The purpose of the organizational chart is to sufficiently specify those duties so that management can quickly assign blame, should another accident occur.

That this approach to management took on a militaristic tone is not surprising. Retired military officers had great influence on the leadership of early businesses. New businesses relied on the technical and managerial contributions of engineers. One of the few and certainly the best source of engineering education in the United States was the United States Military Academy at West Point.

The era of management that began in the mid-1800s can be characterized as "management by results" (Joiner and Scholtes, 1985). Since managers could no longer do the work themselves or direct others in the doing of the work, managers exercised their authority by holding people accountable for results. This train-wreck model evolved in the United States over the years after 1840. In the 1950s, management by results reached its epitome in MBO (management by objectives) and performance appraisal, the Harvardization of train-wreck management.

From the beginning of the Industrial Revolution in England in 1730 up to the present, managers have continually focused on individual accountability for results. These results are E-mailed or laser-printed instead of quill-penned, but the whole approach is not much different from McCallum's *Principles of Administration:* "Great promptness in the report of all derelictions of duty, that evils may be at once corrected ... detect errors immediately but ... also point out the delinquent." Our operations are fine if people would only do their jobs. Management would be easy if it weren't for all the employees.

From today's vantage point it is possible to see the flaws in train-wreck management, but our predecessors took what was indeed primitive and chaotic and gave it order and workability. People like Whistler, McCallum, Frederick Taylor, or Henry Ford in the United States or Darby, the Stephensons, or Brunel in England were pioneers, people of vision and passion who got things done. They did their best and, by and large, what they did was very good. The reign of industrial hierarchy as the best theory of management lasted nearly 200 years.

MEANWHILE, IN JAPAN ...

Around the time of the Western Railroad's train wreck, Japan was experiencing the end of the Shogun era. In 1853, Commodore Matthew Perry sailed into Tokyo Harbor on a U.S. Navy gunboat. Commodore Perry's message: "Open your ports to American commerce." The gunboat's message: "Or else!"

The Japanese have historically been an adaptive people, realistic and flexible while at the same time tenacious and purposeful. Japanese leaders drew two conclusions from Commodore Perry's visit: Japanese ports must indeed be opened to foreigners, and Japan must undertake a more modern approach to militarization. This latter adaptation ultimately led to World War II and military defeat. It also led to yet a new chapter of adaptation—and a new paradigm of leadership.

If the previous era of American management can trace its start to a Massachusetts train wreck, the origins of the new era of management can be attributed to General MacArthur's desperate need for radios. During his administration of the occupation of Japan after World War II, MacArthur had to find a method for communicating with all the Japanese people. The story is reported in Crawford-Mason and Dobyns (1991).

> MacArthur wanted reliable radios, a lot of them, so that the occupation forces' orders and propaganda programs could be heard in every town and village in occupied Japan, and when Japanese manufacturers in the 1940s couldn't give the general what he wanted, he sent for Americans to teach them how.
>
> Think of that: one man wanted a radio that worked, and the world economic order changed.

The irony of a Japan unable to produce good radios, and relying on American teachers to learn how, is an amazing and humbling lesson for us. The Americans who went to Japan were Homer Sarasohn, a systems and electronics engineer, and later Charles Protzman and Frank Polkinghorn, engineers from Western Electric.

Sarasohn and Protzman placed the early emphasis on getting the factories up and running and teaching the importance of viewing production as a system. They taught a 32-day course to senior executives who were ordered to attend by the MacArthur administration.

Sarasohn recommended to the MacArthur administration that W. Edwards Deming be invited to teach quality control. MacArthur's administration, in turn, arranged for JUSE to invite Deming to Japan. JUSE, the Japanese Union of Science and Engineering, had been founded in 1946 by Ichiro Ishikawa.

Deming was a protégé and colleague of Walter Shewhart, who had pioneered statistical applications at Western Electric in the 1930s. During the war, Deming and others had developed a course in quality control techniques called SQC, or Statistical Quality Control, that they taught to 35,000 engineers and technicians in U.S. war industries.[1] Deming and Shewhart were both well known and highly respected by Japanese technical and industrial leaders.

The moment had been prepared for by the work of Sarasohn, Protzman, and Polkinghorn. The audience—now including people well beyond the communications industry—was ready. Deming was going to deliver his message to eager and respectful listeners.

Deming arrived in Tokyo on Friday, June 16, 1950. For the next several weeks he gave almost daily lectures to groups ranging in size from about 200 to about 600—"some of the best classes I've ever had," Deming would comment later.

On the evening of Thursday, July 13, 1950, Deming had a historic dinner with the presidents and top officials of the 21 leading industries. A few years earlier some of these executives had been required by the MacArthur administration to attend lectures by Sarasohn and Protzman. This time they came in response to an invitation by Ichiro Ishikawa, a leader among his peers and father of the legendary Kaoru Ishikawa who would become the leader of the quality movement in Japan for the next four decades.

The group of 21 industries represented most of Japan's power and wealth. Deming was later told that 80 percent of Japan's capital was in that room at the Industry Club in Tokyo. What he told them was persuasive because it was clear to them that Deming himself believed what he was saying. What struck them more was that his words and manner suggested that this man was not another victor giving orders to the vanquished: This man was a colleague who genuinely respected the Japanese and cared about their well-being. The industrial leaders were intrigued and arranged for another meeting with Deming a few weeks later. Of this first meeting at the Industry Club on July 13, 1950 Deming would later say, "That was the birth of the new Japan, if a date can be put on it" (Kilian, 1992, p. 23).

What Deming taught the Japanese in 1950 and in his subsequent trips to Japan—some 27 trips in all—have evolved into his philosophy of management, summarized in his works (1986, 1994). This philosophy, along with lessons learned from some of Japan's masters, is a major part of what is presented in this book. But here, in brief, is a description of what Deming taught the Japanese in 1950 (Kilian, 1992):

[1]After the war, the use of SQC virtually disappeared from American industry. Deming has said that one of his biggest mistakes was to teach quality only to those who made American products, not to the American managers, who made policy.

- *The marketplace is now global.* There must be international standards[2] of quality and an international language for describing quality.
- *The customer is all-important.* Seek to cultivate long-term relations with your customers. Seek to continuously understand consumer needs when designing and manufacturing products.
- *Quality is determined by managers.* The quality of products and services must reflect consumer needs. Products must be uniform, be consistent, and perform dependably. The quality of the product cannot be better than the intentions and specifications of management. Quality results from the way managers lead.
- *Production is a system.* The supplier is your partner. Make the supplier a partner and an integral part of the system. The customer is also part of the system, the most important part of the system. Statistical quality control must be applied to all the stages of the system.
- *The chain reaction.* If you improve your processes and product, your costs will decrease and you will capture the market with better quality and lower prices, thus allowing you to stay in business and provide jobs and more jobs.
- *Japan must see itself as a system.* All of Japan is a system. There must be trust and cooperation throughout Japan. A common commitment to quality, trust, and cooperation must sweep through Japan "like a prairie fire. All Japanese on fire! Everyone will win!"

FROM THE FIFTIES TO THE PRESENT

Japan took Deming's message to heart. Within months they began to notice improvement. Within four years some of Japan's products began to make progress in the world market. (Deming had predicted it would take five years. The Japanese proved him wrong!)

In the United States, we went from discounting Japanese products ("You'll never be able to get spare parts!") to noticing, and becoming disconcerted by, the shrinking U.S. market share in key industries.

Do you know what these groups of products have in common?

[2]Dr. Deming was not referring to anything like ISO standards.

automobiles
cameras
stereos
medical equipment
color TV sets
hand tools
electric motors
machine tools
food processors
microwave ovens
athletic equipment
computer chips
industrial robots
electron microscopes
optical equipment

What they have in common is that in the 1970s the United States lost 50 percent or more of its world market share in each (Wheelwright, 1984). By the 1980s, Americans were hollering "unlevel playing field" and looking for trade sanctions against Japan.

While the United States was whining, Japan learned about improving quality more rapidly. JUSE was promoting the quality philosophy—called TQC for Total Quality Control—and was presenting annual awards to individuals who contributed to quality and companies that achieved certain described standards of quality. The award was, and still is, called the Deming Prize. Since it was first awarded in 1951, approximately 60 individuals and 160 organizations have won the Deming Prize.

In 1980, NBC presented a television documentary, produced by Clare Crawford-Mason with reporter Lloyd Dobyns, titled "If Japan Can, Why Can't We?" Using the typical measures of TV success, market share and ratings, it was not a hit. But in terms of its impact on American business, it was a thunderbolt. It captured an audience of business leaders. The United States discovered the existence of this obscure 80-year-old statistician who was revered and respected by Japanese leaders. The quality era finally arrived in America.

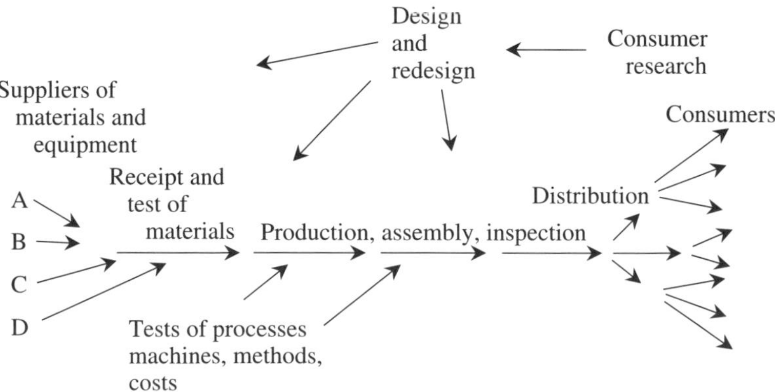

Figure 1-2. Diagram used by Dr. Deming at his lectures in Japan during the summer of 1950.

Style of management	Events & philosophies that have influenced American business
1840 – 1890 "Train-wreck" management	• Discovery of anthracite coal in Western Pennsylvania • End of the era of cottage industries • Mass production (coal-fueled machines) • Mass distribution (railroads) • First factories (1850)
1890 – 1920 "Train-wreck" management	• Scientific management • Henry Ford • Production lines • Assembly lines • Waves of immigrant workers
1920s "Train-wreck" management	• Walter Shewhart • Statistical process control chart • Rise of labor unions
1930s "Train-wreck" management	• The Great Depression • Hawthorne experiments • Human relations school of management (Western Electric)
1940s "Train-wreck" management	• W.E. Deming and others teach SPC to U.S. war industries
1950s "Train-wreck" management adopts MBO and performance evaluation	• SPC and human relations disappear in U.S. • Deming teaches the Japanese industrial leaders • TQC begins in Japan • Deming Prize
1960s and 1970s "Train-wreck"/MBO in the U.S., TQC in Japan	• Douglas McGregor's "Theory X" and "Theory Y" • Herzberg on motivation • Japanese economy flourishes • U.S. begins to lose market share
1980s "Train-wreck" management/MBO, early stirrings of Quality management in the U.S.	• "If Japan Can, Why Can't We?" NBC White Paper • TQM begins in U.S. • Baldrige prize • "TQM" becomes a fad in the U.S.
1990s • "Train-wreck" management still dominates • Some emergence of Quality management • Some decline of Quality management	• Quality bashing in the U.S. • "TQM" fades as a fad • Quality holds firm, however, in thousands of organizations
?	

Figure 1-3. Our management heritage.

A GENERATION IN TRANSITION

Since the late 1980s, the baby boomers have been becoming the world's managers. Through no choice of their own, they have also been selected by a convergence of events to be the generation that leads the transition from the 1840s premises of management to 1950s premises. This generation of managers will have a difficult time with the transition. There are not many current models. None of the baby boomers grew up in schools or other organizations where the new philosophy was even taught, let alone practiced. The boomers will be making it up as they go along. Their assurance can come from knowing that this philosophy has been developed, tested, and proven for decades. They are not guinea pigs, just, perhaps, inelegant learners.

There is a peculiar learning curve related to the mastery of this new philosophy. The conventional learning curve is depicted in Figure 1-4. The Deming transformation's learning curve, however, resembles the curve in Figure 1-5.

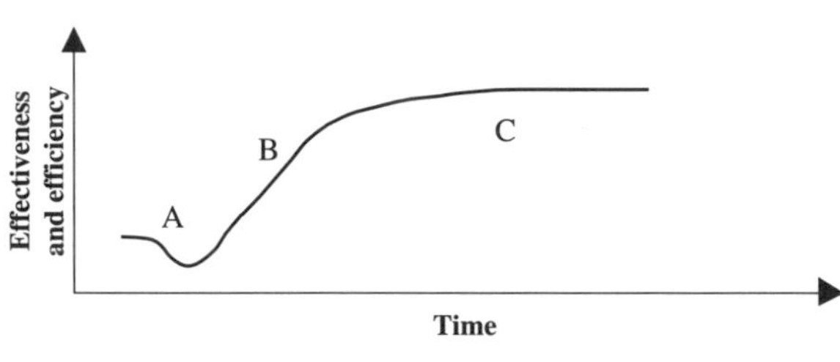

A = A slight time loss of productivity while adjusting to the new way
B = Then a rapid increase in effectiveness and efficiency as the new method is mastered
C = Then a plateau at a higher level

Figure 1-4. The conventional learning curve.

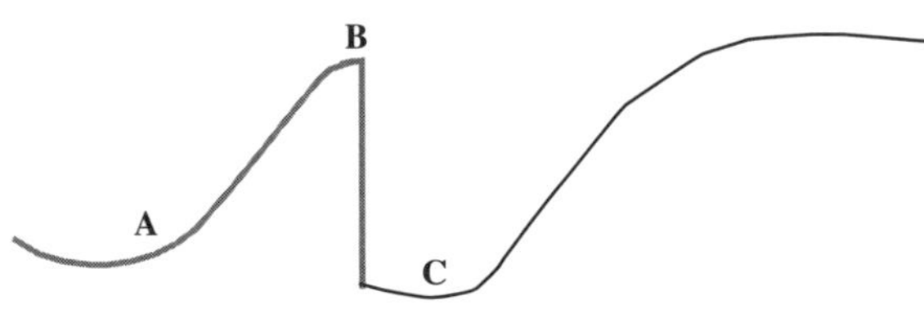

A. The illusion of learning
- Mastering the rhetoric
- Grafting programs onto the old organization
- Knowing enough to be dangerous
- The same old premises are at work

B. Sufficient understanding to see that "we don't know much"
- The "A-ha!" experience
- The beginning of the integration of knowledge and know-how

C. Real learning begins

Figure 1-5. Transformation's learning curve.

At first I thought this observation was a product more of my own overactive cynicism than of objective observation. But I began to observe it frequently in many managers in almost every company with which I worked. I concluded that this false learning curve was not imaginary. It is a predictable pattern. The phenomenon can be described as shown in Figure 1-6 (top of facing page).

Dr. Deming emphasized that we move from unconscious incompetence (area 1 in Figure 1-6) to conscious incompetence (2), a sign of great progress. This allows us to move from conscious incompetence to conscious competence (3), and then to unconscious competence (4).

Myron Tribus, an articulate teacher of Deming's philosophy who learned these levels of competence from a speaker named Mike Vance and taught them to Dr. Deming, has commented that this transition from the false learning curve to the real learning curve is a transition

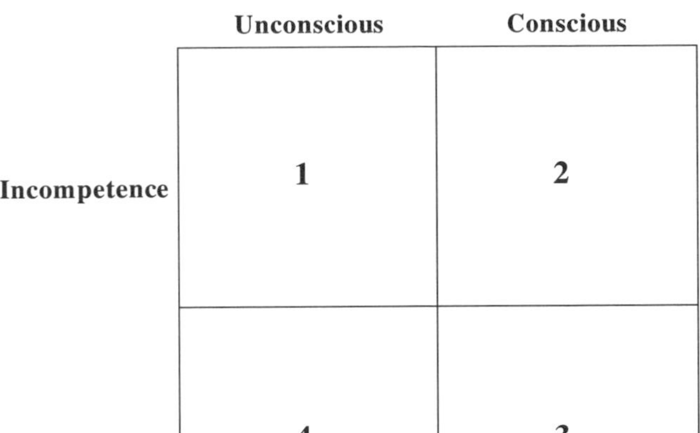

Figure 1-6. Competency matrix.

"from knowledge to know-how." That seems to be a pretty fair description. What I observed among clients and others seeking to apply the new philosophy was that they had an abundance of education and training, were able to sling around new jargon ("rules of the funnel," "common cause," "special cause," and "PDSA" used as an acronym for both noun and verb) and talk about "customers"—internal and external—like these were some recently discovered subspecies of the human race. There would be lots of teams and projects, usually too many. The managers would sit through the obligatory wordsmith-a-mission-statement sessions. There would be lots of hype and activity. But the managers themselves did nothing much new: no new systems, no new relationships, no new approaches to planning, problem solving, decision making, budgeting, etc. I kept wondering when I would begin to see *them* transform. Instead I saw the continuation of the old ways of managing, what one of my client-partners described as "common-cause stupidity."

Then, almost magically, after about a year I began to notice some signs of something new: managers asking smarter questions, applying principles learned a year earlier to current circumstances, and saying to me, "You know that systems stuff you were teaching last year? I think I finally get what you meant."

I tried to figure out what caused the lifting of the veil, but there were no common patterns or themes. The only thing these managers had in common was this yearlong period of dormancy, and then a gradual awakening.

What can we learn from this notion of the false learning curve?

In September of 1989, I had an opportunity to lecture to the students of Dr. Noriake Kano at Tokyo Science University. Dr. Kano is one of the leading teachers of TQC in Japan and one of the consultants and reviewers for the Deming Prize sponsored by the Japanese Union of Science and Engineering (JUSE). In his class I presented my observation about the false learning curve attributable to those seeking to learn the quality philosophy. When I finished, Dr. Kano raised his hand and asked:

"Mr. Scholtes, you say the false learning curve lasts for about a year?"

"Yes, Dr. Kano."

"Mmmmmm... You must be very good!"

("What the hell does he mean by that?" I thought to myself.)

Dr. Kano continued, "I think it takes three years!"

For me, this was one of those wonderful epiphanies, a sudden revelation: What I had been observing, but was suspicious of as being a product of my cynicism, Dr. Kano had also been observing. I felt a great sense of reassurance and affirmation from this. Furthermore, I had been observing this in American managers; Dr. Kano had been observing it in Japanese managers (whom we all know have a gland that secretes quality).

Dr. Kano's remarks extended the period of the false learning two years beyond what I had estimated, but his comments gave me hope. This phenomenon of the false learning curve seems to be a real and predictable occurrence, and it is temporary. It will pass if you give it time and patience, and you must persist. I fear a lot of CEOs will conclude, after a year or two, "We tried it, but it doesn't work here."

- *Be patient.* Most often we will notice progress only by looking back at how we were two or three years ago.
- *Be persistent.* Don't ever give up! Don't get restless and look for a new management philosophy du jour.
- *Be humble.* The arrogant organization will find it difficult to learn anything. Acknowledge our inadequacies. Instead of assured pronouncements, offer hypotheses that need data for support.
- *Be inelegant.* Give yourself permission to be inept and ask dumb questions. Don't try to fake it. Rather seek to learn it.

SUMMARY

Some factors and features of our organization have been with us so long, we tend to see them as having been around forever. We are so used to them that we never think to question whether they are useful or necessary.

In the United States, managers didn't exist until 1840. Factories didn't start operating until 1860. The typical organization chart was not brought down from Mount Sinai by Moses. Each of these things has a history and there are reasons why they made sense. Managers, factories, and organization charts continue to make sense, but a very different sense from when they started being used.

In 1950 Deming "reengineered" the way we think about work and leadership, about organizations, indeed about the world and life itself. In effect, Dr. Deming taught us that everything is a system, and we are part of it. We function at our peril when we are unaware of systems. We have discovered a new way to think, and we need this new way to understand what is happening and to know how to function in the world.

In the next chapter we begin to look at some new competencies that leaders must have. Many of these "new" competencies are old competencies that must be pulled out, dusted off, and relearned.

CHAPTER ONE ACTIVITIES

Discuss the following questions with others with whom you work:

1. What is quality?

2. What are the basic principles of quality?

3. Contrast your response to Question 2 with what Dr. Deming taught the Japanese in 1950.

REFERENCES

Chandler, A.D. 1977. *The visible hand.* Cambridge, MA: Belknap-Harvard.

Crawford-Mason, C., and Dobyns, L. 1991. *Quality or else.* Boston: Houghton Mifflin.

Deming, W. Edwards. 1994. *The new economics.* Cambridge, MA: MIT.

Deming, W. Edwards. 1986. *Out of the crisis.* Cambridge, MA: MIT.

Joiner, B., and Scholtes, P. 1985. *Total quality leadership versus management by results.* Madison, WI: Joiner Associates Incorporated. Included in a collection of Joiner Associates articles titled *A practical approach to quality,* published by Joiner Associates.

Kilian, C. 1992. *The world of W. Edwards Deming.* 2nd ed. Knoxville, TN: SPC Press.

Kolesar, P.J. 1994. What Deming told the Japanese in 1950. *Quality Management Journal,* Fall, 9–24.

Koyanagi, K. 1952. *Statistical quality control in Japanese industry.* Tokyo: Nippon Kagaku Gijutsu Remmei (JUSE).

Mann, N. 1985. *The keys of excellence.* Los Angeles: Prestwick Books.

McGregor, D. 1960. *The human side of enterprise.* New York: McGraw-Hill (25th Anniversary Edition, 1985).

Tribus, M. *Quality first.* Alexandria, VA: AQPI. This is a collection of articles written by Dr. Tribus from 1981 through 1987.

Wheelwright, Steven C. 1984. Strategic management of manufacturing. *Advances in Applied Business Strategy,* 1, 1, 1–15.

Ordering information

Joiner Associates Incorporated, 3800 Regent Street, P.O. Box 5005, Madison, WI 53705-5445. Fax: (608) 238-2908

Quality Management Journal, ASQC, 611 East Wisconsin Avenue, P.O. Box 3005, Milwaukee, WI 53201-3005. (800) 248-1946

2 THE NEW LEADERSHIP COMPETENCIES

INTRODUCTION

In America and Europe we have an almost insatiable appetite for fads. We seem more interested in what is *new* than in what is *good.* Consequently we have a disposable mentality: If what we have doesn't seem to work, we throw it out and find something new. This obviously applies to fashion and music. Unfortunately, it seems also to apply to relationships such as spouses and employees. We live in a time of the management philosophy du jour.

To some, the approach to management described in this book may seem vaguely familiar enough that a manager may conclude, "Been there, done that." The quality movement, from about 1982 through about 1992, used some of these notions. But, by and large, the teachers of TQM didn't understand the philosophy in the first place and trivialized it in the second place. TQM, I repeat, is the *trivialization* of an important new way of thinking. In this chapter I will describe the new approach to leadership as it has been developed by its pioneers over the last 50 years, without the barnacles and affectations that have attached themselves to this profoundly important and revolutionary way of thinking.

Here are some of the current fads and their accretions:

- We must *empower* our people.
- We must put them into *teams.*
- We must put them into *self-directed groups.*
- We must *motivate* them.
- We must offer them *incentives.*
- We must *hold them accountable.*
- We must *reengineer* and *reinvent* them.

All this fails to appreciate *systems* and the importance of mastering systems in order to get the important daily work done. To understand systems is to understand this:

> ***All of the empowered, motivated, teamed-up, self-directed, incentivized, accountable, reengineered, and reinvented people you can muster cannot compensate for a dysfunctional system. When the system is functioning well, these other things are all just foofaraw. When the system is not functioning well, these things are still only empty, meaningless twaddle.***

A well-run organization with well-functioning systems allows people from top to bottom to do work of which they can be proud.

When we can work well together doing worthwhile work we can create a joyful workplace as well. The approaches described in this book will create pride and joy in the workplace. The current foofaraw and twaddle that pass for management philosophy won't bring pride and joy, only cynicism and resentment.

This chapter is loaded with concepts that some readers may need time to assimilate, especially those who are new to these ideas. The ideas aren't particularly difficult to understand. They are, however, tightly packed. The reader is encouraged to stay with this chapter and take it in one mental morsel at a time.

In this chapter we will examine the new leadership competencies. These are areas of understanding and proficiency needed by managers in the new paradigm. Walking down a street, I noticed someone wearing a T-shirt showing the word "paradigm" with a red diagonal slash mark through it. I acknowledge this word has been overused and misused. In this case, however, it is exactly the right word. The leadership philosophy begun by Deming in Tokyo in 1950 is the first fundamentally new management philosophy since 1840, the equivalent of the transition from Newton to Einstein. In fact, Deming may represent an even greater departure from past ways of thinking. *U.S. News and World Report* (1991) included Deming in a list of revolutionary thinkers that includes, among many others, St. Paul (Christianity is not just for Jews), Copernicus (the earth is not the center of the universe), Darwin (we are not specially created, only the most advanced of the life forms), and Freud (there is much about ourselves that we don't understand and can't control or predict). Deming's contribution to the discontinuity of human thought is this: Everything is a *system* and we are part of it.

Let us first briefly examine the *old* competencies: aptitudes needed to survive and excel in the *old* organization.

1. *Forcefulness.* Part of a manager's responsibility was to control the workforce, making people do what they may be otherwise inclined to ignore. Good managers could look their people square in the eye and get them to respond.
2. *Motivator.* The "softer" side of forcefulness was the ability to inspire your people to do great work. The judicious combination of carrots and sticks, of inspiration and exhortation, was the manager's stock-in-trade.
3. *Decisiveness.* To make quick decisions in the absence of information was routinely expected of the old-style manager.
4. *Willfulness.* Good bosses knew what they wanted and were dogged in their pursuit of it.

5. *Assertiveness.* A good boss was outspoken. Old-style leaders could not show weakness or ignorance lest their people run all over them.
6. *Result- and bottom-line-oriented.* Bosses held people accountable for meeting quotas and standards and achieving measurable goals. Maximizing ever-increasing profits every quarter and minimizing ever-diminishing costs: These were the goals.
7. *Task-oriented.* Managers kept everyone busy and occupied. No slacking off, no socializing. People don't really want to work and, left to themselves, will screw off. Therefore, be their conscience and taskmaster.
8. *Integrity and diplomacy.* Good bosses covered toughness with tact and amiability. Be honest, fair, and respectful while letting your people know that you know what to do when things get out of hand.

You get the idea. We have all worked in such environments and know managers who excel in this set of behaviors. These are still the prevailing expectations of managers. These old competencies aren't wrong. Rather, they are simply inadequate or, in some cases, irrelevant.

THE NEW COMPETENCIES

The new competencies are different in nature. They are based on very different premises, assumptions, and beliefs about people and organizations.

Anyone familiar with Deming's *System of Profound Knowledge* will recognize these approaches. What I present as "the new competencies" is an interpretation of and elaboration on his work, the great legacy for which I have the deepest respect and gratitude (see also Deming, 1994).

Competency 1: The Ability to Think in Terms of Systems and Knowing How to Lead Systems

We are used to thinking of organizations in terms of their structure, the chain of command, who reports to whom. (See Figure 1-1.)

Cherokee Wisdom and Leadership Competencies

According to Cherokee tribal lore, there is an ancient formula for success:

- *Clear intention:* You must know what your purpose is and persist in its pursuit.
- *Skillful means:* You must have good methods and be skilled in their use.
- *Affirmation:* Your task must have integrity, it must not clash with fundamental values, it needs support from the tribe and from your own heart.

Figure 2-1. Cherokee wisdom (adapted from: Dhyani Ywahoo. *Voices of Our Ancestors: Cherokee Teachings from the Wisdom Fire.* Boston: Shambhala, 1987).

Eons ago these were the new leadership competencies. They still are. Our "new" insights help us to rediscover and deepen our understanding of these fundamentals for success.

Deming has taught us to see *systems,* as represented in Figure 2-2.

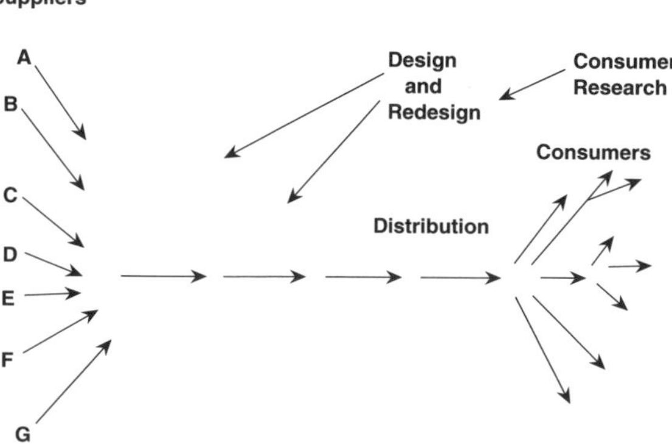

Figure 2-2. Deming's systems view.

The New Leadership Competencies

1. The ability to think in terms of systems and knowing how to lead systems.
2. The ability to understand the variability of work in planning and problem solving.
3. Understanding how we learn, develop, and improve, and leading true learning and improvement.
4. Understanding people and why they behave as they do.
5. Understanding the interdependence and interaction between systems, variation, learning, and human behavior. Knowing how each affects the others.
6. Giving vision, meaning, direction, and focus to the organization.

What Is a System?

The following are some characteristics of a system:[1]

1. A system is a whole composed of many parts (e.g., a car).
2. The systemic unit has a definable purpose (e.g., a car's purpose is to provide personal transportation).
3. Each part of the system contributes to the system's purpose but no part by itself can achieve that purpose (e.g., an automobile engine cannot provide personal transportation all by itself).
4. Each part has its own purpose. But when it affects the whole system it is dependent on other parts. The parts of the system are *inter*dependent.
5. We can understand a part by seeing how it fits into the system. We cannot understand a system by identifying each part or the entire unassembled collection of parts.
6. Looking at the interactions among the parts might help us understand how this system works. But to understand *why* this system exists, we must look outside the system, usually at human events and larger systems. (Why is the steering wheel on the left in some countries and on the right in others?)
7. To understand a system we must understand its purpose, its interactions, and its interdependencies. When you take a system apart, it loses its essential characteristics. *Analysis*

[1] I am indebted to Russell Ackoff for most of what is in this list.

involves looking at the parts. *Synthesis* involves looking at the whole.

8. When we look at an organization, we are looking at a complex social system as well as a technical system.
   - The organization has its interests, purpose, and interacting, interdependent parts.
   - The organization is but one interacting, interdependent part within even larger systems (e.g., the business, the industry, the economic community, the nation, the world).
   - Within the organization are interacting, interdependent parts (e.g., departments, divisions, teams, individuals), each of which has its interests and purpose that may affect, in a positive or negative way, the organization's ability to achieve its purpose (Figure 2-3).

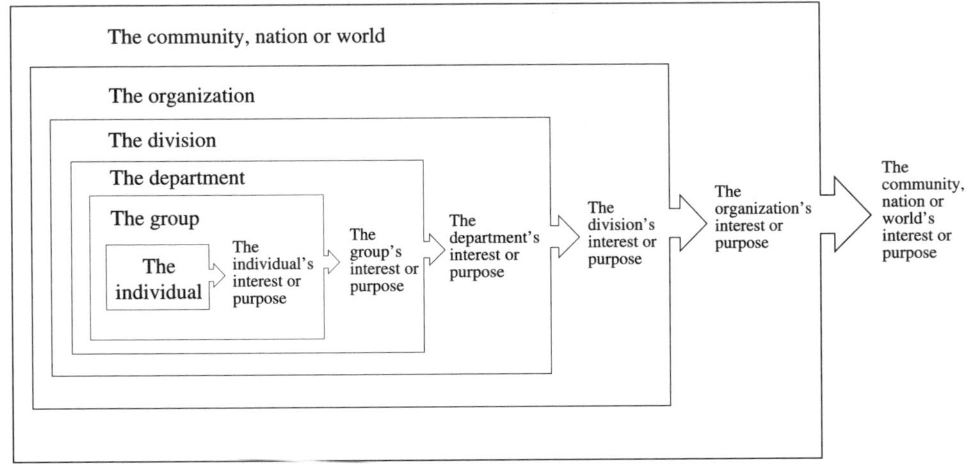

Figure 2-3. Systems in systems in systems.

   - To technical and mechanical interactions, organizations add the complexity of social interactions—relationships, teamwork, collaboration, cooperation, community, etc.

Any current situation is the net result of the interaction and interdependence of various factors, forces, and events, as shown in Figure 2-4.

As we have said, the system consists of the dynamic interaction of various forces and factors that result in some complex situation. If you wish to understand your current situation—whether it is what you want or don't want—you need to understand your system.

The *purpose* of the system is inextricably linked to the notion of systems. Without a defined purpose you cannot determine whether your system is functioning well, poorly, or not at all. Without a clear purpose you won't know how to improve or redesign the system.

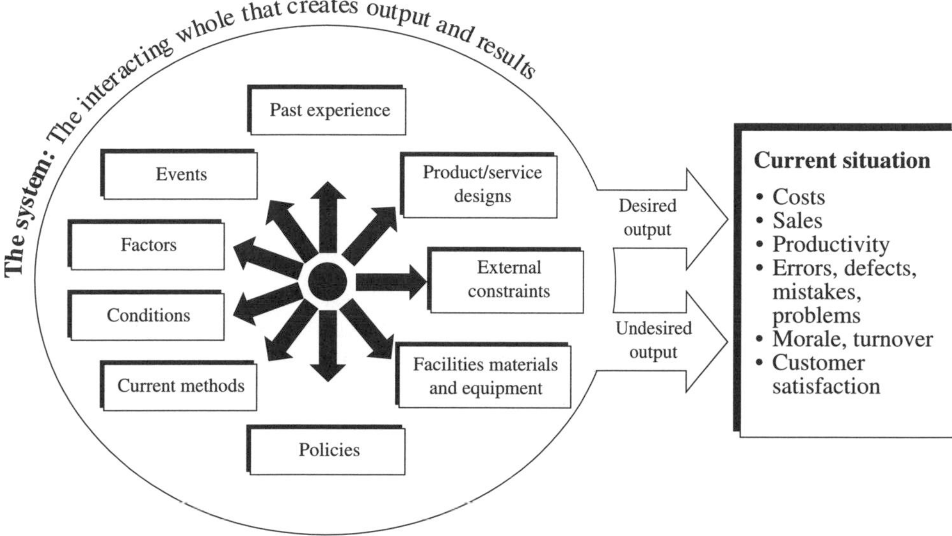

Figure 2-4. The system as an interacting whole.

An inconstant purpose results in a chronically dysfunctional system. For systems to respond flexibly to necessary shifts in focus, there must be subsystems that plan those shifts and assure flexibility of response.

The system is the method by which you achieve results. The failure to achieve desired results is caused by the inadequacy of the method or system.

Without conscious attention to *systems,* we will focus on *people.* That is what we have been trained to do. Rather than understanding and improving our systems, we seek better results by exhorting and seeking to motivate our people. When we don't understand systems, we equate improving our people with improving our systems.

People are not the same as organizational systems. They work in systems, but the systems existed before most of the people were hired and will continue after the current employees are gone. Improving systems takes a concerted, well-planned, usually cross-functional effort led from the top of the organization. When a system is changed, people need to change what they do. However, changing what people do will not necessarily change the system.

Applying Systems Thinking

When thinking about systems in the abstract, it is easy to get lost in esoterica. The practical value of systems thinking, however, is powerful. Consider these statements:

> Costs are out of control! I want you all to find ways to reduce costs! Start by buying less expensive supplies and materials and cut down on travel expenses!
>
> Reshaping this piece will cost us money! I don't care if it *would* make it easier and cause less breakage for the people in assembly! We won't do it!
>
> To improve sales during these last four weeks of the quarter, I am offering a free 36-inch television to anyone who sells 25 percent above his or her quota!

Systems thinking will help us avoid overly simplistic interpretations and solutions to complex problems. In an age of sound bites and bumper stickers, we are encouraged to look for slogans and scapegoats, not the deep, system-based explanations of what is happening and why. If we want to run a business and improve our daily work, we must understand systems. More than understanding systems, we must develop systems reflexes and systems instincts.

"Costs are out of control." Are they? How do you know? Competency 2 addresses the issue of how indicators (such as costs) vary. But while we are exploring the first competency, "systems thinking," we will consider costs as a system.

The I-am-not-making-this-up Department

The market for a particular type of paper had gone soft because of the recession. The paper company headquarters sent word to the plant manager that inventories for this product were too high; therefore, the machines making this product should be slowed down. The plant manager tried to protest, but in the autocratic style of this company he was told to just "follow instructions."

What the plant manager knew was that when this machine ran too fast, it produced many defects in the paper, and the product had to be scrapped (or "broke" as they say in the paper industry). This machine was running too fast.

In better times when demand was high, the orders to the plant manager were to "speed up the machine," which the plant manager also tried unsuccessfully to protest. So, obeying orders, the plant manager slowed the machine. This, in turn, resulted in fewer defects and greater productivity, more paper that couldn't be sold, bigger inventories, and even fuller warehouses. The plant manager? He was fired for disobeying orders.

This is an example of the tragic consequence of the ignorance of systems on the part of headquarters' managers.

Costs are the net output of a series of factors and interacting, interdependent events. If the costs are truly "out of control," then one or more factors or events or interactions in the series are "out of control." The statement about costs quoted earlier asserts that costs are "out of control," a determination that will require data to support it. The speaker, however, leaps to a solution ("Start by buying less expensive materials and cut down on travel expenses!"), without an indication of what the *cause* of the problem is, if indeed there is a problem. It could be that the cause of the problem is that the inferior, inexpensive materials already in use cause breakdowns, defects, rework, and delays. Buying cheaper goods might only make matters worse.

The second quotation ("Reshaping this piece will cost us money!...") illustrates, again, the absence of systems thinking. Because "reshaping will cost us money," the idea is rejected. Reshaping the piece will make assembly easier and result in less breakage. However, the manager quoted is concerned about the budget for which *he or she* is accountable, and gets no credit for ease of assembly or reduced breakage. The remuneration policy rewards managers only for optimizing *their* part of the system. So *this* manager does well but the larger system suffers.

In the third quotation, the sales manager offers an incentive (a free 36-inch television) to encourage the sales force to increase sales and help make the quarterly quota. What is wrong with this way of thinking? It assumes that:

- Quarterly quotas are an effective way to increase sales.
- The quarterly quotas are achievable.
- The salespeople have the information, knowledge, and resources needed to increase sales.
- The sales force is functioning at a diminished capacity, consciously or unconsciously withholding a certain amount of effort.
- A full effort must be coaxed or coerced out of them.
- In order to give their full effort, sales personnel need some kind of material incentive.
- These material incentives (36-inch TVs) are effective.
- Forcing sales this month won't have a detrimental effect on next month's sales.
- The product targeted by the quota is what customers need.
- Pushing quotas will do no long-term harm to your relationships with your customers.

This sales manager looks at sales and sales representatives and sees not a system with a built-in capability, but people who need to be manipulated and co-opted. If managers learned to see a *system* of sales, they could seek ways to improve the *system* to get better sales results, rather than resorting to carrots and sticks aimed at "motivating" people. We will explore systems thinking in more depth in Chapter 3.

Competency 2: The Ability to Understand the Variability of Work in Planning and Problem Solving

A psychologist attached to the Israeli air force had heard reports that the flight instructors were being abusive toward the student pilots: offering few compliments, giving public reprimands, screaming, and using abusive language. The psychologist took on as a project an effort to develop "kinder, gentler" flight instructors (Kahneman and Tverski, 1973, McKean, 1985).

In his first encounter with a flight instructor, the psychologist was told by the instructor that "kinder-gentler" didn't work: His compliments to the student pilots generally led to deteriorated performance. Reprimands, however, usually led to improvement.

The psychologist was troubled—but unconvinced—when he heard essentially the same story from the other flight instructors. He decided to observe what happened, to see for himself what effect compliments and reprimands had on the performance of the student pilots.

The results were a shock to the psychologist. The performance of the student pilots generally improved after they were reprimanded and, indeed, got worse after they were complimented. What the flight instructors claimed seemed to be true. Based on student pilot performance, he could no longer advocate using more "positive reinforcement" or urge the flight instructors to avoid the harsher responses.

The psychologist gave up this project and moved on to other work. However, the results of this study troubled him. He couldn't let go of this problem, even though he gave up the project. During the following year, he studied other things. In the midst of his other activities, he learned something that led him to reexamine the abusive flight instructor problem.

The psychologist had been studying the concept of *variation.* Recall Figure 2-4, the system as an interacting whole. Learning to fly an airplane is the result of a variety of interacting conditions, factors, and events. These factors are not stable. Each varies from day to day. The weather varies, the planes—each with its own system of interacting parts—vary, the flight instructor varies, the student pilot varies. There are innumerable factors that go into the performance of a student pilot and no one will ever know all of them. The net results will be variation.

With his new learning and perspectives in mind, the psychologist reexamined the performance of the student pilots and how performance related to the interventions of the flight instructors. The new results, interpreted with a different perspective, yielded a dramatically different conclusion: Flight instructor reprimands did *not* result in improved performance nor did compliments result in worsened performance. What was going on was *common cause variation.*

Dr. Deming taught us that there are two types of variation. Common cause variation is built into the system and is the net result of multiple influences, many of which will never be known. Most variation—the problems, defects, errors, accidents, mistakes, waste, scrap, and rework that we suffer on a daily basis—is common cause variation, built right into the system. Deming calls the other type of variation *special cause variation,* a unique event that is attributable to some knowable influence.

Most variation in our organizations is common cause variation built right into the system. But it is a common, though misguided, managerial reflex to regard anything that goes wrong as a special cause attributable to some person. This is what the flight instructors did. They attributed "good days" and "bad days" to the *pilots,* not to the built-in varying capabilities of the system.

Look at Figure 2-5 and ask, "When is a flight instructor most likely to pay a compliment?" Probably on days 2, 4, 8, or 12. And when will the flight instructor reprimand the student pilot? Probably on days 6, 9, 13, and 15. In a system of common cause variation, when performance is high, it is far more likely to go down than up. When performance is low, it is unlikely to stay low. That is the nature of variation and the intervention of the authority figure has nothing to do with it.

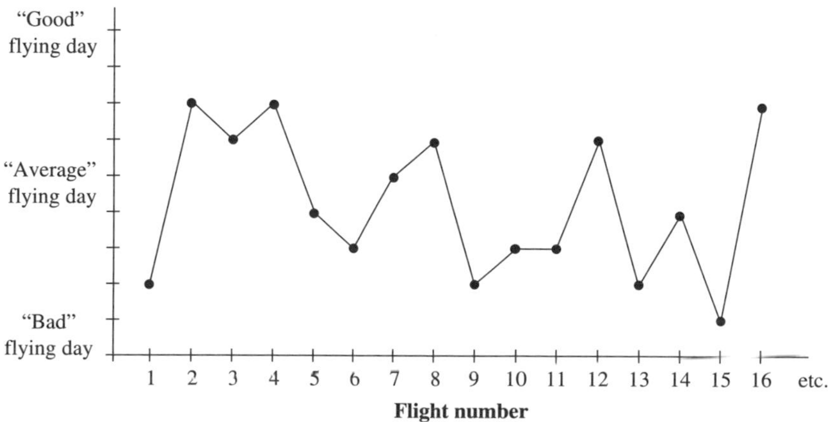

Figure 2-5. Variation in a student pilot's performance.

Common Cause and Special Cause

As you read this text there are innumerable minor distractions that affect how well you can concentrate: background noise or activity, your own state of mind or health, the condition of the material you are reading, etc. The net effect of all of these is variation in your ability to concentrate, all built into the "system" with a predictable range and average of performance—if indeed your ability to concentrate could be measured. Now suppose lightning strikes a tree next to your house, accompanied by a deafening clap of thunder, or a child runs to you crying, or someone rings the doorbell. Or suppose all of these things happened at once. These distractions are extraneous to the system. They are peculiar and identifiable. The former set of factors affecting your ability to concentrate are common cause and the latter are special cause factors.

When they are unaware of the existence of variation built into the system and have only an *illusion* of knowledge, managers develop the equivalent of superstition. Suppose that at the end of a "bad" day, the flight instructors had the student pilots kiss the fuselage. What is likely to happen to the student pilot's performance the next day? It will improve, not because of kissing the fuselage but because of variation. Now, no flight instructor would have student pilots kiss the fuselage after a bad day. That would be superstitious! Instead they reprimand them. That is not considered superstitious.

How should managers respond to problems? It depends whether the problem comes from common cause variation or special cause variation. Without carefully gathered and skillfully analyzed data the manager won't know what kind of variation he or she is dealing with. If the problem results from common cause variation—and most do—then getting rid of the problem will involve changing the system, process, or method of work. If the problem derives from a special cause of variation, then the manager must use data to seek out the cause of the problem and eliminate that problem at its point of origin.

When a manager fails to understand variation or, worse yet, doesn't even acknowledge its existence, serious and chronic problems result:

- The manager sees trends where there are no trends. ("Costs are out of control!")
- The manager misses trends where there are trends. ("We have had a few problems with deliveries but nothing unusual.")
- The manager attributes the cause of problems to any individual nearby at the time the problems took place, even if that individual had no control over the event. ("Because of recent flash floods, we have fired our weatherman!")

- The manager gives credit to individuals for making improvements and performing well when, still, they had no control. They were just lucky. ("This award goes to our school nurse because of whom, during this past school year, there were no reported cases of measles. Congratulations, Miss Bliss!")
- The manager does not understand past performance and is not able to predict future performance.
- The manager does not understand the current systems, their vulnerabilities, their capabilities, or whether the systems need to be improved or replaced.

In a World Without Data, Opinion Prevails

If the world were a logical place, we would expect to see a correlation between assertiveness and objective truth.

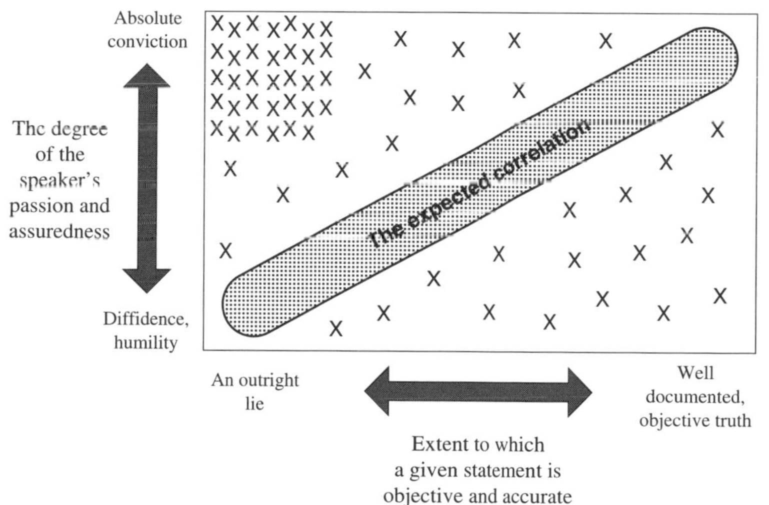

Figure 2-6. Assertiveness and truth.

The shaded area represents what would be an ideal and logical correlation. The X's represent what we commonly observe in everyday life.

Discourse is usually cloaked in the rhetoric of rationality. However, data is a necessary ingredient to rationality, particularly data showing variation. Without data, opinion prevails. Where opinion prevails, whoever has power is king. The ultimate correlation, therefore, is more likely between assertiveness and clout, not assertiveness and objective truth. It is possible that managers who wish to hold on to the illusion of power may resist a statistical view of work.

Why Are People So Resistant to Using Data in Planning and Problem Solving?

This will be addressed further in Chapter 6. Here are my theories about this dilemma:

- Math and statistics have traditionally been taught in such a way that the only point of interest is whether students will be bored to death or scared to death. By the time people become managers, they have taken a vow of statistical abstinence.
- The conventional use of statistics in business is related to financial measures (unless, of course, you are in the business of sports broadcasting, where statistics are often the only things to talk about).
- Statistics other than financial data are not seen as relevant data for executives and leaders. Data showing variation in the systems, processes, and other key indicators are given a lesser status and left for people of lesser status to attend to. Executives ignore these data.
- As a way of avoiding any statistical work, we resort to defensive strategies such as ridicule. The most common excuse—"There are lies, damned lies, and statistics"—is a cliché. (No one ever says "lies, damned lies, and the annual budget," which would probably be more true.)
- Data are not asked for. When executives and top-level managers expect data and ask questions that can only be answered with data, data will start becoming the language of the realm. This, of course, would require that executives understand data and apply them.
- Too often there are plenty of data that are useless and ignored or useful and still ignored. Many companies, such as Ford and GM, have gone through a measurement overhaul, purging the unuseful data and reducing reports by as much as 90 percent. Only the significant few remain. To do this, however, requires a knowledge of systems and statistical thinking.

Competency 3. Understanding How We Learn, Develop, and Improve; Leading True Learning and Improvement

Lifelong learning and improvement for individuals, organizations, and communities are no longer optional. Consider the following (I am grateful to Malcolm Knowles for this concept).

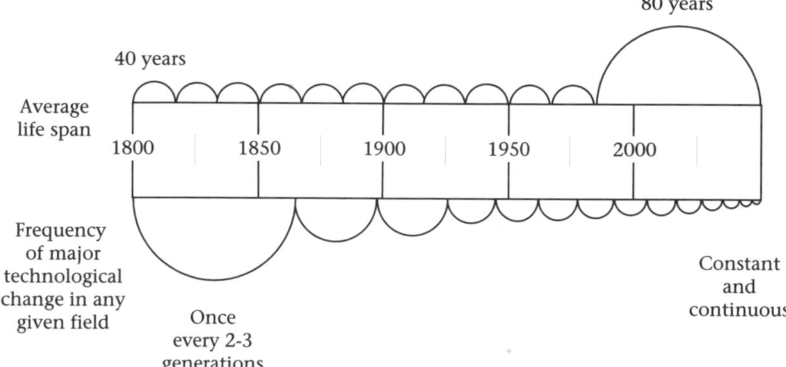

Figure 2-7. Two concurrent phenomena.

Over the course of history, as illustrated in Figure 2-7, there have been two trends related to learning. One is the increasing life span. The other is the frequency of technological, economic, social, and political change. As life span has increased so has the frequency of change. The implications:

- Education is no longer an undertaking of our younger years that is applied in our adult years. Learning must be lifelong.
- Education no longer consists of a single set of lessons that endure over several generations. The lessons change continuously within our individual lifetimes.
- Our schools must lead students. The root of the word *educate* is the Latin word for *lead.* Schools must *lead* students into *learning how to learn.* This is not at all the same as teaching.
- Our organizations and communities must be centers of lifelong learning. We must radically rethink the notion of on-the-job learning.
- Organizations without systems of continuous learning are probably doomed to obsolescence.

How Learning Takes Place: Theory and Application

Here are two quotations, each from renowned statistical thinkers. These quotations appear to contradict each other, but they say the same thing:

"All theories are wrong, but some are useful."—Dr. George Box

"All theories are right, in some world."—Dr. W. Edwards Deming

Theory? Hypothesis? Hunch? Guess?

These are statements or opinions that are in need of proof or at least improvement. A recipe is a theory that suggests that if you follow these directions you will have the dish you desire. The only way to learn if the recipe theory is valid is to use it. Then you can improve on the recipe and test that theory as well. A checklist is also a theory. The theory is that if you complete every item on the checklist, things will go well. When things don't go well, we have learned that our checklist needs improvement. In the same way, an annual plan or an annual budget is also a theory.

What each is saying is that the proof of a theory is in its successful application. Theories by themselves prove nothing. "Costs are out of control!" is a theory. It means nothing until tested against an application, in this case data that will verify whether or not costs are out of control.

Theory by itself teaches nothing. Application by itself teaches nothing. Learning is the result of dynamic interplay between the two.

Figure 2-8 illustrates the basic dynamic of learning.

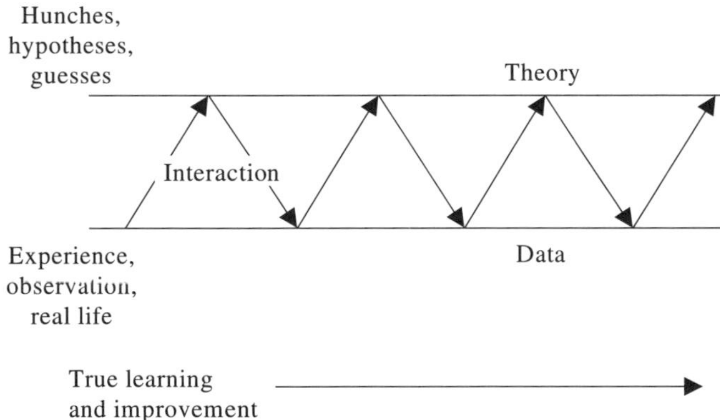

Figure 2-8. Theory and application.

We have something in mind that we believe to be true:

- Costs are out of control!
- Complimenting student pilots is detrimental to their performance.
- People will work harder if we offer incentives.

- Our television commercials will result in increased sales if we feature hyperactive people talking at a manic pace.
- We must hold our teachers accountable!

These are hypotheses. Most managerial dictums are hypotheses. A hypothesis by nature is useless unless proven by data. To apply data or any other observable test, we must define what it is we are looking for. The ability to operationally define our hunches allows us to look for data that confirm or contradict our assertion. For example, what exactly does "out of control" mean? For that matter, what is a "cost"?

Asserting an opinion as a fact is a lot easier. Pretending that our assuredness reflects objective truth is certainly convenient. However, if we want to understand what is truly going on and learn what is necessary to improve the situation at its source, we need to test our beliefs against data. If we don't do this we will not identify and eliminate the chronic causes of problems. At best we will only provide ourselves with "temporary symptomatic relief." Managers must see themselves as experimenters who lead learning, not dictators who impose control. Something that Dr. Deming taught the Japanese serves to underscore the manager's role as an experimenter and the leader of the learning cycle. It is the PDSA cycle.

The PDSA cycle is a never-ending cycle of learning and improvement that Deming developed, based on what he learned from his mentor, Walter Shewhart. Deming taught it to the Japanese in 1950. He called it "the Shewhart cycle" and the Japanese call it "the Deming wheel."

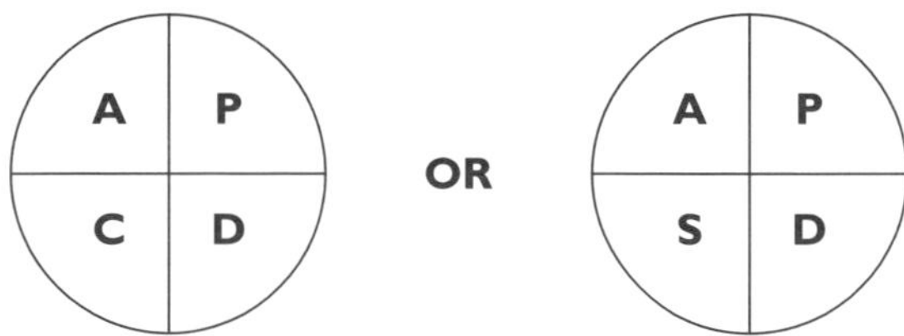

Deming preferred the word "study" to the word "check," which he believed implied "constrain." The Japanese have called it PDCA for decades. The application of PDCA and the spirit and intent of PDSA are nowhere more pervasive than in Japan. I have chosen, however, to defer to Dr. Deming's terminology.

Figures 2-9 and 2-10 make more explicit the connection between PDSA and the nature of true learning.

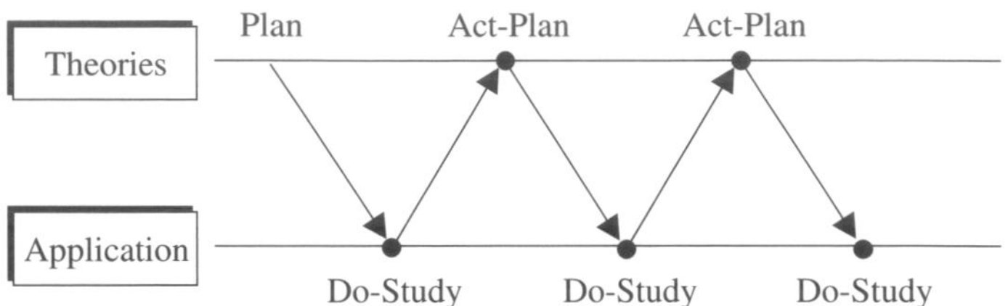

Figure 2-9. Learning and PDSA.

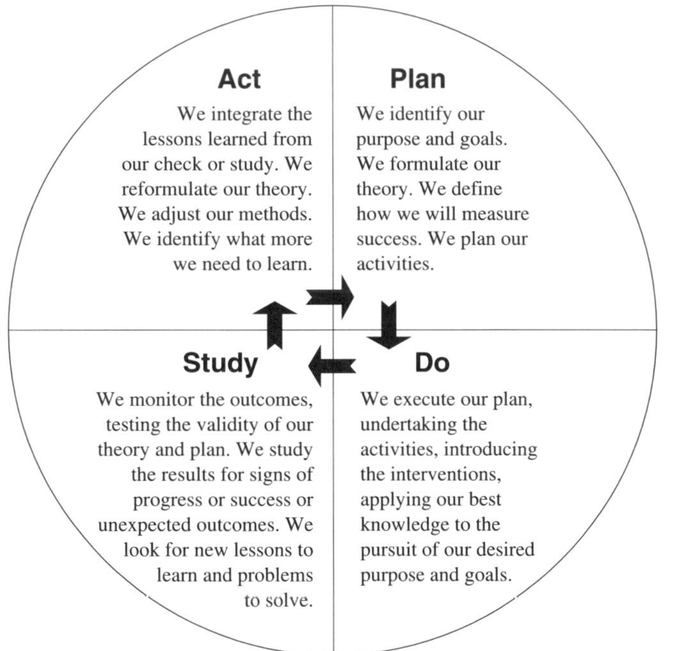

Figure 2-10. The ongoing cycle of learning and improvement.

The PDSA cycle may be used to test changes associated with long-term goals (our five-year plan, our vision and values) or with shorter-term cycles (our weekly staff meeting). PDSA can be applied to any recurring activity, such as our annual planning process or everyday work in regularly recurring processes—billing, order taking, materials handling. We cannot promise that nothing will go wrong, but PDSA builds forgiveness into our work and a promise that we will learn from things gone wrong.

Not All Learners Learn Alike

Much has been written in recent years on the different ways in which people learn. Our traditional classrooms seem based on the unspoken premise that all students learn in exactly the same manner. This may have been sufficient 200 years ago when there wasn't much to learn and education was finished in a few years. But now, when learning how to learn is important, a student must learn how he or she learns best and then make sure his or her learning needs are met in the learning environment. Teachers must expand their teaching methods beyond how they were taught, or how they learn best, to accommodate different kinds of learners. One approach to understanding learning differences is taught by Dawna Markova who, with Anne Powell, wrote *How Your Child* Is *Smart* (1992).

There are many theories about learning differences that have led people to think of themselves as visual, auditory, or kinesthetic learners. Traditional definitions of these types of learners are:

- Visual learners
  - — Visual learners learn first by watching and reading and writing.
  - — The written word is important.
  - — Students express themselves through charts, graphs, and pictures.
- Auditory learners
  - — Auditory learners learn first through hearing and conversing.
  - — The spoken word is important.
  - — Students express themselves through discussion, conversation, and sounds.
- Kinesthetic learners
  - — Kinesthetic learners learn first by doing it—experience and activity.
  - — Objects, actions, and feelings are important.
  - — Students express themselves through movement, gestures, and touch.

Markova's *The Open Mind* (1996) is an approach to understanding learners and how they learn. An important insight offered by the open mind approach is that *all three* perceptual channels—visual, auditory, and kinesthetic—are essential to each person's learning process. They are triggers to three brain wave patterns, which correspond to three different kinds of mental functioning. According to this approach, the three perceptual channels work together in one of six possible personal thinking patterns: AKV, AVK, VKA, VAK, KAV, and KVA.

A learner's pattern is the most comfortable and functional sequence in which to receive and process auditory, visual, and kinesthetic information. A person is most comfortable learning with the first channel in his or her pattern, but needs the other two kinds of input as well to learn most effectively.

While people who consider themselves to be auditory learners may be comfortable learning with a lecture approach, the information will "stick" when they have also had something to look at and something to do in the learning process. Similarly, kinesthetic learners may get energized by hands-on activities and simulations, but their active learning will be enhanced by follow-up that includes reading and discussion, for example.

Training programs are usually based on the premise that "we all learn the same way." Trainers must realize that learning will be most effective, long-lasting, and retrievable when all of our senses have been used in the process. Offering a variety of learning options may meet the needs of more learners in the training process.

Some comments on the process of learning:

- The emphasis is on learning and how the learner learns, not on teaching and how the teacher teaches.
- Teaching can take place without it resulting in learning. It is possible—and not uncommon—for learning to take place without teachers and teaching.
- The old adage was, "If the student hasn't learned, the teacher hasn't taught." I don't see the truth or usefulness of that statement. I prefer to say, "If the learner hasn't learned, the system is not yet adequate."

Applying Understanding of How We Learn, Develop, and Improve

Without understanding how we learn, develop, and improve, leaders create a number of vulnerabilities for themselves and their organizations:

- Not understanding the difference between change and improvement, managers introduce and allow others to introduce interventions that are illusions of progress and create only a temporary infusion of optimism, not real improvement.

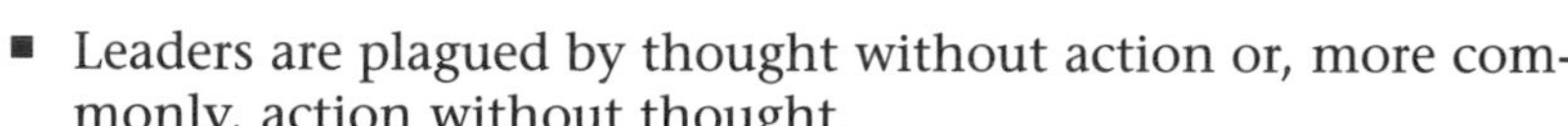

- Leaders are plagued by thought without action or, more commonly, action without thought.
- Problems remain unsolved. At best they disappear for a while only to reappear. People don't know why the problems disappeared or why they reappeared.
- The organization that doesn't know how to learn doesn't know how to improve, how to improve learning, or how to improve improvement.
- The organization becomes a victim of the current fad, whatever management program du jour is currently in vogue. People become cynical, having learned that this fad will come and go only to be replaced by another. Thus, they take none of them seriously.

Competency 4. Understanding People and Why They Behave as They Do

We Americans like to see ourselves as sensitive to people. "People are our most important asset" is the boast of many managers. Our rhetoric is humanitarian. When looked at closely, our premises, reflexes, relationships, and leadership behavior are not.

Why People Do What They Do

To a great extent, people behave in a way consistent with how we expect them to behave. In his landmark work, *The Human Side of Enterprise* (1985), Douglas McGregor described the two sets of managerial assumptions and how they affect employee behavior. (See Chapter 9, p. 298.) More recently Dov Eden explored the same subject in a fascinating book, *Pygmalion in Management* (1990).

If a manager wants to know why people do what they do, a good starting point is for the manager to examine his or her own expectations. There is a good likelihood that self-fulfilling prophecies are at work.

Motivation

How can managers motivate their people? They can't. Frederick Herzberg established this thirty years ago (1966, 1968). It is the ultimate management conceit to believe that we can motivate people. Motivation is not some substance we can infuse from the outside, like a bone marrow transplant.

All of our efforts to motivate our people are based on commonly shared myths. Managers can, it is true, *de*motivate. Suppose your boss came in tomorrow and told you, "Because we're trying to cut

Knute Rockne: The Great Motivator

Didn't Knute Rockne motivate the Fighting Irish, in his stirring half time speech, to "win one for the Gipper"? The never-asked alternative question: "Would Notre Dame have won the game without the speech?"

I submit that what won the game was the training, conditioning, and coaching that began years before the fateful game. The system won the game, not the oratory. But my version, I admit, would not have made as good a movie.

costs, we are reducing your salary by 50 percent." Such an announcement might result in less effort on your part and a worsened performance. You would be demotivated. Suppose your boss made a different announcement: "Beginning tomorrow, your salary will be doubled!" Will you be happy? I should think so! Will you be motivated? Will you do a better job? No, you won't. There may be a temporary "halo effect" while—after the manner of a special cause—you pay closer attention, put in extra hours, and put in some extra effort. But this likely will not last long (not even the joy of more money will last) and you will quickly return to common cause variation in your performance. Consider the implications of someone being able to motivate you to a higher level of performance through some kind of reward. What this would say about you is that you have been withholding some reservoir of effort, waiting for it to be bribed out of you. None of us would say that about ourselves. Nor do we say that others are holding back, waiting for a bribe. However, with our contests and merit pay and incentive bonuses, we *act* as though it were true.

In his important book, *Punished by Rewards,* Alfie Kohn (1993) reminds us of Harry Levinson's observation that between the legendary *carrot* and *stick* stood a *jackass.* The efficacy of the carrot and stick motivational approach, if there is any efficacy at all, seems to be limited to that species. But managers commonly accept as unquestioned truth the belief that people must be motivated through a combination of promises of reward (carrots) and threats of punishment (sticks). What a cynical and perverted view of people, especially in a country that sees itself as humanitarian.

Herzberg calls such motivation KITA (for "kick-in-the-pants"). There are positive KITA (carrots) and negative KITA

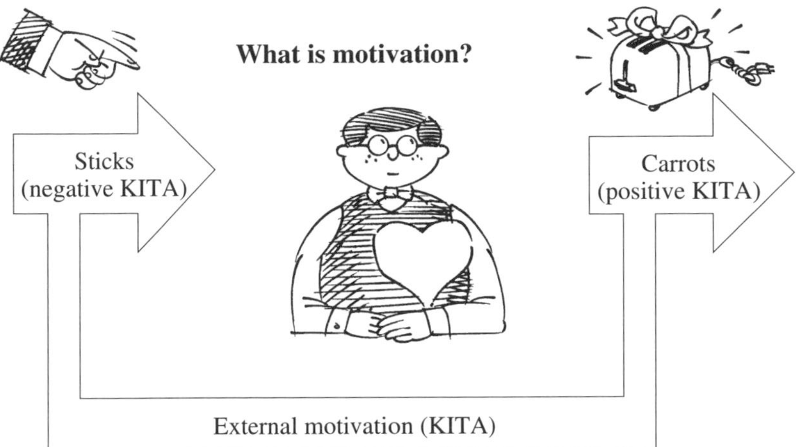

Figure 2-11. External and internal motivation.

(sticks). The problems with both positive and negative KITA, according to Herzberg and Kohn:

- They don't work (except for short-term, noncomplex conformity).
- They are detrimental to the relationships between:
  - — The motivator and the one to be motivated
  - — The one to be motivated and his or her peers

As pictured in Figure 2-12, KITA locks the manager and the subordinate in a parent–child relationship. When rewards are a matter of internal competition among coworkers, they create winners and losers and adversarial relationships among those who should be colleagues. Imagine the impact of competition on teamwork and collaboration, as well as among managers who claim to be humanitarian.

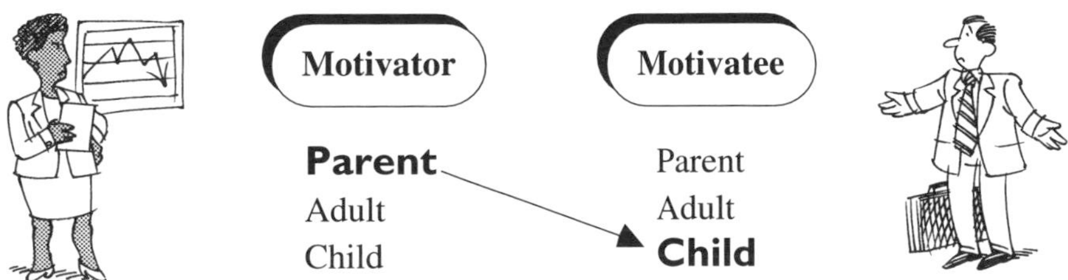

Figure 2-12. The relationship between the motivator and the motivatee.

Reading for Pizzas: External Motivation versus Internal Motivation

My friend Dave from Indianapolis was upset. His daughter Emily had been a good student, an avid reader ... that is, until Pizza Hut got into the reward business. It seems Pizza Hut provided teachers with coupons for free pizzas to be awarded to a student when he or she had completed ten books. Dave's daughter started reading shorter and less challenging books or just skimmed longer books, so she could get more coupons.

Meanwhile, Emily's classmates also started reading more books. Even those who were not readers started reading. The books they read were short and simple, but at least these kids were reading *something*. The students who, like Emily, were avid readers, switched their reading preference to short, simple books.

Eventually, however, Pizza Hut's reading-for-pizzas campaign ended; and so did the reading by those who used to be avid readers of challenging books as well as by those who didn't read.

"What my wife and I unwittingly allowed Pizza Hut to do," said Dave, "was substitute their *external* motivation for our daughter's *internal* motivation. They replaced *her* reason for reading and then eventually their substitute reason was removed." With pizza coupons no longer available, the kids in the class felt that there was no longer a reason to read.

This story—a true incident—demonstrates a fallacy of *all* incentive programs. Research on rewards, merit and incentive pay programs—among adults as well as children—shows them to be ineffective and, as in Emily's case, even harmful.

To many this will come as a shock. Reward, incentive, motivational, and merit programs are almost always sincere, well-intentioned efforts to recognize the good that people do. How could they be the wrong thing to do? How could they be ineffective and even harmful? To read more about this from a valuable resource, with a wealth of rigorous documentation, read *Punished by Rewards* by Alfie Kohn. (Excerpted from *Small Business Forum*. Madison, WI: UW Extension. Winter 94/95, p. 71 ff. "Reward and incentive programs are ineffective—even harmful."—Scholtes)

Relationships

Understanding people requires understanding relationships. Leading people requires establishing personal relationships, nurturing these relationships on a daily basis, and encouraging others to form and nurture relationships as well.

What is a relationship? By relationship I mean a good, old-fashioned, one-to-one, personal relationship, face-to-face, first name to first name. Some characteristics of this kind of relationship:

- You listen to each other's stories. You are able to tell your stories to each other.
- Each respects the other and knows how to show respect in ways the other wants respect to be shown.
- Each knows the other well enough to know what the vulnerabilities and hot buttons are. Each cares enough about the other to avoid those vulnerabilities and hot buttons.

It is obvious that no one person can have this kind of relationship with everyone else. However, it is possible to have an organization where everyone is known and has relationships with others. No one should be unconnected. We spend too much of our lives in our workplaces to experience an isolated and solitary existence for long periods of time without human contact and interaction.

The nature of the manager–employee relationship in most organizations is patronizing and paternalistic. Eric Berne is the founder of transactional analysis, whose writings unfortunately became associated with the psychobabble of the 1970s human potential movement. He deserves better. Berne popularized and significantly developed the teachings of Freud. Berne taught that each of us has three "ego states," three postures in relation to others:

- *Parent:* at best is nurturing and supportive; at worst is judgmental and controlling.
- *Adult:* at best is realistic, logical, and rational; at worst is affectless.
- *Child:* at best is playful and creative; at worst is rebellious and spiteful.

Most managers assume the stance of parent, giving those around them little choice but to assume the position of child. Figure 2-13 de-

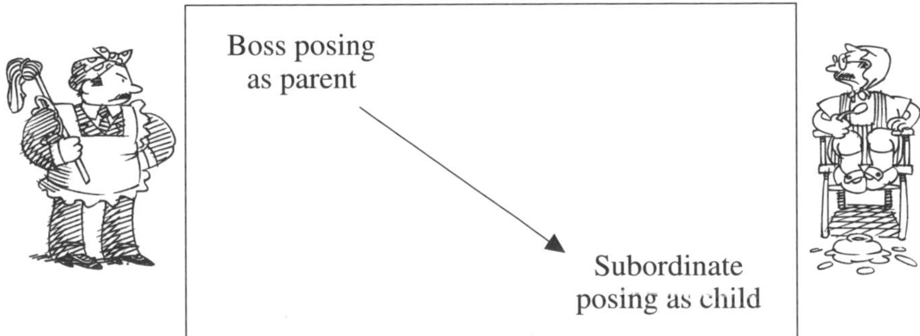

Figure 2-13. The boss–subordinate relationship in a conventional organization.

picts this relationship. Sometimes it happens that subordinates assume the role of child, making it difficult for the boss to take any stance other than parent. The unspoken message from the parent-boss to the subordinate-child, in the conventional paternalistic relationship, is "I'm OK, you're not OK!"

In relationships there are four possible positions, as pictured in Figure 2-14.

	I'm not OK	*I'm OK*
You're OK	I'm not OK, you're OK	I'm OK, you're OK
You're not OK	I'm not OK, you're not OK	I'm OK, you're not OK

Figure 2-14. I (the boss) am OK, you (the employee) are OK.

"OK" means basically competent and reliable; having high value as a person and an employee. "Not OK" means incompetent and/or unreliable; untrustworthy as an employee and/or a human being.

Only one of the positions in Figure 2-14—I'm OK, you're OK—represents a healthy relationship with the world around us. The other three represent different forms of social pathology. The conventional, paternalistic boss–subordinate relationship is based on a form of social pathology:

- *I'm* OK, *you* need motivation.
- *I'm* OK, *you* need carrots and sticks.
- *I'm* OK, *you* need performance appraisal.
- *I'm* doing my best, *you* need to be given incentives in order to get you to make an effort.

Managers intervene with their employees' behavior in ways they would deem unnecessary for themselves. Because they were expected to be the stern taskmasters, managers in the old paradigm were encouraged *not* to get personal with subordinates. Contrast this with Tom Chappell, president of Tom's of Maine, who encourages the forming of personal relationships with and among his people and who believes in the power of listening to people as they tell the stories that convey who they are and what the values are that shape them. Tom Chappell wants his employees to know each other not merely by job category, but in a way that brings each one into each other's lives. Peter Block calls this "connectedness." At Tom's of Maine they seek to create not only a business but a community of people. The notions of personal relationships and community are then extended to customers, suppliers, owners, financial partners, the local community, and government. "I... found myself thinking about... my company not only as a private entity but in relation to other entities—employees, financial partners, customers, suppliers, even the earth itself. Living in a community, we are relational, and we have obligations that go along with those relationships" (1993, p. 16). Tom Chappell had discovered for himself and his company the human side of systems thinking.

Trust

An understanding of people and relationships requires an understanding of trust. Trust requires the coexistence of two converging beliefs, as pictured in Figure 2-15. When I believe you are competent and that you care about me, I will trust you. Competency alone or caring by itself will not engender trust. Both are necessary.

Each is demonstrated over time. Thus relationships take time to unfold. When something happens that leads me to doubt either your competence or your caring, it will take a while to rebuild trust.

When the starting point between individuals or groups is distrust, there needs to be a thoughtful series of activities that will allow each party to test its willingness to believe in the other's competence and caring. When you are starting to work with parties to an adversarial relationship, begin by doing simple, low-risk activities. For example, learn something new together. Gradually plan your coopera-

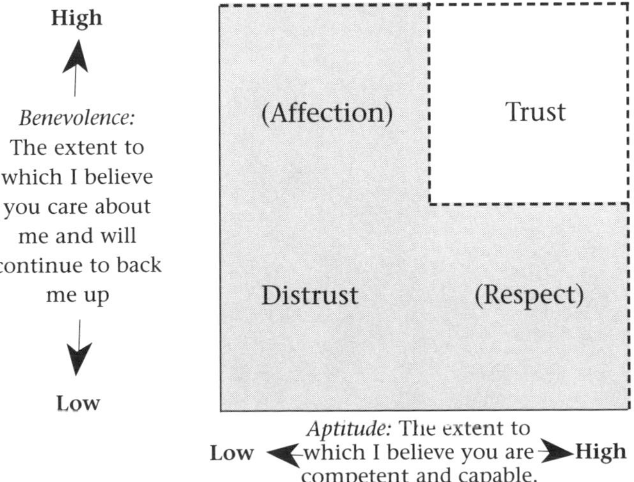

Figure 2-15. Trust, respect, affection.

tion around activities that are more and more challenging. The small increments of risk and trust won't seem like great steps forward. But the slow, steady progress over time can be substantial indeed. (I am grateful to Liz Freeman and Roland Coates for the ideas on which these comments regarding trust-building activities for adversaries are based.)

Competency 5: Understanding the Interaction and Interdependence between Systems, Variability, Learning, and Human Behavior; Knowing How Each Affects the Others

The list of new leadership competencies presented earlier in this chapter is based on Dr. Deming's system of profound knowledge, though phrased slightly differently. In Figure 2-16, I have chosen to use Dr. Deming's terminology. The meaning is the same.

While we have explored each of the four areas of profound knowledge separately, it is essential to understand that the four areas are an interactive, interdependent *system* of knowledge. One cannot fully understand or apply one area of profound knowledge without understanding the other three and how all four areas impact upon each other.

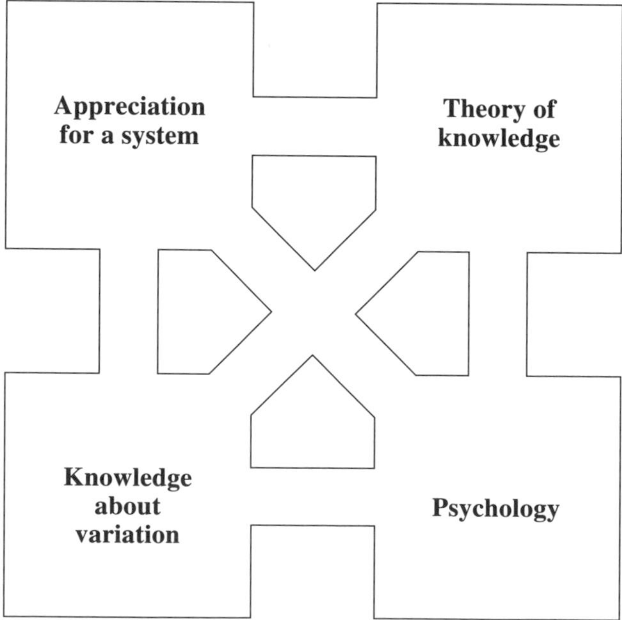

Figure 2-16. Dr. Deming's system of profound knowledge.

One of my first experiences in applying Deming's philosophy was with the City of Madison, Wisconsin Motor Equipment Operation. Motor Equipment was responsible for maintaining and repairing city vehicles, ranging from police cars to garbage trucks, snow plows, and Zambonis. I had developed some expertise in the areas of organization development and teamwork. I worked with the late Dr. Bill Hunter, a statistician from the University of Wisconsin, who was also very knowledgeable about Deming's philosophy.

In the first meeting with the people from the First Street Garage, where motor equipment was located, we asked them, "What are your biggest problems?" "Morale!" was their immediate and universal response. I didn't want to work on morale problems because they are symptoms of something else and working on them usually involves a lot of useless complaining. I got them to agree to defer working on the morale problem.

They started to work on two other projects: customers' feedback and cycle time. The immediate customers of the Motor Equipment Operation were the other municipal agencies that needed their vehicles to be up and running: the Police Department, Parks Department, Streets Department, etc. The Motor Equipment people did surveys and interviews of their customers to learn their perceptions regarding the services of Motor Equipment. They identified the chief customer complaints and the customers' priorities (which types of jobs should take priority over others). Much to their delight, the Motor Equipment people also learned that, for the most part, the customers were pleased with their service.

The cycle time project studied how long it took from the time a vehicle broke down until it was back in service. They identified all the stages of the downtime process and how much time each consumed. Then they spun off some subprojects aimed at reducing the cycle time. For example, one effort was aimed at reducing the time spent waiting for parts. After six or eight weeks of involvement in such activities, I suggested at a meeting, "Now let's talk about the morale problem." "What morale problem?" they responded.

The original presented problem, morale, was part of the *psychology* area of the system of profound knowledge. I suggested, instead, activities focused on understanding the *system,* beginning with the customers, who are the end point and purpose of the system (a second area of profound knowledge). The study of the system and cycle times inevitably involved studying *variation* in the components of cycle time: which delays were due to unique (special) causes and which were built into the current system (common cause). This is, of course, a third area of profound knowledge. Knowledge of the system and variation allowed them to focus on *improvements* dealing with the systemic causes of problems. Because of their expanded knowledge of customers, systems, and the methods of improvement, the Motor Equipment people made dramatic improvement on problems that had plagued the operation for decades. (Learning, knowledge, and improvement are the fourth area of profound knowledge.) All of this led to excitement, pride, great motivation, and an evaporation of the morale problem.

The example of the Israeli air force flight instructors described earlier in this chapter is an example of interacting areas of profound knowledge. Because the flight instructors didn't understand variation, they attributed all problems to the student pilots. Because problems were simplistically attributed to the student pilots, the instructors couldn't understand the systemic nature of the problems, and so missed the opportunity to make real improvements in the pilots' capabilities. The additional and unfortunate by-product of this culprit mentality was, undoubtedly, unnecessary stress, anxiety, guilt, and anger for the student pilots and needlessly impaired relationships between them and the flight instructors. Such strained relationships presumably would get in the way of the instructors and pilots working together to improve the learning process. Thus, the interactions within the system of profound knowledge go on and on.

Anything of importance, whether it is a problem to be solved or an accomplishment to be attained, involves an understanding and application of all parts of the system of profound knowledge. We must learn to see all four areas as interactive, interdependent, and concurrent.

Today, problems and needs are complex. We cannot make progress by applying simplistic solutions to complex problems. The system of profound knowledge allows us to see those complexities more clearly and deal with them more realistically. To Justice Oliver Wendell Holmes has been attributed the statement, "I wouldn't give a fig for the simplicity on this side of complexity, but I would give my life for the simplicity on the other side of complexity" (Cawthon, 1996). Justice Holmes, perhaps, was articulating the need for profound knowledge.

Competency 6: Giving Vision, Meaning, Direction, and Focus to the Organization

In order to maintain the cohesiveness of an organization and the integrity of its systems, all the members of an organization need to know the following:

1. Who are we?
2. What business are we in?

Solipsism: Obscure and Wonderful Word #1

Solipsism is the belief that nothing exists outside of yourself. If you, while reading this book, believe that this book and everything around you are figments of your imagination, you are solipsistic… and a little loopy; get help!

Engine Charlie Wilson, former CEO of GM, once said, "What is good for GM is good for America!" Engine Charlie was indulging in solipsistic thinking on behalf of GM.

Grades in school may be another example of solipsism. The purpose of a school is learning. We create a surrogate indicator of learning: grades. Then we collude with each other to pretend that grades are an accurate indicator that learning has or has not taken place. We no longer even question the legitimacy of grades.

Another example: sweeps week. Twice a year there are weeklong surveys of TV viewership. The ratings during sweeps week are important because they determine what the networks charge for advertising. The solipsism is this: We pretend that the programs during sweeps week are representative of the networks' regular fare and that the ratings during sweeps week are indicative of something real.

Another example: *The Discipline of Market Leaders,* a book that made *The New York Times* list of best-selling books. This occurred because those behind the book were able to identify which stores around the country were used by *The New York Times* as their sample for calculating which books were best sellers. By buying up their book at these stores, they could artificially inflate the figures. The solipsism: pretending that *The New York Times* list accurately depicts the sales of books (and that the volume of sales of books is an accurate measure of what is worthwhile to read).

Organizations often indulge in solipsistic thinking when they engage in planning. Managers pretend that the only important measures—of customer satisfaction or business success—are the measures that they as managers agree on. The history of business is replete with companies that met their goals and targets… and still failed. This was because their measures were reflective mainly of their inner world, their solipsism.

Leaders must be sure their measures of success or failure reflect the real world outside themselves and their organization. There is a difference between having a vision and suffering from a hallucination.

3. What businesses are we not in?
4. Where are we headed in the long term?
5. What are the priorities for the short term?

6. What values and principles should be characteristics of all our relationships and all of what we do?
7. What is my own personal job and how do my functions and operations fit into the larger purposes and systems of the organization?
8. What is the best way to do my job and what is expected of me? By whom? What is a "good job" and who defines it?
9. How will improvements to my job be accomplished? Who will do the improvements and by what methods? Will I be involved in these improvements? How?
10. What sources and forms of feedback are available to help me know how I'm doing?

Conventional organizations pay scant attention to these issues. The answers to the first six questions, dealing with organizational purpose and direction, are often ambiguous and constantly shifting. With no purpose there can be no system. With an unclear or inconstant purpose the system will suffer from chaos and dysfunction. Chapters 5 and 6 address the first six questions. If the answers to the first six

Inch-Deep, Mile-Wide Thinking

I worked with one company that had 88 top priorities for the year. At midyear they realized they had accomplished none of the priorities, so they dumped some and added others—maintaining a total of 88. Near the end of the year, when it was clear that they would accomplish nothing of substance, they vowed to do better in planning for the following year. They brainstormed a list of priorities—about 80 of them—and then tried to reduce the list. But it became like Congress at budget time—each manager lobbying for his or her own pet project, trade-offs, and compromise. No systems thinking.

Realizing that they were repeating the mistakes of the previous year, they sought to knuckle down and reduce the priorities to a doable few. Sad to say, all they accomplished was to take the excessive number of priorities and group them into categories and declare each category a priority. They went from about 80 priorities to about 10 priorities, each of which had multiple subpriorities. Nothing changed except the complexity of the sentences in their goal statements. I decided not to interfere with this "inch-deep, mile-wide" process. Instead I limited my work with them to only one of the subpriorities. We went, successfully in this case, "a mile-deep-and-an-inch-wide" on that one priority.

questions on our list (those that deal with organizational purpose and direction) are unclear and inconstant, the answers to the last four (dealing with individual purpose and direction) will also be unclear and inconstant. Organizational ambiguity leads to individual confusion. Questions 7, 8, 9, and 10, dealing with an individual's clarity and purpose regarding his or her job, will be looked at in Chapter 4.

Dr. Noriaki Kano is a professor of management science at Tokyo Science University and one of the leading teachers of quality in Japan. He has worked with many managers of American companies. His advice to us: "Americans tend to go an inch deep and a mile wide. You must learn to go an inch wide and a mile deep." We must learn to do fewer things thoroughly rather than many things inadequately. Creating direction and focus for an organization requires that leaders consider all the worthwhile things to do and say no to most of them.

While Chapters 4, 5, and 6 look at this in more practical detail, for now I am simply suggesting that knowing how to give direction and focus is an essential and necessary competency for contemporary leaders. Leaders who don't know how to provide direction and focus to their organizations on a daily basis are incompetent.

SUMMARY

Life is not simple. Organizations are complex systems of social networks and technical processes. Simplistic approaches will not help resolve complex problems. The first thing a leader must learn to do is think differently.

In this chapter we have looked briefly at a handful of competencies leaders will need to make things happen, get things done, create products and services people can be proud of, and create an environment of joy at work.

We have skimmed the surface of systems thinking, one of the six new leadership competencies. In the next chapter we take another look at systems and draw some practical conclusions for leaders.

CHAPTER TWO ACTIVITIES

Questions for discussion

1. How do you motivate employees?

2. How does your answer to the previous question differ from what is described in Chapter 2?

3. **A.** What have you learned lately? (Some understanding or skill that is new to you.)

   B. How did you learn it?

   C. Is this typical of how you best learn?

Radar chart for self-assessment

- Below is a radar diagram, a form for recording one's own relative competence regarding various capabilities. The capabilities correspond to the new leadership competencies described in this chapter.
- The radar chart consists of 18 areas of competence divided into six categories.
- This chart is divided into four concentric circles or levels. Level 1, close to the center, indicates almost total ignorance of the competency. Level 4 indicates a high degree of mastery and application.

Directions

- For each competency, place a dot on the corresponding "spoke" on the radar chart indicating your current level of understanding and application.
- When you are done, connect the dots. The resulting picture will look like an erratic spiderweb, showing your strengths and your opportunities for further development.

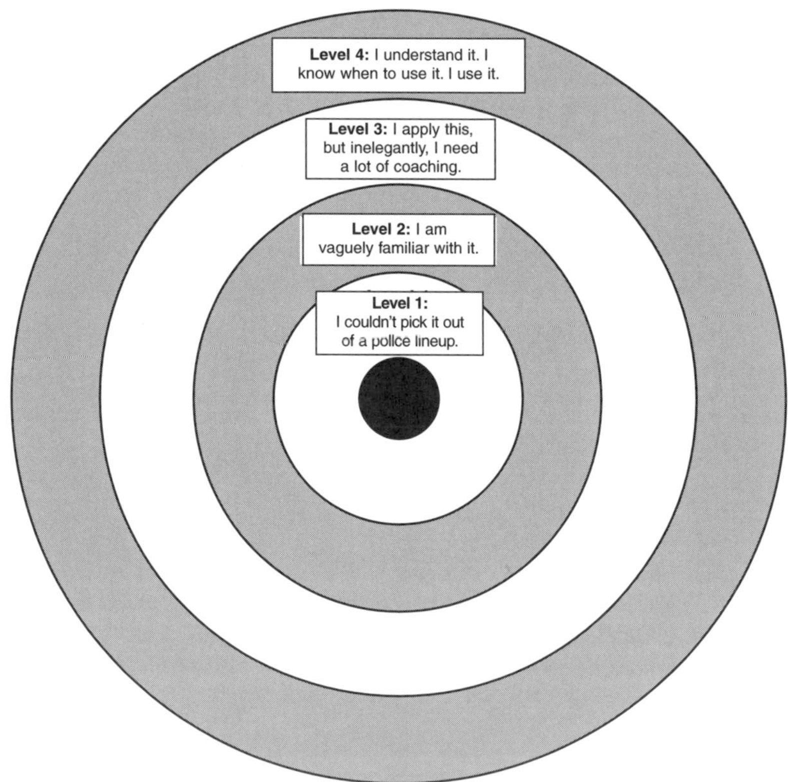

Some Suggestions

- You might ask a trusted colleague to do a radar diagram indicating his or her perception of you.
- If you are part of a team, you might have each individual do a chart on a blank overhead transparency. Then lay the individual diagrams on top of each other, project them onto the screen and see where the collective, self-perceived strengths and development opportunities are.

The Competencies

A. Systems thinking

1. Understanding the difference between systems and such things as structure and policy
2. Reflexes to see contexts and flows
3. Instincts to seek systemic causes, not culprits

B. Variability of work

4. Knowing the difference between common cause and special cause of variation
5. Knowing how to respond to common cause variation and to special causes
6. Gathering various important data in appropriate time-ordered charts

C. Learning

7. Understanding when a statement is theory or opinion versus fact, and acting accordingly
8. Knowing how different people learn differently
9. PDSA
10. Providing systems and resources for lifelong learning
11. The difference between change and improvement

D. Psychology and human behavior

12. Understanding and applying the concepts of internal versus external motivation and demotivation
13. Developing relationships and community within the organization and with those outside
14. Developing and nurturing trust

E. Interactions

15. Seeing the interdependence between systems thinking, variation, learning, and human behavior

F. Vision, meaning, direction, and focus

16. Starting with clarity of purpose
17. Going an inch wide and a mile deep
18. Developing and continuously communicating a clear sense of direction and focus

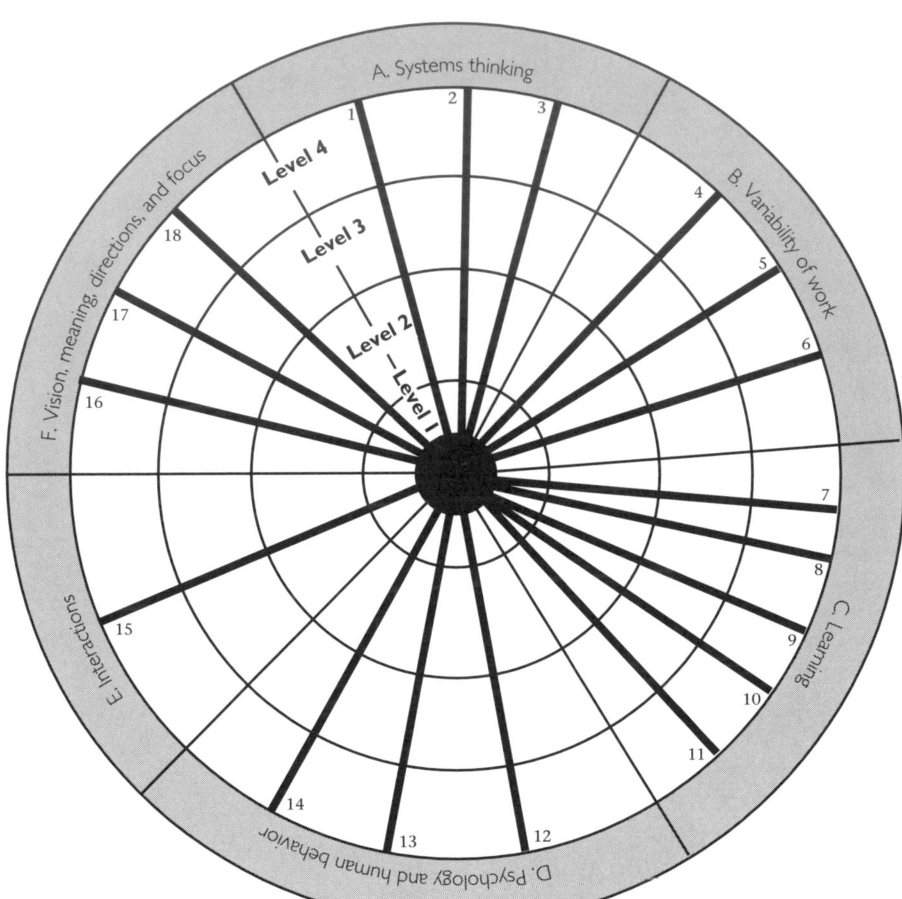
A. Systems thinking
B. Variability of work
C. Learning
D. Psychology and human behavior
E. Interactions
F. Vision, meaning, directions, and focus
Level 4
Level 3
Level 2
Level 1
1
2
3
4
5
6
7
8
9
10
11
12
13
14
15
16
17
18

REFERENCES

Ackoff, R. 1994. *The democratic organization.* New York: Oxford University Press.

Ackoff, R. 1991. *Ackoff's fables.* New York: John Wiley & Sons.

Ackoff, R. 1986. *Management in small doses.* New York: John Wiley & Sons.

Ackoff, R. 1981. *Creating the corporate future.* New York: John Wiley & Sons.

Beer, S. 1981. *Brain of the firm.* New York: John Wiley & Sons.

Berne, E. 1974. *The structure and dynamics of organizations and groups.* New York: Grove Press.

Berne, E. 1972. *What do you say after you say hello?* New York: Grove Press.

Berne, E. 1964. *Games people play.* New York: Grove Press.

Block, P. 1993. *Stewardship.* San Francisco: Barrett-Koehler.

Borwick, I. 1969. Team improvement laboratory. *Personnel Journal,* January.

Boulding, K.E. 1985. *The world as a total system.* Newbury Park, CA: Sage.

Cawthon, D.L. 1996. Leadership, the great man theory revisited. *Business Horizons.* May 15.

Chappell, T. 1993. *The soul of a business.* New York: Bantam Books.

Cheaney, L., and Cotter, M. 1991. *Real people, real work.* Knoxville, TN: SPC Press, Inc.

Deming, W.E. 1994. *The new economics for industry/government/education.* Cambridge, MA. MIT CAES.

Dobyns, L. 1995. *Better management for a changing world.* A four-part video series featuring Dr. Russell Ackoff with Lloyd Dobyns. Contact: CC-M Productions, 8510 Cedar Street, Silver Springs, MD 20910, (800) 453-6280, www.cc-m.com

Eden, D. 1990. *Pygmalion in management.* Lexington, MA: D.C. Heath and Company.

Gall, J. 1986. *Systemantics,* 2nd ed. Ann Arbor, MI: The General Systemantics Press.

Herzberg, F. 1968. One more time: How do you motivate employees? *Harvard Business Review.* January-February.

Herzberg, F. 1966. *Work and the nature of man.* Cleveland: World Publishing.

Joiner, B.L. 1994. *Fourth generation management.* New York: McGraw-Hill.

Jongeward, D. 1973. *Everybody wins.* Reading, MA: Addison-Wesley.

Kahneman, D., and Tverski, A. 1973. On the psychology of prediction. *Psychological Review,* 80, 237–251.

Knowles, M. 1970. *The modern practice of adult education: Androgogy versus pedagogy.* New York: Association Press.

Kohn, A. 1993. *Punished by rewards.* New York: Houghton Mifflin.

Langley, G.J., Nolan, K.M., Nolan, T.W., Norman, C.L., and Provost. L.P. 1996. *The improvement guide: A practical approach to enhancing organizational performance.* San Francisco: Jossey-Bass Publishers.

Laszlo, E. 1972. *The systems view of the world.* New York: George Braziller Inc.

Markova, D. 1996. *The open mind.* San Francisco: Conari Press.

Markova, D. 1991. *The art of the possible.* Berkeley, CA: Conari Press.

Markova, D., and Powell, A. 1992. *How your child* is *smart: A life-changing approach to learning.* San Francisco: Conari Press.

Maurer, R. 1996. *Beyond the wall of resistance.* Austin, TX: Bard Books.

McGregor, D. 1985. *The human side of enterprise.* New York: McGraw-Hill.

McKean, K. 1985. Decisions, decisions. *Discover,* June, 23–32.

Neave, H. 1990. *The Deming dimension.* Knoxville, TN: SPC Press Inc.

Quinn, D. 1992. *Ishmael.* New York: Bantam/Turner.

Scherkenbach, W. 1991. *Deming's road of continual improvement.* Knoxville, TN: SPC Press Inc.

Scholtes, P. 1994. *Learning and leadership.* Salisbury, Wiltshire: The British Deming Association.

Senge, P. 1990. *The fifth discipline.* New York: Doubleday.

Tveite, M. 1995. *The Deming philosophy: New ways to think about the world.* Salisbury, Wiltshire: The British Deming Association.

U.S. News and World Report. 1991. 10, 15:52.

Wheeler, D. 1993. *Understanding variation.* Knoxville, TN: SPC Press Inc.

SYSTEMS THINKING: THE HEART OF TWENTY-FIRST-CENTURY LEADERSHIP

INTRODUCTION

In the previous chapter we explored systems thinking as a new management competency. In this chapter we look at systems and systems thinking in more depth.

Before we continue, let me establish some loose definitions of terms, at least what I mean by them. *Systems thinking* refers to the general reflex or habit of conceiving of reality in terms of interdependencies, interactions, and sequences. It is a way of thinking at the broadest macro-level (the galactic system) or the smallest micro-level (the genetic DNA system). Most of us work with systems somewhere in between those two extremes.

Beyond the generic use of the word *systems,* I use different words to differentiate different scales of systems or systems thinking:

- *System* refers to interactions and interdependencies on a large scale. Systems consist of subsystems or, if they're small enough in scope, processes. What is the point at which something is no longer a system or a subsystem but becomes a process? I don't know. (When does a ship become small enough to be called a boat?)
- *Processes* refer to the components of a system. Processes have purposes and functions of their own, but by themselves processes cannot accomplish the purpose of a system.
- *Methods* refer to components of the process that have their own purpose and function but the value of the method is seen only through its interaction with other methods that make up the process.
- *Steps* refer to components of a method. One event in a sequence that interacts with the other steps to serve the purpose of the method.

An example:

- System
  - Macro-system:
    - PepsiCo's international operation
    - The worldwide Pizza Hut chain
    - A regional Pizza Hut organization
  - System:
    - One Pizza Hut restaurant
    - One restaurant's kitchen operation
  - Micro-system

- Making pizzas

- Process
  - Macro-process: Making a specific pizza
  - Process: Making pizza dough
  - Micro-process: Rolling out pizza dough
- Method
  - Rolling out pizza dough by feeding it through a machine that flattens it, or
  - Rolling it out by hand, or
  - Spinning it in the air
- Step
  - Dusting the surface with cornmeal before rolling out the pizza dough

THE SIPOC MODEL

What all of these systems, processes, methods, and steps have in common is the SIPOC model. The SIPOC model (Figure 3-1) is another version of Dr. Deming's systems view (see Figures 1-2 and 2-2).

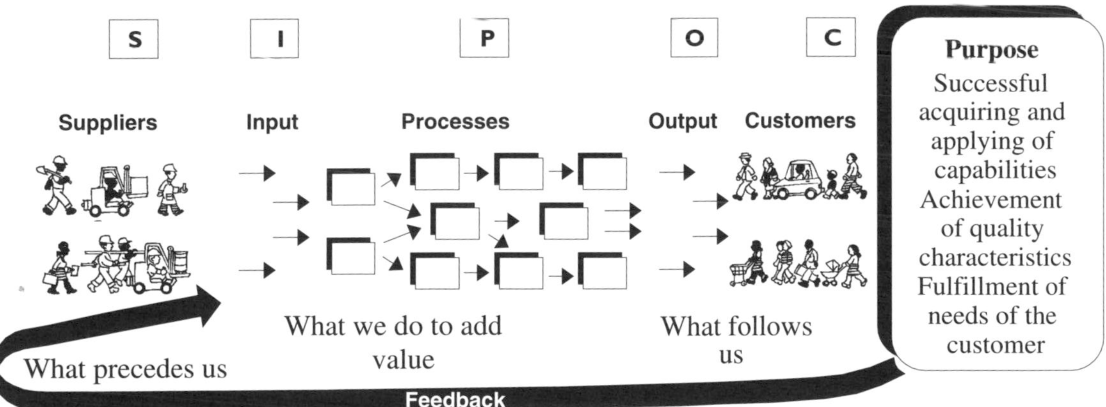

Figure 3-1. The SIPOC model.

The SIPOC model begins with purpose. Without a purpose there is no SIPOC, there is no system. "Clean off the table, please." Unless the context makes it evident, the purpose of this request is not sufficiently clear to let you know what method (steps/process/system) to use. The table-cleaning methods appropriate for playing cards, eating, or performing surgery would be quite different.

The SIPOC Model

The SIPOC model is an elaboration on Dr. Deming's systems diagram (Figure 1-2). SIPOC is an acronym for Suppliers, Input, Process, Output, Customers. This entire chapter is a detailed look at the SIPOC model. (By the way, I pronounce it SEE-pock.)

Learning to apply SIPOC is an indispensable first step in understanding how the new philosophy applies to people's daily work. Your job—and the jobs of all the people in your organization—consists of a collection of SIPOCs. Your work and theirs is part of a flow with steps that precede the work and steps that follow. To help you and your people begin to see work in its larger *systemic* context, you must see it as a SIPOC within larger SIPOCs within still larger SIPOCs. The activities at the end of this chapter and the end of Chapter 4 are designed to help people come to grips with the SIPOCs of their work.

One chronic problem with our organizations, work units, and the jobs of individuals is that the purpose is often unclear or constantly changing. Such inconstancy and ambiguity make it impossible to have a system. Ironically, without a system it is impossible to deal with change. More about that later.

Once the purpose is clear, we can then identify the customers—those whose needs must be served—and learn from them what output, goods, or services they need. Then we can design a process or method suitable to produce that output, and we can therefore identify what input from which suppliers is necessary. In the broadest sense, input includes not just the usual materials and supplies but also policies and plans; customer and market research; organizational structure; leadership style; values, mission, and vision; communication modes, methods, and styles; and education and training resources. Inputs include all those material objects, the environment, various factors and conditions, the tangibles and intangibles that are needed to make the process work in a manner that both delights the customer and serves the purpose of the organization.

SIPOC also includes feedback: loops of information that inform those working within the system as to how well the system is functioning. Without system-based feedback there will be no improvement. Feedback is the mother's milk of improvement.

If we were to examine any part of the process in the SIPOC model, we would discover a microcosm of the whole, a SIPOC within the SIPOC, a step within a method within a process within a system. Dr. Deming has taught us that everything is a system, and we are part of it.

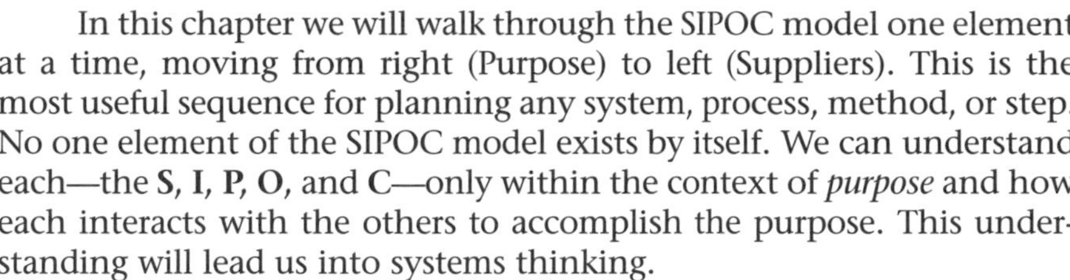

In this chapter we will walk through the SIPOC model one element at a time, moving from right (Purpose) to left (Suppliers). This is the most useful sequence for planning any system, process, method, or step. No one element of the SIPOC model exists by itself. We can understand each—the **S, I, P, O,** and **C**—only within the context of *purpose* and how each interacts with the others to accomplish the purpose. This understanding will lead us into systems thinking.

PURPOSE

Purpose tells you and the world why you exist, what business you are in and, by implication, what business you are *not* in. Purpose is best defined from a customer's point of view. Rather than simply describing your products and services, describe the benefit or capability your customers acquire as a result of interacting with you. Your purpose is related to these benefits and capabilities that accrue to your customers. Therefore, the purpose of your kid's lemonade stand might be described as "pedestrian refreshment." That is the reason the customer buys the lemonade. Lemonade, therefore, is a means to an end defined by the customer's benefit. Here is an example [I am grateful to Dr. Noriaki Kano for this story]:

> Konica Camera had a problem: They wanted to develop a breakthrough product but the feedback from their customers would lead to only minor improvements.
>
> In one meeting when Konica's managers were discussing the problem, Mr. Takanori Yoneyama, the chairman of Konica, offered this observation: "Perhaps we are asking the wrong questions. We ask for feedback on our *camera*. But people don't purchase our camera in order to own a camera. They buy a camera in order to take *pictures*. We see ourselves as manufacturing and selling cameras. Customers see us as a source for acquiring the capability to take photographs. Perhaps we should start seeking feedback on the *pictures*."
>
> Sitting down with customers' photographs was a revelation. The pictures were pretty bad: out of focus, too light, too dark, one superimposed upon another. In each case the customer blamed not the camera, but themselves. "You have a very good camera. I am simply not a very good photographer."
>
> From this feedback Konica was able to invent the error-proof camera: automatic focusing, lens opening, adjustment, film forwarding, flash, etc. Now customers love both the camera *and* their photographs.

The purpose of your organization, therefore, is related to the benefits or capabilities acquired by your customers as a result of their inter-

> The highest use of capital is not to make more money but to make money more for the betterment of life.
>
> —Henry Ford, 1931

action with you. If buggy-whip manufacturers saw their purpose as providing the capability for vehicular acceleration, they would more likely have survived the transition from the horse and buggy to the era of the horseless carriage. A purpose based on customer capability can provide a beacon of stable focus and direction during times of turbulent change in technology or the market.

It is my firm belief that the purpose of an organization, if it is to survive, should be altruistic, not self-aggrandizing. By altruistic I mean focused on doing good for society. By self-aggrandizing I mean a purpose focused primarily on profitability and return on investment.

If my primary purpose were to maximize shareholder gain, I could justify buying underpriced stock, gaining control of a company, closing its factories, laying off its employees, selling off its assets, and maximizing my profits. This has been acknowledged by Wall Street as smart business, or at least the unfortunate by-product of the free enterprise system.

I think it should be a felony.

I am not against profits or return on investments. They are necessary means to an end. When they become an end in themselves, however, a business is likely to begin hurting its customers, its employees, the quality of its goods and services, the community, the environment, and its own long-term survival. The business can begin to lose its *soul*. (See Chappell, 1993.)

When a business is altruistic, when it is committed to serving (rather than exploiting) customers and society, such an elevating purpose can create and sustain excitement and commitment among leaders, managers, employees, stockholders, and—most importantly—customers. (See Customer-In Thinking in the next section.) The purpose of the organization must, in my belief, describe, in Herzberg's words, "work worth doing." Such a business, if it is well-led, is also likely to prosper.

THE CUSTOMER

Moving from right to left in the SIPOC model (Figure 3-2), we next look at customers. The customers are those who benefit from the

Customer

Purpose

- Successful acquiring and applying of capabilities
- Achievement of quality characteristics
- Fulfillment of needs of the customer

Figure 3-2. SIPOC, moving right to left.

goods and services you supply. Customers are those who acquire the new capabilities you offer. Conversely, customers are those who are disappointed or angry over the inadequacy of your goods or services, because it is the customers who fail to gain a new or improved capability from your goods or services.

Customer-In Thinking

The perspective of a system creates a different attitude and approach to customers: *customer-in thinking.*

We conventionally think in terms of "product-out," as pictured in Figure 3-3.

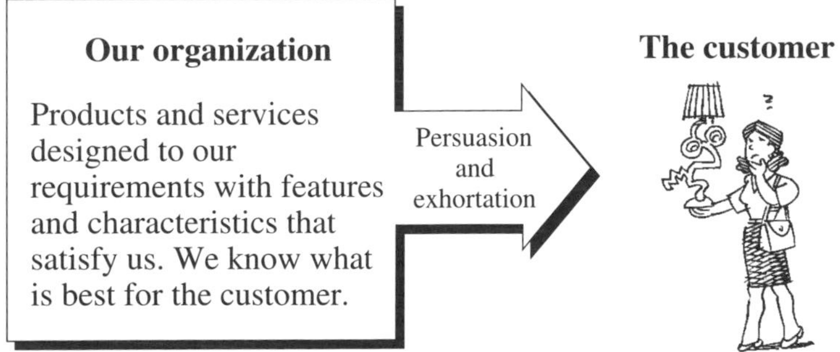
Our organization
Products and services designed to our requirements with features and characteristics that satisfy us. We know what is best for the customer.
Persuasion and exhortation
The customer

Figure 3-3. A product-out mentality.

The product-out mentality is at best tactful arrogance. (And often it is not done at its best.) Whenever you as a consumer are made to feel stupid or manipulated, you are on the receiving end of product-out mentality. In the product-out organization, the marketing department is focused on sales: What can we do in the naming, de-

> **Customers**
>
> Customers are the "C" of SIPOC. This chapter will devote quite a bit of attention to customers. They are an organization's reason for being. Without customers' feedback, you cannot know if you are doing a good job. In Chapter 2 and again in Chapter 9, we discuss motivation. When an organization and its people lose sight of *customers* they have lost a sense of altruism about work. Without the motivation inherent in doing good for the customers, managers are more likely to resort to artificial motivation such as contests, incentives, etc. This is ultimately destructive to the company, its employees and, worst of all, its customers (see Chapter 9). Attention to customers is pivotal. Therefore, considerable attention is given to customers in these pages.

scribing, packaging, positioning, and advertising of this product or service to take advantage of the buying habits of potential customers? The dark underside of a product-out mentality is organizational self-absorption, isolation, and haughtiness. (If an idea is any good, we have already thought of it. If we didn't think of it, it isn't any good!) We have all had to deal with such organizations.

A Customer-In Mentality

When internalized in our everyday routines and reflexes, systems thinking will lead us to customer-in thinking (Figure 3-4.) The cus-

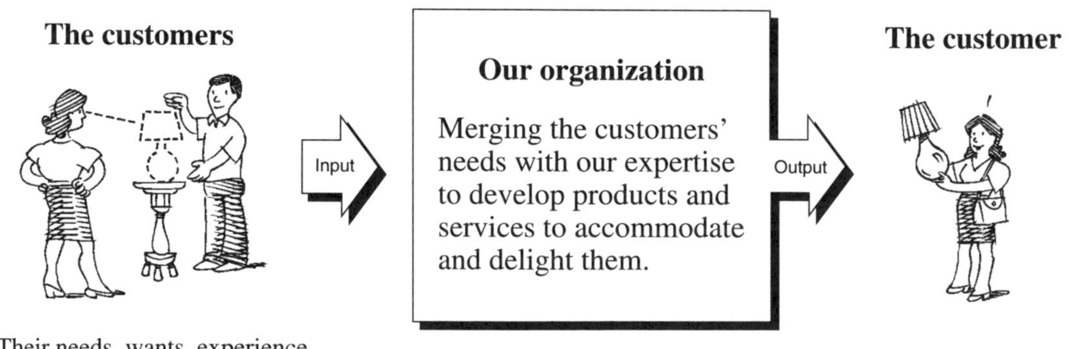
The customers
Input
Our organization
Merging the customers' needs with our expertise to develop products and services to accommodate and delight them.
Output
The customer
Their needs, wants, experience, definition of a "good job"

Figure 3-4. A customer-in mentality.

tomer-in mentality is outward-focused rather than narcissistic, other-centered and not self-centered. Customer-in is characterized by thoughtfulness (What else can we do for them?), responsiveness, empathy, and altruism. It is the best way to create new products and services. If you understand the day-to-day experiences of your customers, you can imagine products and services that they might not even think of. Customer-in thinking increases the likelihood that customers get what they need and need what they get.

In a customer-in organization, marketing becomes focused on real customer research: research not just on sales strategies, but research on customers and their needs and experiences.

Some Important Notions about Customers

A. Purchasers are not necessarily customers. The fact that some person or group pays for a product or service does not make them customers. By paying my cable TV bill, I am a purchaser of MTV and Beavis and Butthead. I am, however, most certainly not a customer of MTV, Beavis, or Butthead, a fact to which, I suspect, MTV is spectacularly indifferent.

B. You don't have a be a customer to be important. Stockholders, insurance companies, elected officials, and contributors to United Way are all extremely important in different aspects of this nation's everyday life. But, from a systemic point of view, each is a *supplier,* not a *customer.* The systems do not exist to serve *their* needs. Their role is to help systems serve the needs of the customers. When suppliers start seeing themselves as customers, the needs of the true customers are likely to be displaced and subordinated.

Hospitals to Moms: Give Birth and Go

New goal considered: six hours and then out

A mother in a Chicago suburb gave birth to her third child and underwent tubal ligation. Twenty-four hours after she entered the hospital, she was released. Maternity stays in the hospital may be further cut to 12 or even 6 hours if insurers and managed care providers get their way.

—Based on a story from the *Chicago Sun-Times,* June 18, 1995

Are the needs of the customers being displaced by the needs of the purchasers?

"Fresh" Feedback

Honda dealers in the Cleveland area provided free cellular phones in new cars, with the customer service number programmed into the phone. They wanted customers to tell them what was going wrong or what suggestions they had as the need was occurring. They didn't want to require customers to remember the problem until the next survey was mailed to them.

C. When suppliers and customers disagree, or when customers disagree with each other, it is likely that the organization's purpose isn't clear. The purpose of the organization should describe why it exists, what business it is in, and what business it is *not* in. Suppliers must consent to the purpose and agree on who the customers are and what needs the customers have ... consistent with the organization's purpose.

D. When we "listen to the customer," we must commit ourselves to listening to—even seeking out—dissatisfied customers. This might include:

- Contacting customers who stopped being our customers.
- Contacting customers who chose not to be our customers in the first place.
- Contacting customers who choose neither us nor our competition, but deal with their situation in some other way (or let their needs remain unsatisfied).
- Seeking out immediate feedback: making it easy for customers to complain when the dissatisfaction is fresh in their minds.

E. Customer complaints are "gifts from God," in the words of one company manager. A complaint provides an opportunity to learn. Positive feedback feels better, provides a boost to your spirits, and reminds you that the customer cares; but compliments don't offer an opportunity to learn.

Models for Listening to the Voice of the Customer

There are multiple ways by which we can listen to the customer. Sometimes the customer contacts us. For example:

- Complaints
- Questions

- Warranty calls
- Service requests

Sometimes we initiate contact with the customer:

- Focus groups
- Surveys
- Interviews

Described below are two ways to sort out what you hear from your customers. (Although we are looking here at customers *outside* the organization, these might be useful for feedback from *internal* customers as well.)

The Needs/Gets Matrix

	Customer Needs	*Customer Doesn't Need*
Customer Gets	The customer gets what the customer needs	The customer gets what the customer doesn't need
Customer Doesn't Get	The customer doesn't get what the customer needs	The customer doesn't get what the customer doesn't need

Figure 3-5. The needs/gets matrix.

This suggests two questions to use when exploring the customers' experiences with your products or services or your competitors' products or services:

- What are you getting that you don't need?
- What do you need that you are not getting?

The Kano Model

Dr. Noriaki Kano of Tokyo Science University, adapting some early work of Frederick Herzberg, has developed a framework for identifying, from a customer's viewpoint, those characteristics that describe your products or services. This is adapted from an article by Dr. Kano and others (Kano et al., 1996), in which they suggest three kinds of characteristics:

- *The basics:* These are the "must be" attributes of your products or services that create no delight when they are present but cause anger when they are not. Customers have every right to expect their cars will start when they turn the ignition key. When a car starts, customers don't celebrate (at least they shouldn't have to). When it fails to start, however, they will be angry. Most customer complaints are related to the basics. Ask your customers what the basics are for your products or services. They will be more than happy to tell you.
- *Performance-related:* The more present these characteristics are, the less angry, and eventually the more satisfied your customers will be. When miles per gallon are terribly low, a customer will likely be angry. When they are very high, customers become boastful. Often these characteristics have to do with size, speed, capacity, user-friendliness, value for price, accessibility of service, etc.
- *Delight characteristics:* The very minimal presence of these characteristics creates satisfaction among customers. These are, from a customer's point of view, unexpected, thoughtful, and delightful surprises. Cars now feature equipment that monitors the nearness of objects in front of you as well as your alertness as a driver. This technology will automatically warn you when you are too near an object or too drowsy and even slow down your car. Delighters often become basics be-

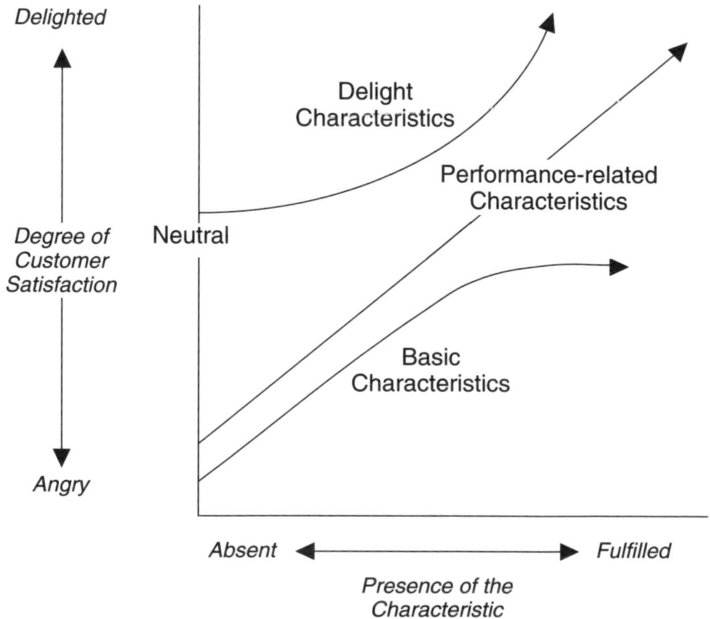

Figure 3-6. The Kano model.

fore too long. Television remote controls and electronic ignitions in automobiles were delighters when they were first introduced. Now they are basics.

A good rule of thumb: If you haven't taken care of the basics, don't work on the delighters. It does no good to have all the automatic sensors on a car that doesn't start. Figure 3-6 illustrates the Kano model.

THE CUSTOMER CHAIN

When we look at customers systemically, we see a less simplistic picture of the customer. Who is our customer? The answer to that is usually a complex sequence and network of people, organizations, and systems that depend on our good work. Who is the customer of the fourth grade?

- The children in the class
- The parents and families of the children
- The fifth grade
- Middle school
- High school
- Trade schools
- Colleges
- Universities
- Future employers of these fourth graders
- The communities in which they are living and in which they will live

All of these have expectations and needs for the fourth-grade students. All of them, in one way or another, are customers.

The customer chain is a systemic concept that describes customers in a way depicted in Figure 3-7.

Figure 3-8 shows a chain of customers related to a manufacturing business: coffee-maker production. Who is the customer of the coffee-maker manufacturer? The entire chain. To which "voice of the customer" should the coffee-maker manufacturer listen? All of them! Can the maker of the equipment rely on the national wholesaler to represent the rest of the chain? No! This manufacturer will go belly up if it responds only to the needs of the organization that pays its invoices, the wholesalers.

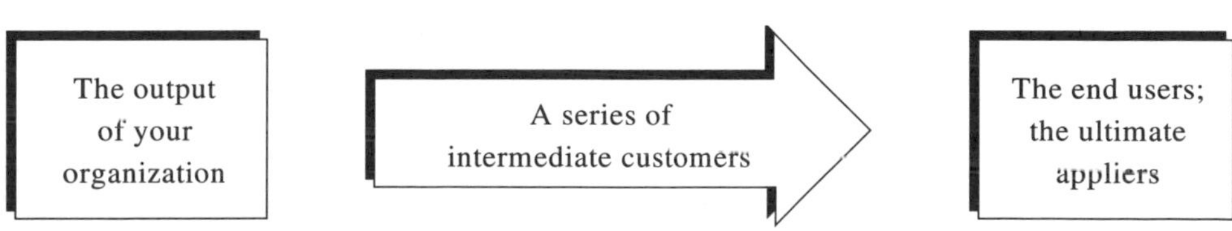

Figure 3-7. The customer chain.

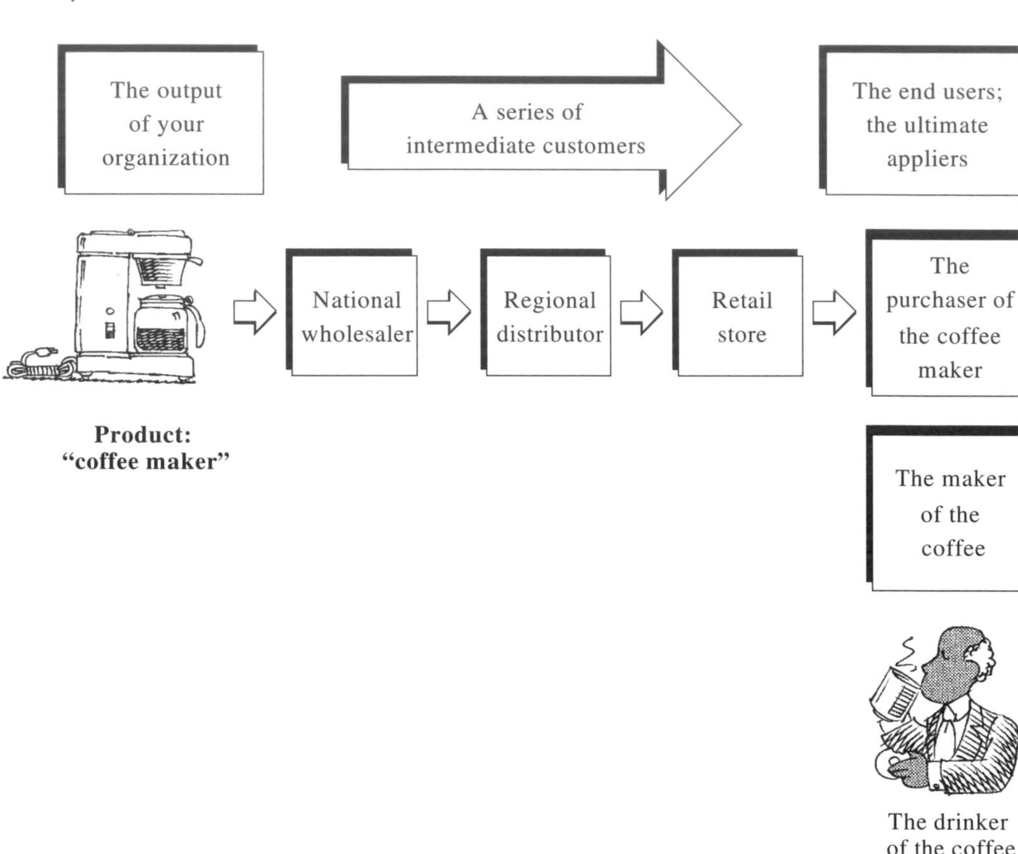

Figure 3-8. The coffee-maker producer's chain of customers.

In the early stages of struggling with the new management philosophy, organizations frequently try to make themselves a subspecies. "That may work for coffee-maker manufacturers or for fourth grades, but we are different! We have a very complicated set of customers, and they have conflicting expectations!" To this I say, "We all have complex chains of customers. That's just the way life is." It always seems easier to see someone else's systems and chain of customers than to see your own. Bring someone in to help you see your systems, if you don't see them.

When Customers Are Hard to Define

It is especially hard to identify the customer when the customer seems to be an abstraction ("all the citizens of the state" or "future generations"). Here are some guidelines for identifying hard-to-identify customers.

1. Break down the organization's work into discrete services, functions, or products. For example, a city police department might be viewed in terms of such services as patrolling a particular neighborhood, responding to a 911 call, and arresting an intoxicated driver. These are separate services, each with its own chain or network of customers.

2. For each separate product or service, ask: What is its purpose? Why would anyone want this product or service to be available? As Konica Camera concluded, people want a product for the capability it provides. Therefore, what capability is provided to whom as a result of people receiving the services that you offer?

3. For each separate service, ask:
   - What is next in the flow of work? Who gets it after this part of the organization is finished? Those who handle the 911 calls, for instance, pass information on to the patrol officer, one of their customers.
   - Who ultimately receives the product or service (the last stop in the chain)?
   - Who benefits from this particular service?
   - Who is the user or consumer of this product?
   - How do those who benefit from this product or service use or consume what we supply? Sometimes it is only in the application that we can gain clarity about who the customers are or what they want. With regard to police service, who in the neighborhood (a generic customer) is more interested in auto safety or vandalism or gang fights? These priorities might indicate different specific customers.
   - What capabilities are acquired and how or when are those capabilities applied? We may find different customers at the point where capabilities are applied. For example, students in school acquire capabilities that are applied elsewhere and later. If we look at the time and place where these capabilities are applied, we might identify others, in addition to the student, who have expectations about the content and effectiveness of that student's education. Another example: I buy life insurance. The capability I acquire is a form of security. The point of application, however, occurs when I am dead and gone. Therefore, who is the customer of my life insurance? Whose needs should it serve? Look at the point of application.

We have been looking at the SIPOC model and have dwelt on the notion of customers. Without customer feedback there will be no sustainable definition of a "good job." Without customers who are delighted, there will be no sustainable organization. Customers must be the focal point of everything a system does.

OUTPUT

We have been working backwards—right to left—in the SIPOC model (see Figure 3-9). We have discussed the importance of a clear, constant, and altruistic purpose. The purpose will help us identify who our customers are. We have explored who the customer is and have seen that in reality the notion of customer is more complex than is commonly believed.

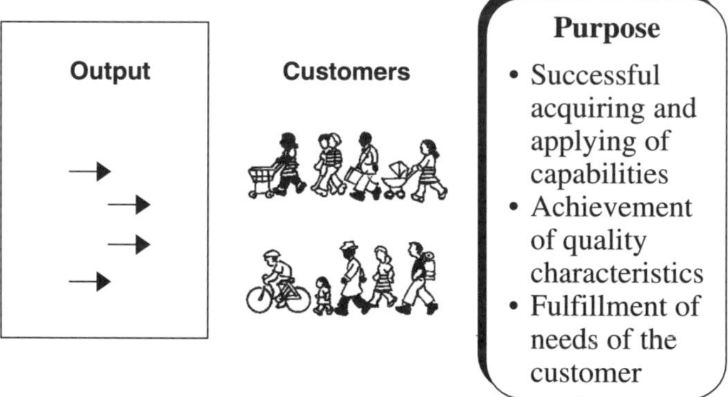

Figure 3-9. SIPOC, from right to left.

If we are to delight our customers with ideal products and services, we must identify our complex chain of customers and learn to understand them continually. Understanding our customers' needs will allow us to define the output needed to make our customers boastful. Here we explore the notion of output.

The output of our organization is the net result of our systems, processes, and methods. For better or worse, we get—and, more importantly, our customers get—what the system is capable of giving us. From our customers' point of view, the output, the goods and services, either delights them, angers them, or, more often, leaves them somewhere in between those two extremes. From the organization's point of view the net output is seen as sales, services delivered, revenue, costs, expenses, net profits, cash flow, return on investment, market

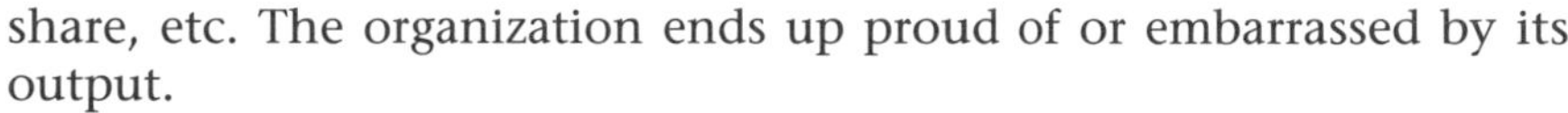

share, etc. The organization ends up proud of or embarrassed by its output.

The point here is twofold:

- Customers have the final say as to the quality of your output. If you want to know if you are doing a good job, ask the customers. They alone know.
- Whether your output is good or bad, it is, nonetheless, the only output of which your systems, processes, and methods are currently capable. If you want better output, you must improve the systems, processes, and methods.

An expansion on the second point regarding output is that the system must be appropriate to the scale of effort. The process and methods appropriate to your kid's streetside lemonade stand, with an output, let us say, of 50 six-ounce cups of lemonade, will not work when he or she is expected to provide 5,000 six-ounce cups of yellow and pink lemonade each in regular or sugar-free varieties. You cannot accomplish this greater scale of output by simply making 100 times more effort. This, of course, is obvious. But if it is so obvious, why do managers so often seek to increase the output of factories or the service workload by simply exhorting people to do more and work harder? If you want more or better output, you must create systems, processes, and methods that generate more and better output.

PROCESS

In the SIPOC model, process refers to the interacting systems, processes, and methods: conditions and factors that convert, for better or worse, inputs into outputs.

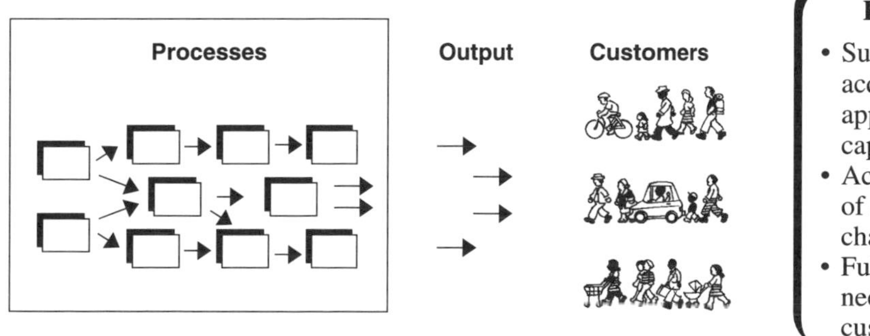

Figure 3-10. SIPOC from right to left.

The Internal Chain

Just as outside customers can be described in terms of a chain of customers, there is also an internal chain in the organization that has its internal supplier-customer interdependencies.

A company making printing paper has these basic operations in its internal chain:

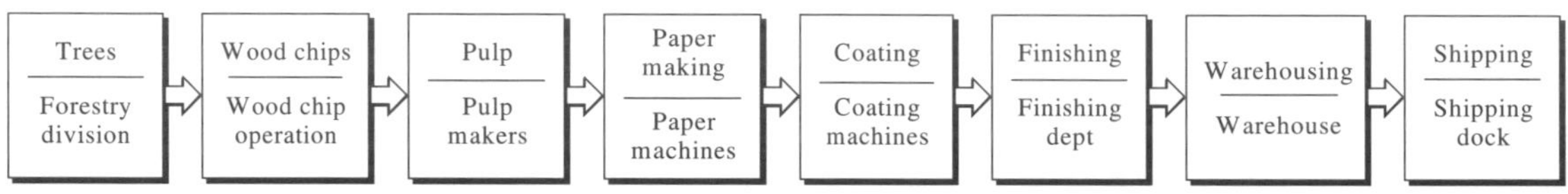

Figure 3-11. The internal chain: paper manufacturing.

Some basic guidelines for the internal chain:

- Don't pass errors, defects, or unfinished work on to the next phases of the operation: your internal customers.
- Set up "feedback loops" by which you and your internal customer routinely monitor data on those attributes that are important to both the internal customer and other customers in the internal and external chains. Begin with having your internal customer describe the attributes of your work that are most important to him, her, or them (key quality characteristics).
- Your purpose is not simply to please your internal customers, but for you and your internal customers to please the outside customers, that is, the outside *chain* of customers.
- The challenge for each link in the chain is to learn to convert the internal and external customers' definition of a good job (key quality characteristics) into those attributes of your system or process (key process indicators) that, when in control, will dependably produce the output desired by both internal and external customers.

  For instance, in our paper company example (as described in Figure 3-12), there will be a need for feedback loops both from the *outside* customer chain and between *internal* operations. Your external and internal customers tell you how they define a "good job" and you design and maintain a process that routinely delivers what they want. Sometimes you will find that you can't do that. Therefore, you work with customers, internal and external, to find ways for them to accomplish their purpose and get what they need through some alternative design or method.

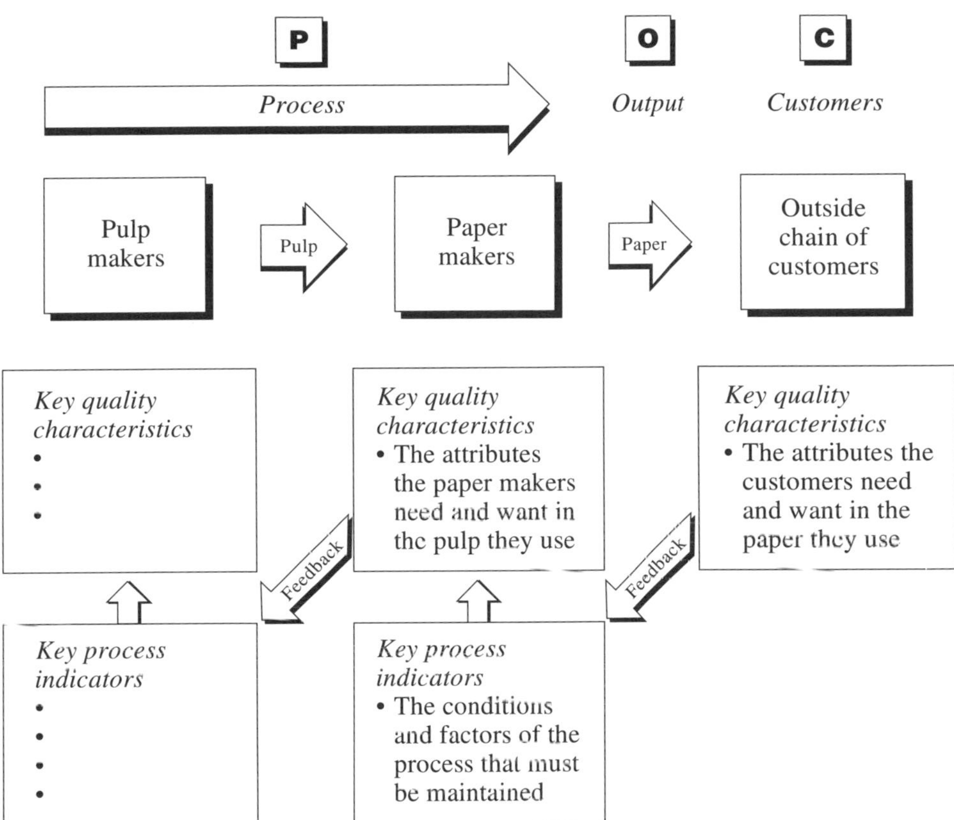

Figure 3-12. The need to convert your customers' Key Quality Characteristics—the customers' definition of a "good job"—to the Key Process Indicators of your work, those attributes, factors, and conditions that, when in control, will routinely deliver to the internal (and external) customers what is important to them when and how they need it.

- In this view of work, managers must attend to the spaces between the operations, the arrows that indicate either transitions or feedback loops. In this view, the role of leadership is to create an environment and routines for transitions and feedback, to maintain the heartbeat, inhalation, and exhalation of the system. (See Chapter 4 for more on feedback.)

GEMBA: A NOTION TO HELP PUT *PROCESS* IN PERSPECTIVE

As we examine the notion of *process* within the SIPOC model, we now look more closely at process and a companion concept called *Gemba*. Gemba creates a clearer context and perspective for the notion of process. Many find that the concept of Gemba haunts them when they think of work and the workplace.

The word Gemba, used by the Japanese, is derived from two Chinese words. There is no English equivalent.

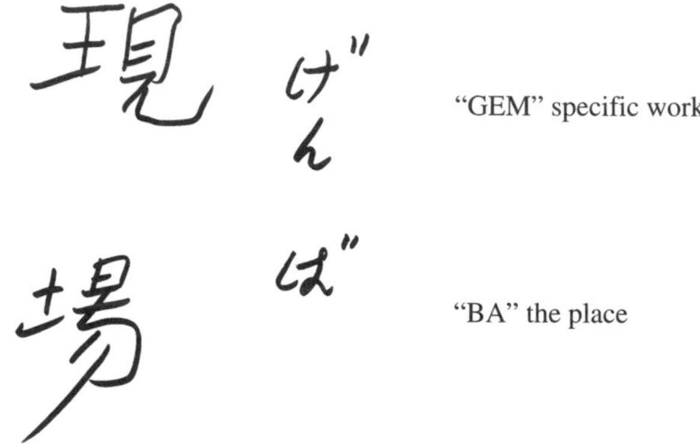

Figure 3-13. Gemba. (LCDR K.C. Moon of the U.S. Navy provided the drawing of the Chinese characters. My thanks to him.)

Gemba is the assembly of critical resources and the flow of work that contribute to those efforts that directly add value to the customer. This is illustrated in Figure 3-14.

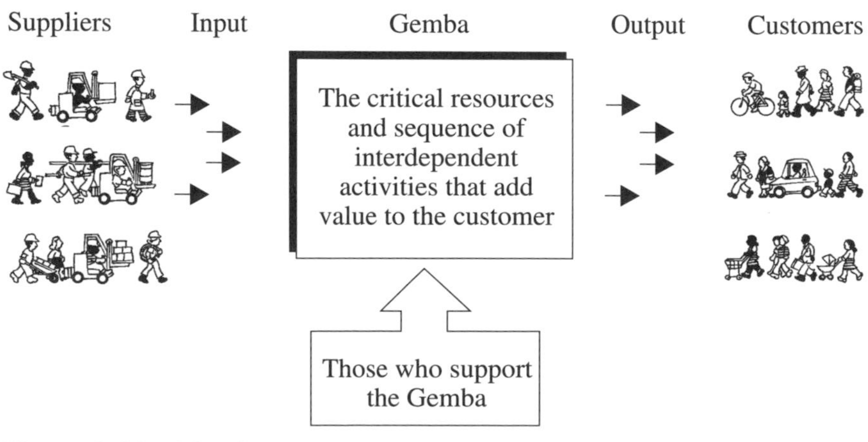

Figure 3-14. The Gemba.

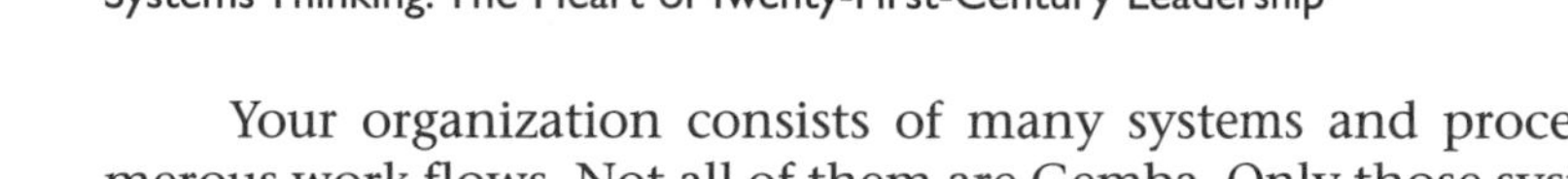

Your organization consists of many systems and processes, numerous work flows. Not all of them are Gemba. Only those systems and processes directly related to a flow of work that adds value to the customer is Gemba.

Some Comments on Gemba

The Gemba's measure of success is customer delight. The success of the rest of the organization is how well it serves the Gemba.

The purpose of this distinction between Gemba and non-Gemba is not to establish yet a new hierarchy of importance among people, a new internal pecking order. The purpose is to define the organization's systems and identify which functions should systemically serve others.

- Gemba takes the general concepts of system and processes and extracts the system or processes directly involved in producing value on behalf of a customer.

These are the Gemba	**These are not Gemba but provide services to the Gemba**
• Product or service design • Product development activities • Service development activities • Potential customer contact and sales • Delivering products or services • Instructional and other after-delivery services for the customer • Routine customer maintenance services	• Most management services • Customer research • System or process design • Human Resources • Plant or facilities repair and internal maintenance • Payroll and other financial services: accounts payable and accounts receivable • Purchasing • Administrative services • Training • Budgeting • Management information services • Production planning • Service delivery planning

- Relatively few of your people are doing Gemba work. Everyone else is engaged in work that supports the Gemba. Almost all non-Gemba people work with information.
- "Everything is felt in the Gemba" is a Japanese expression that describes the interactive and interdependent nature of an organization's systems, processes, policies, plans, and decisions.

Implied in the Gemba perspective is that the Gemba deserves some priority of attention: Whatever else you do, take good care of the Gemba. In Chapter 4 we look more closely at the care and feeding of the Gemba.

The Poetry, Music, Spirit, and Rhythm of the Gemba

Musicians, actors, dancers, and athletes will talk about those times when their work just flows, when it has a life and spirit of its own, and the artist or athlete just tries to stay with it and not interfere. At these times people work together as though reading each others' minds, each knowing the next move the other will make. They describe how they and their partners, building off each other, accomplish things they never could before in ways they never did them before.

This smooth, almost intuitive flow of great work is a form of poetry in motion. Call it a true experience of teamwork. This kind of teamwork does exist in the Gemba. "Sometimes we're really rolling; we're really in a groove," says Bill Warner, a manufacturing engineer at a large equipment production facility. This experience of teamwork takes time. It needs people who like their work and know how to do their jobs very well. It requires a true relationship among members of the team, people knowing each other and caring about each other.

Managers can help this kind of teamwork develop and sustain itself by seeing the importance of such teamwork, creating an environment where such teamwork can flourish. Managers can then help most by staying out of the way of teamwork. When managers don't understand systems, Gemba, and the importance of teamwork and relationships in the workplace, they are liable to do things—usually un-

Poetry in the Gemba

... There is in manufacturing a creative job that only poets are supposed to know. Someday I'd like to show a poet how it feels to design and build a railroad locomotive.

—Walter Chrysler

aware and often with good intentions—that disrupt the teamwork and the rhythm of the Gemba.

> We trained hard—but it seemed that every time we were beginning to form up into teams, we would be reorganized.
>
> I was to learn later in life we tend to meet any new situation by reorganizing, and a wonderful method it can be for creating the illusion of progress while producing confusion, inefficiency, and demoralization.
>
> —Petronius Arbiter
> 65 A.D.

In his book, *Flow,* Mihali Czikszentmihalyi (1990) offers this perceptive insight into conditions that create and sustain *flow.*

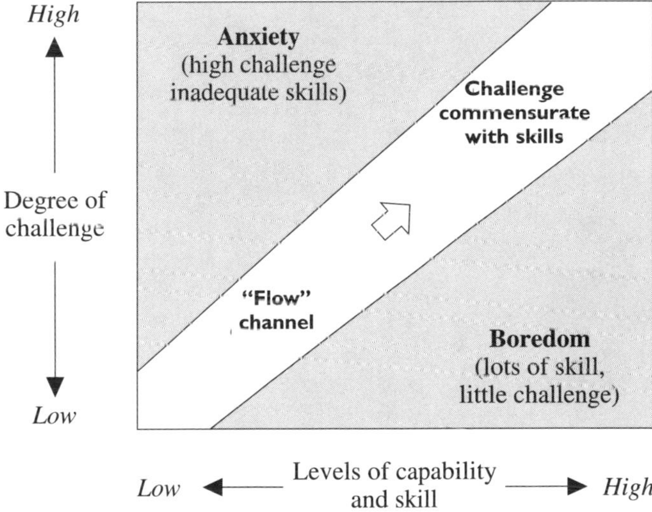

Figure 3-15. Conditions affecting flow.

Flow, suggests Czikszentmihalyi, occurs when there is neither anxiety nor boredom. Anxiety occurs when the challenge of the moment exceeds our capabilities. Boredom occurs when we are capable of doing considerably more than the challenge presented to us.

The implications for leaders are these:

- How to maintain the level of challenge in order to avoid boredom.
- How to increase the level of skill in order to avoid anxiety.
- How to know when there is a need to restore congruence between challenge and capability.
- How to involve people in the increasing of skills and the increasing of challenge.

There is, I believe, a direct correlation between what Czikszentmihalyi describes here and what Herzberg says about motivation and demotivation. Anxiety and boredom are *de*motivating. Flow is motivating.

SUPPLIERS AND INPUT

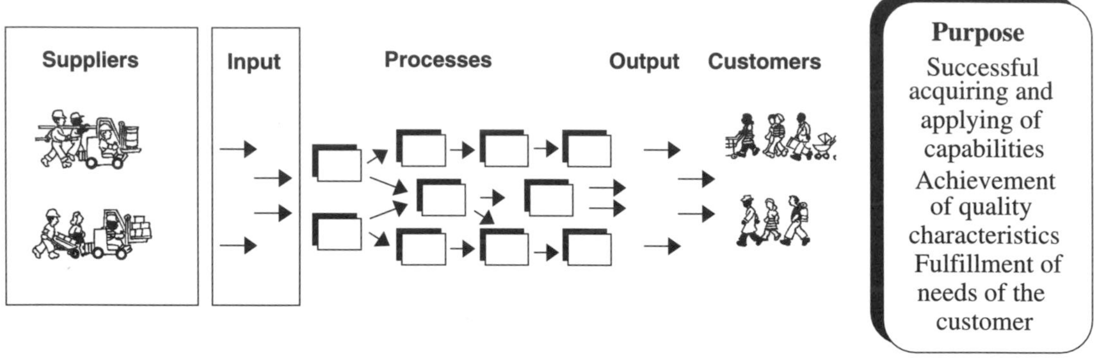

Figure 3-16. SIPOC, from right to left.

Just as there are external customers and internal customers, each of which can be seen in terms of chains of customers, there are also external and internal suppliers, each part of their own chains. And just as you cannot afford to deal only with the first customer in the chain of customers, it is wise to deal with more than simply the last supplier. This is especially true of the major suppliers of the *core resources*. We will look more closely at core resources in Chapter 4.

Elective and Nonelective Suppliers

The difference between internal and external suppliers is probably obvious. One is inside your organization, the other is not. What has more impact on you, however, is whether or not you have a *choice* of suppliers. For example, in my paper company example (see Figure 3-11), there is an internal supplier of pulp to the paper makers. For the paper makers the important question is, "Must we acquire pulp only from this internal supplier?" If they must, then the paper makers are dealing with a nonelective supplier. In a perfect world this should not make a difference. But a common experience is that it is much harder to deal with nonelective suppliers, whether they are internal or external.

Win–Win Regulators

The Department of Revenue of the State of Wisconsin is responsible for regulating the state's breweries, distilleries, and producers of wine. (Yes, there is Wisconsin wine!) The licensing agency, applying Deming's philosophy, started pursuing a nonadversarial approach to their regulatory function. The result: better relationships, better problem solving, better cooperation, and win–win collaboration with the producers of alcoholic beverages.

Russell Ackoff (1994, pp. 142–167) makes this point and argues that corporations would do better if internal suppliers were forced to survive in an open market, without corporate protection regarding their internal customers. (This is a step that I am not ready to advocate. I fear it will subvert the larger systems.)

There are also outside nonelective suppliers. Regulatory agencies, for example, are usually outside, and they supply regulations and constraints. They are also nonelective. If you don't like their regulations, you cannot shop around for another regulatory agency.

Part of understanding how to lead a system is taking on the responsibility to sit down with suppliers and work out win–win strategies to serve the interests of both the supplier and you who are supplied. This applies as well to working with regulatory agencies. Sometimes to help regulators be better regulators, you may have to approach them, as you would with any other supplier, to help them learn how to become systems-focused suppliers. You may want to band together with other organizations that labor under the restrictions of the same regulators, to work out a new arrangement with this supplier of dysfunctional regulations.

Whether the suppliers are internal or external, your systems and ultimately your customers require a smooth, well-functioning flow between the suppliers and you. This is the job of managers: to assure the smooth flow of work from the suppliers to the process, through the process, and from the process to the customers.

Managers are the ultimate internal suppliers to the organization. Managers supply definition, meaning, direction, focus, plans, priorities, communication, equipment, material, methods of work, smooth flow, continuity, moral support, and a good working environment to the organization's employees. Managers, in other words, are suppliers of the *system*. As Myron Tribus says, "Managers work *on* the system. Workers work *in* the system."

There are two questions that I suggest suppliers ask their customers, whether these suppliers be external or internal, elective or nonelective. I also recommend that supplier-managers ask these questions of their employee-customers (see Figure 3-5):

1. What are you getting that you don't need?
2. What do you need that you're not getting?

SIPOC AND THE ORGANIZATION

Leading such dynamic concepts as systems, SIPOC, and Gemba represents a fundamentally different approach to leadership, requiring new leadership competencies (see Chapter 2). The sense of organization is fundamentally different as well. Let us take a look at an organization.

I think there is no simpler view of an organization than that pictured in Figure 3-17. An organization is:

- An aggregate of people ...
- Working within systems and processes ...
- To accomplish some purpose.

This describes all kinds of organizations: work, church, social, civic, and political organizations.

Traditionally we have sought success by inducing our people to work smarter or work harder. We have tried to motivate them, reorganize them, given them measurable objectives, empower them, and hold them accountable. We have taken for granted that to improve our chances for success, we must improve our people.

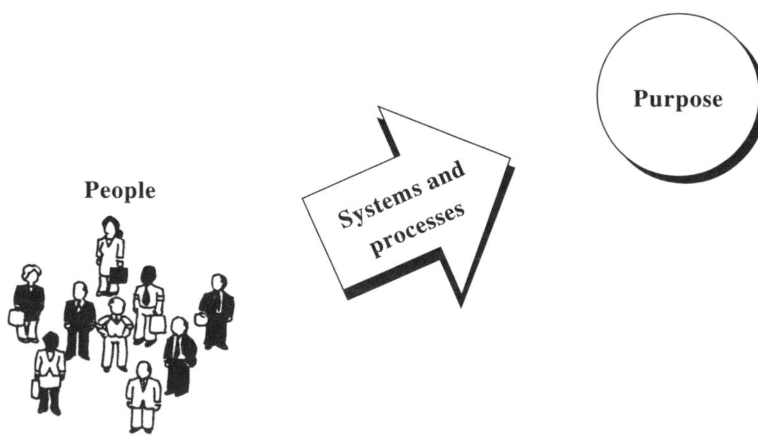

Figure 3-17. The basics of an organization.

Beginning in 1950 we began to think differently. We began to understand systems. We began to realize that to improve the chances for success, we must improve our systems and processes. If we improve our systems and processes, the work of our people will necessarily improve.

Our people work within a large system containing many interdependent, interactive "givens" over which they have little or no control. Even individual managers have limited ability to change the system. Some of the givens that compose the system are:

- Product or service design
- The work facility
- Process design
- Machines
- Materials
- The methods of work
- The equipment
- The policies
- The budgets
- Staffing levels
- Priorities
- Long- and short-term goals and plans
- Training
- The work environment
- Communication systems

At least 95 percent of your quality problems can be attributed to these givens of your organization. Less than 5 percent result from people committing errors. Human error is a negligible source of our problems. Yet because we don't understand systems, we act as though human error were the primary cause of our problems.

Obstacles to Systems Thinking

There are conditions and practices in the organization that make systems thinking difficult for the organization's leaders:

- Isolation from the customer: product-out thinking creates a more inward, narcissistic focus.
- Divisional and functional managers have little awareness of, and no sense of responsibility for, the entire system, only for their individual functional units.
- Divisional and functional managers, and the people who work in their units, are often remunerated based on how well they help their own functional units succeed.
- Plans don't cut across units, nor is planning done cross-functionally.
- Success is measured not by measures important to the customer, but by measures important only to managers.

Yet Another Person Lacking Profound Knowledge

In an interview on C-span on May 19, 1996, Jerry Jasinowski, the president of the National Association of Manufacturers, made this comment regarding the Value-Jet crash in the Florida Everglades:

"I believe that we will learn that—as in most of these incidents—it will be pilot error."

Mr. Jasinowski, of course, was wrong in his prediction. Will it do any good to hold him accountable or try to motivate him to make more accurate predictions?

- Short-term thinking: looking ahead only to this month, this quarter, or this year.
- Fostering and sustaining an environment of blame.
- Scrambling to be important and look good as an individual or a unit.
- Actions are not well planned, nor are they monitored or studied to see if they accomplish what was intended. We simply do things, and often do not see the *system* behind the problems we seek to solve. As a result, today's solutions become tomorrow's problems.

Approaches to Systems Thinking

We can develop systems-minded organizations first by backing away from everyday work and asking some basic questions, as suggested by the SIPOC model. Then we can zoom in closer and closer and ask other SIPOC-related questions regarding daily work.

Some basic, large-scale, long-term questions suggested by the SIPOC model are:

- What is our purpose?
- What capabilities do we provide our customers?
- Who are, or should be, our customers?
- What do they want? What do they need?
- How do we know?
- How can we maintain awareness of customer needs and market shifts on a daily basis?

- Given what we know about our customers, what output (goods and services) with which features and attributes must we provide?
- Given these outputs, what systems, processes, and methods must be in place?
- How do we know?
- How do we monitor these systems, processes, and methods to assure ourselves that they are in control and will reliably, consistently, and flawlessly deliver the output needed by our customers?
- Given these systems, processes, methods, and output, what input do we need?
- Which suppliers can best provide us with the needed input?
- How do we know?
- How will we monitor the input from our suppliers?

Chapter 8 looks at *systems* of questions as well as systemic questions that leaders must ask. Chapter 7 looks at setting up and maintaining the indicators we must monitor, tracking both the *key quality characteristics* important to the customers and the *key process indicators* that tell us how well our systems are working. Chapter 5 looks at how to identify meaning and priorities for the organization and how to communicate direction and focus throughout the enterprise. In Chapter 6 we look at how to plan and implement large-scale systemic change: the systems needed for systemic change. At the beginning of this chapter you read, "Ironically, without a system it is impossible to change." This will be explained in Chapter 6. In Chapter 4 we zoom in on everyday work, looking at it systemically.

We develop a systems-minded organization, therefore, by pulling back and asking systemic questions about the whole enterprise and the larger systems—for example, the market—in which it operates. We zoom in on the everyday work and ask systemic questions about daily work. We organize ourselves around those questions and the pursuit of those answers.

The massive scale and rapid rate of change in our world demand a wholly new approach to leadership. Leaders can no longer be experts and autocrats. Leaders must understand systems, lead systems, and think systemically. To lead your systems systemically is to lead your organization into the new century.

SUMMARY

All work can be characterized by the simple yet useful SIPOC model. Work has a specific purpose—to serve customers. Work is achieved through processes performed at the Gemba. These processes require inputs provided by suppliers. Looking at work this way and understanding and integrating these components is a fundamental responsibility of a twenty-first century leader.

In this chapter we have provided some practical examples of work as a system and shown some helpful ways to use systems thinking to understand and improve workplaces.

In Chapter 4 we take a closer look at the processes by which the daily work is done.

CHAPTER THREE ACTIVITIES

1. **What is the purpose of your organization?**
   - Don't refer to financial goals.
   - Describe who you are and what you do. (Can your purpose be inferred from your activities?)
   - No "motherhood" statements (statements that would describe just about any organization).

2. **What *capabilities* do your customers acquire (or improve) as a result of interacting with you?** (Don't describe your products or services but what your customers can do as a result of receiving your products or services. How are they better off for having interacted with you?)

3. **Who are your competitors?** (Either organizations that provide products or services similar to yours, or alternative ways people satisfy the needs or gain the capabilities that you provide.)

4. A. Who are your current customers?

   B. Who should/could be your customers, but currently are not?

   C. Who, by your choice, are not your customers?

5. **Identify the major products and services that benefit your customers and serve your purpose.**

Product or Service	*Benefit/Capability Acquired by the Customer from This Product/Service*

Choose a specific product or service and enter it here:

6. **Examine the chain of customers for that product or service.**

Who Receives It from You?	*List the Intermediate Customers:*	*Who Is the End User or Beneficiary?*
	■ ■ ■ ■ ■ ■ ■ ■ ■ ■ ■	

Example: A manufacturer of coffee makers.

Who Receives It from You?	*List the Intermediate Customers:*	*Who Is the End User or Beneficiary?*
The wholesaler	▪ The regional distributor ▪ The retailer ▪ The purchaser ▪ The maker of the coffee	The drinker of the coffee

7. Applying the Kano Model.

	What Are the Basics to These Customers?	*What Are the Performance-Related Characteristics?*	*What Are, or Could Be, the Delights?*
The receiving customer			
The intermediate customers			
The end consumer			

Guidelines:

- Don't speculate about these. Go out and ask customers.
- Use the data you already have. For example, customers usually complain when a basic has been neglected.

8. **Identify customer feedback loops.** These are routine methods or systems with which you elicit information from your customers and record the data in ways useful for improvement.

	Reactive Customer Feedback—Initiated by the Customer (e.g., Customer Complaints, Inquiries, Service Requests)	*Proactive Customer Feedback—Initiated by You (e.g., Surveys, Focus Groups, Service Visits)*
Describe the established routine for capturing and processing customer data		
Describe a realistic routine that might be established		

Enter a specific product or service

9. **Gemba I: Mapping the process.** Describe the general flow that develops and delivers this product or service.

How Do You Know When the Process Has Started?	*Identify the Flow of Work*			*How Do You Know When the Process Is Completed and Successful?*
	Early Stages	*Middle Stages*	*Late Stages*	

10. Tracing a basic key quality characteristic back through the process.

A. Select a basic characteristic for the end user or beneficiary of this product or service (see Figure 3-6).

B. Where does this basic get assured or violated? Identify where in the process things can go wrong so that the basic is violated.

Start	*Early Stages*	*Middle Stages*	*Late Stages*	*End*

Some guidelines:

- If necessary, use a more complex form of flowchart such as a deployment flowchart (see Figure 4-5).
- Your purpose is to identify *where* in the process things go wrong, **not** *who* messed up. Look for systemic causes, not culprits.
- Start at the *end* of the process, asking, "What goes on here that contributes positively or negatively to this basic customer characteristic?" Then *work backward* into the process.

REFERENCES

Ackoff, R. 1994. *The democratic organization.* New York: Oxford University Press.

Arbiter, P. The quotation can be found in *The Macmillan book of business and economic quotations.* 1984. Michael Jackman, editor. New York: Macmillan.

Chappell, T. 1993. *The soul of a business.* New York: Bantam Books.

Czikszentmihalyi, M. 1990. *Flow: The psychology of optimal experience.* New York: Harper & Row.

Ford, H. The quotation from Henry Ford can be found in *The Macmillan book of business and economic quotations.* 1984. Michael Jackman, editor. New York: MacMillan.

Gale, B.T. 1994. *Managing customer value: Creating quality and service that customers can see.* New York: Macmillan.

Gitlow, H., and Gitlow, S. 1994. *Total quality management in action.* Englewood Cliffs, NJ: Prentice Hall.

Hagy, M., and Hagy, M. 1994. *Under new management: Organized common sense.* Philadelphia: Atlantic Alliance Publishing.

Kano, N. 1996. "Business strategies for the twenty-first century and attractive quality creation." A paper delivered at The International Conference on Quality, October 15–18, in Yokohama.

Kano, N., Seraku, N., Takahashi, F., and Tsuji, S. 1996. Attractive quality and must-be quality. In *The best of quality,* vol. 7, pp. 165ff. Milwaukee: ASQC.

Mowery, N., Reavis, P., and Poling, S. 1994. *Customer focused quality.* Knoxville, TN: SPC Press.

Vandermerwe, S. 1993. *From tin soldiers to Russian dolls.* Oxford, UK: Butterworth-Heinemann.

4 GETTING THE DAILY WORK DONE

INTRODUCTION

If visitors from another planet were to hover over our workplaces, viewing us with some kind of barrier-penetrating vision, they would observe earthlings, individually or in groups, engaged in various activities. In some workplaces they may see an observable flow of work that produces a product: Wood enters one end of the factory and furniture comes out the other end while in between, people do various things to convert wood into furniture. Sometimes earthlings in obvious pain enter a building and later emerge with less pain while in between, these earthlings received services that appear to relieve their discomfort. In other workplaces, however, the entry points and departure points are not so observable, nor is what takes place in between. The alien visitors would need some other means to discover what is going on.

A Reminder of What the Gemba Is

In Chapter 3 we introduced the notion of Gemba. In this chapter we explore the Gemba more deeply.

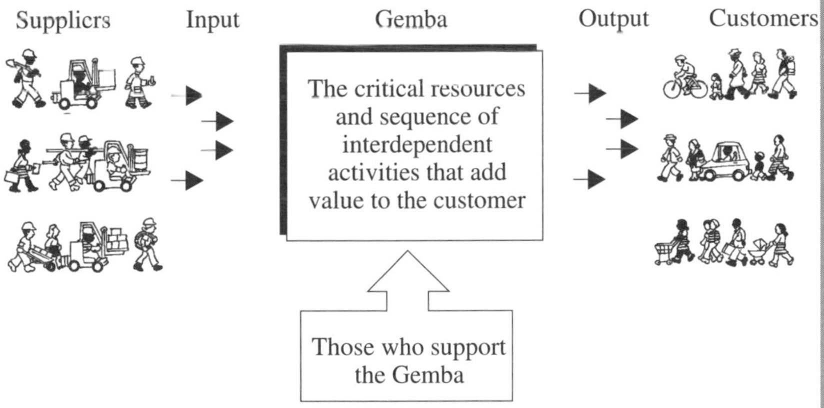

Suppliers Input Gemba Output Customers

The critical resources and sequence of interdependent activities that add value to the customer

Those who support the Gemba

Figure 4-1. The Gemba.

The Gemba consists of those systems, processes, and work flows about which your customers care the most. These are the processes that develop, add value to, and deliver goods and services to your customers. Customers are those who use, apply, and benefit directly from the Gemba's products and services.

The process of examining everyday work involves adopting an almost alien-visitor perspective. We observe and analyze the workplace to see who is doing what and why. The alien-visitor perspective allows us to ask naive or dumb questions.

With a reestablished perspective on what is the important flow of everyday work, we can identify some guidelines for everyday work, learn to standardize everyday work, and remove waste from the workplace. We will explore these issues in this chapter.

Everyday improvement of daily work requires some monitoring and feedback processes, which we will look at in this chapter as well as in Chapter 7. The workers monitor their own work and get feedback from the system within which they work. This, we will see, is not at all like traditional evaluation of the worker's performance. *Feedback* is systems-based data useful for improvement. *Traditional performance evaluation,* on the other hand, is the personal judgment of one individual by another, higher-ranking individual, serving the purpose of establishing a relationship of control by the one judging over the one judged. More about this in Chapter 9.

All of Chapter 4 is focused on the smooth flow of work, particularly that part of work that we identified in Chapter 3 as the Gemba. Most of what we say here will also apply to the non-Gemba activities. However, as we emphasized in Chapter 3, the purpose and value of other work must be viewed in terms of its contribution to the present Gembas and future Gembas. We end Chapter 4 with a look at practical ways to create an environment of teamwork and processes for internal collaboration between the various parts of an operation that must work together in a smooth, continuous flow.

Figure 4-2 shows the flow of initiatives you might undertake in working to improve daily work. It also describes the flow of this chapter.

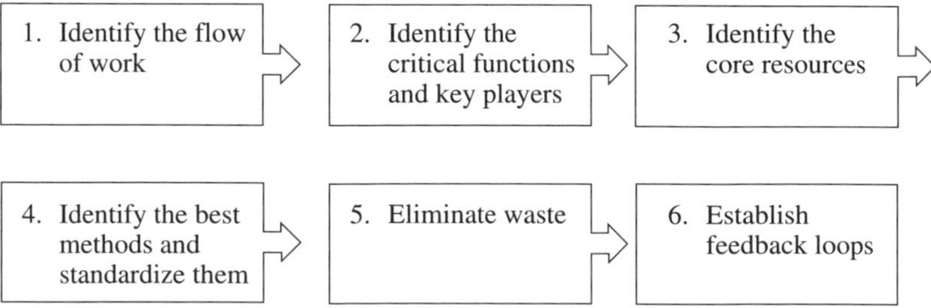

Figure 4-2. Six initiatives for getting the important daily work done.

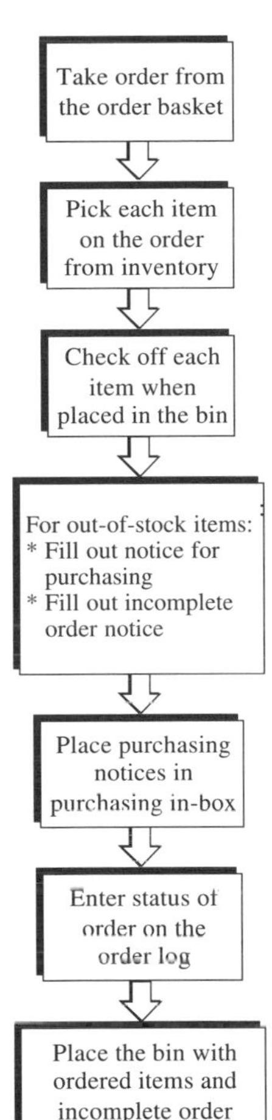

Figure 4-3. The simple flowchart.

EXAMINING THE GEMBA

The Uncluttered Flow of Work

Work, on a large scale (a system) or on a small scale (a process or method), can usually be pictured as a flow of events or activities. The *flowchart* is a graphic representation of the interdependent sequence or flow of phases, activities, events, or steps involved in some undertaking. There are at least six variations on the flowchart. (See Figures 4-3 through 4-8.)

Six Types of Flowcharts

1. The Simple Flowchart (Figure 4-3)

A *simple flowchart* describes the steps in order, moving either left to right or sometimes top to bottom, as shown in Figure 4-3. The simple flowchart can include as much or as little detail as your purpose requires.

2. The Top-Down Flowchart (Figure 4-4)

A *top-down flowchart* describes the basic five or six steps in sequence from left to right across the page and up to five or six substeps in sequence vertically below each step. The top-down flowchart thus displays the simple flow and adds another level of detail, all contained on one page.

I first learned about this type of flowchart from Brian Joiner, to whom I am grateful.

3. The Deployment Flowchart Figure 4-5)

A *deployment flowchart* shows time in the vertical sequence of the steps. But the deployment flowchart also shows the interactions between different individuals or groups. Each active participant in the process is listed at the top of an individual column and the action, while flowing downward on the page corresponding to time, moves laterally under the column corresponding to the group or individual involved in that step.

I am grateful to Myron Tribus, from whom I first learned about the deployment flowchart.

4. The Opportunity Flowchart (Figure 4-6)

The *opportunity flowchart,* which I learned about from Heero Hacquebord, shows the simple flowchart of the value-adding steps of a task running downward in time sequence on the left side of the page. Whenever a step in the process adds no value but only cost, it is dis-

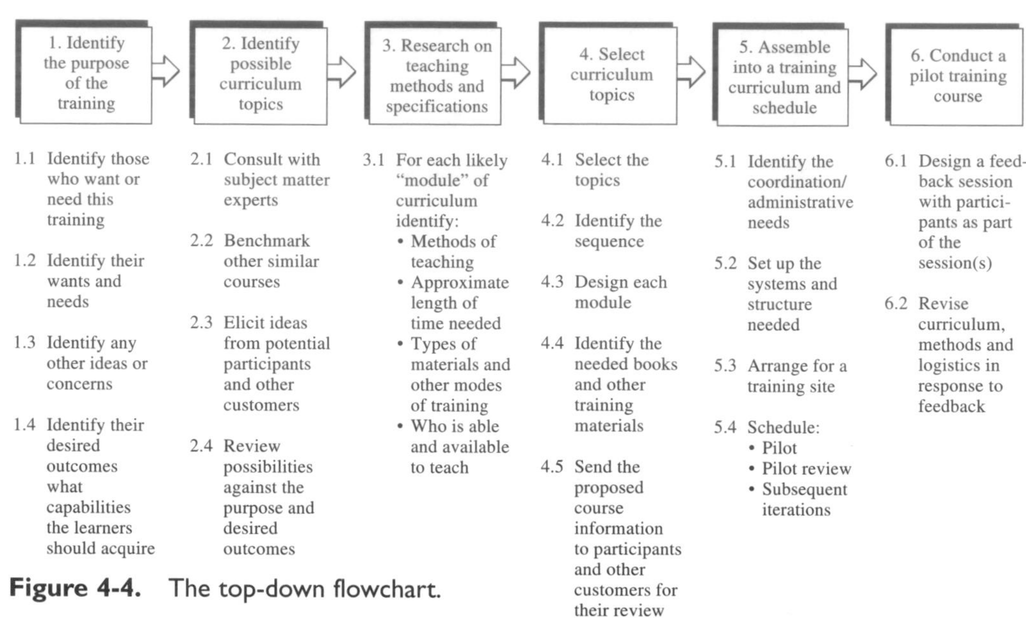

Figure 4-4. The top-down flowchart.

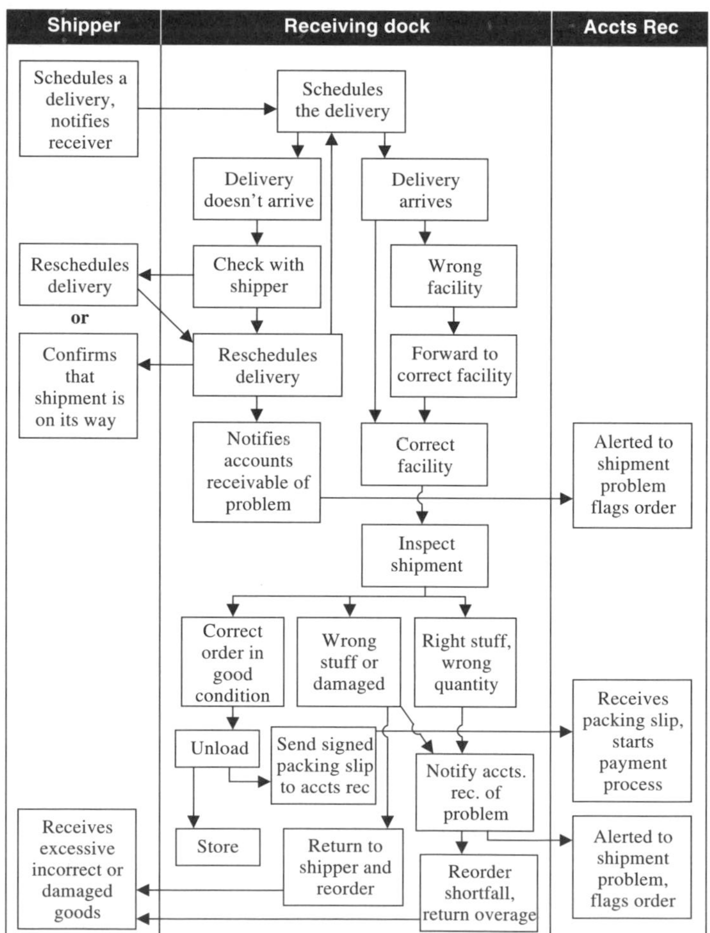

Figure 4-5. The deployment flowchart.

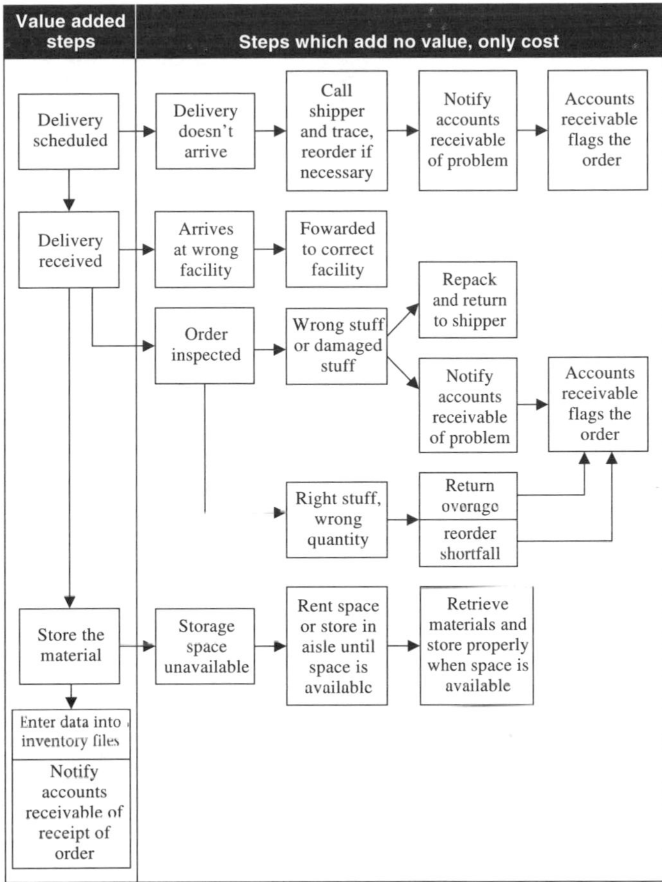

Figure 4-6. The opportunity flowchart.

played to the right. Inspection steps or rework, for example, are not part of the left-side downward flow, but are on the right, cost added only, side. Figure 4-6 shows the same flow of work described in Figure 4-5, but displays the data using the opportunity flowchart's format.

5. The PERT Chart (Figure 4-7)

The *PERT chart* is a flowchart displayed with great detail, showing perhaps many concurrent flows of work, called paths. Elapsed time is estimated between steps in each path. By adding up the cumulative estimated time for each individual work flow, one can identify the critical path, that work flow that will consume the most time. The critical path is the flow of work that determines how long a task will take, the path in which you can least accommodate delays or in which you may need more resources. (PERT is an acronym for Planning Evaluation Review Technique.)

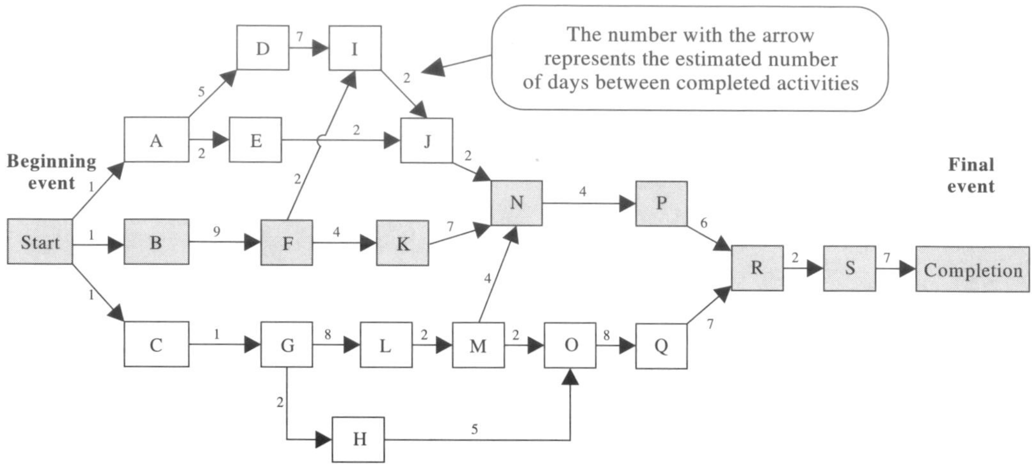

In this PERT chart, the critical path is the shaded boxes (40 days).

Figure 4-7. The PERT chart.

6. The Decision Tree (Figure 4-8)

A *decision tree* is not so much a flow of activities as a sequence of decisions in which the next decision to make depends on which decisions were made before it. Sometimes, other types of flowcharts include decision-tree choices in the flow of activities.

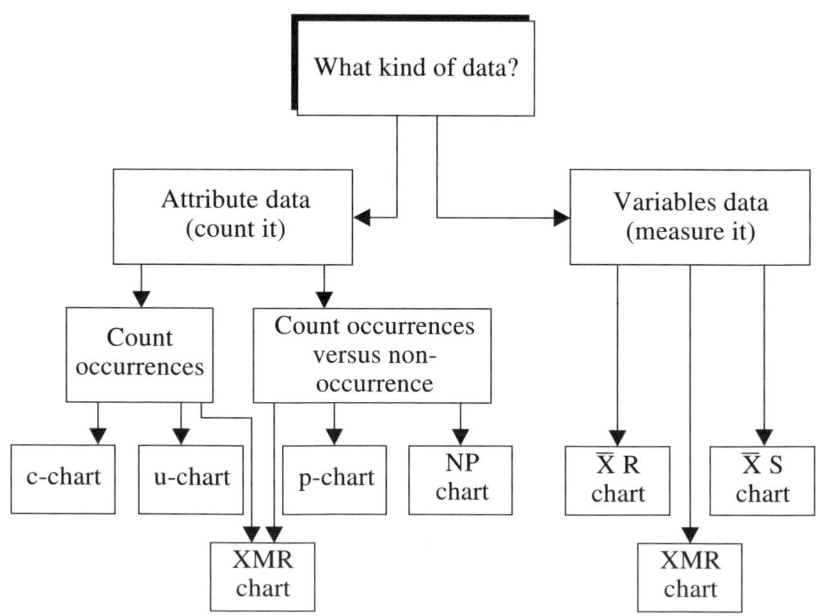

Figure 4-8. The decision tree: a summary map for selecting a control chart.

Some Tips for Doing Flowcharts

1. Decide the end point and starting point.
2. Decide the level of detail, reflecting the purpose of your flowchart and its audience.
3. It often helps to start at the end and work backward toward the start. (This is called backward chaining.)
4. Use Post-its™ or another type of sticky notes. Putting each step on its own Post-it™ will save time and aggravation.

Flowchart Your Gemba Processes

Involve people doing the work in constructing a flowchart of their Gemba process. It might help to have an outsider take part—the visitor from another planet—who can ask naive questions.

The activity by itself is liable to bring improvement. Making a flowchart will help people become aware of what was previously done unconsciously. It will bring out undiscovered variations in methods, provoke discussions, and possibly encourage studies to determine which method works best.

Creating deployment flowcharts of the Gemba processes will describe the internal supplier–customer relationships. This can lead to discussions between interdependent participants in the Gemba regarding, "What are you getting that you don't need and what do you need that you are not getting?" (See "Breaking Down Barriers" later in this chapter.)

While it is useful to develop flowcharts for all your important recurring processes, the important perspective to maintain is that the non-Gemba processes must be subordinate to the Gemba processes. It may be important to look at those points where non-Gemba processes have contact with the Gemba and ask:

- What is the purpose of this contact with the Gemba?
- Are these points of interface necessary?
- How do they help the Gemba?

If they are necessary, ask:

- How can they become a greater opportunity to provide useful service to the Gemba?
- How can they be made minimally intrusive and disruptive?

As we will see, moving through this chapter, we are trying to maintain a smooth, uncluttered flow of work in the Gemba, to avoid disrupting its momentum and rhythm, to keep it humming efficiently and undisruptedly. After all, the Gemba is "the customer's work."

Critical Functions and Key Players

As you review the work flows, you will note two obvious types of important factors: human resources and nonhuman resources. In the section titled "Core Resources," we will discuss the equipment, machinery, and other important nonhuman resources. Here we discuss the human skills and capabilities needed to keep the Gemba (or other non-Gemba functions) running.

There are people doing things throughout the workplace. Each person is important. It is easy to lose sight of this when examining the workplace through this lens we call Gemba. Gemba creates a perspective regarding the subordination of processes and functions, not of people. People who use their superordinate function to patronize those in subordinate functions are indulging their own egos. They are not creating teamwork, not building and sustaining systems to serve customers.

Here we are not looking at *all* roles and functions, not even all of those at work in the Gemba. We are examining the Gemba to find the *critical* factors (what Tim Fuller calls the key leverage points), those specialized and pivotal roles and functions: the doctor in the clinic, the press operator in a printing company, the purchasers and salespeople in a wholesale distributor, and others. Some Gembas are so people-dominated that it is relatively easy to identify the key players, the pivotal roles and functions. Some Gembas are machine-dominated and some may have relatively few highly skilled people involved, as discussed later in Chapter 4.

Identifying Critical Functions and Key Players

Once again we will talk about the Gemba, although what we say will also apply to non-Gemba work. Our purpose here is to provide one focus for our efforts to maintain an uncluttered flow of work.

1. *Which participants in the work flow are directly serving the customer or directly adding value to goods and services that are working their way through the process on their way to the customers?*
2. *Which of these participants are difficult to replace because of the breadth or depth of knowledge and mastery of skills necessary to perform the function?*
   - Some obvious examples: doctors, lawyers, skilled programmers, master chefs, and architects.
   - There are gradations of necessary skill and knowledge. Cab drivers in London take three years to acquire what is called "the knowledge." In some sales organizations the training of a new salesperson may require only three hours. In oth-

ers it may take three years. We are trying to identify those positions or functions that require a more demanding level of skill.

3. *Which of these value-adding, highly skilled participants directly affect the capacity of your organization to serve the customer?* ("Customer demand is so strong that if we could find more skilled machinists we could increase our business by 40 percent.")

Elsewhere (Chapter 9) we will discuss related issues such as how to pay those with such indispensable and hard-to-find levels of skill. Here we are simply examining the workplace to identify the critical factors and leverage points. So far in our examination of the Gemba, we have looked at the flow of work, the sequence of interdependent steps that can be described using one or another form of flowchart. Then we have looked at the critical functions and key players: participants in the Gemba who perform indispensable functions requiring a high degree of mastery.

Next we look at the core resources, the nonhuman leverage points in the Gemba. As we mentioned above, some Gembas are people-dominant, some are equipment-dominant, and some are both. In the following section we look at the nonhuman critical resources that we call the *core resources.*

Figure 4-9 pictures the concept of critical functions, key players, and core resources.

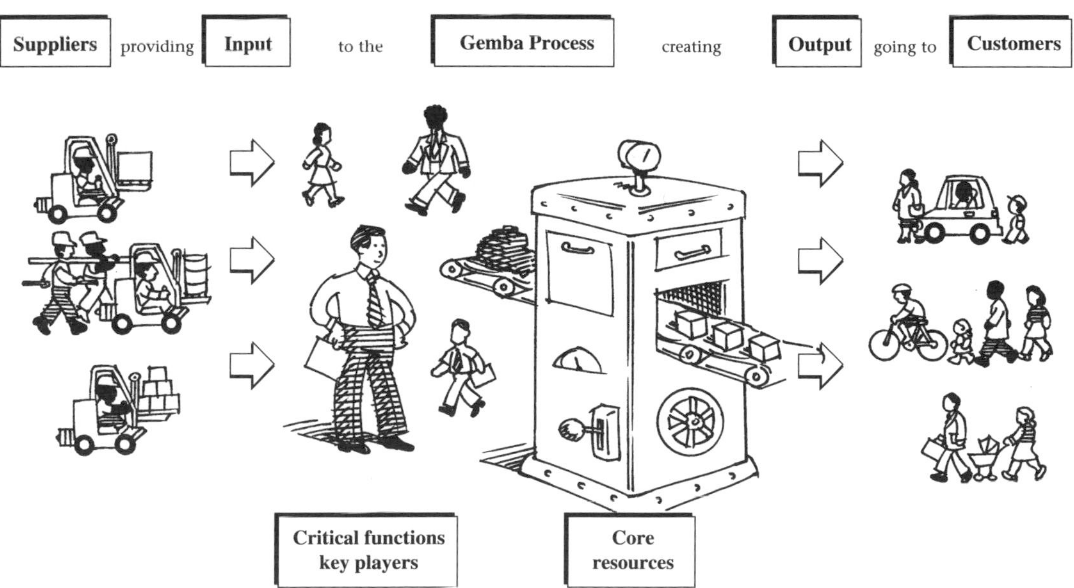

Figure 4-9. Critical functions, key players, and core resources.

Core Resources

As we examine the Gemba, we must also look at those core resources other than people. Here we look at the equipment and machinery, the facility or workplace where the Gemba work is performed, the layout of the work space, the materials, supplies, ingredients, environment, and procedures of the Gemba.

We don't consider every single item under these types of resources. Similar to our examination of the critical functions and key players, we look for those core resources that are critical factors, the indispensable factors that contribute to successful outcomes in the Gemba.

Our purpose in examining these core resources is to provide another point of view when we seek to create an uncluttered flow of work.

These approaches are also applicable to non-Gemba workplaces. Again, however, we are trying to maintain a Gemba-as-priority perspective on work. Some questions to ask when examining the core resources:

1. Which core resources directly add value to the customers or to products and services on their way to the customers? For example:
   - A printing press in a printing company
   - A kiln in a pottery factory
   - An MRI in a hospital
   - The floor of a dance hall
2. Among those core resources that are value-adding, which are expensive to purchase, install, and maintain? For example:
   - A $15 million paper machine
   - A pizza oven
   - A printing press
   - Ski lifts and snow machines on a ski hill
3. Which core resources can create delays or bottlenecks or otherwise limit your capacity to serve the customer?
   - The organization and layout of the warehouse in a mail order operation

- Appointment scheduling and the speed of records access in a doctor's office
- The adequacy of the supply of food and various ingredients as well as clean dishes, glasses, and utensils in a restaurant

4. Which core resources are characterized by safety and worker-friendliness? The Gemba and other workplaces must be safe and ergonomically sound. We owe this to our workers, our customers, and the communities within which we work. In our examination of the workplace, we should ask questions such as the following:
   - What environmental dangers do we create with our processes? What are the systemic causes?
   - What frequency and patterns of injuries and accidents (or near injuries and accidents) do we experience in our workplace? What are the systemic causes?
   - To what work-habit or ergonomically related syndromes are our workers subjected? For example:
     — Carpal tunnel syndrome for typists
     — Back problems for factory and warehouse workers
   - What can we learn from industry research on the safety and ergonomic issues to which the people doing our types of work and work processes are vulnerable?

We want to identify those core resources that have impact on the precision, accuracy, completeness, timeliness, customer-friendliness, and overall quality of our goods and services as well as the safety and worker-friendliness of our processes. In all of these except for the safety and ergonomic issues, which must predominate everywhere, we should give priority to the Gemba. We should have a reasonably clear picture of the flow of work, the critical functions and key players and the core resources of the Gemba. For the entire workplace, not just for the Gemba, we need a keen awareness of the safety and ergonomic needs and issues.

Figure 4-10 displays some of what we have described thus far, showing examples from a variety of Gembas. This is not intended to be a complete listing of all the important factors. Rather, it shows some examples to stir up your own thinking for your own workplace.

Types of work	Critical functions and key players	Core resources	Non-Gemba resources	Internal supplier—Gemba	Internal customer—Gemba
Making a pizza in a restaurant kitchen	The chef	• The oven • The recipe • The ingredients • The work space (counter-tops, etc.) • Etc.	• Chef's uniform • Music	• The wait staff process • Purchasing • Utensil-washing	• The wait staff process • The home delivery process
Treating cardiac arrest in an hospital emergency room	• E.R. doctors • E.R. nurses	• Defibrillators • Medications • Miscellaneous equipment • Syringes • Etc.	• Waiting area for relatives	• Emergency services (ambulance, medivac) • Lab services (X-ray, etc.)	• Operating room • Intensive care • Rehab center • Etc.
Arresting an intoxicated driver	• Police officer • Breathalizer operator	• Police car • Breathalizer • Etc.	• Holding cell	• 911 and dispatch • Patrol officer processes	• The county prosecutor or city attorney • Detox centers
Making facial tissues (e.g., Kleenex™)	• Paper machine operators • Box machine operators	• Paper machine • Box machine • Pulp and other ingredients • Box material • Etc.	• Posters and slogans • Lunchroom • Inspection processes	• The pulp making process • The wood supplier process	• Cartoning process • Warehouse and shipping processes
Making a commercial loan	• Loan officer	• Computer • Policies • Forms • Etc.	• Gift calendar for the customer	• Credit check process • Credit info process	• Loan clerk • Monitoring processes

Figure 4-10. Examples of Gembas and some of their critical factors or key leverage points.

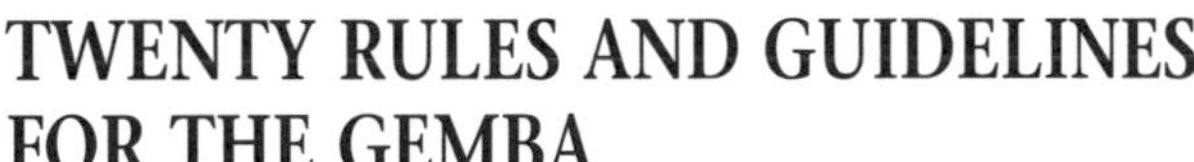

TWENTY RULES AND GUIDELINES FOR THE GEMBA

Gemba Guidelines

Here is a list of the 20 guidelines for the Gemba.

1. Give priority to the Gemba.
2. Focus on clearing out and cleaning up the Gemba.
3. Make sure the core resources, especially those with key functions and roles, are almost always busy doing Gemba work.
4. Study the Gemba processes and core resources.
5. Make changes to reduce costs in the Gemba (without compromising quality).
6. Streamline the Gemba and organize the work.
7. Identify and eliminate waste in the Gemba.
8. Don't keep the Gemba waiting.
9. Don't interrupt or disrupt the Gemba.
10. Error-proof the Gemba; make it more robust.
11. Standardize recurring Gemba tasks when the important factors are controllable.
12. Address the out-of-control factors in the Gemba.
13. Make changes in the Gemba to increase throughput.
14. Identify the key process indicators and routinely monitor them.
15. Maintain continual education and training for the Gemba.
16. Make the Gemba "hum" with communication.
17. Develop in the Gemba the reflexes, habits, and processes for continual PDSA.
18. Attend to the human needs of the Gemba people (and everyone else as well).
19. Make the Gemba a fun place to work.
20. Assume that "everything is felt in the Gemba."

1. *Give priority to the Gemba.* As I have emphasized already, the Gemba is the heart of your organization and it must take precedence over everything else. While these principles and guidelines apply and will be helpful all over your organization, apply them first in the Gemba and work outward from there.

2. *Focus on clearing out and cleaning up the Gemba.* There are two categories of work that apply here.
   - *Systemic cleaning up and clearing out:* Look at the actual work flow and make changes that will eliminate unnecessary and non-value-adding steps. The opportunity flowchart may be a useful tool for this.
   - *Physical cleaning up and clearing out:* When the Gemba is neat, tidy, and well-organized it will be harder to lose things and easier to find things, and generally more pleasing to the eye.
3. *Make sure the core resources and especially those with key functions or roles are always busy doing their Gemba work.*
   - In a medical clinic or law office, you don't want everyone else occupied while the doctor or lawyer sits idle. Make sure the core resources are occupied with Gemba work.
   - You don't want a $15 million paper machine sitting there doing nothing.
   - If there is excessive variability in the earlier steps, resulting in core resources standing idle, work to reduce this variability, making a more predictable flow.
   - Schedule the work of the core resources carefully, so that it is occupied with the most important work in the most efficient way.
4. *Study the Gemba processes and core resources.*
   - Your Gemba people must be students, experts, and masters of the Gemba work.
   - Your Gemba people should know the factors necessary to make the process function well even under unstable conditions. They should know more about your equipment and machinery than the designers and manufacturers of it.
   - Your Gemba people should be masters of the sciences and methods that result in the best output for your customers.
5. *Make changes to reduce costs in the Gemba.*
   - Reduce waste, scrap, and rework.
   - Reduce, reuse, and recycle materials (without compromising quality).
   - Study ways to use less (materials, time, space, personnel, etc.) with equal or better results for the customer.
   - Let the customers share in the savings.

Aisin Seiki and the Ozashiki

Aisin Seiki is part of the Toyota family, partly owned by the auto giant and a supplier of various parts.

Aisin Seiki challenged the Deming prize, winning it in 1972.

In their Nagoya water-pump plant, one of their 1980 improvement themes was to clean up the plant, making it like the Ozashiki, the parlor in the typical Japanese home that was kept spotless (in case visitors should stop by). Aisin Seiki spent five years pursuing this goal.

I had an opportunity to visit this plant in 1985, along with several other American visitors. In spite of its manufacturing operations (drilling, grinding, stamping, etc.), the plant was spotless, no grease, no dust, no filings. Almost every worker had his or her work station decorated homelike with flowers, trees, pictures, clocks, and other amenities. Throughout the plant were islands used by the workers for eating lunch, taking breaks, and having meetings. These were built and are maintained by the workers themselves. Some are quite spectacular with trees, tables, goldfish ponds and fountains.

Each work station had formfit storage for tools, warning systems telling when drills should be changed and systems to assure the reorder of parts when the supply was low. Their just-in-time system applied not only to the component on which they were working, but to the drills, etc. which they used in their work.

How did they keep the place so clean? Their three minute clean-up period for each shift, with each worker cleaning up his or her own area, seemed inadequate to explain a degree of cleanliness that would make even my mother envious. They constructed some dust and filing collecting apparatus around their machinery. The workers have learned how to prevent dirt and litter in their ordinary work equipment and methods.

The effect of such cleanliness is increased quality and productivity. In a preventive mode, the absence of dirt and disarray can help avoid missing parts and lost tools or distraction from a worker's concentration. A side effect of Aisin's cleanliness, pointed out by the plant manager, has been increased pride and self-confidence of the workers and supervisors. A series of signs erected Burma Shave-style by workers on the plant floor reads, "We are proud/Of our TQC corner/To the world." The English wasn't elegant, but the message was eloquent. They have every right to be proud. Photographs taken five years before show that this was a typical grungy plant. Now it's an Ozashiki. (From Scholtes, 1986.)

6. *Streamline the Gemba and organize the work.*
   - Draw a floor map of the Gemba and trace the patterns of movement (fast-motion video might be useful for this study). Look for opportunities to reduce movement by redesigning the layout.
   - Have a place for everything and have everything in its place. Use signs, labels, and outline drawings to make things easy to find and easy to return to their places.
   - Locate the frequently used equipment and supplies for easy access.
   - Have ready access to what is needed for the current cycle or task, for example, all the parts needed for assembling one unit. Create a means for just-in-time availability of what will be needed for the next task or cycle.

Specs or Drop Test: Studying the Process

A European-based electronics corporation had subcontracted with a Japanese television manufacturer. Months of protracted meetings and negotiations had resulted in numerous standards and specifications that the Japanese company was expected to meet under the terms of the contract.

Several weeks after the specifications were completed, a representative of the Japanese manufacturer (JM) contacted the project manager for the European corporation (EC).

JM: In one section of the standards you describe the exact specification of the packing material that must surround the television set in the carton.

EC: Yes?

JM: You also describe as a standard that the carton must withstand a certain drop test without damage to the television set in the carton.

EC: Yes?

JM: If we can meet the drop-test standard, must we still conform to the packing specifications?

EC: No. The drop test is the more important measure.

JM: Very good! We have designed a packaging method that will withstand the drop test and reduce the size of the carton.

EC: Oh?

JM: And with a smaller carton we can put more units on each skid and increase the units per shipment with no increased shipping cost.

EC: Oh?

JM: And we will, of course, pass the savings on to your company.

This true story demonstrates a commitment to improvement and customer delight.

7. *Identify and eliminate waste in the Gemba.*
   - Know the different types of waste and how to reduce or eliminate them.
   - See "The Different Kinds of Waste" later in this chapter.
8. *Don't keep the Gemba waiting.*
   - Don't keep the key people waiting.
   - Eliminate bottlenecks.
   - Maintain the smooth, uncluttered flow of Gemba work.
9. *Don't interrupt or disrupt the Gemba.*
   - Study the types and patterns of interruption and devise methods to reduce or eliminate them, or handle the issue without interrupting the flow of work.
10. *Error-proof the Gemba; make it more robust.*
    - Find methods to make the Gemba more:

— Mistake-proof	— Flexible
— Omission-proof	— Adaptable
— Inadvertence-proof	— Simple
— Tamper-proof	— Endurable
— Easily taught	— User-friendly
— Easily learned	— Versatile
— Tolerant of variation	— Durable
— Forgiving	— Rugged
— Resilient	— Sustainable

    - Accomplish these through systemic changes, not through exhortations and slogans.
11. *Standardize recurring Gemba tasks when the important factors are controllable.*
    - See the next section, "Standardization."
12. *Address out-of-control factors in the Gemba.*
    - Give priority to the negative effects of these uncontrollable factors.
    - Study the patterns of out-of-control-ness: When? Where? Under what circumstances?
    - Determine the systemic causes of the factor that is out of control.
    - Redesign the system or process to eliminate the cause, avoid its impact, or at least reduce the likelihood of its occurrence.

Eliminating Waste in the Gemba

This case is based on real improvement efforts that took place at a mid-sized manufacturing facility.

Before the streamlining

- A fairly typical manufacturing and assembly layout. The entire operation was housed in two buildings.
- The main assembly area was long (150 ft.) with several long stretches when the product was moving from one station to another while no work was being done on it during the transition.
- Large stacks of inventory
  — Parts waiting to be supplied to assemblers
  — Parts standing near the assemblers
  — Parts waiting to be supplied to manufacturers
  — Parts standing near the manufacturers
  — Finished products waiting for orders and shipment

After the streamlining

- All operations were moved into one facility. This was done by reducing movement distances, compacting operations, and dramatically reducing inventory and the space needed to store it.
- Main assembly line was reduced in length to one-fifth its previous span. Empty transitional space was eliminated (on the *first day* of the effort). Inventory was removed from the line area. Subassembly loops were created in compact work areas adjacent to the main assembly line.

The flow of work

This took several months, but manufacturing, subassembly, and main assembly became so synchronized that there were no accumulations of parts or subassemblies waiting to move forward. Everything was a smooth flow—just-in-time.

Inventory

The smooth flow allowed a dramatic reduction of inventory. The smooth flow extended backward to the suppliers who provided a slower, steadier flow of materials and parts on an as-needed, just-in-time basis.

Time cycles and product inventory

The time cycles and pace of work were adjusted to reflect orders from the customers. The time cycles for manufacturing and assembly were reduced so that production could be more immediately responsive to requests from the customers. Instead of "pushing" the product through to the warehouse where it sat and waited for orders, the operations managers could reduce the finished-product inventory and extend the notion of smooth flow directly to the customers. Now, customer demand "pulls" products through the system with less waiting and need for storage. "We make our products just-in-time, not just-in-case," said one manager.

(Continued on page 114.)

Before the streamlining

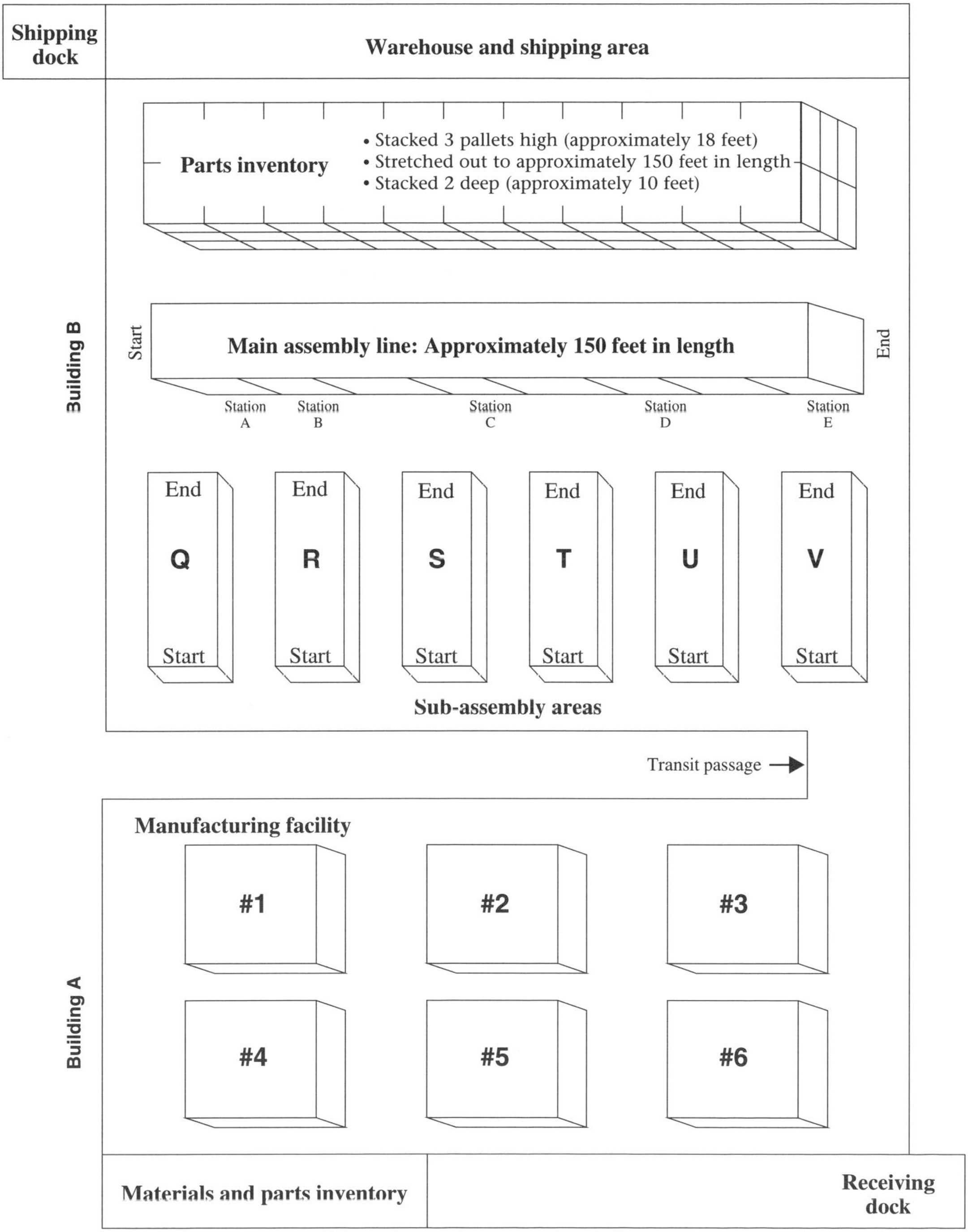

(Continued from page 112.)

Staging areas

The Gemba operators don't fetch parts. Each operator in the main assembly area, subassembly areas, and manufacturing areas have staging tables. These tables are designed with silhouette outlines of each part needed for that assembly operation. The operator has ready access to one complete set of parts. When that set of parts is used—when a cycle has been completed—a new set of parts replaces it on a just-in-time basis. This replacement task is done by a highly mobile *parts coordinator.* (The Japanese name for this role is "water spider.") The role of parts coordinator is filled only by very experienced and knowledgeable former operators. The work of the operators and assemblers, therefore, is not disrupted. The flow is unbroken.

Ergonomics

The replacement of materials and tools reflects efficient, safe movement. Before, for instance, an assembler needed to walk back and forth to a bench to pick up a drill when needed. After streamlining, the drill and other such tools were hung in holsters or slings attached to the line platform, inches from the operator's hand. One of the operators said to me, "I do less work now and get more done!"

This example is a composite of three improvement efforts I have either been part of or witnessed. Such streamlining took several months of intense effort, though some streamlining was accomplished in the first day. The methods used are based on the approaches of the Kaizen Institute.

You will note that in the example described above, the following types of waste were addressed:

- Overproduction
- Excess inventory
- Waiting
- Unnecessary motion

(See Bohman, 1992.)

13. *Make changes in the Gemba to increase throughput.*
    - Study ways to improve the capacity of the Gemba and increase its capability to do Gemba work.
    - Increase the capacity of the core resources and key participants.
    - Eliminate pauses and bottlenecks.
    - Off-load non-Gemba tasks to non-Gemba personnel, freeing up the time of the Gemba's key players to do the critical functions.
    - A word of caution: If the Gemba work is flowing efficiently, you must work to avoid a bottleneck in the steps immediately following.

After the streamlining

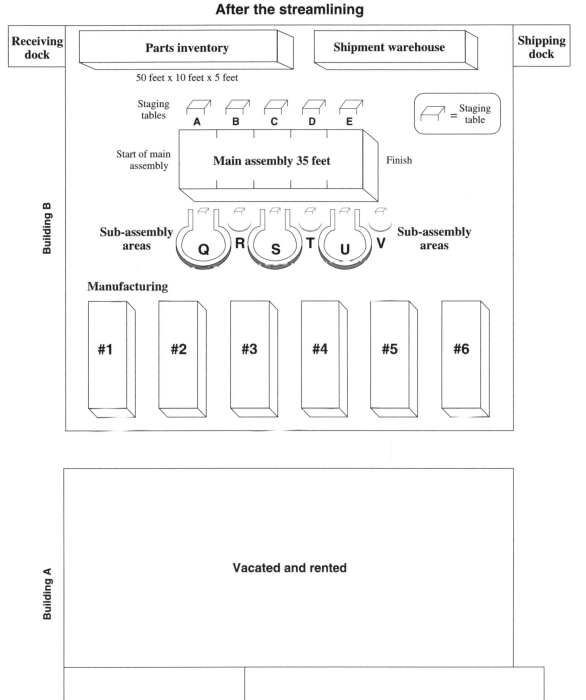

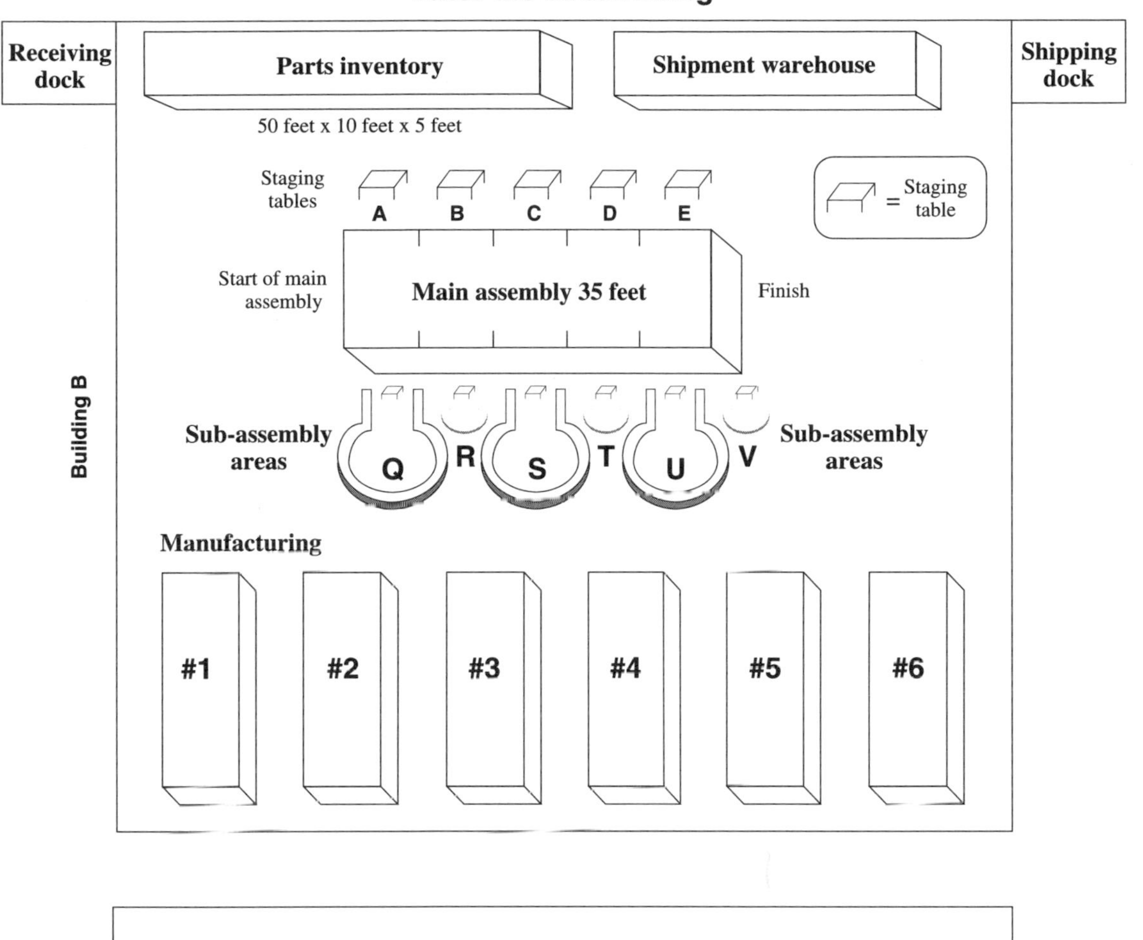

Building A

Vacated and rented

Quick Response

Some comments from Rajan Suri, Director of the Center for Quick Response Manufacturing at the University of Wisconsin–Madison.

> One of the biggest competitive edges a company can have is speed in the delivery of their products. Companies that are not able to do this will lose market share.
>
> If you want to be efficient, you should have 10 to 15 percent idle capacity so you don't have a big backlog and can serve (your customers) faster.
>
> Reported in the *Wisconsin State Journal,* December 1, 1996.

14. *Identify the key process indicators of the Gemba and routinely monitor them.*
    - Learn what the Gemba's "vital signs" are. Record the data in an appropriate manner and analyze and interpret the data appropriately.
    - Get help from someone well versed in statistical applications.
    - Create *systems* for collecting, recording, and analyzing the data. (Chapter 7 examines some of these issues.)
15. *Maintain continual education and training for the Gemba.*
    - Use multiple modes and means to assure that people learn what needs to be learned.
    - If you must err, err on the side of too much education, training, and communication.
    - Devise ways to educate, train, and communicate that are both effective and minimally disruptive of the Gemba and its work.
16. *Make the Gemba "hum" with communication.*
    - Successful projects and teams have continual communication within the group and between the group and its surrounding systems.
    - Communication must be through varied modes and media. Ask, "What must be communicated to whom and how do they best learn?"
    - Let the Gemba "hum" with communication and "blossom" with visual displays of work and progress.

17. *Develop in the Gemba the reflexes, habits, and processes for continual PDSA.*
    - PDSA is a continual cycle of *planning, doing, studying,* and *acting* (see Chapter 2). It builds forgiveness and learning into things gone wrong. We cannot guarantee that we will never make a mistake. We can, however, guarantee that we will learn from our mistakes.
    - With PDSA there is no failure. Mistakes are an opportunity to learn. Mistakes are what we discover when we *study.* Then we react, and adjust the process in response to what we have learned. We can then *act,* provided we have sufficient data to know what response is appropriate. The data we gather, the studying we do, and the adjustments we make allow us to prepare more effectively for *planning* the next cycle.
    - In the Gemba, we learn to continually study the key indicators of the process (KPIs) and the key quality characteristics (KQCs), attributes of the products and services important to our customers. We use this data to learn how to adjust the process without tampering with it (Deming 1994, Chapter 9).

Komatsu: Foolproofization

One of the Deming award companies we visited in 1985 was Komatsu, a heavy-equipment manufacturer. In their Awazu plant we saw examples of error-proofing. For instance, a unit moving through an assembly area has a credit-card-size mag card attached to it. Programmed into the mag card are instructions to the various tools and equipment on the assembly line.

At one station the worker tightens bolts with an impact wrench. Before doing the task the worker inserts the mag card into the machine that controls the equipment. This programs the equipment so that the bolts are automatically tightened to the proper torque—neither too tight nor too loose. The equipment also counts the bolts as they are tightened, notifying an operator who tries to forward the assembly with a missing bolt.

Komatsu identified the most common mistakes in their process and built error-proofing into their methods when possible.

Pete Gillespie's Barber Chair

One of my manager heroes was Pete Gillespie. Pete was president and CEO of a Chicago paper merchant, buying paper from paper mills and selling it to users. I knew Pete when I had a summer job in his warehouse. Pete had a spare office next to his work office and it contained a barber chair and haircutting supplies. One way Pete kept in touch with the men in his company was to give them free haircuts.

He was a good barber, though he apparently never learned to cut women's hair. Everyone—managers, sales personnel, hourly workers, and even the summertime warehouse help—would make an appointment to have a haircut by the CEO. During the haircut, Pete Gillespie chatted and got to know his people.

The lesson here is not that managers should become barbers, but that managers should find ways appropriate to them to keep in touch with their people.

18. *Attend to the human needs of the Gemba people (and everyone else as well).*
    - Make the Gemba safe and ergonomically sound. Do this not through slogans and exhortation but by removing the systemic causes of injuries and health hazards.
    - Have nearby break space and accommodations for meals, meetings, and training.
    - Allow for people's needs to socialize and communicate spontaneously.
19. *Make the Gemba a fun place to work.*
    - Remove the sources of "un-fun."
    - Develop things that are fun.
    - Let the Gemba people lead in this effort.
20. *Assume that "everything is felt in the Gemba."*
    - All the diseases in the organization create symptoms felt in the Gemba.
    - All the well-intentioned plans and decisions made elsewhere for various reasons will create repercussions in the Gemba.
    - A rule of thumb: Do nothing without first asking, "How will this have impact on the Gemba?" If your response is, "It will have no impact on the Gemba," then look deeper. There is something you have missed.
    - See Petronius Arbiter's quote on page 79.

STANDARDIZATION

Much of our work consists of repetitious work: changing a roll on a printing press or changing a roll on a cash register, closing the books every year or closing the office every night, running a weekly meeting or running an annual conference.

Repeatable tasks can be studied and improved. We can determine the most efficient, most reliable, easiest, safest, and most productive way we know to do this work. Then we can document that method, teach it to everyone involved in this task, and reinforce its continual use in a variety of worker-friendly ways.

Standardizing a task around a single best method results in a better product and service for customers, greater ease in training new workers, and improved ability to solve problems and improve the process even more. While the best-known method is being used as part of the routine, employees can continue to study the task to come up with an even better method. The effort thus keeps going.

Everyday PDSA

When a noted Japanese teacher of quality was visiting a U.S. city, he was invited to visit a local hospital. The top managers of this hospital were avid followers of Dr. Deming, sincerely applying the quality philosophy throughout their organization. It was they who wished to meet with this visiting Japanese expert.

When the visiting expert arrived at the hospital at the appointed time, only one of the hospital's managers showed up. The woman coordinating the meeting on behalf of the hospital was embarrassed and apologetic. She asked to reschedule the meeting for another time.

"Certainly," was the Japanese teacher's response, "but first let us learn from today."

"How shall we do that?" the woman asked.

"Why did so few show up today?"

"Perhaps because it was so close to the holidays. People may have taken the day off. But they had agreed to this date! I don't know."

"How could you find out?"

"Ask them, I suppose."

"Maybe we should do this: You conduct an investigation to find out the various causes why this meeting didn't occur. Then call me up next week and we will discuss a plan for the next meeting."

The visitor's reflex was PDSA. An unsuccessful meeting was an opportunity to learn. Data was important, not speculation. Improvement was important, not blame or apology. Learning was important, not simply another attempt without new understanding of what is necessary for success.

Gathering Points

When communicating with employees, managers can use the equivalent of a product-out approach or a customer-in approach. Product-out means, "This is what *we* want to communicate to them and here is how *we* want to communicate it." Customer-in means, "Here is what *they* believe is important for them to know and this is how *they* learn about things."

One company, wanting to communicate production changes, decided on multiple methods of communication. They asked people on the floor how they usually heard about things. Unexpectedly, most people said "At the picnic tables outside, during lunch and breaks." Therefore, the managers included this medium in their communications system: Printed announcements were left on the outdoor tables, and someone from planning was available out there to answer questions.

Where are your organization's "gathering points"? Pick places where almost everyone goes and where they are likely to wait idly. These are often the places where informal socialization occurs: fax machines, coffee stations, copy machines, restrooms, elevators, etc.

What Is a Standard?

A standard is a documented, best-known method to perform some task or process. A standard combines technological knowledge and process know-how, putting them in written form so everyone can use them. The purpose of a standard is to:

- Make it easier for people to do their jobs.
- Avoid the known pitfalls in a task.
- Assure safe operations.
- Make it easier to teach new employees.
- Make it easier to track down the cause of a problem.
- Eliminate unnecessary variation caused by too many methods being used to accomplish the same task.

Characteristics of a Good Standard

- *Clear and specific.* It describes precisely what steps to take, when to take them, how to do them, why to do them, what to monitor, and how to respond to signals of problems.
- *Designed for the uninitiated.* It should be understandable by new and not fully trained employees. Design it for those who fill in when the regular process operator is home sick.
- *Realistic.* It must be workable and easily followed and understood, and must include nothing unnecessary or contradictory.

- *Agreed-upon.* The standard should come from a consensus of those who must use it. They should study the methods and use data to determine which one method will work best.

Questions to Ask When Something Goes Wrong

- Do we know where in the process the problem occurred?
- Does that part of the process have a standard method?
- Do all the people working in that part of the process know the standard method?
- Is the standard method routinely used? This should not be seen as or used for the purpose of uncovering a culprit. Even if a single individual didn't use the standard, we should consider this an opportunity to improve the process:
  - — Perhaps that individual has developed a better method.
  - — Perhaps something is inadequate in our training process.
  - — Perhaps the standardized method is not suitable for this type of worker (because of height, left-handedness, etc.).
  - — Perhaps there is a rarely occurring special cause of which we have been unaware.

In Order to Develop a Standard:

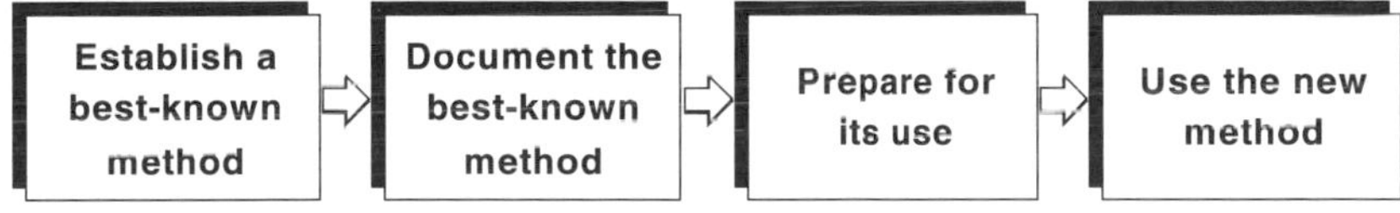

Establish a best-known method	Document the best-known method	Prepare for its use	Use the new method
• Use data to support which method is best • Make the method as "inadvertence-proof" as possible • Involve those who will be using the new method • Build consensus around the new method	• Use flowcharts and standardized process charts • Show how to do the new method, what problems to monitor, how to react to signals of problems • Use manuals, checklists, and graphic instructions • Use instructional displays at the exact spot where the new method will be used	• Prepare to train people in the new method • Train the trainers • Prepare materials – For the current employees – For future new employees • Plan the details for launching the new method • Decide how progress and success will be monitored	• Use a little hoopla for the first day/week/month of use • Monitor the new method to learn if it is: – Being used consistently – Resulting in an improved process and improved results

A Standardized Process Chart

Shown in Figure 4-11, a standardized process chart is a way to document the critical information regarding a process or task after it has been standardized. Ideally, tasks or subtasks should fit on one page.

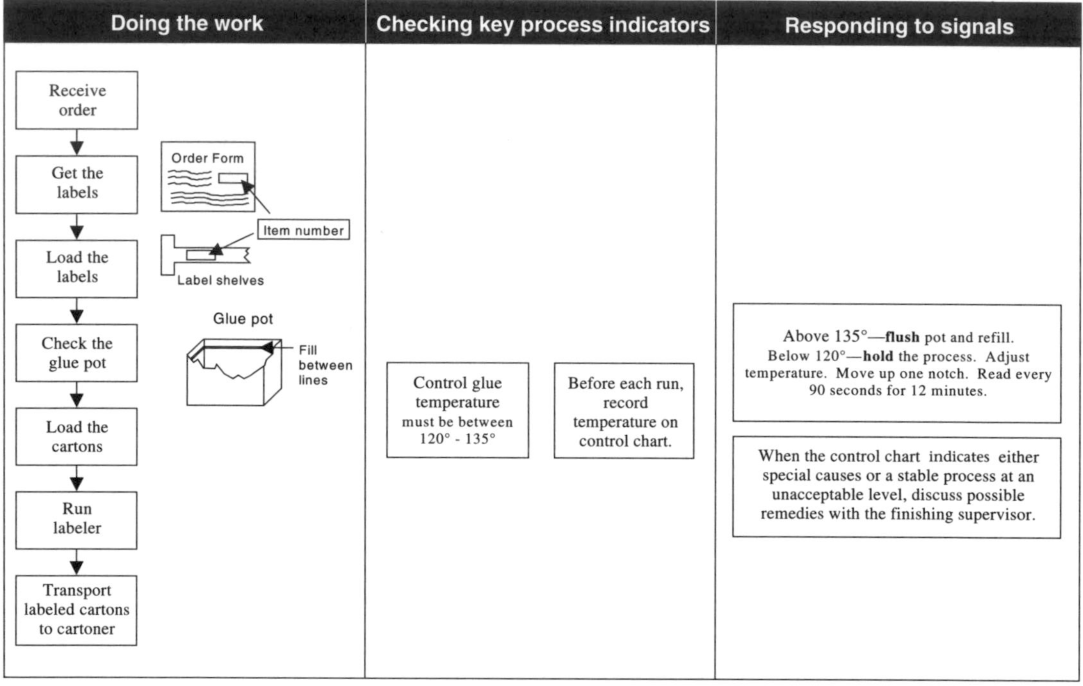

Figure 4-11. An example of a standardized process chart for a carton labeler operator.

Because the process depicted in Figure 4-11 is a single-person process, this standardized process chart uses a simple flowchart in the left-hand section. If the standardized process required interaction between several people, a deployment flowchart would be appropriate (see Figure 4-5).

For this particular worker (this is a real example from a real workplace), running the carton labeler represents only one of several tasks. Rather than a conventional job description, the employee has a sheaf of standardized process charts describing the 15 or so processes involved. Thus the worker knows what jobs to perform, how to do each, what is important to check or monitor, and how to respond to the signals observed while observing the key process indicators. Contained on one page is the *do, study, act* information for a PDSA cycle.

Keeping a Straight Stack

It is important to know how to translate customer needs (key quality characteristics) into points of control in the process (key process indicators). My favorite example of this occurred in the early 80s at a Kimberly-Clark plant in Neenah, Wisconsin.

Kimberly Clark's Kleenex™ tissues advertised the feature "pull up one, up pops another." It is one of their key quality characteristics.

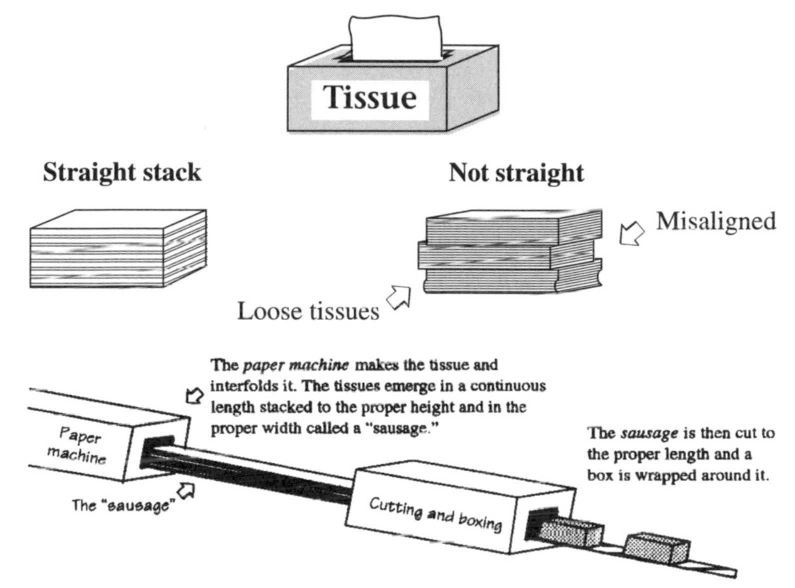

If the stack is not straight, it fouls up the cutting and boxing process or it may survive that part of the process and get boxed up but not provide the important customer feature—"pull up one, up pops another"—because the tissues are trapped in the box.

Only two veteran operators knew how to consistently keep a straight stack and they were near retirement. Therefore, the operators set up a project to study what these men did. The veteran operators ran the machine on intuition and instinct. They couldn't explain what they did. So the project consisted of two sets of observers, one for each veteran operator, taking notes and writing down what these experts were responding to (sometimes a subtle change in the sound of the machine) and how they responded.

It took a few weeks to get what the operators did down to a standardized method, but they got it done. As a result, every operator kept a straight stack.

This particular operator knows from experience that this process has three vulnerabilities: wrong labels, empty glue pot, and glue that is too hot or too cold. Each of these opportunities for error is addressed in this standardized process chart with a little more detailed description and the instruction to enter the glue temperature on a control chart. In this case, the mechanism controlling glue temperature is sufficiently erratic that the worker is using data entered on a control chart to determine if this equipment can be kept in control or should be replaced.

Figure 4-12 describes the standardized process chart format.

1. Doing the task	2. Checking key process indicators	3. Responding to signals
This section uses a flowchart to describe the sequence of activities and—if appropriate—the flow of work between interactive groups and individuals. More detailed information may be included here or, if necessary, referenced here.	Many processes have critical steps that need to be monitored by the operator. These steps have "key process indicators" (KPIs) vital signs that indicate whether or not the process is in control and on track. These should be used sparingly, only when you know of a point of vulnerability.	• A KPI informs you that an adjustment is necessary. The instructions for response are placed in this part of the chart. • This describes immediate responses for the operator as well as who to inform regarding the performance of the process, in case more than process adjustment and control is necessary to avoid problems.

Figure 4-12. The format for the standardized process chart.

Guidelines for the Standardized Process Chart

1. The chart should ordinarily describe, on a single page, a specific task or operation. If your operation is too long to fit on one page, break it down into subtasks, and put each on a separate page.
2. Eventually people's jobs—at least the greater proportion of their jobs—can be described using a series of these charts.
3. Avoid needless effort. Focus on what is important and useful. Add detail where and when it is needed.
4. Start where you are feeling pain. Use this chart first on processes with which you are experiencing problems. Monitor only those indicators that you know from experience are

important to monitor. Columns 2 and 3 don't need to be filled out on every standardized process chart.

5. Don't overdo it! If you initiate a standardized process chart blitzkrieg in your organization, you will drive people crazy. Do some pilot standardization activities. Gradually expand the effort, learning as you go. Let groups and individuals standardize processes one at a time at a workable pace, starting with those processes that need standardization most.
6. The same format can be used to describe a supervisor's or manager's job. Figure 4-13 shows one of the larger work flows coordinated by the finishing supervisor, the carton label operator's boss. Note that one of the processes in this system, "Packages product in labeled cartons," shows where the carton labeler operator fits into the finishing system.

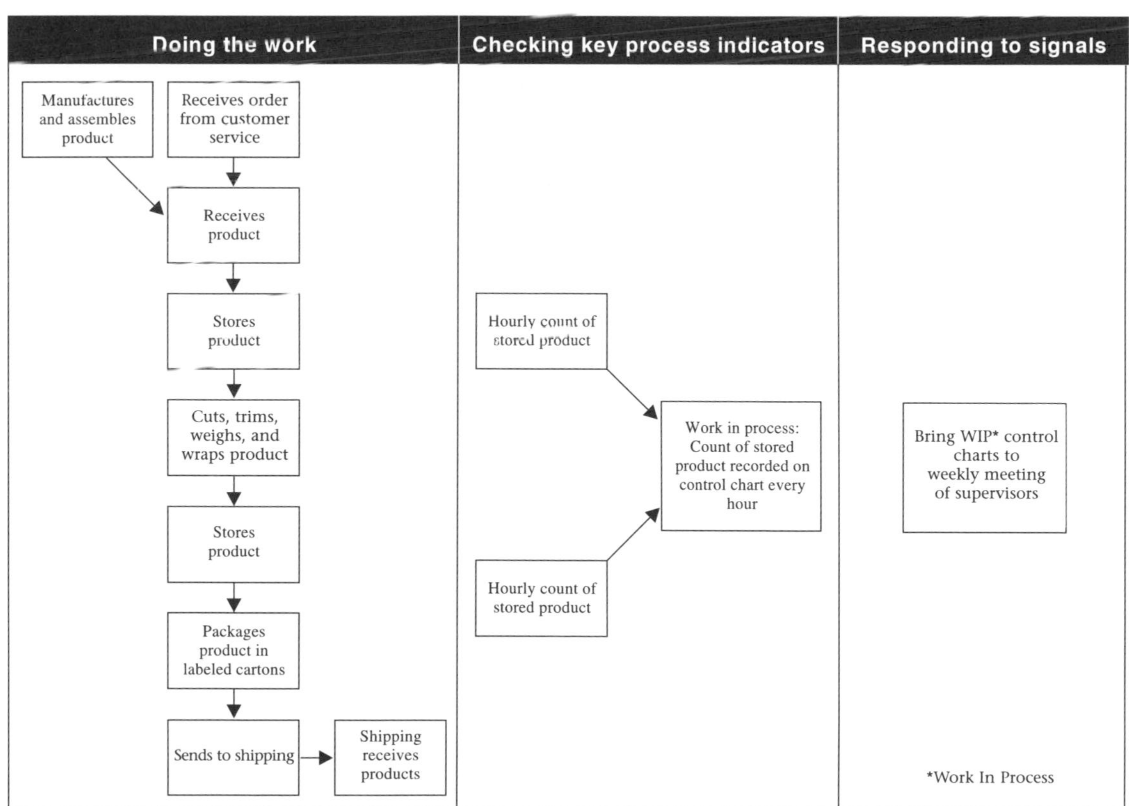

Figure 4-13. The finishing system managed by the finishing supervisor.

ISO 9000

On the surface, ISO 9000 (or its automotive equivalent, QS 9000) seems like the right thing to do. You must make your processes consistent, document the consistent processes, and have your consistent processes certified by an ISO inspector. Then you are ISO certified. Voilà!

What is wrong with ISO?

- The pursuit of quality is a long and arduous journey, requiring a holistic, integrated, systemic approach. Standardizing is a good thing to do. That is what this section is all about. However, standardization must be an effort guided by a larger context. ISO offers no greater purpose or larger context or system.
- A company can have consistent standardized processes that, though they are documented and certified, end up infuriating the customer. ISO doesn't attend to whether your customers are displeased. If one of your certified processes subverts another of your certified processes, you can still have those processes approved by ISO. If you are doing the wrong thing, ISO asks only that you do it consistently.
- There is a certain paternalism and a tone of distrust inherent in ISO. ISO implies that companies won't do this standardization effort, or at least won't do it correctly, unless the "ISO police" are there to inspect and approve it. It is an example of the "teacher checking your homework" syndrome. ISO displaces your company's internal motivation to do good work with ISO's external motivation. This is inconsistent with the spirit of quality. Who is it who has decided that you must be certified into good work? Who decides that "we are fit to declare you to be OK?" You don't decide. Your customers don't decide. The *ISO police* decide!
- ISO assumes that each inspector is consistent in his or her methods with all the other inspectors. However, those who have been inspected have reported wide disparity. Just like teachers checking homework, there are easy markers and hard markers. ISO inspections themselves, it seems, are not standardized.
- ISO is positioned as something you must do to export to Europe. Not true! There is no single standard for all of Europe. Also, some European countries do not insist on such standards.
- Becoming ISO certified or recertified is expensive and bureaucratic. You will be faced with a dilemma should you improve one of your certified processes: Do you use the certified, unimproved process or do you use the uncertified but better process? If you choose the latter, do you incur the expense of recertification, or do you just do it anyway?

When using a flowchart such as this to review their jobs, managers need to pay attention to the *arrows,* the transition points in the systems. Managers usually get in trouble when they manage "inside the boxes." Managers should rely on their Gemba people to do the work inside the boxes. Managers manage the arrows and the white spaces.

Managers may also be useful in helping the Gemba units establish and maintain feedback loops between each other. Managers should also work with them to create feedback loops with the outside customers. (See "Feedback Loops" later in this chapter.)

Last Comments on Standardization

There is a delicate line to walk when dealing with standardization. On the one hand we want methods of work that are usefully constraining, that eliminate needless variation in method and, therefore, in output. While people may think of their jobs as art forms, dependent on their own unique and individual genius, seldom is this the case. While we want to eliminate art-form-like caprice and needless variation from work, we do not want to make work oppressively rigid and obnoxiously bureaucratic. Between these is the fine line. By involving people in the standardization of work we can remove some of the oppressiveness of it. People are less likely to balk at standards *they* have devised. Recognizing that we need not standardize everything should help. Also, agreeing to begin with those processes that we all acknowledge need to be standardized should help. The ideal is for people to take charge of their own standardization effort. Myron Tribus recalls a conversation with Mr. Sasaoka of Yokagawa Hewlett-Packard when the president of YHP described how they required each new worker to rewrite the instructions that describe how to perform the standardized work processes. The new worker is probably a good judge of how much standardization is necessary and how much is too much.

THE DIFFERENT KINDS OF WASTE

Having identified the flow of work, the critical functions, key players, and core resources, and having discussed how to standardize the recurring processes, we now explore another aspect of daily work: waste. Many of the rules and guidelines identified previously focus on such items as clearing out and cleaning up the Gemba, making changes to reduce costs, streamlining the Gemba, and identifying and eliminating waste. We will address these issues in this section.

There are some principles we should keep in mind as we seek to make the Gemba (or any other part of the operation) more efficient and productive:

Standardizing Sales

Perhaps more than other professionals, salespeople are inclined to see themselves as a unique subspecies of the human race. "This stuff may work with those other people," they protest, "but salespeople are different. What we do is intuitive. We have to use our instincts. There is no system here. It's an art form!"

Such was the response among the salespeople at one very high-tech product/service organization. They provided very sophisticated financial systems software tailored to the needs of the user. These salespeople also had to be very technically astute.

"Do you go out and make sales calls?" I asked. They responded in the affirmative.

"So let's look at that sales call this way." I drew on the flipchart:

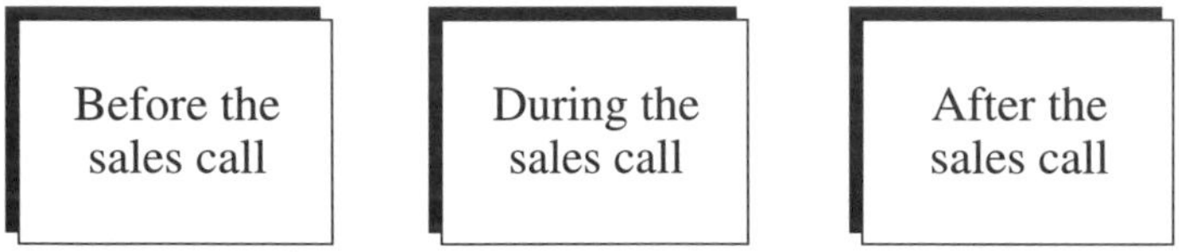

Before the sales call	During the sales call	After the sales call

"What is important to do before the sales call?" They offered various answers, which I listed. Some items caused discussion among the salespeople, not so much disagreement among them as an awareness of interesting differences in their approaches.

Then we moved on. "What is important during the sales call?" I asked. They offered several items, but when one salesperson said, "The presentation is the most important part of the call!" everyone agreed.

"What constitutes a good presentation?" I asked. The salespeople started listing a number of factors. Once again they mostly agreed, though there were some interesting variations. Then I asked two important questions:

- "Who decides what is a good presentation?" It took them a while to say, "The customer does!"
- "And how do your customers define a 'good presentation'?" Silence.

So we devised a little research project for the sales force: Talk to customers about sales presentations they have seen. What made some better and some worse? How can our presentations be improved? What are you, the customer, getting in our presentations that you don't need? What do you need that you're not getting?

What happened here? The salespeople started looking at their work as a *process* aimed at customers, a process that can be improved with feedback from the customer.

We didn't use the words "system" or "process." Nor did we need to debate the issues of intuition and art form. But we started examining the system called selling. Also, these salespeople got excited about the exploration.

The Different Kinds of Waste

1. Overproduction
2. Excess inventory
3. Transportation
4. Waiting
5. Unnecessary motion
6. Overprocessing
7. Correction
8. Complexity
9. Bureaucracy

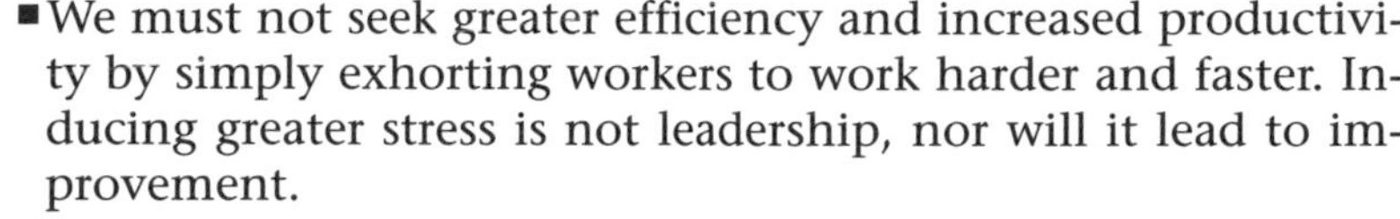

- We must not seek greater efficiency and increased productivity by simply exhorting workers to work harder and faster. Inducing greater stress is not leadership, nor will it lead to improvement.
- We must not achieve increased efficiency and productivity by compromising the functionality of our systems and processes. Short-term productivity gains may create long-term chaos.
- We should not achieve greater efficiency and productivity at the cost of reduced customer satisfaction.

How, then, can we increase efficiency and productivity? *By reducing or eliminating waste.* This must be done not by edict but by careful study and well-planned efforts.

Waste Plus Complexity and Bureaucracy

1. *The waste of overproduction*
   - Making more than you need
   - Having more capacity than you can possibly use
   - Having more space than you need
2. *The waste of excess inventory*
   - Having more materials, supplies, ingredients, and components than you need
   - Excessive levels of work-in-process

SOME COMMENTS ON OVERPRODUCTION AND EXCESS INVENTORY

- The ideal is a constantly moving flow, where nothing waits or accumulates. The best way to determine the appropriate levels of production capacity, inventory, or work-in-process is to start with patterns of customer demand. Then conduct time-order statistical studies to create profiles of the variation in your systems. Learn the range, average, and patterns of variation on the demand for products or services, the cycle times for total production, and the times for each phase within the total time cycle.
- Determine the levels of production, inventory, and work-in-process with data based on current actual performance, not hunches, wishes, and dreams.
- When your improvement plans include specific interventions to reduce cycle times or increase capacity, then a commensurate adjustment in the levels of production, inventory, and work-in-process may be appropriate.

3. *The waste of transportation*

The time it takes to get your products or services from you to your user/customer is waste.

COMMENTS ON TRANSPORTATION WASTE

- You may consider transportation as inevitable. From the customer's point of view, however, it is waste. An example:

  Kikkoman used to transport soy beans from the United States to Japan, brew soy sauce, and export the bottled soy sauce back to the United States. In the late 1970s Kikkoman defied tradition and built a production and bottling plant in Wisconsin, thus eliminating a lot of transportation waste.
- You may never eliminate all transportation waste (unless you find a way to "beam" your products and services to your customers), but you should continually seek ways to reduce it.

4. *The waste of waiting*

Waiting wastes many things: people's time, idle facilities, equipment, and other unused resources. Waiting interrupts the flow and rhythms of work. Assemblers can't complete the assembly of a unit. Managers can't complete plans because of information that is not ready. Builders can't continue building because needed materials are late, and because the builders are late, the plumbers and electricians are delayed on this job and on all the other jobs on which they are expected to work.

SOME COMMENTS ON WAITING

- As you explore the Gemba, look for signs of waiting. Ask the Gemba workers how often they must wait, for what types of delay, for how long.
- Don't keep the Gemba waiting. This is rule #1. For example, keeping a materials handler waiting is more harmful if it results in keeping an assembler waiting. Keeping a manager waiting is less harmful than keeping a machine operator waiting.
- Good planning and process knowledge should virtually eliminate all waiting. Collect data on the causes of waiting. Start with the type of waiting that consumes the most time. Find the systemic causes of the waiting and eliminate them.

5. *The waste of unnecessary motion*
   - Poor layouts that require unnecessary or excessive movement
   - Physical distances that require unnecessary or excessive movement

- Poor ergonomics
- See the example "Eliminating Waste in the Gemba" (pp. 112-114)

SOME COMMENTS ON UNNECESSARY MOTION

- Sometimes it is useful to draw a floor plan of your office or shop and trace the physical movement of a job as it works its way through the work space. An alternative method of conducting this study is to use a fast-motion video. (See Figure 7-12.)
- Does the layout of the office or shop reflect the logical and smooth-flowing sequence of steps in a process, or are workers required to double back to perform intermediate steps? Are the tools and equipment within easy reach of the person using them: no stretching, stooping, or walking back and forth to retrieve items?

6. *The waste of overprocessing*
   - Steps that add no value
   - Empty busy-ness, make-work
   - Multiple inspections, multiple signatures
   - Skeuomorphs (see sidebar)

SOME COMMENTS ON OVERPROCESSING

When developing a flowchart of the process, it is useful to ask the purpose of each step. ("Why do we cut off the ham shank?") Then ask whether this purpose continues to be relevant. This may help to identify unnecessary steps and indications of overprocessing.

7. *The waste of correction*

Deming once said, "Let's make toast American style. You burn. I'll scrape!" The waste of correction is the waste involved in inspecting for mistakes and errors and then in undoing and redoing things gone wrong: scraping burnt toast, remedial activities in school, damage control, inspection and correction, apologizing to the customers (necessary, perhaps, but an indicator of waste).

AN EXAMPLE OF OVERPROCESSING LEADING TO CORRECTION LEADING TO OVERPROCESSING

In a company that manufactured boards for printed circuits, one step in the process involved copper plating and a later step involved brushing the copper. When asked what they were doing and why, those doing the brushing said, "We're brushing the copper plate to get it down to the proper thickness. We have to do this because the group doing the plating puts too much on."

> **Skeuomorph: Obscure and Wonderful Word #2**
>
> An activity or artifact that continues in use long after its original purpose has disappeared. The great-grandmother cut off the shank of the ham because the oven was too small. The grandmother, mother, and daughter continued to cut off the shank—because of tradition, not because of the size of their ovens. (My gratitude to John Norrie of the British Deming Association for introducing me to this word.)

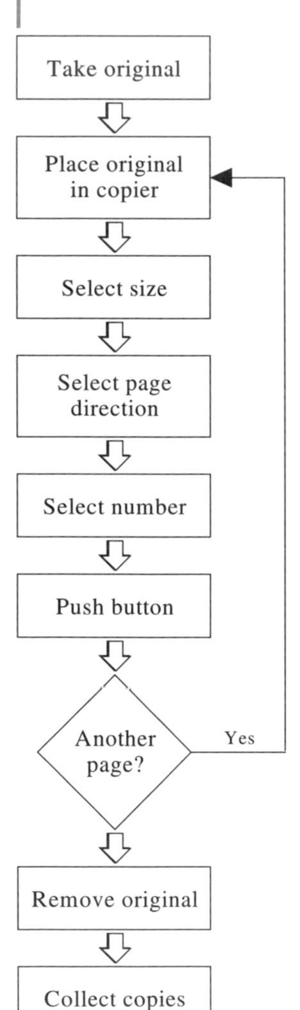

Figure 4-14. A copy machine process with no errors.

We walked up the line to where the operators were dipping the boards into the plating tank and asked them to describe what they were doing and why. They told us.

Then we asked, "How do you know how much copper plating to put on?"

They explained and added: "But, of course, we always add a little extra."

"Why?" we asked.

"Because those folks down the line are brushing the hell out of it!"

8. *Complexity*

Complexity is a combination of waiting, unnecessary motion, and correction. Complexity is work that is added because the task wasn't or couldn't be completed correctly with the first effort. This notion was first introduced by Tim Fuller (1985).

Figure 4-14 is a simple flowchart of a copy machine process with no errors occurring. Now look at that same process when errors occur (Figure 4-15).

The copy machine process is displayed using an opportunity flowchart (see Figure 4-6) with the errorless steps on the left flowing downward and the complexity to the right of the vertical divider.

9. *Bureaucracy*

Bureaucracy is a peculiar combination of other forms of waste. Russell Ackoff (1991, p. 3) says a bureaucracy is an organization whose principal objective is to keep people busy doing nothing. Bureaucracy as a form of waste is the result of what happens when people with no real work to do impose needless demands on those who have real work to do. In other words, when the non-Gemba imposes unnecessary work on the Gemba you have the form of waste called bureaucracy.

Bureaucracy has to do with both unnecessary work and needless constraints. The notion of constraints might be viewed in the context of a continuum, as seen in Figure 4-16.

Value added

Cost added only

Take original
Copier in use?
Wait?
Leave
Glass dirty?
Clean
Place original
Select size
Select page direction
Select number
Out of toner?
Find toner
Know how to add toner?
Add toner
Get help
Toner added
Out of Paper?
Find paper
Box open?
Knife?
Load paper
Load paper?
Open box
Find knife
Push button
Find help
Another page?
Copy made?
Quality OK?
Stop copier
Adjust?
Remove original
Req'd number?
Find problem ?
Adjust
Collect copies
Find help

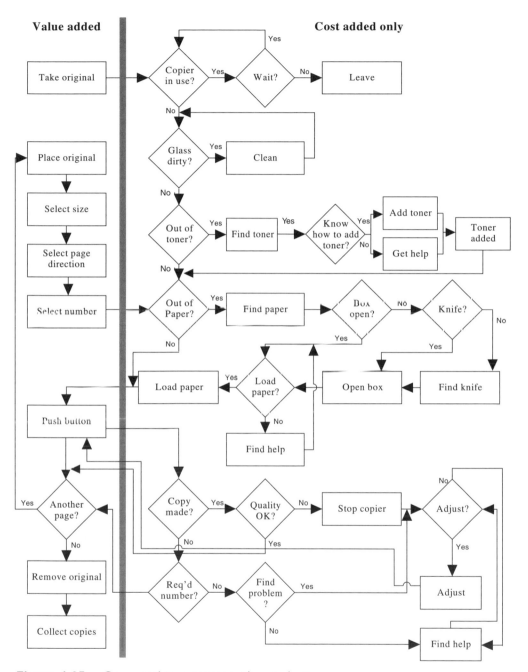

Figure 4-15. Copy machine process with complexity.

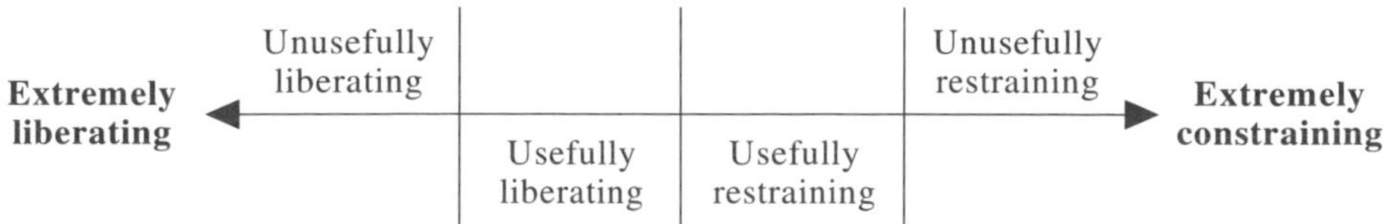

Figure 4-16. The continuum of constraints.

Liberating

- An increased variety of options. "Unusefully liberating" is when an organization disables itself with too many options (too many products, services, or priorities; an inch-deep and a mile-wide approach).
- One of the requirements for creativity is a form of useful liberation, permission to break the rules (within some stated structure and boundaries).

Constraining

- A decreased variety of options, imposing new limitations.
- Useful constraining is also part of the requirement for creativity. Useful constraints provide direction and focus to people's creative effort.
- "Unuseful constraint" is a way of defining bureaucracy. Bureaucracy consists of limitations without purpose or limitations that are detrimental to accomplishing the purpose of an undertaking. Bureaucracy consists of limitations that get in the way of serving the important needs of the customer.

We tend to blame government or other regulatory agencies for most bureaucratic constraints. My observation is that, by far, most bureaucracy is generated from within, constraints devised not by government but by a company's own lawyers, accountants, labor negotiators, or HR people.

One Officer's Response to Bureaucracy

Gentlemen:

Whilst marching from Portugal to a position which commands the approach to Madrid and the French forces, my officers have been diligently complying with your requests, which have been sent by H.M. ship from London to Lisbon and thence by dispatch rider to our headquarters.

We have enumerated our saddles, bridles, tents and tent poles, and all manner of sundry items for which His Majesty's Government holds me accountable. I have dispatched reports on the character, wit, and spleen of every officer. Each item and every farthing has been accounted for, with two regrettable exceptions for which I beg your indulgence.

Unfortunately the sum of one shilling and ninepence remains unaccounted for in one infantry battalion's petty cash and there has been a hideous confusion as to the number of jars of raspberry jam issued to one cavalry regiment during a sandstorm in western Spain. This reprehensible carelessness may be related to the pressure of circumstances, since we are at war with France, a fact which may come as a bit of a surprise to you gentlemen in Whitehall.

This brings me to my present purpose, which is to request elucidation of my instructions from His Majesty's Government, so that I may better understand why I am dragging an army over these barren plains. I construe that perforce it must be one of two alternative duties, as given below. I shall pursue either one with my best ability, but I cannot do both.

1. Train an army of uniformed British clerks in Spain for the benefit of the accountants and copy-boys in London, or perchance
2. To see to it that the forces of Napoleon are driven out of Spain.

Your most obedient servant,
Wellington

A Tale of Two Taxis

This story is an example of bureaucracy at work. In this case it involves a policy commonly used by cab companies to the detriment of their customers.

I arrived home from a business trip late one night. The airport was almost closed. I looked out at the cab stand and it was empty. So I called my preferred cab company. I will call it "Yellow Cab." When I walked out to where the cab would pick me up, there was a woman waiting. I learned from her that she had called "White Cab."

A white cab pulled up; the woman walked over and conversed with the driver and walked back to where she had been waiting.

"What happened?" I asked.

"Oh, he can't pick me up. The driver who bid on my call is on his way. He will pick me up."

"Isn't that ridiculous!"

Then a yellow cab pulled up and the same thing happened to me. So there she was waiting for a white cab and there I was waiting for a yellow cab; there was a yellow cab looking for a fare but not allowed to pick me up, and there was a white cab looking for a fare but not allowed to pick her up. We each could have gotten into the other's cab and everything would have been OK.

Who was this policy meant to serve? Certainly not the customer. It punishes the customer. The policy was devised to avoid internal disputes between cab drivers within each respective company. Needless to say, it has to do with how the drivers are paid.

I walked over to the driver of the yellow cab and asked, "What's the worst that will happen if you give me a ride home?"

"Another driver will be mad at me!" he responded.

"What's worse for Yellow Cab," I responded, "to have one driver mad at another or to have a customer mad at Yellow Cab?"

He called his dispatcher and got permission to pick me up.

I never did find out what happened to the woman.

FEEDBACK LOOPS

So far in this chapter we have explored several topics related to getting the important daily work done:

- Understanding the importance of the uncluttered flow of work
- Identifying the critical functions, key players, and core resources
- Rules and guidelines for leading Gemba work
- The importance of the standardization of recurring daily work
- Different types of waste that must be removed from and reduced in the Gemba

In this section we will explore the importance of establishing feedback loops. We mentioned the subject of feedback loops in Chapter 3, in the discussion of process. See Figure 3-12 for an illustration of feedback loops.

Everyone in the Gemba needs a clear sense of direction and focus. Everyone in the Gemba and elsewhere needs clarity about "how we are doing." In the hierarchically driven organization this was accomplished by individuals being evaluated by their bosses: "This is how *I* (your boss) perceive *you* (my subordinate) to be doing." In a systems-conscious organization, the individualized hierarchical set of activities is replaced by systems- and process-based activities. This is described in the table presented in Figure 4-17.

	Systems focused organization	*Hierarchically focused organization*
1. Who gets the feedback?	One part of the system or process	An individual
2. Who gives the feedback?	Outside customers and/or inside customers, subsequent parts of the system or process	His or her boss
3. The form of the feedback?	Data on key indicators of quality as identified by the external/internal customers	Rating, rankings, and judgments regarding conformance of the individual to the manager's standards and objectives
4. The purpose of the feedback?	Improvement	Management control

Figure 4-17. Feedback: New and old.

In order to maintain a well-functioning system or process, managers need to encourage people to establish and maintain feedback loops: ongoing, routine processes by which customers (external and internal) share data with their important suppliers (internal or external). Feedback loops also need to be established between people and their own work processes. Workers in a given part of the system or process monitor data on those key indicators that keep them informed on how well the process is functioning. Figure 4-18 describes the typical feedback processes in which workers are routinely engaged.

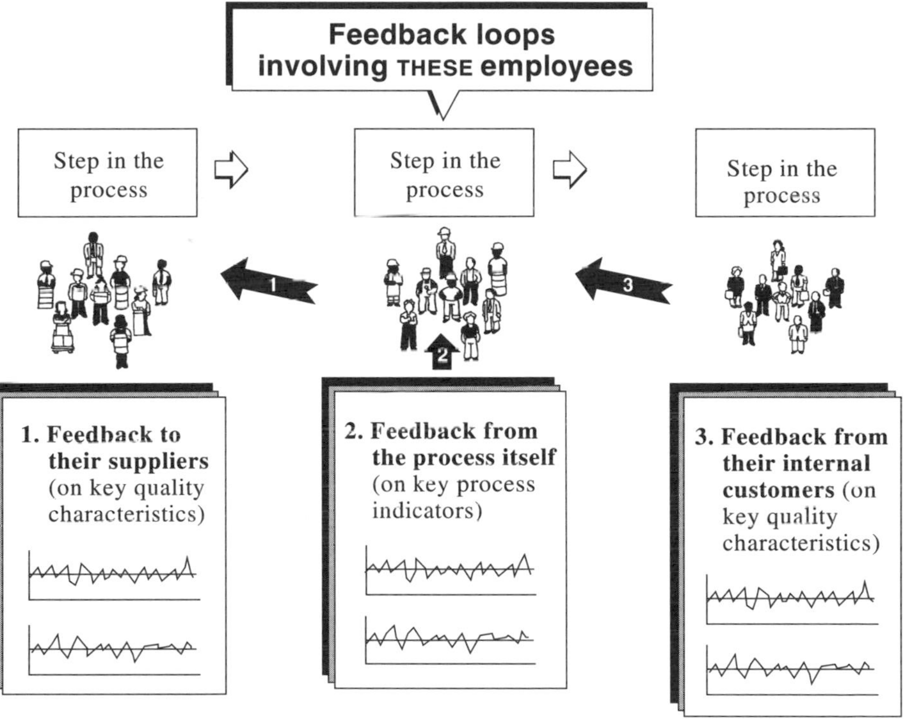

Figure 4-18. Feedback loops.

BREAKING DOWN BARRIERS

This final section of Getting the Daily Work Done explores the need to create relationships of interdependence between the functional units. Perhaps the biggest obstacle to the uncluttered flow of work and the creation of feedback loops is our traditional practice in Western organizations of allowing, even encouraging, our managers to function autonomously. Figure 4-19 illustrates this point, showing the functional ramparts.

Figure 4-19. The functional ramparts.

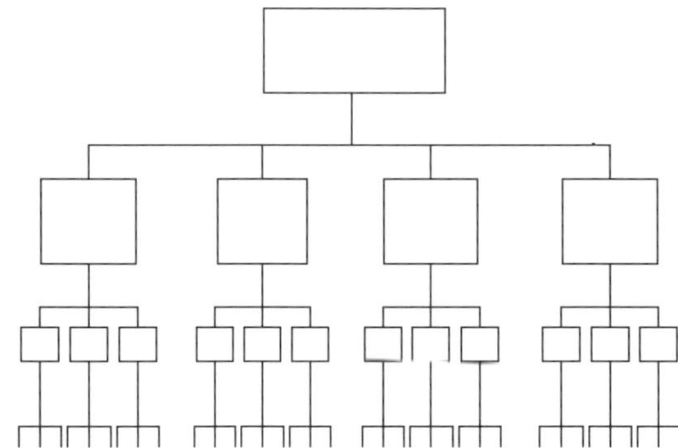

Figure 4-20. The mentality that fosters functional ramparts.

The characteristics of a rampart mentality are:

- Independent managers, functioning in isolation with relative autonomy: "I don't interfere with your domain. You don't interfere with mine."
- Each entity is run by a manager, doing the best he or she can, accountable for its successful operation.
- Internal competition is often encouraged.

- Interaction and interdependence are difficult:
  - — Rambo mentality: "I must be tough and independent." (See David Couper's quotation on page 220.)
  - — There are no precedents, models, or methods for interdependence.

If we exist within a hierarchical framework (and most Western managers and workers do), we are vulnerable to the mentality of functional ramparts.

And yet we seem to get work done. We have for well over a century and a half. The way we get work done is to coax, cajole, or coerce it through the rampart-separated hierarchy as shown in Figure 4-21.

This flow of work through the organization is at best needlessly complicated: too many steps, too much bureaucracy, too many opportunities to pass errors and defects on to another unit. When the hierarchical managers are people with inflated egos who have been set in competition against each other, the flow of work becomes even more impeded. Usually, the impediments are subtle but nonetheless real. ("If our unit added this step and its expense to *our* process, it would make things easier, faster, and cheaper for George's operation. But let's not volunteer to increase our costs!")

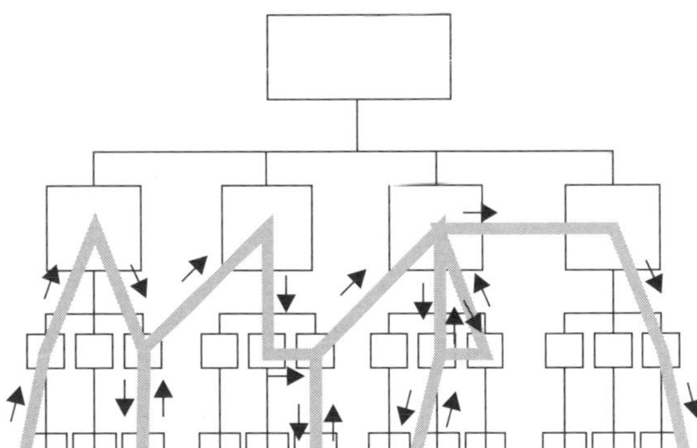

Figure 4-21. Work making its way through the rampart-separated hierarchical organization.

Figure 4-21 illustrates many typical organizational processes.

- New product (or new service) development
- The work flow from order to delivery
- The work flow from customer complaint to resolution and systems improvement to prevent future problems
- The making of a product from raw materials through manufacturing through subassemblies through final assembly

An Example of Breaking Down Barriers

A manufacturing company uses complex and very expensive machinery to make its product. This machinery requires a sophisticated knowledge of mechanical engineering, chemical engineering, electronics, and hydraulics. The machine was a continuous system with eight separate subsystems managed by eight different superintendents on each shift. Figure 4-22 is a picture of the system.

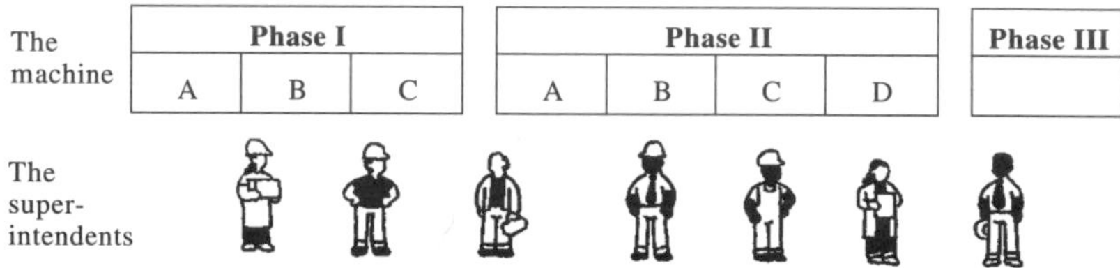

Figure 4-22. The old system.

Each superintendent was an experienced senior operations director and each was a proud and relatively autonomous manager. Each would say, "I own this part of the operation. I'm in charge of it!"

Then disaster struck. The superintendents had been exposed to such notions as continuous improvement. They had begun to learn some of the quality philosophy and improvement methodology. They each knew enough to be dangerous.

During a scheduled shutdown, different superintendents responsible for the separate operations made independent "improvements" that resulted in a system no longer capable of making a product.

- When they went to start the machine back up, it no longer worked.
- No single person knew all the complex interactions between the old system and the various innovations introduced to the system.
- No single individual even knew all of the changes introduced by the various superintendents.
- All they knew was the system no longer worked and no one knew why, and it was costing them millions of dollars each month in lost revenue.

It took about nine months to sort out all that had gone wrong and return the system to its pre-shutdown efficiency and production quality.

In response to this experience, the independent superintendents were formed into a *Priority Team* as illustrated in Figure 4-23.

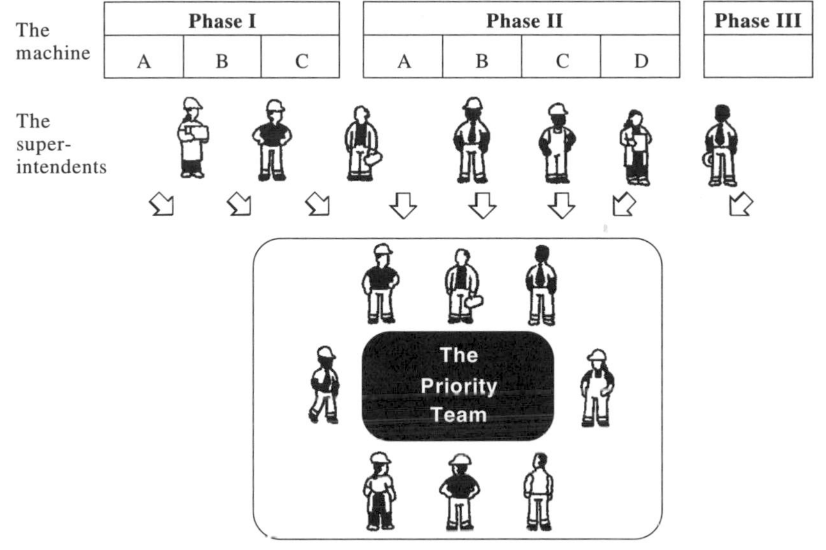

Figure 4-23. The priority team.

- The priority team collectively managed the process. No one superintendent "owned" any one part.
- Any proposed improvements had to be proposed to and approved by the entire priority team.
- Proposed improvements required a certain amount of homework before proposal. The review process followed an adaptation of the 7-Step Method. This is displayed in Figure 4-24 (see pages 142-143).

This was more than merely the forming of a team. This is what one superintendent described as a culture change. It required a major shift in the way the superintendents conceived of their work, did their jobs, and related to each other. They needed to shift:

- From functionally autonomous to interdependent
- From lone experts to a collaborative team
- From impulsive to disciplined
- From the use of experience and instinct to the use of data
- From separate functions to a systems mentality

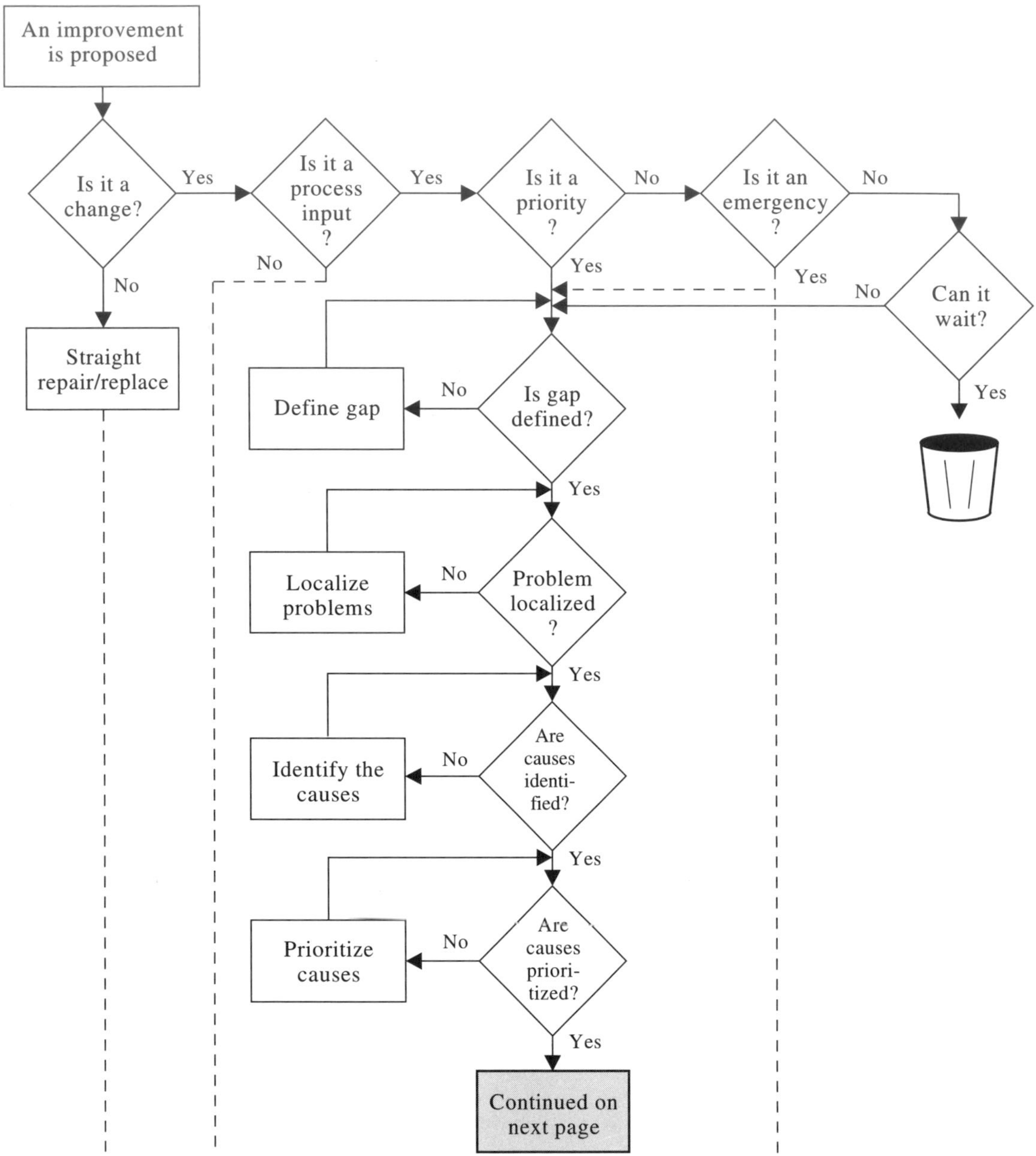

Figure 4-24. The proposed-improvement decision tree.

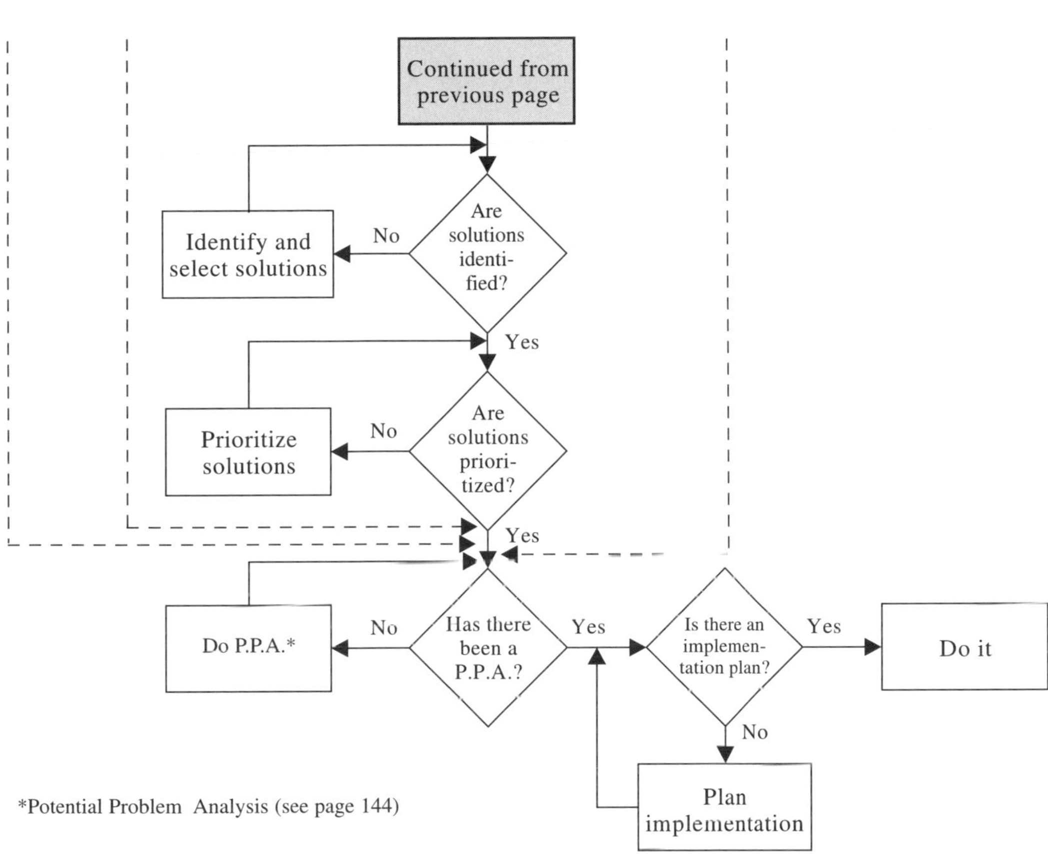

Figure 4-24. *(Continued)*

Indeed, many of these require complex systems for their successful accomplishment. But the addition of a rampart mentality and bureaucracy enormously increases the likelihood of errors, delays, breakdowns, defects, and out-and-out failure.

Thus we see the relevance of Deming's Point #9: *Break down barriers.* "Break down barriers between departments. People in research, design, sales, and production must work as a team to foresee problems of production and in use that may be encountered with the product or service" (Deming, 1982, pp. 62–67).

The Proposed-Improvement Decision Tree includes adaptations of the following:

- The 7-Step Method (see also Diagram 8-6):
  - — The original source for this is Kume (1985). Kume calls this method the QC Story.
  - — Brian Joiner and I developed an alternative version of Kume's QC story. It is called the Joiner 7-Step Method and is published by Joiner Associates.

- Kepner and Tregoe (1981). Potential Problem Analysis, Is/Is Not Analysis, and other methods are described in *The New Rational Manager.*
- Some expressions that may need explaining:
  - *Change* refers to something other than a replacement. Changing a burnt-out bulb with an identical new bulb is *replacement.*
  - *Process input* refers to a change that affects the process (a new type of heat regulator) rather than a change external to the process (a new ladder attached to the side of the machine).
  - *Priority* refers to already identified priorities, part of the annual planning process.
  - *Gap* refers to the disparity between what you need and what you have (almost synonymous with "problem").
  - *Localize:* Similar to Kepner-Tregoe's Is/Is Not Analysis, this is an analytical process by which you narrow the problem's possible causes by using data to look at patterns of occurrence: when does it happen versus when not, where versus where not, etc.
  - *PPA,* or Potential Problem Analysis (Kepner-Tregoe): Asking "What could go wrong?" and planning around it.

The Challenge of Interdependence

Most of us weren't raised to think in terms of interdependence, though its place in American culture goes back to barn raisings and quilting bees. But as work became more depersonalized and hierarchical, and as managers became more autonomous and internally competitive, we lost our sense of mutuality. Perhaps the greatest challenge facing today's leaders is to learn to help people understand and appreciate their interdependence. There are two generic categories of interdependence: social and systemic. We are *socially* interdependent because as humans we need each other: No man is an island. We are *systemically* interdependent because that is how good work gets done. In Chapter 2, we explored social interdependence, discussing the importance of relationships. In this chapter, and especially in this last section, we have discussed systemic relationships.

People in your organization need to ask each other—particularly at those points where their work intersects—"What do you need from me that you are not getting? What are you getting from me that you don't need?"

Look at the functional ramparts pictured in Figure 4-19. If we were to show them as interdependent functions, we might use a matrix like the one in Figure 4-25. There are 72 cells in the matrix shown in Figure 4-25.

Customers / Suppliers	1 Design	2 Marketing	3 Sales	4 Purchasing	5 Finance	6 Technical Service	7 Production	8 Human Resources	9 Engineering
A Design									
B Marketing									
C Sales									
D Purchasing									
E Finance									
F Technical Service									
G Production									
H Human Resources									
I Engineering									

Figure 4-25. The matrix of functional interdependence.

For each, ask:

- What is the nature of the interdependence?
- What does the customer (1 through 9) need from the supplier (A through I)?
- What systems, processes, and routines need to be put in place to routinely review interdependencies and provide what is needed to each other?
- What appropriate feedback loops need to be in place?

I first saw this approach presented by Ed Baker as a process he developed for managers at Ford Motor Company. I am grateful to Dr. Baker for this idea.

SUMMARY

Getting the daily work done requires setting priorities and establishing routines. We need a sense of Gemba, the flow of work that matters most to the customers. We need to keep the Gemba flowing without interruptions, clutter, or waste. In order to maintain reliability and consistency, we need to study our processes and establish uniform, standardized methods based on what we know to be the current best way to do the work. To maintain the integrity of our work and to continually improve our systems and processes we need to foster a spirit of collaboration and interdependence among our various, previously independent units. We must create an environment that makes it safe for one part of the system to give feedback to a preceding part of the system and we must establish processes—feedback loops—that make such feedback a routine occurrence.

This is all hard work. There is nothing glamorous or esoteric about it. However, there is nothing in leadership that compares with the joy of creating and sustaining a workplace that "hums," where a caring group of people delivers excellent goods and services to delighted customers. There is nothing like it!

CHAPTER FOUR ACTIVITIES

Enter the specific product or service: [ ]

1. The heart of the Gemba: The critical functions and key players.

Critical functions and key players are the indispensable human roles and capabilities that add value to work on its way to the customer. Some characteristics of the critical functions and key players are as follows.

- They are technically challenging roles and functions.
- People with these roles and functions are highly trained and skilled.
- They are difficult to replace.
- They are directly involved in work that serves the outside customer.

For example: Accounting and accountants are critical functions and key players in an accounting firm. But however useful and important, accounting and accountants are not critical functions or key players in a manufacturing organization.

As they apply to the product or service listed above, identify the critical functions and key players:

Designing the Product or Service	*Developing It, Assembling the Component Parts*	*Delivering the Product/Service to the Customer*	*Providing Follow-up or Support Services to the Customer*	*Getting Feedback from the Customers*

This alternative framework may be useful.

Early in the Flow of Work	*In the Middle Stages*	*In the Late Stages*	*At the Point of the Customer's Application or Use*

2. **The heart of the Gemba: The core resources.**

Core resources are the nonhuman, indispensable Gemba resources: facilities, equipment, machinery, workplaces, etc. Core resources are objects that contribute directly to work on its way to the customers. For example: A copy machine is a core resource in a copy shop (Kinko's). But however indispensable it may be, a copy machine is not a core resource in a restaurant.

Enter the specific product or service:

With regard to the product or service listed above, identify the core resources:

Designing the Product or Service	*Developing It, Assembling the Component Parts*	*Delivering the Product/Service to the Customer*	*Providing Follow-up or Support Services to the Customer*	*Getting Feedback from the Customers*

This alternative framework may be useful.

Early in the Flow of Work	*In the Middle Stages*	*In the Late Stages*	*At the Point of the Customer's Application or Use*

3. Supporting the Gemba.

Your organization has Gemba work—work on its way to the outside customer—and non-Gemba work. Here we explore how the non-Gemba functions support the Gemba.

Enter the specific product or service: ____________________

The Gemba

The beginnings → The flow of work that adds *direct* value on its way to the customer → The endings

↑ Not the Gemba, but supporting the Gemba

Identify the Key Functions, Services, and Resources in Your Organization That Are Not Gemba, but Support the Gemba	*For Each Key Non-Gemba Function, Service, or Resource, Describe How Each Contributes to the Success of the Gemba*

Some guidelines:

- Many of these will be managerial, administrative, financial, maintenance, and HR functions.
- These will tend to serve *all* Gembas, not just the one you have identified.
- There will be some non-Gemba functions that seem to support no Gemba. Consider this interesting and useful information.

4. **Identifying waste.**

Enter the specific product or service:

For each stage of the Gemba process, identify examples of waste.

Early Stages	*Middle Stages*	*Late Stages*	*At the Customer's Point of Application*

Types of waste:

1. Overproduction—more output, space, capacity, etc., than you need
2. Inventory—more supplies than are necessary
3. Transportation—more distance than necessary between the end of one step and the beginning of the next
4. Waiting—bottlenecks, things not ready
5. Unnecessary motion—long reaches, complicated movements, inefficient paths
6. Overprocessing—unnecessary steps, empty rituals
7. Correction—"scraping burnt toast," rework, remedial steps
8. Complexity—all the waste involved when something doesn't go right the first time (multiple forms of waste)
9. Bureaucracy—unuseful and unnecessary constraints imposed on the Gemba

5. **Creating standardized processes.**

Enter the specific product or service:

Step 1: Use a flowchart to create a map of the process.

Step 2: Have the people involved in each part of the process come to agreement on the best way to do that part.

A. Use data to determine which method is best.
B. Make each part as error-proof as possible.
C. Draw a new flowchart for each part.
D. Each part should work with people working on other parts to assure alignment and integration.
E. Prepare new manuals, checklists, and graphic instructions.
F. Plan and implement training in the new method.
G. Monitor the new method to see whether it does what you want to accomplish and avoids what you don't want.

6. **Document the standardized process.** Below is a standardized process chart format for documenting a standardized process.

1. Doing the Task	*2. Checking Key Process Indicators*	*3. Responding to Signals*
This section uses a flowchart to describe the sequence of activities and, if appropriate, the flow of work between interactive groups and individuals. More detailed information may be included here or, if necessary, referenced here.	Many processes have critical steps that need to be monitored by the operator. These steps have key process indicators (KPIs), vital signs that indicate whether or not the process is in control and on track. These should be used sparingly, only when you know of a point of vulnerability.	■ A KPI informs you that an adjustment is necessary. The instructions for response are placed in this part of the chart. ■ This describes immediate responses for the operator as well as whom to inform regarding the performance of the process, in case more than process adjustment and control are necessary to avoid problems.

Document the process with the following form:

1. Doing the Task	*2. Checking Key Process Indicators*	*3. Responding to Signals*

Some guidelines:

- The chart should ordinarily describe, on a single page, a specific task or operation. If your operation is too long to fit on one page, break it down into subtasks and put each on a separate page.
- Eventually people's jobs, at least the greater proportion of their jobs, can be described using a series of these charts.
- Avoid needless effort. Focus on what is important and useful. Add detail where and when it is needed.
- Start where you are feeling pain. Use this chart first on processes with which you are experiencing problems. Monitor only those indicators that you know from experience it is important to monitor. Columns 2 and 3 don't need to be filled out on every standardized process chart.
- Don't overdo it! If you initiate a standardized process chart blitzkrieg in your organization, you will drive people crazy. Do some pilot standardization activities. Gradually expand the effort, learning as you go. Let groups and individuals standardize processes one at a time at a workable pace, starting with those processes that need standardization most.

7. **Establishing internal feedback loops.**

Enter the specific product or service:

Below is an illustration of feedback loops:

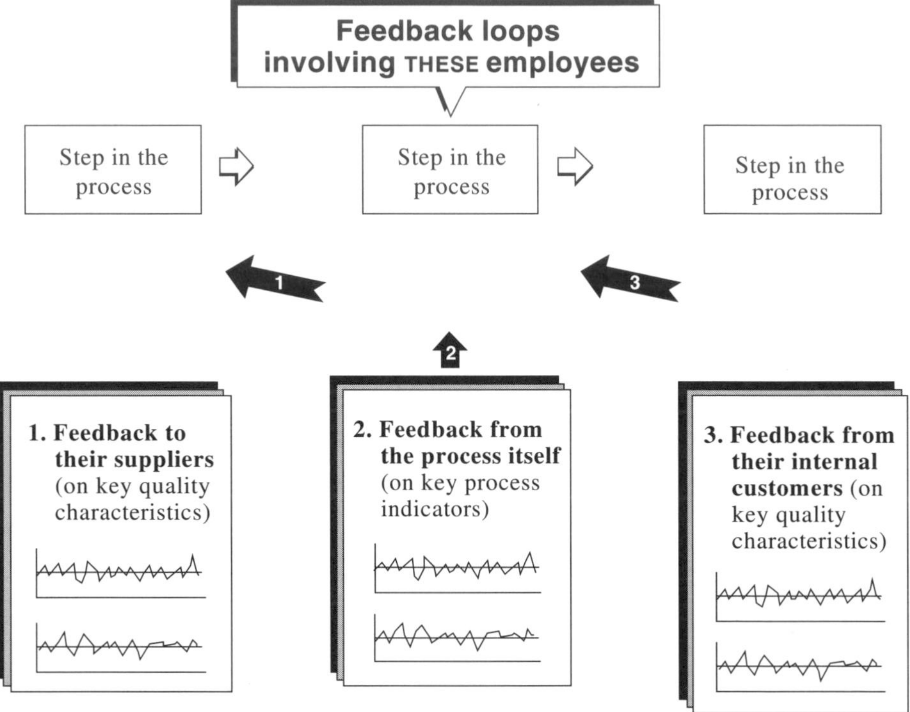

Helping your employees set up feedback loops

1. *Have employees redefine their jobs in terms of the processes in which each is involved.*
   - Sometimes the process or the step in the process involves a group or a team, sometimes an individual acting alone.
   - Have the group or individual explore information such as that described on page 155, *the job and its process.*

The Job and Its Process	
Use this form to organize information on the various tasks related to your job. While you may be tempted to speculate about the answers to #4 and #7, there is no substitute for finding out directly from internal and external customers.	
1. Name one task, operation, or function that is part of your job.	
2. Show what percentage of your time is taken up by this task.	
3. List those who share in this task.	
4. How does this task contribute to the satisfaction of the outside customer?	
5. Describe how often this process completes a full cycle (one cycle per hour, day, week, month).	
6. Who are the internal customers of this process?	
7. How do these internal customers define a good job by you? What are their important needs?	
8. Who are your suppliers (internal and external)?	
9. How do you define a good job? What are your important needs from them?	

Note: Start with the most important single task and carry this planning process through to completion. Then move on to the next most important. Don't overdo this. Move slowly, learning as you go. This may be done one process at a time.

2. *Planning with the customer: Part I*

Those involved in the process described above in "The Job and Its Process" meet with their internal customers. The following is a format that may prove useful for this discussion.

Planning for Feedback from the Internal Customer: Part I	
Describe or name your internal customer: ______	
What process will you be describing? ______	
1. List the basic expectations of your internal customer. (The absence of these characteristics provokes anger.)	
2. List those characteristics that result in greater internal customer satisfaction the more those characteristics are present.	
3. Describe how these characteristics relate to the needs of the outside customer.	
4. What data will indicate the presence of this characteristic? What signal will be a measure of successful fulfillment of this characteristic?	
5. How will this data be gathered, recorded, and analyzed? Who will record what data, how, and when?	

Some notes:

- "Basic" in #1 refers to the basic characteristics as defined by Dr. Kano (see Chapter 3).
- Answering #4 and #5 will require some knowledge of statistics and the application of statistical methods. Chapter 5 will touch upon this, but your organization should make use of knowledgeable experts to help you design such measurement systems.
- Chapter 5 will also provide some sample indicators that may be the basis for feedback loops. Ultimately, however, you will need to join with your customers to identify and design your own.

3. *Planning with the customer: Part II*
   - How often will we meet to review the data on the indicators?
   - Who will set up these meetings and prepare the agenda?
   - When we continually improve the characteristics of our interaction:

A. *How Might We Inadvertently Create Problems for the Outside Customer?*	*How Can We Avoid This? Detect This? Respond to This?*
B. *How Might We Inadvertently Create Problems Elsewhere in the System?*	*How Can We Avoid This? Detect This? Respond to This?*

Suggested agenda:

A. Review the agenda.
B. Review data on the chosen characteristics.
C. What does the customer get that he or she doesn't need?
D. What does customer need that she or he doesn't get?
E. Additions and revisions to indicators.
F. Meeting evaluation.
G. Schedule the next meeting.

Some notes:

- Parts I and II provide some direction and guidance for an initial discussion between an internal supplier and his, her, or their customer.
- Try this out, and revise it as you see fit. The important part of this effort is the communication about what is important and agreement on how to create a workable feedback process between you.

REFERENCES

Ackoff, R. 1991. *Ackoff's fables.* New York: John Wiley & Sons.

Bohman, J. 1992. Power-tool maker borrows from Japan. *Wisconsin State Journal,* March 8 (Cox News Service story).

Brassard, M. 1989. *Memory jogger plus.* Metheun, MA: GOAL/QPC.

Deming, W.E. 1994. *The new economics for industry/government/education.* Cambridge, MA: MIT-CAES, Chapter 9.

Deming, W.E. 1982. *Out of the crisis.* Cambridge, MA: MIT-CAES.

Fuller, T. 1995. Why many improvement projects fail. *The Chicago Quarterly Review,* 1, 4, Winter. This article, with some adaptations, was also published in *The Public Sector Network News,* 2, 1, Summer 1995, under the title "Focus on the work: Pick improvement projects that really help your agency's operations."

Fuller, T. 1985. Eliminating complexity from work. *National Productivity Review.* Autumn.

Gass, K.C. 1995. *The procedural system.* LaCrosse, WI: Specialized Quality Publications.

Gitlow, H., Shelly, A., and Oppenheim, R. 1989. *Tools and methods for the improvement of quality.* Homewood, IL: Irwin.

Goldratt, E. 1990. *Theory of constraints.* Great Barrington, MA: North River Press.

Goldratt, E. 1984. *The goal.* Croton-on-Hudson, NY: North River Press.

Imai, M. 1997. *Gemba Kaizen.* New York: McGraw-Hill.

Imai, M. 1986. *Kaizen.* New York: McGraw-Hill.

Ishikawa, K. 1988. *Introduction to quality control.* Tokyo: 3A Corporation.

Ishikawa, K. 1985. *What is total quality control?* Englewood Cliffs, NJ: Prentice Hall.

Ishikawa, K. 1982. *Guide to quality control.* Tokyo: Asian Productivity Organization.

Joiner Associates. 1990. *The Joiner 7-Step Method.* Madison, WI: Joiner Associates.

Juran, J. 1988. *The quality control handbook,* 4th ed. New York: McGraw-Hill.

Kepner, C.H., and Tregoe, B.B. 1981. *The new rational manager.* Princeton, NJ: Princeton Research Press.

Kerridge, D., and Kerridge, S. 1996. Dr. Deming's cure for a sick system. *Journal for Quality and Participation,* 19, 7:24–27. (Original title: Diseases of the system. Old Aberdeen Scotland. E-mail: dfk@rsc.co.uk)

King, B. 1988. *Better designs in half the time.* Methuen, MA: GOAL/QPC.

Kume, H. 1985. *Statistical methods for quality control.* Tokyo: AOTS.

Mizuno, S. 1988. *Management for quality improvement: The 7 new QC tools.* Cambridge, MA: Productivity Press.

Nakajo, T., and Kume, H. 1996. Studies on the foolproofing of operation systems: The principles of foolproofing. In *The Best of Quality,* vol. 7, ch. 11, pp. 185ff. Milwaukee: ASQC Quality Press.

QIP Inc. and PQ Systems. 1993. *Total quality transformation improvement tools.* Dayton, OH: PQ Systems.

Scholtes, P. 1994. *The methodology of improvement.* Madison, WI: Scholtes Seminars and Consulting.

Scholtes, P. 1988. *The team handbook.* Madison, WI: Joiner Associates.

Scholtes, P. 1986. My first trip to Japan. *Center for Quality and Productivity,* Report 5. Madison, WI: University of Wisconsin.

Snee, R.D. 1993. Creating robust work processes. *Quality Progress,* February.

Swanson, R.C. 1995. *The quality improvement handbook.* Delray Beach, FL: St. Lucie Press.

Tribus, M. 1990. *Deployment flow charting.* Los Angeles: Quality and Productivity Inc.

Weisbord, M. 1991. *Productive workplaces.* San Francisco: Jossey-Bass Publishers.

Wellington. The letter from the Duke of Wellington was written in the August of 1812 somewhere near Salamanca, Spain. This and other dispatches from Wellington were published by Clowes of London in 1837. Currently this letter is in *The War Times Journal: Archives: Wellington,* 1997, London.

Wilson, R., and Harson, P. *Process mastery.* (This book is not yet available from a publisher. Contact: Ray Wilson, 6448 Blossom Lane, Indianapolis, IN 46278.)

Ordering Information

Introduction to Quality Control by Kaoru Ishikawa. JUSE Press, Ltd., 3-A Corporation, Shoei Building, G-3, Sarugaku-Cho 2 Chome, Chiyoda-ku, Tokyo 101, Japan.

Memory Jogger by Michael Brassard and Diane Ritter. GOAL/QPC, 13 Branch Street, Methuen, MA 01844, (508) 685-3900.

The New Rational Manager by Charles H. Kepner and Benjamin B. Tregoe. Princeton Research Press, P.O. Box 704, Research Road, Princeton, NJ 08540.

PQ Systems, Inc., P.O. Box 750010, Dayton, OH 45475-0010, (800) 777-3020 or (513) 885-2255.

Statistical Methods for Quality Improvement by Hitoshi Kume (ISBN #4-906224-34-2 C0034). The Association for Overseas Technical Scholarship (AOTS), 30-1 Senju-azuma 1 Chome, Adachiku, Tokyo 120, Japan.

Theory of Constraints by Eliyahn M. Goldratt. North River Press Inc., Box 309, Croton-on-Hudson, NY 10520, (914) 941-7175.

5 GIVING MEANING, PURPOSE, DIRECTION, AND FOCUS TO WORK

INTRODUCTION

True North! We hear a lot about true North. We must, without doubt, have a sense of direction, a steady and reliable indicator that tells us where we are and which direction to go in order to get to our destination. The captain of the ship must know which way is true North, and must also know about the prevailing currents, winds, and tides, the presence of reefs and other barriers, the patterns of weather—what storms to avoid and how to ride through the ones that can't be avoided. The captain must understand the characteristics and capabilities of the ship and its crew, and must know how to lead. *True North is good, but it is not enough.*

The workplace is filled with ambiguity and uncertainty. People have always had to deal with the inconstancy of their leaders, migrating from one fad to another. Workers learned to hang on because "This, too, shall pass." I've heard this described as the BOHICA syndrome. "*B*end *O*ver *H*ere *I*t *C*omes *A*gain!"

But now the uncertainty is dramatically different. People's employment is at stake in the current management fad. Downsizing has always been with us and each instance has its own set of causes. While I tend to agree with Russell Ackoff (1996), who says that downsizing is immoral, I recognize that sometimes downsizing is a tragic inevitability. Perhaps what is immoral is not the downsizing itself but the lack of leadership that brought the organization to this inevitable choice.

Between 1990 and 1995 nearly 30 percent of United States workers who lost their jobs lost them because of downsizing or shutdowns (Cognetics Research Group, 1996). Why this sudden rush of downsizing? Why are so many corporations downsizing now? In this decade? Much of the epidemic of corporate restructuring and massive layoffs seems to be the result of a virus-like fad spreading through the country. CEOs and boards of directors want to appear to be proactive, in control, and accountable, taking decisive action, biting the bullet, and making the tough choices. As a result, they end up putting a whole lot of people out of work. They think they are leading the organization into being lean and mean. Instead, it becomes emaciated and vicious. Even more worrisome is the apparent indication that downsizing improves nothing, either in the short term or the long term (Ackoff and Pourdehnad, 1997).

Purpose and Direction

What is missing too often in our corporations is a sense of purpose and direction, a definition of who we are and a description of where

Questions for Downsizers

1. How do you know you must downsize?
2. How do you know how much downsizing to do?
3. How do you know it must be permanent?
4. To what other remedies have you resorted before downsizing? For example:
   - Reduced shareholder gain?
   - Reduced executive-level salaries and bonuses?
   - Reduced workweek?
5. What data do you have to show that downsizing will be an effective remedy?
6. What savings have you realized through applying the methodologies of systems and process improvement?
7. What are you doing to provide those who lose their jobs with a dignified and humane transition process?
8. What are you doing to console and support those who survived the downsizing?
9. What are you planning to do in order to:
   - Maintain continuous, clear, honest communications with your workforce on the ongoing status of the company?
   - Restore trust?
   - Restore a sense of mutual loyalty?
   - Assure this will not happen again?
10. Have you apologized to your people for this?

we are heading. We need values, principles, and priorities that guide us when we run into obstacles and setbacks. We need systems providing continuity of effort and other systems providing nimble responsiveness to change. In other words, corporate America needs leadership.

In Chapter 2 we offered the following list of questions the members of an organization need to have answered:

1. Who are we?
2. What business are we in?
3. What businesses are we not in?

4. Where are we headed in the long term?
5. What are the priorities for the short term?
6. What values and principles should be characteristics of all our relationships and all of what we do?
7. What is my own personal job and how do my functions and operations fit into the larger purposes and systems of the organization?
8. What is the best way to do my job and what is expected of me? By whom? What is a "good job" and who defines it?
9. How will improvements to my job be accomplished? Who will do the improvements and by what methods? Will I be involved in these improvements? How?
10. What sources and forms of feedback are available to help me know how I'm doing?

Chapter 4 addressed the last four questions. In this chapter and in Chapter 6, we will deal with the first six questions.

Goals, Forecasts, Facts of Life, and Process Capability

Suppose that your organization is faced with a problem, let us say an excessive cycle time from order to delivery.

Let's examine the difference between goals, forecasts, facts of life, and process capability as they relate to cycle time. Presume your largest customer has said to you, "If you don't reduce the cycle time between our order and your delivery to no more than four days, we will take our business elsewhere. You have six months to do this and keep our business!"

This Is a Fact of Life

If something doesn't change there will be an inevitable consequence, something over which you have no control ... a fact of life.

Goal

A goal reflects how you would like things to be. You might arbitrarily decide that the order to delivery cycle should be reduced to no more than three days. That would be nice!

The goal, however, does not necessarily reflect reality and usually accomplishes nothing. In fact, a goal may do harm. If the goal is unrealistic but people are held accountable for achieving it, some stress and distortions may affect the work and the reporting methods.

Process Capability

By using data, particularly control charts, you can see the current performance of the system and whether the variation is common cause or special cause. You can discover some of the patterns that affect cycle time. From this you can devise strategies to deal with the problems at their source and look forward to reducing the cycle time.

The process capability may look like the chart in Figure 5-1.

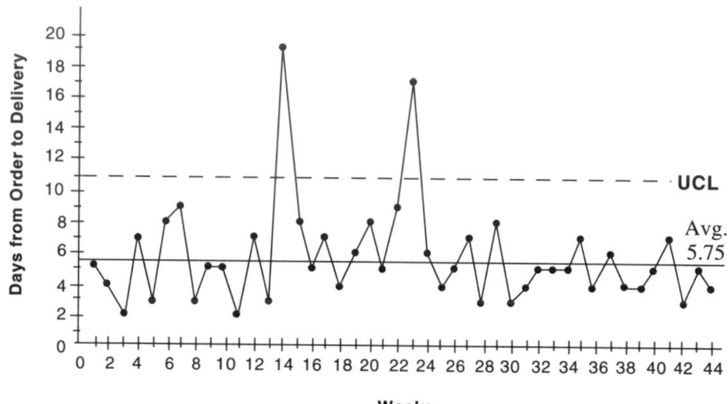

Figure 5-1. The current capability of the order-to-delivery system.

The data tell us that the current process ranges from 2 to 19 days, averages 5.75 days, and is unstable (two special causes). The difference between the fact of life (customer's need) and our capability is considerable. The customer wants a four-day upper limit. Our process capability is an average of 5.75 days. Of 44 deliveries, 28 of them exceeded four days.

Forecasts

A forecast is a prediction based on an understanding of two factors:

- *Theory.* The data on cycle time can help lead to theories on why the cycle takes as long as it does. This will lead to theories on how to improve it.
- *Data.* In this case the data can prove or disprove your theories.

The combination of legitimate data and confirmed theories may allow you to make realistic forecasts—not guesses, not hunches, but data-based and theory-based projections of future performance.

In the case of our cycle time project, we may be able to forecast that by getting rid of the special causes, we can bring our average down to 4.94 days. To make a more optimistic forecast would require a knowledge of specific methods of improvement that would allow us to realistically calculate a better turnaround time.

Management is prediction. Prediction requires, among other things, an understanding of your current capabilities and a theory on how to improve.

Daily Work versus Breakthrough Improvement

The difference between daily work and breakthrough improvement can be seen in Figures 5-2 and 5-3. In Figure 5-2 we see the 12-month history of output for an organization. This is described here in terms of only one indicator, customer service visits, shown in their cumulative amount. This same kind of graph could be used to picture products manufactured, sales, caseloads, or any other key indicator of an organization's work.

Figure 5-2 describes the current capability of the system regarding this particular indicator. If various factors inside and outside the organization remain stable—an unlikely occurrence—then the capability of the system will stay the same. Figure 5-3 takes that data and adds to it.

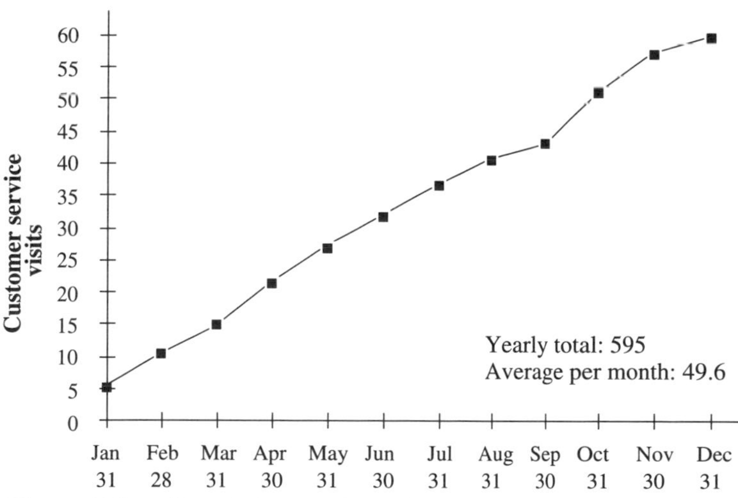

Figure 5-2. Cumulative number of customer service visits.

Depicted in Figure 5-3 is a projected improvement, a level of output beyond the capability of the current system. Figure 5-3 highlights the need for two distinct management systems, not nec-

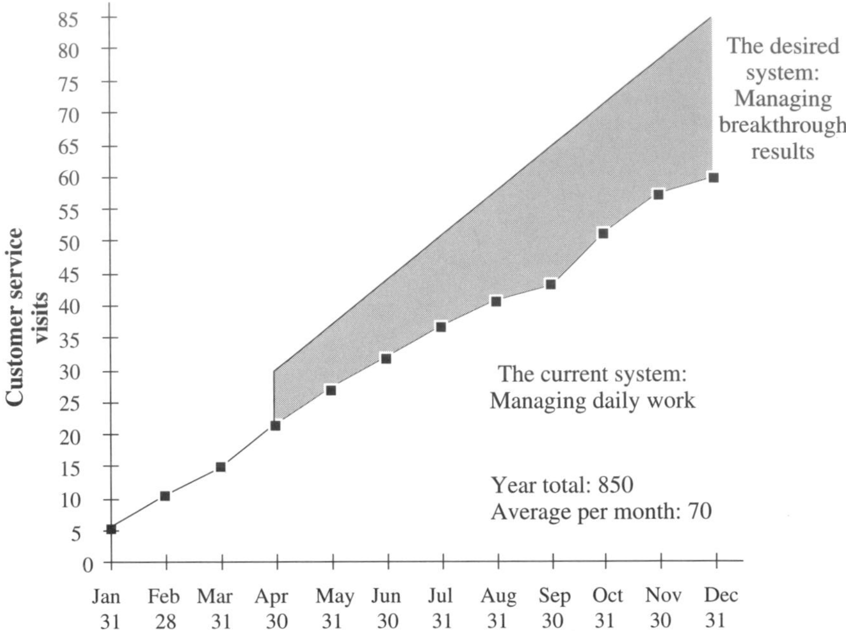

Figure 5-3. The desired capacity of our system of customer service visits.

essarily different management personnel but two different sets of functions, roles, processes, and methods needed by the managers. One is *managing daily work*. This was addressed in Chapter 4. The second management system is *managing breakthrough improvement,* the focus of this chapter and Chapter 6.

Breakthrough improvement involves a *system* of interventions. Earlier we stated that without a system, it is impossible to change. This chapter and the following chapter focus on the systems needed for breakthrough improvement.

DIRECTIONLESSNESS AND PURPOSELESSNESS

Directionlessness and purposelessness start at the top. If your people have no sense of mission, purpose, values, or focus it is because the leaders either lack these or inadequately communicate them. Another reason that the workforce has no sense of direction and purpose is the inconstancy of management: too many directions, the program du jour, the latest BOHICA.

I know a company that one year focused on high-performance management. The results were disappointing, so two years later the push was high-performance organization. In neither case was the *purpose* clear. It was a buzzword, fluff on the outside with no content on the inside. This is what happens when marketing infiltrates management.

Why Aren't Our Middle Managers Leading?

I was part of a team of consultants working with a Fortune 500 company. We had worked with them for over a year: lots of training, lots of planning sessions. The managers seemed to know and understand everything they needed to know and understand. But not much change was occurring. Why? While we were discussing this, I was doodling. The doodle almost began to draw itself. This is what I ended up with:

We were working with division vice presidents, mostly one or two levels down from the CEO, COO, and the Chairman of the Board. The ambivalence was in this top group. Until they made up their minds and chose which path to take, the rest of the organization would wait.

Change versus Improvement

Leaders are faced with complex challenges when they look at change. Some of the issues related to change are:

1. Is this change a *fact of life*?

   Is this change part of the inexorable sweep of nature, economics, science, technology, or political forces over which no one has control? Is this a change that, for better or worse, will happen with us or without us? Some examples:

   - Trying to keep up with the changes in communications and computer technology.
   - Adjusting to the demographic impact of the baby boomer bulge that works through the population.
   - The challenge of dealing with a deteriorating environment and diminishing natural resources.

Rapid Technology

Figure 5-4 pictures an example of technological change shaping the lives of people and businesses. For most of human history, from the time when humans learned to tame animals until about 1830, the speed of human transportation was limited by the speed of a horse, a little over 40 mph. Then, beginning in the mid-1980s, technological advances allowed us to travel at ever-increasing speeds.

Figure 5-4 shows not only the rate of travel but also the rate of change. The implications that this explosion of rapid change has for learning have been discussed in Chapter 2. The speed of change is given an insightful review by Stafford Beer in *Brain of the Firm.* I have adapted some of his ideas here.

The exponential curve of the speed of human transportation

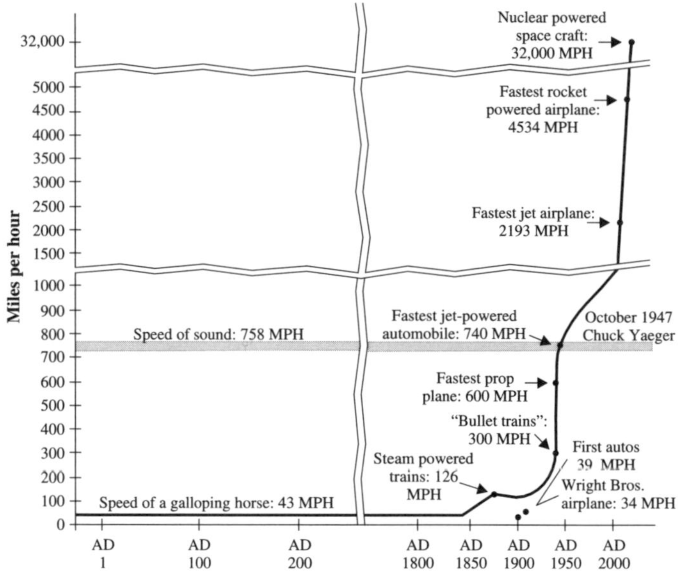

Figure 5-4. The speed of human transportation.

This graphic describes only what has happened to the speed of transportation. Add to that all the other rapid transformation—in communications technology, medical practice, etc.—and we can quickly see why the scope, scale, and speed of change are beyond the current capabilities of our contemporary organizations and conventional approaches to leadership.

2. Is this a change over which we have any control?
   - Are there optional responses?
   - Is one alternative to simply opt out?
3. Is this a mere change or is it an improvement?
   - My observation is that 95 percent of most organizational changes initiated by managers have nothing to do with improvement!
   - How do we know the difference between a mere change and an improvement?
   - Who is better off because of this change? Why? How will we measure "better off"?
4. What is the purpose of the change?
   - If the change is a solution, what is the problem? What are the causes of the problem? Is there a connection between our proposed change (solution) and the discernible causes of the problem?
5. What scale and scope of change are necessary, sufficient, desirable, or inevitable?
   - Changing the entire organization: its purpose, outputs, systems, processes, functions, roles, and structure?
   - What parts of the organization will be directly affected, and how will this have indirect impact on the rest of the system?

From Purpose to Structure: What Gets Changed and Why?

Let's look more closely at the scale and scope of an organization and, therefore, the possible changes that might take place in an organization. Figure 5-5 displays a sequence of organizational concepts and dynamics that shape and are shaped by each other. It is a blank-slate organizational model, indicating the likely sequence in which one might design an organization from scratch.

Some comments on this model:

1. *Purpose:* Without a clear and constant purpose, nothing else will fall into place. (See Chapter 3.)
2. *Systems:* The notion of *systems* includes all the elements of the SIPOC model: supplier, input, process, output, and customer. (See Chapter 3.)

3. *Functions: Functions* is not synonymous with *jobs*. Some jobs consist of several functions and some functions require several jobs. Function is a discrete category of tasks: invoicing, order entry, assembly, quality control, etc. Here we try to describe the system by identifying the sequences of interdependent functions.
4. *Capabilities:* In order to perform the functions, you need certain capabilities, some of which are equipment driven (e.g., a computer or construction equipment), others that are personnel driven (e.g., cooking, programming, sales, etc.), and some that may be either one or both (e.g., welding, mailing, etc.). These are still not yet jobs, but the capabilities around which jobs must be formed.
5. *Roles/jobs:* Here we describe the positions, roles, or jobs we create in order to distribute the needed capabilities in a way suitable for performing the functions. Some jobs require several capabilities and some require only one. Some roles are involved in many functions, some in only one.
6. *Structure:* The purpose, systems, functions, capabilities, and jobs must now be integrated and supported. The structure does not precede these but rather is designed specifically to make them work: Form follows function. Structure involves:
   - Reporting relationships
   - Pathways for formal communication
   - Divisions, departments, groups
   - Policies
   - Ongoing teams
   - Modes of management and leadership
7. *Personnel:* Whom will you select to work with you?
   - Whom will you recruit?
   - Whom will you hire?
   - Whom will you promote?
   - Whom will you fire?

What Gets Changed and Why

When someone proposes a change in the organization, use Figure 5-5 to locate where in this scheme the proposed change will take place and ask, "Why?" and "Why there?"

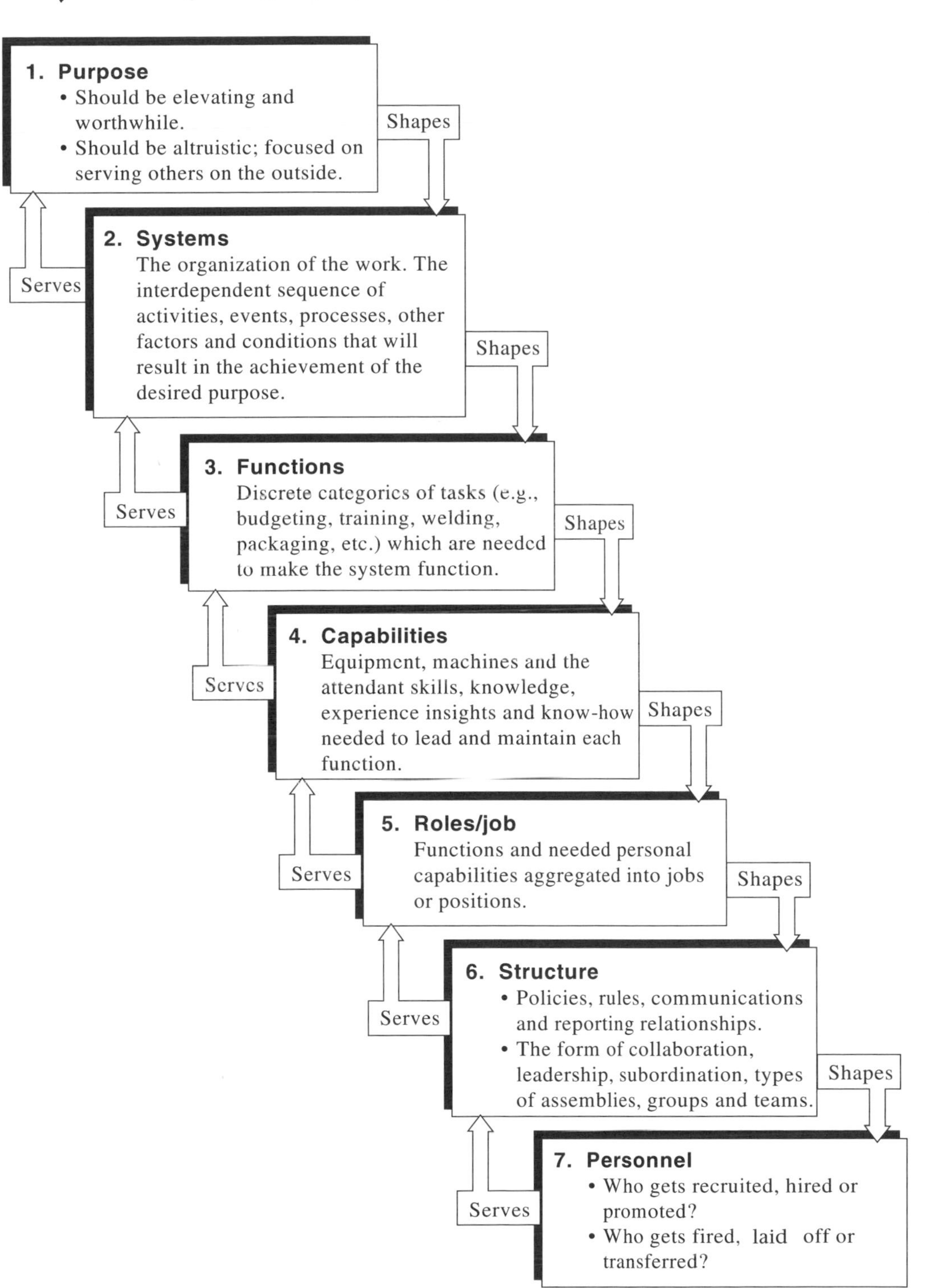

Figure 5-5. From purpose to personnel: A model for organizational development.

- If the purpose changes, then everything else must necessarily change.
- Nothing will improve by changing the structure or the personnel (for instance, setting up new teams, firing a manager, or altering who reports to whom) if the problem lies elsewhere. A new organizational structure will not ordinarily improve a dysfunctional system or an ineffective purpose.
- America's knee-jerk reaction to organizational problems is to change the personnel or change the structure. George Steinbrenner fired Billy Martin as manager of the Yankees. Then he fired Billy's replacement and rehired Billy. Then fired Billy. Then rehired Billy. Were these changes or improvements? And why did Mr. Steinbrenner believe that working at the level of personnel was what was needed to improve the team?
- Sometimes bringing in a new manager does bring in new capabilities and provides an occasion for the reexamination of purpose, systems, functions, capabilities, roles, and structures—a more *systemic* view of the organization. If those who fired and hired managers themselves had a more systemic view of the organization, they could better decide when and why to replace management personnel and what to look for in new leadership. Unfortunately, all too often there is no systems view. A changeover in management occurs, but the same old problems continue under the new regime.

PURPOSE: CREATING A SHARED VISION

A shared vision is the glue that holds people together and keeps them moving forward despite adversities. An elevating purpose gives a greater meaning to work and turns menial tasks into a tedious but necessary part of important work. "The assembly worker on the line in this plant is not just finessing a door, he's building a car," one plant manager said to me. "And we make sure our people know and see and meet and talk to our customers, the people out there who will own this car, use it, and depend on it. So he's not just finessing a door, not even just building a car. He's serving the transportation needs of people." This plant had routine programs whereby the plant personnel went out to dealers and met customers on the showroom floor and back in the service area, learning to look at their products through the customers' eyes. This plant also had customers receive delivery of their cars there in the plant at a ceremony attended by the plant personnel.

Peter Senge said (1990, p. 206), "A shared vision is not an idea.... It is rather a force in people's hearts, a force of impressive power." It fills, in Senge's words, "... their desire to be connected in an important undertaking."

Purpose, Vision, Mission

I know of people who vigorously insist on the differences between purpose, vision, and mission, and how statements presenting each must be approached in distinctly different ways. Maybe so. However, in my experience, organizations have used these interchangeably with no harmful effects.

What is important, I think, is that companies find ways to say to themselves and to the world around them, "This is who we are, this is what we do, and this is where we are headed." The short statements are easier to remember. The longer statements can elaborate on the slogan. What is important is the impact on those who hear it; it should ideally create excitement, learning, focus, boundaries, challenge, and commitment.

Rallying Cries

Many companies have short phrases that serve to tell the employees about themselves and their work:

- "Komatsu of the world" expands the workers' vision of the company and their work.
- Toyota: "Cars for the world to love."
- Marshall Fields, the retailer: "Give the lady what she wants."
- Ford: "Quality is job one."
- Herman Miller does not just make fine furniture; it seeks "to be a gift to the human spirit."
- My own small company, Scholtes Seminars and Consulting, has as its elevating purpose, "creating pride and joy at work."

Of course, slogans such as these become hollow if you are not good at what you do. Sears Roebuck boasted, "Satisfaction guaranteed or your money cheerfully refunded," even when customers in its auto service centers were getting ripped off.

Visions without a method aren't visions; they are hallucinations.

For some useful insights on this topic, see Collins and Porras (1996).

Unfortunately, most direction-setting statements stir up little excitement. They are exercises in wordsmithing the obvious: "We will provide maximum value to our customers!" This is the mission statement of a major high-tech manufacturer; not exactly a bold, defining statement.

A Process for Developing Purpose/Mission/Vision/Values

For the developing of a shared vision, there must be a shared process. But I believe that the initial draft must start at the top of the organization and then be circulated throughout.

The organization leaders prepare to develop the first draft. In a retreat setting with a facilitator on hand, the leaders share with each other their thoughts on the following:

1. What do you like about what you do here?
2. What do you like about our industry or profession?
3. What do like about our company when it's at its best?
4. What legacy do you want to leave behind—your personal contribution to this organization?
5. What legacy do you think we, collectively, should leave behind?

Some guidelines for discussing these questions are:

- Each leader should speak from the heart.
- Take one question at a time, each individual speaking to that question in round robin fashion.

What Makes a Good Purpose, Mission, Vision, Values Statement?

- It is from the heart.
- It is ennobling, appealing to our best instincts.
- It says something that applies uniquely to you and is not a generic, usable-by-anyone statement.
- It gives sufficiently clear direction that a year from now you can discuss, in specific terms, what progress you have made.
- It has staying power. It will be an appropriate statement for years to come.

- No disagreement is allowed, just words of support and understanding and questions for clarification.
- When you have completed going around the group addressing one question, look for common themes and record them. Then move on to the next question.

When you have completed the discussion on all the questions, review what you have said, especially on the common themes. Formulate a series of statements describing "things that are important to us." Circulate this list among your people with a description of where the list comes from and what you intend to do with it. Ask people in their work groups to read it, discuss it, ask for clarification, and add anything that they agree, by consensus, is important to say.

When the group of leaders receives these responses, they use them to refine their original list of statements. The leaders then discuss the content of statements of purpose, mission, vision, and values. The leaders should probably not compose the statements. The writing would be better off done by one individual given the task of expressing the thoughts of the leaders. The leaders should then approve the draft of their direction-setting statements. The draft is then circulated throughout the organization for feedback and input.

The leaders review the responses from the organization and create the final version, again through a group process.

TEAMS, PURPOSE, AND SYSTEMS

There is a difference between teams and teamwork. *Teams* refers to small groups of people working together toward some common purpose. *Teamwork* refers to an environment in the larger organization that creates and sustains relationships of trust, support, respect, interdependence, and collaboration. It is a mistake to confuse the two. It is relatively easy for a leader to set up teams. But creating and sustaining an environment of teamwork is vastly more important and enormously more difficult. A contrary environment will ruin teams (see the quotation from Petronius Arbiter, p. 79).

Teams aren't new. Some managers may see the forming of teams as a major step forward in their organization, but they probably feel the same way about indoor plumbing. What is new about teams is this: *Teams are systems and are part of a system.* Without an understanding of the systemic contexts within teams and surrounding teams, the potential of teams will never be realized and they will probably fail.

In Chapter 3 we discussed the interdependence of purpose and systems. Without a purpose there is no system. There is a similar interdependence between purpose and teamwork. Without purpose there is no team, only an aggregate of individuals with no reason to be together. There is another interdependency between teamwork and systems. A team with a purpose but no method will end up well-intentioned but unsuccessful, an effective way to undermine teamwork. This three-way interdependence can be pictured as in Figure 5-6.

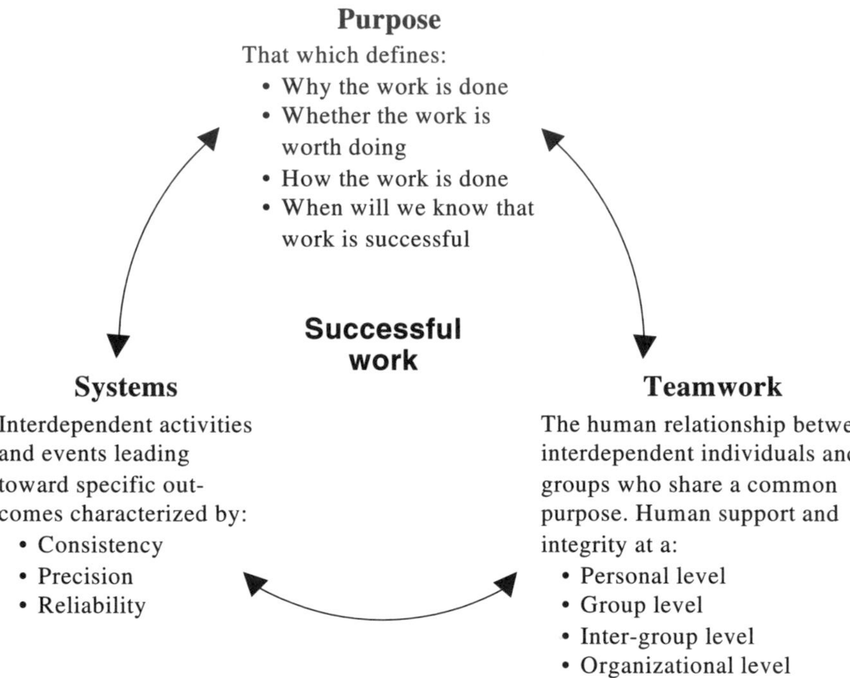
Purpose
That which defines:
• Why the work is done
• Whether the work is worth doing
• How the work is done
• When will we know that work is successful
Successful work
Systems
Interdependent activities and events leading toward specific outcomes characterized by:
• Consistency
• Precision
• Reliability
Teamwork
The human relationship between interdependent individuals and groups who share a common purpose. Human support and integrity at a:
• Personal level
• Group level
• Inter-group level
• Organizational level

Figure 5-6. The interdependence between purpose, systems, and teamwork.

We depicted in Figure 2-3 how each group is but one system within larger systems. In Figure 5-7, a different diagram makes a similar point. The team pictured in Figure 5-7 is probably just one of several teams in the organization. Each team may have its own purpose and each purpose may be worthwhile. A common problem I observe in organizations, however, is a multitude of teams or groups, each serving its own, presumably worthwhile, purpose, but with nothing to align them. They may be okay individually but collectively they go nowhere. (See Figure 5-8.)

Purpose and vision can help align teams, giving a common set of guiding points of focus. This is pictured in Figure 5-9.

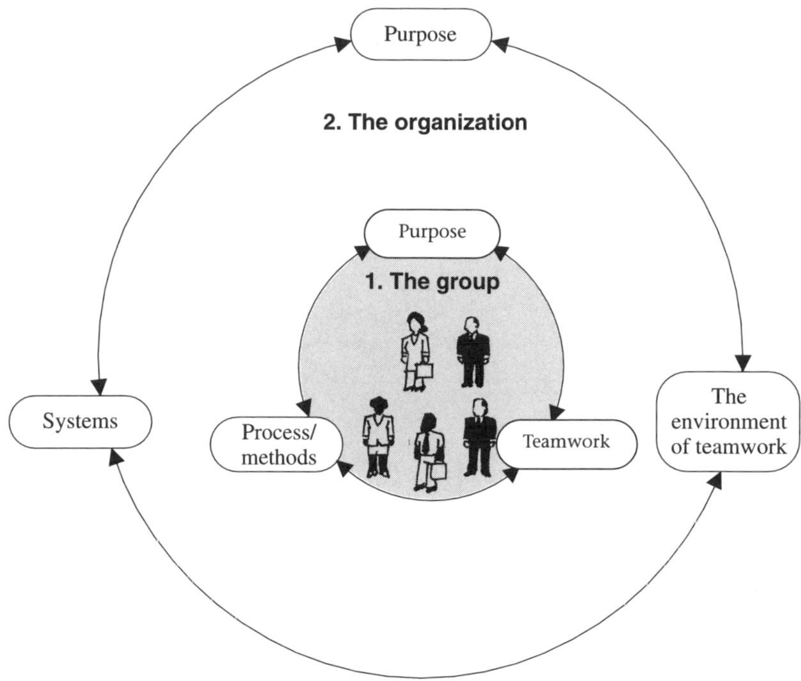

Figure 5-7. Teams and systems.

Figure 5-8. Groups or teams going their separate ways within the organization.

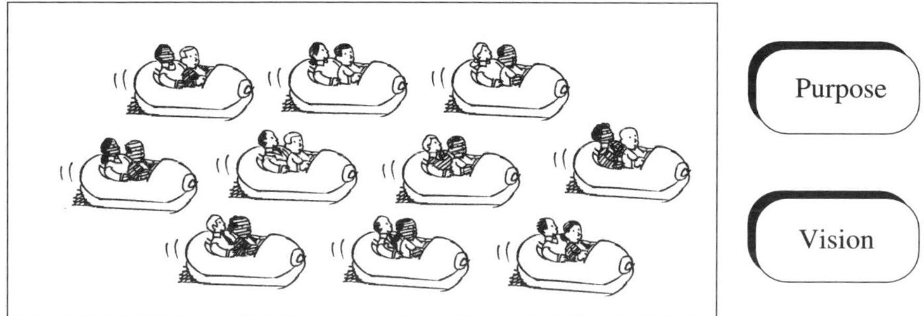

Figure 5-9. Aligning teams using purpose and vision.

This is useful but not enough. Beyond a common purpose and vision, the various groups and teams within the organization need to participate in common priorities and an integrated plan of action. There must be a network of activities linked together to accomplish something of major importance to the organization and its customers. This is pictured in Figure 5-10.

Figure 5-10. Teams that are aligned and integrated into a common system of improvement.

We refer to this source of integration and alignment of effort that directs and focuses the whole organization as *breakthrough improvement.* We describe it in Chapter 6. First we will examine another factor commonly associated with change: culture.

Organizational Culture: Perhaps an Oxymoron

Culture is an anthropological word. Culture is what Margaret Mead learned when studying the mating habits of island tribes. What, therefore, does someone mean when referring to an organization's culture?

It is my observation that using the word "culture" often takes ordinary dysfunctional behavior and elevates it to something ethereal. "We don't work in teams. It's not part of our culture." When some behavior is described as culture it is rendered inaccessible and, therefore, those who are characterized by this behavior need not take responsibility for it. It is the organizational equivalent of the word "personality."

Aside from organizational culture being an excuse for obnoxious behavior, what might it mean?

What Is Organizational Culture?

If it means anything, culture should describe the day-to-day experience of the ordinary worker. Culture is what makes the experience of working at one company different from doing the same work at another company offering similar services or products.

The organization has often been depicted as an iceberg. In Figure 5-11 we use the iceberg to describe the components of culture.

Arrested Adolescence and Organizational Culture

I was invited to visit a major production facility of a well-known high-tech manufacturer. One of my first appointments was with the director of this facility. He was also a senior vice president of the company.

After introductions, I could tell by his silence that he expected me to initiate the conversation. So I asked him: "You are just beginning to lead this part of the company into applying the philosophy of quality to its approaches. How do you expect your job to change as a result of this?"

His response: "I'm not interested in discussing that Western intellectual bullshit!" Then silence. My question may not have been brilliant, but it deserved a better response than I got. I honestly cannot recall the rest of the conversation. Somehow we got through it. I later visited with friends who worked in this facility and described this incident, commenting on how rude this facility director was.

"Oh," my friend responded, "you don't understand our culture. That's how managers treat people here. It's called 'constructive confrontation.'"

I would call it arrested dysfunctional adolescent social skills, sometimes called being a brat! This company calls it culture and declares it something admirable.

I later learned that in their catalogue of corporate training programs, they offered a course in constructive confrontation. "Okay class, now imagine yourselves to be precocious, spoiled, antisocial, 12-year-old brats...."

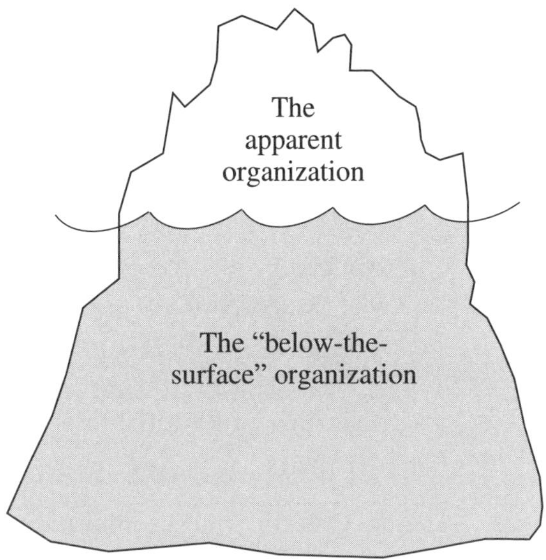

Figure 5-11. The organizational iceberg.

The Apparent Organization

There is the visible, formal, obvious, and officially reported version of the organization. It consists of the products, services, customer segments, and markets; the hierarchical structure and chain of command; the official roles, functions, job descriptions, and accountabilities; the facilities, equipment, machinery, materials, and supplies; the official systems, processes, and methods of work; the official policies, goals, plans, objectives, and standards.

The Below-the-Surface Organization

The informal organization has its unofficial leaders and unwritten rules. The informal organization is shaped by the styles and values of its founder and leaders, and by its history—the residual impacts of past victories and setbacks, old feuds and rivalries. The informal organization has its own communication channels, its grapevine; it consists of unofficial networks and cliques. The informal organization often determines how well-included and respected an employee feels. Inside the official organization and on its perimeter are various unofficial yet influential groups, each with its own unofficial, sometimes unspoken rules of membership. The informal organization makes decisions that can affect whether or not or how well the official decisions are implemented.

The hidden, below-the-surface organization is what determines the average employee's workplace experience. The hidden organization creates and, for all practical purposes, constitutes the organization's culture. The higher in the organization someone is, the less likely he or she is to know or understand what the everyday workplace experience is for the ordinary employee. Even bosses who rose up through the ranks are unlikely to get it. Therefore, the managers are the least likely to understand the culture of their organization though they are the ones most likely to talk about it. Managers may also not appreciate what it takes to change an organization's culture. From an employee's point of view, culture may be pictured as in Figure 5-12.

As an employee:

- I can like my coworkers and the company but dislike my job.
- I can like my job and coworkers but dislike the company.
- I can like my job and the company but dislike my coworkers.
- When I like all three, I am more likely to be energetic, committed, and motivated to do good work.

There is a connection between culture and change.

- Culture often becomes an excuse for *not* changing.

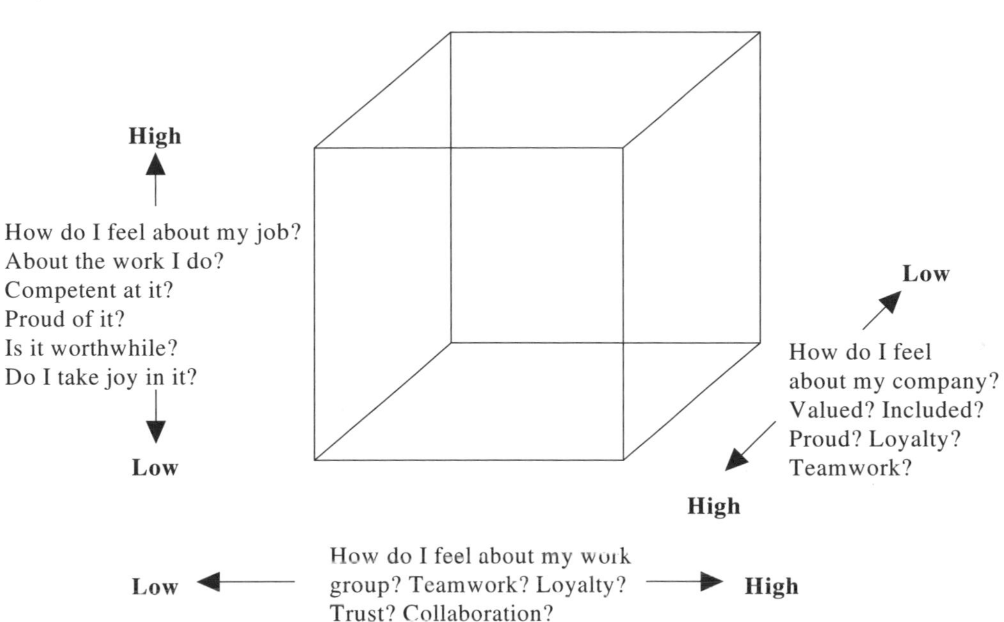
High
How do I feel about my job?
About the work I do?
Competent at it?
Proud of it?
Is it worthwhile?
Do I take joy in it?
Low
Low
How do I feel
about my company?
Valued? Included?
Proud? Loyalty?
Teamwork?
High
Low
How do I feel about my work
group? Teamwork? Loyalty?
Trust? Collaboration?
High

Figure 5-12. Organizational culture from an employee's point of view.

- Culture takes what is ordinary and explainable and elevates it to the ethereal and unattainable.
- Any time you are tempted to use the word "culture," substitute "current behavior" and reflect on how this changes the nature of what had been seen as culture.

SUMMARY

Giving meaning, purpose, direction, and focus to work is the quintessential leadership role. This responsibility of a leader is betrayed by fad-dabbling and ego-dancing.

There is a certain noble poetry to work that can be captured in our statements of vision and purpose. And there can be true esprit de corps when people rally around a compelling common goal. These are what leaders must help us achieve and maintain.

There are three levels of direction setting:

- First, giving clarity and focus to everyday work. This was discussed in Chapter 4.
- Second, the galvanizing force of a shared vision and common purpose; the larger, longer view that shapes us and our future that has been the subject of this chapter.
- Third, the hard work of carefully selecting priorities and planning for their successful accomplishment, which we will discuss in Chapter 6.

CHAPTER FIVE ACTIVITIES

Direction and focus

1. What are your organization's statements of mission, purpose, vision, or values?

2. Are these unique, or are they generic statements that could fit almost any organization of your type?
   - What is unique?

   - What is generic?

3. Are these statements helpful to anyone? If so, to whom and how?

Teamwork and teams

Select one team and answer the following questions with that team in mind.

1. Enter the name of the team.

2. Who established this team?

3. What is the purpose of this team?

4. Who defined its purpose?

5. Describe the problem, need, or opportunity this team was established to address.

6. Why is this problem, need, or opportunity more important to address than other possible targets of your team's effort?

7. What, in general, are you trying to accomplish?

8. Is your team part of a larger effort? If so, describe the larger context and how your team fits into it.

9. How does your team differentiate between those issues that are appropriate for your team to address and those that are not?

10. What are the ultimate measures of success for your team?

11. How will you know if you are making progress?

12. How will you know whether you are making a beneficial difference?

13. How will you know that your current project is completed?

14. Where would you place your team on this continuum?

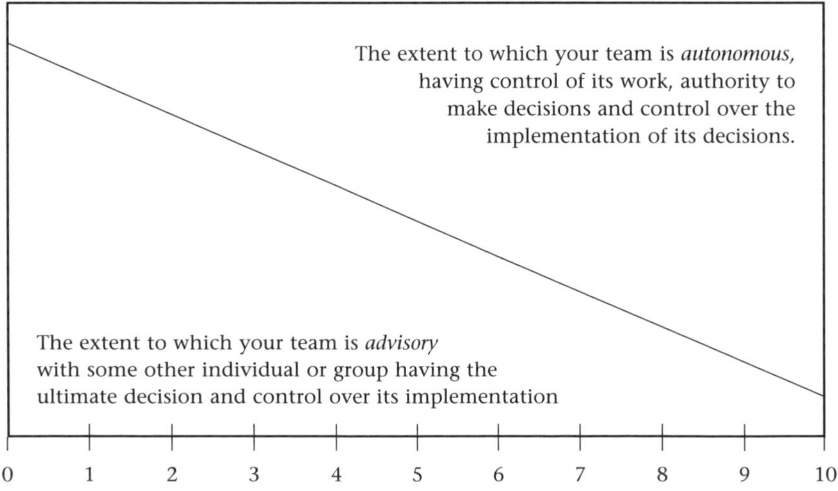

The extent to which your team is *autonomous,* having control of its work, authority to make decisions and control over the implementation of its decisions.
The extent to which your team is *advisory* with some other individual or group having the ultimate decision and control over its implementation
0 1 2 3 4 5 6 7 8 9 10

15. Where on this continuum would the next layer-up of hierarchical management place your team?

16. Characterize your team:

An aggregate of discoordinated, inharmonious individuals	(circle one) 1 2 3 4 5 6 7 8	A synchronized, synergistic, collaborative unit

17. Describe what might help move your team farther to the right on the continuum in Question 16.

Questions on culture

1. What is your organization's culture:
   A. As described by the executives?

   B. As described by managers?

   C. As described by the hourly workforce?

REFERENCES

Ackoff, R. 1996. Report of a presentation October, 1995. *Quality Matters,* the newsletter of the Madison Area Quality Improvement Network, IX, 1, January/February.

Ackoff, R., and Pourdehnad, J. 1997. The irresponsibility and ineffectiveness of downsizing. *Systems Practice,* 10, 1.

Barker, J. 1996. Address to the Association for Quality and Participation's Annual Conference in Portland, Oregon.

Cognetics Research Group. 1996. Annual corporate report on job demographics. *Wisconsin State Journal,* December 26.

Collins, J., and Porras, J. 1996. Building your company's vision. *Harvard Business Review,* September–October.

Juran, J.M. 1995. *Managerial breakthrough.* New York: McGraw-Hill.

Juran, J.M. 1988. *On planning for quality.* New York: The Free Press.

Likert, R. 1967. *The human organization.* New York: McGraw-Hill.

Lippit, G.L. 1973. *Visualizing change.* Fairfax, VA: NTL.

Schein, E. 1985. *Organizational culture and leadership.* San Francisco: Jossey-Bass.

Scholtes, P. 1995. Teams in the age of systems. *Quality Progress,* December.

Senge, P. 1990. *The fifth discipline.* New York: Doubleday Currency.

6 BREAKTHROUGH IMPROVEMENT

INTRODUCTION

In Chapter 5 we provided some guidance for getting ready for change: developing statements of vision, meaning, purpose, direction, and focus. We also mentioned teams and teamwork as prerequisites for change and touched upon the notion of an organization's culture as perhaps an obstacle or perhaps a useful perspective regarding change.

In Chapter 6 we will talk about change and improvement. The leader's job is to know the difference between change and improvement and to know how to lead improvement.

First we will discuss the seven phases of breakthrough improvement, then some principles regarding change and resistance to change.

Effectiveness versus Efficiency

Effectiveness is doing the right thing. Efficiency is doing things right. Peter Drucker, the great student of management, is credited with this insightful distinction. Russell Ackoff claims that it is better to do the right things poorly (inefficient effectiveness) than to do the wrong things well (efficient ineffectiveness). For example, we are becoming more and more efficient at building automobiles in a world that is less and less able to tolerate their existence.

The difference between managing daily work and managing breakthroughs illustrated in Figures 5-2 and 5-3 is relevant here. Daily work is focused on achieving greater efficiencies in the production and delivery of our current products and services. Breakthrough planning may also, indeed, contribute to more efficient production. But the starting point of breakthrough management needs to address the question, "Is this the right thing to do?" This is the point where the issue of effectiveness must be raised and resolved.

The purpose of this chapter is to help leaders step away from the day-to-day and ask questions related to broader systems and longer terms. This is, quintessentially, the leader's job.

BREAKTHROUGH IMPROVEMENT

What follows is a model for planning breakthrough improvement. As George Box has said, "All models are wrong but some are useful." This model may not be right for you. It may not be right for anyone! But if you adapt it to your own situation, it will probably be useful.

A Systems Look at Effectiveness: A New Spin on an Old Cliché

For the lack of a nail, the horseshoe was lost. For the lack of a shoe, the horse was lost. For the lack of a horse, the rider was lost. For the lack of a rider, the battle was lost. With the loss of the battle, the war was lost. By losing the war the tyrant was exiled. And the people found freedom again.

The moral: Sometimes inefficiency is better than efficiency.

We saw in Figure 5-3 the difference between breakthrough improvement and improvement in daily work. Breakthrough improvement involves:

- Doing what we have never done before (new products, new services).
- Producing at a scale we never imagined achieving (more, faster, better).
- Working well beyond the capabilities and capacities of our current systems, processes, and methods.
- Achieving well beyond what could be accomplished by merely trying harder or working faster using our current approaches.
- Designing a new system.

Here are the seven phases of planning for breakthrough improvement:

1. Step back and see what is going on.
2. Step closer and look at your organization's current systems and capabilities.
3. Describe the future, define the ideal.
4. Identify the actions, plan for successful accomplishment, and select the priorities.
5. Mobilize the resources and begin.
6. Leaders shift from planners to reviewers, from decision makers to researchers.
7. The organization learns to improve and integrates what has been learned into future cycles.

Perhaps They Need a Breakthrough Improvement!

Opening a discussion group on the Internet requires approval from the Internet participants. While anyone with an E-mail address can vote, generally there are only 200–300 votes whenever someone asks for approval.

Recently, however, someone asked for approval to open a white supremacists' discussion group. Instead of 300 voters, there were 40,000 voters. (The proposal lost by a 66 to 1 ratio.)

The volunteer who had offered to count the votes needed several months to do what ordinarily would take a few hours. His computer, the address for voting, was at his job. The company's computer crashed three times from the volume of traffic. His boss was very accommodating, allowing the continued use of the office computer after hours.

Someone commenting on the Internet discussion group voting process admitted, "I think we have to come up with a better way!"

We will explore the phases one at a time. For each phase it is important to get a sense of the whole, rather than getting caught up right away in the details.

Phase 1. Step Back and See What Is Going On.

Here we describe not a single event, but ongoing information systems that continually provide data. These data are brought together for various reasons at various times. We describe the convergence of data at the onset of the breakthrough planning process. When the planning process is completed, however, the data-gathering systems continue. Some of the types of converging data are shown in Figure 6-1.

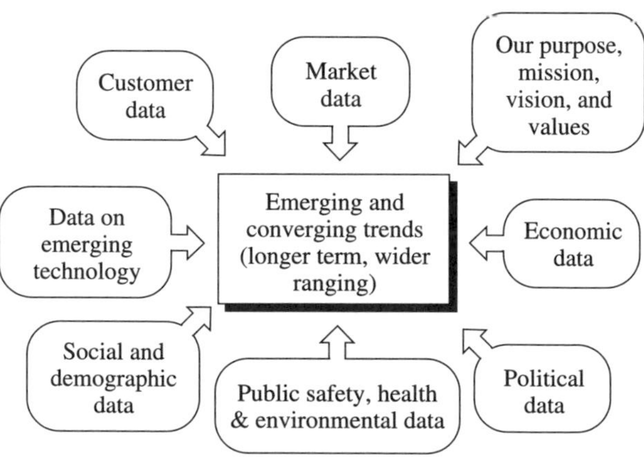

Figure 6-1. Types of converging data.

Each area of data gathering represents a system put in place to routinely monitor the trends important to the organization. Each organization selects what types of data are important for it to monitor. This will obviously vary depending on the purpose, mission, vision, and values of the organization. One of the important leadership roles is to be the visionary: to step away from the everyday urgencies and take the longer, broader view, using data in that search.

Our Purpose, Mission, Vision, and Values

- What progress have we made on these?
- Are events and trends emerging in other areas suggesting any reconsideration of these direction-setting statements?

Market Data

- The market is the entire world in which your products, services, and capabilities are offered. Some of the market consists of those who are currently your customers. Most of the market does not consist of your customers.
- What do you know about:
  - Those in the market who are not your customers? Those who are:
    - Working with your competitors
    - Finding a way to get along without what you or your competitors provide
    - Unaware of what you or your competitors can provide
  - Former customers? Why they left, where they went?
  - Our could-be-but-never-were customers?

Shifts in Mission

In 1995, The Association for Quality and Participation changed its mission to include *communities* as a target for AQP's services.

In 1997, The board of The American Society for Quality Control announced the change of the name of the organization to The American Society for Quality, thus recognizing the broader focus already occurring in ASQC.

Baby Boomers

In 1945, World War II ended, and nine months after the troops returned home, we began to experience a huge bulge in the population (so to speak).

At the beginning of 1996, baby boomers began turning 50 at the rate of one every seven seconds. All sorts of agencies and businesses have had to consider this demographic phenomenon when planning to serve the boomer population.

In New Zealand, morticians have been planning for the onslaught of what they call the "body boomers."

— Benchmark data: What can your competitors provide that you can't (more, better, faster, smaller, cheaper, more user-friendly, etc.)?

- Without understanding both your customers and the market, you will have difficulty identifying breakthroughs and priorities.
- An innovation (what Kano would call "delight characteristics") is almost never suggested by customers. But awareness of customers and their experiences can suggest these types of breakthroughs to the creative leader.

Current Customers

- Any discernible shifts in numbers? Type or segment? Demographic patterns?
- See also the more immediate customer data listed in Phase 2.

Data on Emerging Technology

- What new technology is already out there?
- What characteristics could be designed into not-yet-developed technology that would give you an advantage (or disadvantage if your competitors had it)?

Social and Demographic Data

- How are society and the population changing?
- What can be reasonably projected for 5, 10, or 20 years from now?

Public Safety, Health, and Environmental Data

- What is the predictable availability of natural resources that are necessary for your products or services?
- What safety, health, and environmental damage do you, or could you, cause?
- What are the current and reasonably predictable safety, health, or environmental regulations that affect, or could affect, you?
- What must you do to take care of safety, health, and the environment responsibly and in a timely way, preventing damage rather than doing crisis intervention?

Political Data

- What is happening in local, state, national, or international politics that will have an impact on your suppliers, processes, economics, and markets?
- How can you best monitor those national or international problems and trouble spots that will affect your work?
- Where are problems being resolved and stability restored? Where can you look for new opportunities?

Economic Data

- What are the patterns and trends of economic distribution on a local, national, and international level?
- How will these patterns and trends affect your business?
- What values and responsibilities will you take on regarding fair salaries and wages?
- How will you differentiate between common cause variation and special cause variation in observing and analyzing events in the stock market? In corporate financial performance? In supply, demand, and price fluctuations?

This, of course, is a sample list. Not all will apply to you and other indicators will apply that are not listed here. The important points are these:

- Select the data to monitor and the indicators to watch that are most important to your needs as an organization.
- Treat your list of indicators not as an agenda of discussion topics, but as a list of ongoing data-gathering and analyzing systems.

Phase 2. Step Closer and Look at Your Organization's Current Systems and Capabilities.

Figure 6-2 shows some of the types of internal data to monitor and analyze. These, too, should be seen as ongoing systems for gathering data, not simply discussion topics.

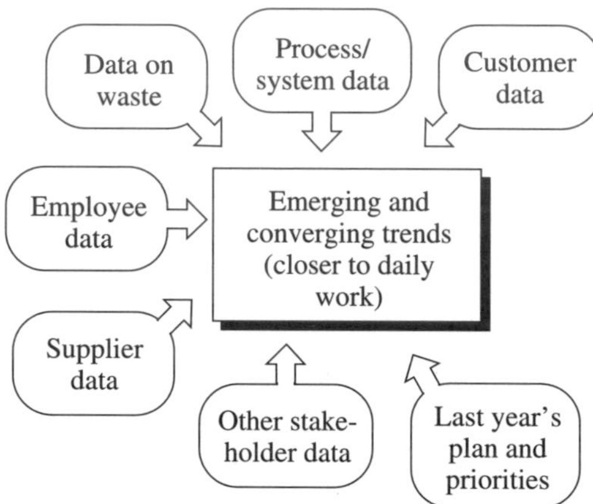

Figure 6-2. Types of internal, daily-work data to analyze.

In Chapter 7 we will explore the issue of measurement in greater detail. Here we look briefly at each type of data.

Customer Data

Some of this data will dovetail with customer data described in Phase 1. The difference is this: Phase 1 customer data looks at longer-term trends. Here we look at more immediate trends. Phase 1 looks at the longer-term future of the market. Here we look at what is happening now with our current customers.

- Using the Kano Model (Figure 3-6), explore the following with your current customers.
  - What are the basics, and how well are you doing on them?
  - What are the performance-related characteristics, and how are you doing on them?
  - What more can you do?
  - What are or could be the delight characteristics? How are you doing? What more can you do?
- What is the frequency of customer complaints, and what are the patterns? (See the sidebar "What to Do with Customer Complaints" in Chapter 7.)

- What have you learned from focus groups and customer surveys?
- How successfully did you predict and anticipate customer-related trends in past years?

Process/Systems Data

- Which major processes are in statistical control; which are not?
- Which processes are in control with a range and average acceptable to your customers? (See Chapter 2.)
- How well have you done at bringing into control those processes that were out of control last year?
- Which major processes are standardized, and which are not? (See Chapter 4.)
- What data do you have on conformance to the key quality characteristics identified by your customers? (See Chapters 3 and 4.)

Waste

What data do we have on any of the following? (See Chapter 4.)

- Waste
- Scrap
- Rework
- Remedial activities
- Breakdowns
- Cycle times
- Output capacity
- Inventory
- Work in process
- Bottlenecks
- Administrative mistakes, omissions, and errors
- Key financial data (profit and loss, cash flow, budgeted or forecast costs or revenue versus actual, etc.)

Employee Data

- What do your people tell you regarding the workability of your systems and process?
- What gets in the way of people doing work they can be proud of?
- What gets in the way of joy in their work?
- What data do you have on employee turnover? Why do people leave?
- What data do you have on the frequency and patterns of grievances?

- On a day-to-day basis, how are you doing with regard to employee safety and health?
- What data do you have on hiring and promotion? How many applications? How many candidates with ideal capabilities? What are the patterns regarding insufficient capabilities?

Supplier Data

- How well are suppliers meeting your key quality characteristics?
- What trends are likely to affect their service to you?
- What data do you have showing which of the suppliers' systems or processes are in control and which are not?

Data on Other Stakeholders

This is a miscellaneous category that includes data from such sources of input as:

- Unions
- Stockholders, stock analysts
- Regulatory or licensing agencies
- Bankers
- Neighbors of your facilities, the communities in which you are located

Last Year's Plan and Breakthrough Priorities

- What did you learn from last year's planning process that you can incorporate in this year's planning process?
- How well did you do on last year's priorities? Are any waiting to be completed?

Sorting Out the Data

The data reviewed in Phases 1 and 2 of breakthrough improvement will provide many clues and signals of possible directions. But it will be somewhat chaotic. The data will need to be sifted and winnowed.

There are various tools and approaches for this sorting-out process. Many of these are described in *The Memory Jogger Plus* (Brassard, 1989). In particular, the affinity diagram (p. 17 ff.) and the interrelationship digraph, also called the relations diagram (p. 39 ff.), are useful. These approaches will help create some order out of the chaos.

In their classic work, *The New Rational Manager,* Charles Kepner and Benjamin Tregoe (1981) explore various ways to analyze problems (Chapters 1 and 2) and analyze decisions (Chapters 3 and 4). Kepner and Tregoe's work represents a synthesis of problem-solving and decision-making methodology as it existed prior to the approaches taught us by Deming, Ishikawa, and others. Kepner and Tregoe's work can be judiciously combined with the work of those engaged in the Quality Movement and become a powerful way to plan, make decisions, and solve problems.

Some Guidelines for Sifting and Winnowing

Look for Confirmation of Your Strengths.

- What you are good at?
- What you are known for?
- Where and with whom do you have the greatest acceptance?
- What capabilities have you mastered?

Look for Indications of Your Vulnerabilities.

- Where are you losing your competitive edge?
- Which trends and technological developments may overtake you?
- Which financial truths and economic trends may leave you exposed?

Look for Opportunities.

- Look for the likely unfolding of events that will put you in a unique position to capture the market and the technology.
- Look for new directions and new capabilities you can offer the market that take advantage of your expertise and unique resources.

Look for Urgencies.

- Problems that may well develop into crises.
- Problems that could spread, affecting other parts of the organization.
- Opportunities that may soon disappear and never pass this way again.

Employee Participation in Breakthrough Improvement

When the priorities are announced at the end of Phase 3, and the plan is shared at the end of Phase 4, they should come as a surprise to no one.

As the process unfolds, there should be continual sharing with employees, input and feedback from them, and involvement by them in the planning.

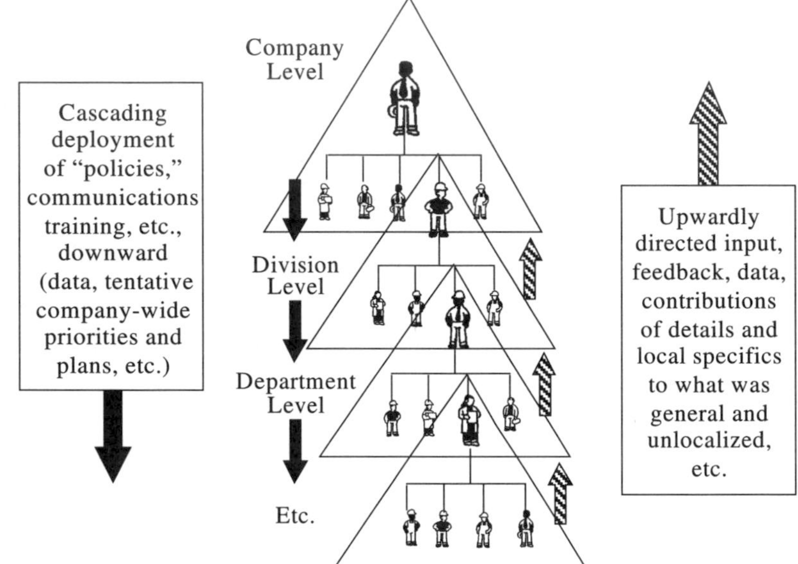

Figure 6-3. Rensis Likert's linchpin model may be a useful approach to developing pathways of participation.

Look for Antecedents That Lead to Consequences.

- What are the causes of the problems? What are the causes of the causes?
- What are the barriers to progress?
- What are the systemic conditions or factors that allow this problem to exist?
- What unmet needs stand in the way of resolving other problems?

In All of This, Use Data: Not Opinions, Not Guesswork, Not Bombast or Passionate Rhetoric ... *Data*!

Phase 3. Describe the Future, Define the Ideal.

By the end of Phase 2 you should have an initial sense of the emerging themes. With this awareness as a framework and background, leaders can begin a process of reconceiving reality. Breakthrough planning requires us to let go of our old assumptions, easier said than done.

In *Creating the Corporate Future,* Russell Ackoff (1981) offers some help with what he calls idealized design (pp. 104–125). The following is an adaptation of his work.

Define the Future Using Idealized Design

1. *Assume that your products, services, systems, and processes have just been destroyed.* They no longer exist. You cannot re-create them. You have left only your organization's purpose and your people's knowledge, experience, and imagination.
2. *Your challenge is to replace what was destroyed with new products, services, systems, and processes;* not to rebuild the old but to start from scratch and begin anew. What was there is gone forever.
3. As part of idealized design, ask the following questions about the products, services, systems, or processes that were just destroyed:
   - What was their purpose?
   - What capabilities did our customers acquire as a result of these products or services?
   - Is this purpose and are these capabilities worth preserving in the new design?
   - What new purpose or capabilities would be important to offer?
4. You are completely free to redesign the product, service, systems, or processes within the following restraints:
   - What you do must be technologically feasible. You may need to use known technology to invent new things, but no science fiction.

     For example: Sony used technology that Texas Instruments had developed for use in hearing aids and applied it to radios—the dawning of the age of transistor radios.
   - It must be operationally workable in the present environment. Once developed, the new technology must be able to function as intended and survive.
   - Assume there are no regulations to prevent you from going forward. However, consider alternative ways to fulfill the legitimate intent and spirit of the regulations.

Define the Ideal

If we can pull it off, here is what we want:

1. The following new network of products: ________________

   ____

   - Providing these capabilities ________________

     ____

   - With these characteristics and attributes ________________

     ____

2. The following new network of services: ________________

   ____

   - Providing these capabilities ________________

     ____

   - With these characteristics and attributes ________________

     ____

3. The following new systems and processes: ________________

   ____

   - Providing these capabilities ________________

     ____

   - With these characteristics and attributes ________________

     ____

4. Our ideal is responsive to the following data that we obtained and reviewed in Phases 1 and 2: ________________

   ____

5. Here is how our customers will benefit from these new products, services, systems, or processes: ________________

   ____

Phase 4. Identify the Actions, Plan for Successful Accomplishment, and Select the Priorities.

At this point we have looked at the current situation (Phases 1 and 2) and defined an idealized future (Phase 3). Now we ask what we must do to achieve our idealized future. We also need to identify the priorities for implementing those activities. The most important question to ask at the start of Phase 4—and to ask repeatedly—is, "What will be necessary to successfully accomplish our goal, our idealized future?"

> **Breakthrough Improvement versus Management by Objectives**
>
> A goal without a method is cruel!—W. Edwards Deming
>
> It is in Phase 4 that breakthrough improvement parts company with MBO. MBO is more or less a wish list, not much different from what we did as kids getting ready for Christmas or a birthday. "Here are my wishes," the boss says. "Now you are accountable for making them come true."
>
> This takes no brains. It is not leadership. This represents the avoidance of thinking and the abdication of leadership.

Figure 6-4 shows a tool and a way of thinking. The tool is called a *tree diagram.* (See Brassard, 1989, p. 71 ff.) It is a way of thinking through the conversion of goals into actions.

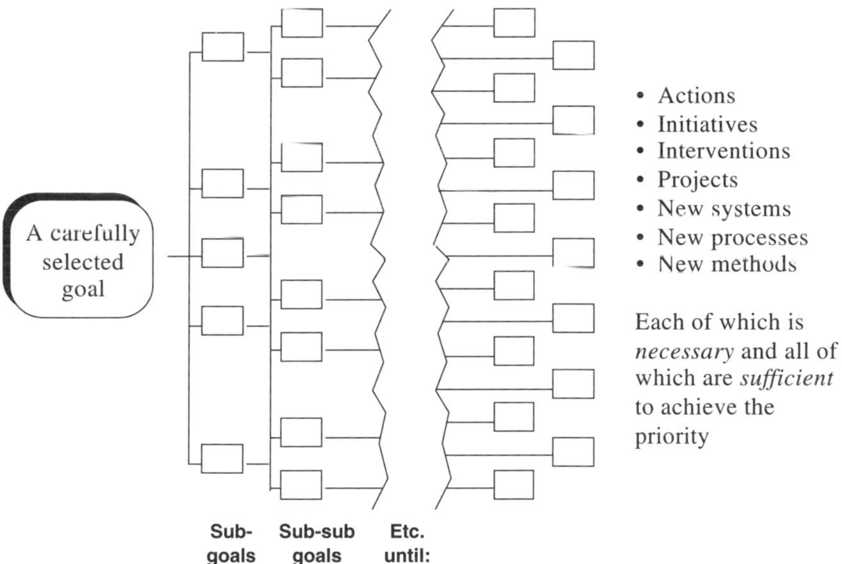
A carefully selected goal
• Actions
• Initiatives
• Interventions
• Projects
• New systems
• New processes
• New methods
Each of which is *necessary* and all of which are *sufficient* to achieve the priority
Sub-goals
Sub-sub goals
Etc. until:

Figure 6-4. A tree diagram describing the conversion of a goal to activities.

When we first ask, "What will it take to successfully accomplish this?" we will undoubtedly end up with a list of subordinate goals. For each subgoal, we repeat the "What will it take" question, perhaps continuing through further sequences of subordinate goals and "What will it take ..." questions. Eventually the answer to "What will it take ..." will be lists of *actions.*

The Systems Side of Change

Usually whatever we propose to change is part of a larger system. It is important, therefore, to look at the systemic implications of any proposed change. Here are some questions to explore:

- What purpose is currently served or desirable benefit acquired by the process or method we propose to change?
- How does whatever it is we propose to change fit in? What larger systems or processes does it support or feed into? What smaller processes or methods fit into it?
- How can the desirable output and benefits of this process continue without the continued existence of this process?
- What should we monitor to assure that we are sustaining the benefits of the old process without suffering its shortcomings?

There are two tests for the items in the tree diagram:

1. Is each item *necessary*? Don't pursue a subgoal or undertake an activity that isn't necessary in order to accomplish the larger, carefully selected goal.
2. Are all the items *sufficient*? Should subgoals or activities be added to make the network of goals and activities sufficient to accomplish the larger goal?

Some of the items on the list of actions may require a team to accomplish, some a natural work group, some a cross-functional team, some an ongoing team, some an ad hoc team especially formed for this project. Other items on the action list won't require a team at all, but can be undertaken by one person acting alone, sometimes with a single stroke of a pen. The nature of the task on the list of actions will indicate the structure appropriate for the effort: team or no team? Who should be involved? The old architectural adage, form follows function, applies here also.

Select the Priorities

Having defined the idealized future and translated these ambitious goals into actions, we must decide where to start: What gets done first and which parts get put off until later? What makes one set of actions more important than another? Here are some criteria. Previously we used these criteria to sift and winnow the data and indicators of possible goals or themes for breakthrough improvement. Here we use the same criteria to organize our action steps into an appropriate sequence.

1. Builds on our strengths.
2. Protects us from our vulnerabilities.
3. Provides us with a compelling opportunity.
4. There is an urgent need to respond.
5. Antecedents and consequences: One action is necessary before others can begin.

One tool to help sort out priorities is the *matrix diagram* shown in Figure 6-5. For more on this tool, see Brassard (1989, p. 97 ff.).

	Criteria for selection					
Sub-goals and actions	**Builds on strengths**	**Protects vulnera-bilities**	**Compelling opportunity**	**Urgent need**	**Chrono-logically antecedent**	**Comments**
List the items from the tree diagram: Use both the last generation of goals and the action list items						

Figure 6-5. Matrix diagram.

Two other tools useful for displaying chronological interdependence are the PERT chart and the GANTT chart, shown in Figures 6-6 and 6-7.

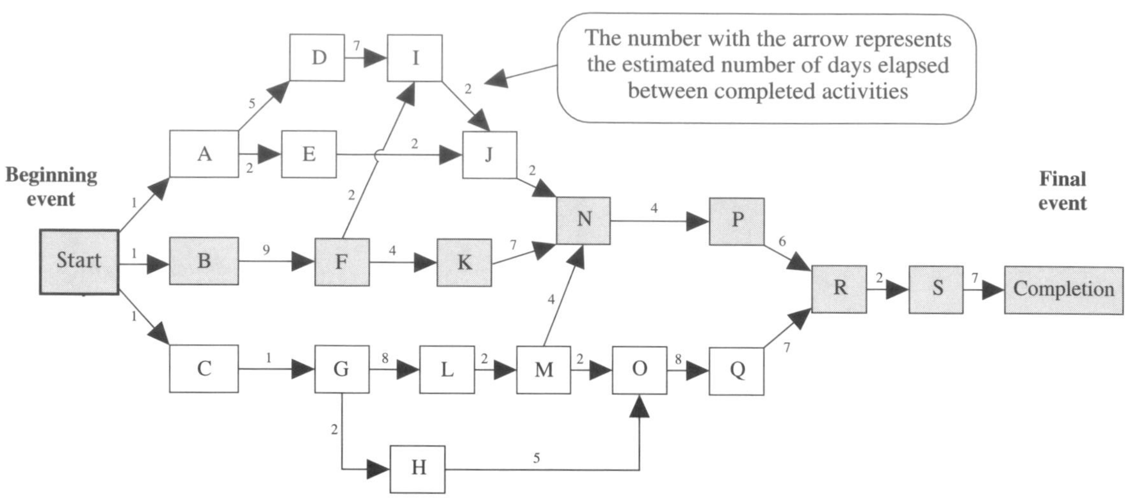

Figure 6-6. In this PERT chart, the critical path is the shaded boxes (40 days).

	Week	1	2	3	4	5	6	7	8	9	10	11	12	13	14	15	16
1. Educate the top managers	Plan		■	■	■	■											
	Actual			▨	▨	▨	▨										
2. Obtain their approval for a pilot test	Plan					■	■										
	Actual						▨										
3. Select the pilot area	Plan						■	■									
	Actual						▨										
4. Develop a training curriculum	Plan				■	■	■	■	■								
	Actual																
5. Identify the trainers	Plan				■	■											
	Actual																
6. Train the trainers	Plan								■	■	■						
	Actual																
7. Schedule the training	Plan						■	■									
	Actual																
8. Identify…	Plan								■	■							

Figure 6-7. A Gantt chart on the introduction of a new measurement system in the company.

The PERT Chart (or Critical Path)

This planning tool became famous when it was used to plan the construction of the first nuclear-powered submarine (which came in under budget and ahead of schedule). PERT is an acronym for Planning Evaluation Review Technique. Critical path—its currently popular name—refers to the longest anticipated single line of activity from start to finish. The Japanese quality teachers consider this one of the seven management tools and call it the Arrow Diagram. This chart was described in Chapter 4 (see Figure 4-7).

For more information on the PERT chart, see Brassard (1989, pp. 97 ff.). Brassard chooses to call this the activity network diagram.

The Gantt Chart

The developer of this chart, Henry Gantt, was a consulting engineer and protégé of Frederick Taylor at the turn of the century. The chart developed by him is a wonderfully visual planning tool that describes the temporal relationships of events that unfold over time. The Gantt chart can be used to describe a macro plan (the construction of a new city) or a micro plan (the construction of one chair that will be placed in one room of one building of that city). The Gantt chart can show projected schedules and actual schedules.

Some guidelines for the use of PERT and Gantt charts:

- In general the PERT chart accommodates complex projects better than the Gantt chart.
- Either chart may, and probably should, be done showing different scales of action: one chart for more generic categories of activity, other charts for the more minutely detailed actions.
- When developing the chart, it is usually easier to start at the end and work backward toward the beginning.
- It is common to discover how unrealistic your anticipated timeline is when constructing a PERT chart or Gantt chart. If you have found that you haven't allowed enough time to get things done, it is generally better to postpone your target date than to arbitrarily shorten the time allowed for each stage in the development effort. Better yet, don't set a target date, at least not until this planning is completed.
- It is also common to discover missing steps when constructing these charts, steps you had not originally anticipated. This is one of the reasons the next guideline is important.
- When doing these plans in their early draft form, use Post-its™ or some other brand of sticky notes. Some clients have told me that this is the most useful bit of advice I have ever given about how to plan. (Faint praise is sometimes worse than no praise at all.)

Phase 5. Mobilize the Resources and Begin.

After Phase 4 we know what has to be done, but we are not quite ready to do it. We must surround our breakthrough improvement with a little infrastructure providing guidance, alignment, and support. Generally speaking, each improvement effort will need two kinds of support, as illustrated in Figure 6-8.

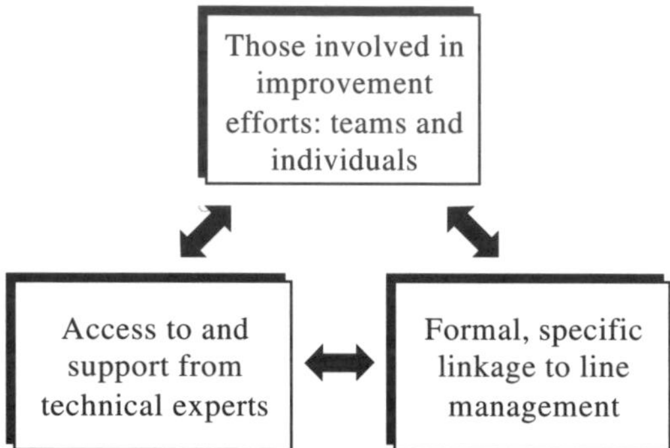

Figure 6-8. Two types of support for those engaged in improvement efforts.

Managerial support and linkage: Contact with and access to the appropriate level of leadership in the organization. A sure recipe for failure is to allow any individual group to drift off like orphans in a storm.

Technical support: Access to various types of expertise, training, advice, and counsel including intrinsic technology (subject matter, product, or service expertise) and expertise in improvement methodology.

One suggestion that I have found successful for offering a structure of support is described in Figure 6-9.

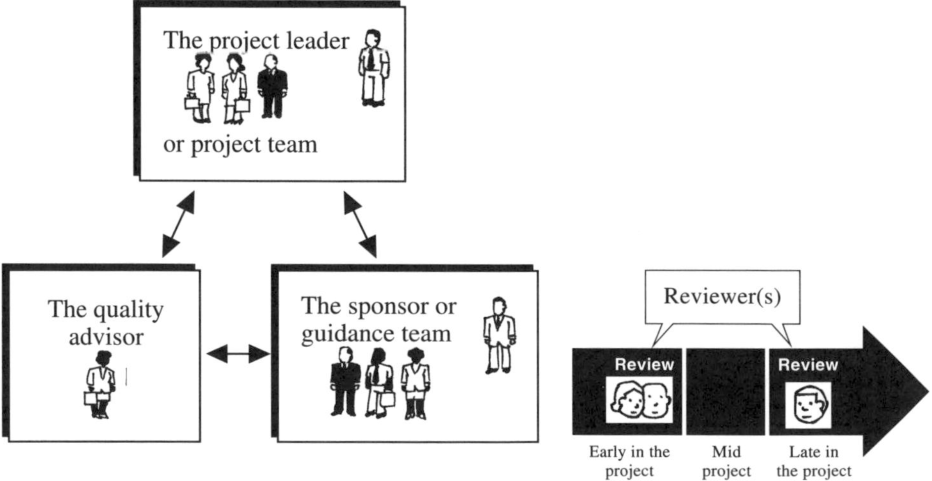

Figure 6-9. A structure of support for improvement efforts.

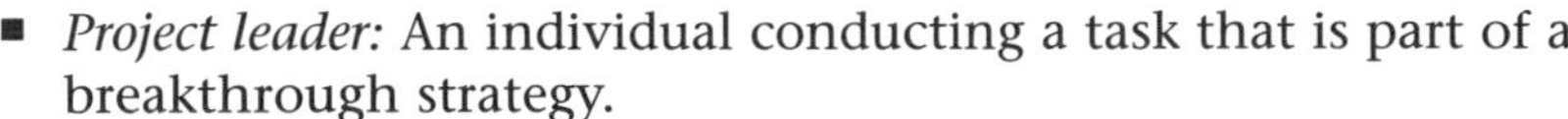

- *Project leader:* An individual conducting a task that is part of a breakthrough strategy.
- *Project team:* A group assigned to an improvement task.
- *Quality Advisor:*
  - — Coaches both those involved in the project and those engaged in giving managerial support. A teacher of the methodology of improvement on a just-in-time basis.
  - — The internal or industry technical advice (called intrinsic technology) is provided by those in or outside the organization who have such expertise and are assigned as consultants to the project or are sometimes actual members of the project team.
- *Sponsor:* Someone in line management who cares about this project has responsibility for the area involved in the breakthrough effort, understands the larger purpose and strategy of the breakthrough effort, and is assigned to be available to the project participants for support and reality checks.
- *Guidance team:* Sometimes the role of sponsor is fulfilled by a team of managers and other appropriate leaders.

  The guidance team most probably will need a designated leader. Sometimes the greatest value provided by the guidance team will be to act as an identified point of contact between those directly involved in the project and line management. Many times the meeting may consist of the project team having an informal check-in with the sponsor or guidance team, updating them on current developments. The sponsor or guidance team may still use the questioning and listening skills discussed in Chapter 8, without the formal review process described later in this chapter. Ideally, the project team and guidance team are partners, working together: The guidance team acts as a reality check and helps to remove roadblocks and elicit the organization's support, and helps the project team prepare for formal written or oral presentations and reviews.
- *Reviewers:* At different times during the project's history, those involved in the project will meet with one or more senior managers for a review. I have also known of occasions when a customer was part of a review. The reviews have various purposes and the reviewer should be selected based on who would be appropriate for a given review with a given purpose. (For more on reviews, see Phase 6 and Chapter 8.)

Therefore, part of organizing for the network of breakthrough improvement efforts is to plan and deploy the support systems surrounding the breakthrough projects. Figure 6-10 is a sample format for displaying this information.

Review dates	This describes planned dates on which some appropriate manager or team of managers will conduct a review of this effort.
Expected completion date	This describes the target date. This is especially useful when other efforts must wait for the successful completion of this effort.
Resources for technical support	This describes how you will receive technical guidance and support; who and how to contact them: Examples: • Your quality advisor is Mary Rose Walsh, 6-4220 • For technical advice reference glue properties, contact W. Warner in the research lab.
Resources for management support	This describes the nature of ongoing contact with line management, whom to contact and how to contact him or her. Example: • Guidance team for this project led by J. Chandler, 3-5483 • Sponsor for this project: W. Terwilliger, 6-5150
Contact person/ phone	This describes who will be coordinating/leading this effort. Whom to contact and how to contact him or her.
Description of the participants (individual/team/ whom to contact)	This describes the structure of participation, who participates, who is involved, who is consulted and any limits to authority. Examples: • A cross-functional team representing sections P, Q, R, & S • Consult Wilson in research. • One person from finance with support from an advisory group • #3 machine day shift; consult other shifts. • Operations team will accept recommendations.
Description of the effort (scope, depth, extent)	This describes the boundaries of the project. Examples: • Establish baseline data on cycle time and recommend next steps • Study leakage that occurs after point H and to point K • Identify causes of surface damage and eliminate the occurrence of them across all relevant function areas • Develop and recommend alternative purchasing policies to help reduce the number of suppliers of routine maintenance supplies
Project Title	This is a short description of the nature of the project. Examples: • #3 machine downtime • Out-of-stock study • Work-in-transit distance reduction • Purchasing policy alignment • Spare parts bottleneck • Missed delivery dates
ID#	This is a reference code for record keeping.

Figure 6-10. The infrastructure surrounding the improvement activities.

Commissioning Those Who Will Begin the Improvement Effort

Along with the information included in the format shown in Figure 6-10, the leaders of the breakthrough effort should communicate the following information to project leaders and team members.

1. The purpose of the team.
2. The problem or need that this team has been established to address.
3. How this effort integrates into a network of other efforts (the tree diagram strategy).
4. What the expectations of senior management are:
   - How we will measure the completion of the task.
   - How we will measure success.
5. What *output* is expected from this effort, who receives that output, and what they expect.
6. What internal and external resources are available to you.
7. What the known boundaries and constraints are:
   - What you have control over (areas of independence).
   - What you do not have control over (areas of dependence).

Along with this information, tell them to begin!

Phase 6. Leaders Shift from Being Planners to Being Reviewers, from Being Decision Makers to Being Researchers.

Up until this point, leaders have been the leaders, orchestrators, facilitators, and promoters of the planning process. The plan is theirs but widespread and frequent participation will be necessary to pick the right priority (Ackoff's "Doing the Right Thing") and to develop a plan for the necessary and sufficient activities (Ackoff's "Doing Things Right"). When the projects have been commissioned and are underway, the leaders switch hats. They become *reviewers.*

In Chapter 2 we examined how learning takes place. Here is a summary of the points that are applicable to the review process:

- Learning and improvement result from the dynamic interplay between theory and experience. The entire breakthrough plan is theory. As it is applied, managers will acquire knowledge. Review is how managers examine how well the theory is working and what needs to be learned so they can do better.

- The PDSA (Plan-Do-Study-Act) cycle is a continual cycle of learning and improvement.

Conducting reviews is one method by which the leaders incorporate study into their breakthrough improvement efforts.

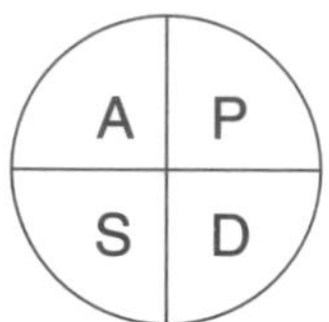

Diagram 6-1. The PDSA cycle.

Diagram 6-2 is a description of the leader's annual transition from planner to reviewer. It is organized according to the PDSA cycle.

The matrix in Diagram 6-2 refers to required capabilities. These are discussed in Chapters 2 and 8. Figure 6-11 is a sample format for planning the reviews. Much of this information would be taken from the form shown in Figure 6-10. Figure 6-10 organizes some basic information on all the projects. Figure 6-11 organizes review information on each project individually. Figure 6-10 is a format intended for use by senior managers and the quality office. Figure 6-11 is a form intended for use by project leaders, sponsors, and assigned reviewers.

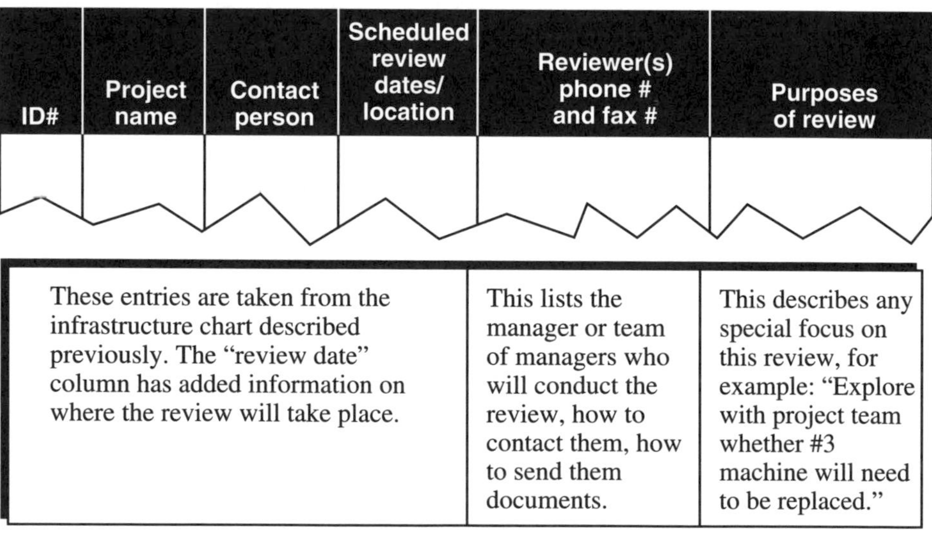

ID#	Project name	Contact person	Scheduled review dates/ location	Reviewer(s) phone # and fax #	Purposes of review

These entries are taken from the infrastructure chart described previously. The "review date" column has added information on where the review will take place.	This lists the manager or team of managers who will conduct the review, how to contact them, how to send them documents.	This describes any special focus on this review, for example: "Explore with project team whether #3 machine will need to be replaced."

Figure 6-11. Information sheet on reviews for each individual improvement effort.

		Activities	Required Capabilities
P	The manager as planner	1. Reviews various data • Customer data • Market data • Process data • Employee data • Long-term plans, last year's efforts and results	• Statistical thinking • Systems thinking and analysis
		2. Analyzes data, develops priorities through interactive methods	• Meeting skills • Listening skills • Inquiry skills
		3. For each priority—and with ample input and participation—identifies all the various interventions, projects and activities that are necessary and sufficient to accomplish that identified goal	• Systems thinking • Improvement strategies • Communication skills • Meeting skills • Inquiry skills • Planning skills
		4. Commissions the various interventions, projects and activities, scheduling review dates for each	• Communication skills • Listening skills
D	The manager as reviewer	5. Takes advantages of opportunities to informally inquire about the activities	• Neutral observation • Listening skills • Inquiry skills • Improvement strategies and methodology
S		6. Conducts formal reviews at scheduled times	• Meeting skills • Listening skills • Inquiry skills • Review infrastructure • Improvement strategies and methodology
A	The manager as planner	7. Integrates learnings into future efforts	• Systems thinking • Statistical thinking and analysis

Diagram 6-2.

Organizing for the Review

For each improvement effort determine the following:

An Overview of Reviews

Inquiry is an informal method by which managers can stay in touch with those involved in improvement efforts or any other activities. The review is a formal inquiry, held at a predetermined place and time. The review (unlike inquiry) cannot happen serendipitously. At the heart of the review process is the PDSA cycle. PDSA guides several direction-setting mechanisms, each operating on a different cycle. During the reviews, the managers may look for indicators relevant to these questions.

1. Mission, vision, values, philosophy; long-term goals and plans; and medium-term goals and plans operate on slow turning cycles. Annual plans and short-term projects operate on faster turning cycles. The longer cycle direction-setters stay more or less in place, however, mostly unaltered over time. But it is appropriate to revisit them from time to time, especially during the annual improvement planning cycle.
   - Are the longer-term cycles still relevant? Still meaningful?
   - Are we making continual progress toward them?
2. Each of the shorter-term cycles involves its own planning, doing, studying, and acting. The review process is relevant to the check step for each of these:
   - What progress are we making toward our annual improvement goals?
   - How well is our strategy working? What adjustments are necessary?
   - How effective is our knowledge and skill in improvement methodology?
   - How successful is this particular improvement effort? What progress has been made?
   - What have we learned that can be transferred to other current and future efforts?
3. Given the various contexts provided by the longer- and shorter-term PDSA cycles, the purposes of reviews may be described as follows:
   - To test the current validity of the mission, vision, values, and philosophy of the organization.
   - To measure progress and assess the current validity of long-term goals and plans and mid-term goals and plans.

- To measure progress toward the accomplishment of the annual improvement plan.
- To test the validity of the strategy behind the annual plan: Is each activity necessary? Are all of them sufficient?
- To look for gaps in our ability to use the various elements of improvement methodology.
- To look for lessons to be integrated into our systems, to be used by (or avoided by) others engaged in improvement efforts.
- To recognize and support the efforts of those engaged in improvement efforts.
- To determine where additional resources may be necessary or useful to bolster improvement efforts.
- To align and realign activities, if necessary, with their original intent and with the larger purpose and strategy.
- To stay in touch with the everyday folks doing the important, real work.

4. Some implications of these purposes for reviews:
   - All of these purposes cannot be pursued at any given review.
   - Different managers, or other staff specialists, are more appropriate for reviewing some purposes, others are the appropriate reviewers for other purposes.
   - There may need to be special reviews of, perhaps, a sampling of projects aimed at pursuing some of the slower-turning, longer-term cycles.
   - Like everything else, reviews have their own PDSA cycle.

The Review Itself

In Chapter 8, we will look at various questions and strategies of questioning that leaders may use. The questions may be used in an informal setting, perhaps even in a casual conversation. Here we examine the formal review: its logistics and process.

The formal review is a scheduled event with presenters, reviewers, and, sometimes, an audience. It is held at a prearranged time and date in a prearranged place. It usually has an established format and agenda. The formal review is conducted by managers; those being reviewed are the individuals or groups involved in various improvement activities.

Earlier I described an infrastructure for an improvement effort that included a sponsor or guidance team (Figure 6-9). My recommendation is that the sponsor or guidance team *not* act in the reviewer role. They may help the project leader or project team prepare for the review, perhaps with a dress rehearsal. However, during the review, I recommend that the sponsor or guidance team be among those who may be asked questions by the reviewers. I recognize that this involves more managers and some organizations simply do not have enough management personnel to accommodate this recommendation.

Figure 6-12 shows a suggested layout for the review location. This is adapted from the setup used by Dr. Ishikawa and other Japanese quality leaders.

Figure 6-12. A suggested room setup for a formal review.

The following participate in the review:

- *The reviewers.* Listen to the presentation and ask appropriate questions of anyone involved: team leader, team members, guidance team members, or quality advisor.
- *Presenter.* Usually the project team leader. Because the team leader is commonly the presenter, most questions are likely to be directed to him or her. It is reasonable, however, for the presenter to redirect questions to some other appropriate party. Sometimes the leader of the guidance team or the sponsor may introduce the presenter.
- *Others.* This is optional. However, it may be useful to have other interested parties in attendance. For example, future presenters, workers in the area under study, other managers and staff personnel, customers, suppliers, etc.

Some recommended elements of the review process:

- *Orientation for presenters.* The review can be a fairly intimidating experience, even with the most benevolent of reviewers. Whoever will be presenting should be coached and briefed about:

  — How to prepare materials for the review.

  — What to expect at the review itself.

  It is suggested that this orientation be conducted by the quality advisor and, if possible, by one of the reviewers.

- *Orientation for reviewers.* Reviewers new to the review process will also need to be coached in such areas as:

  — What questions are likely to be most appropriate (and inappropriate)?

  — What are the specific steps of the review? How does it unfold? Who does what?

  This orientation is ordinarily conducted by the quality advisor or a knowledgeable senior manager.

- *Preparation and distribution of presentation materials.* The presentation should ordinarily be in an improvement story format using an overhead projector or power-point projector. A hard copy of the overhead presentation should be made available to the reviewers one week in advance. Extra copies should be made available for others on the day of the presentation. The improvement story format has graphic displays showing what the team has learned and accomplished. For more information on the improvement story format, see *The Team Handbook* (Scholtes, 1988, pp. 4–27). There it is called the story board format.

Figure 6-13 is a deployment flowchart of the suggested review process.

Some notes on this process:

- Reviewer mentions what he or she liked.

  — This may seem contrived but, contrived or not, it seems to help establish a less severe tone to the proceedings.

  — The comments should obviously be sincere and directly relevant to the work of the project and the presentation of the work: "I found your before-and-after data, put in the form of back-to-back histograms, to be particularly useful."

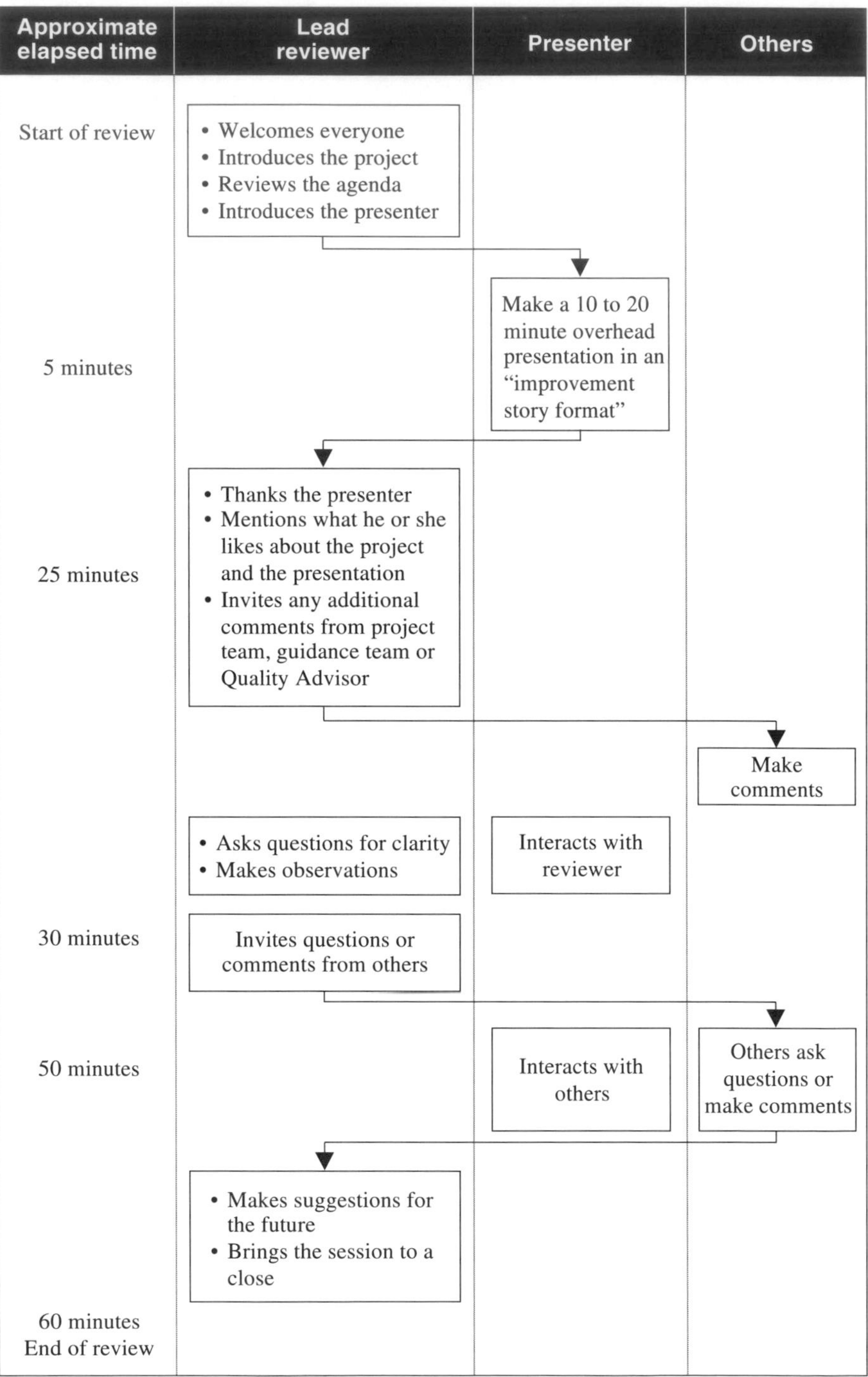

Figure 6-13. The review process: During the review.

- Reviewer asks questions for clarity. For example:
  - "When you say 'prompt response,' what exactly do you mean by that?"
  - "On page 4, the chart on the top of the page: I know that the passing of time is recorded in the horizontal axis. Would you explain what is described on the vertical axis?"
  - "How do you know that your definition of 'on time' is the same as the customer's?"
  - "Please explain the connection between your solution in Step 4 and your identified causes in Step 3."
- Reviewer makes suggestions for the future.
  - This should be done gently, offering bits of advice rather than orders from headquarters. "May I suggest that you revisit Step 2 and do more stratification and localization? Use a Pareto chart, for instance, to show where the damage is most likely to occur."

Figure 6-14 displays what might take place immediately after the review. This builds a study step directly into the review process.

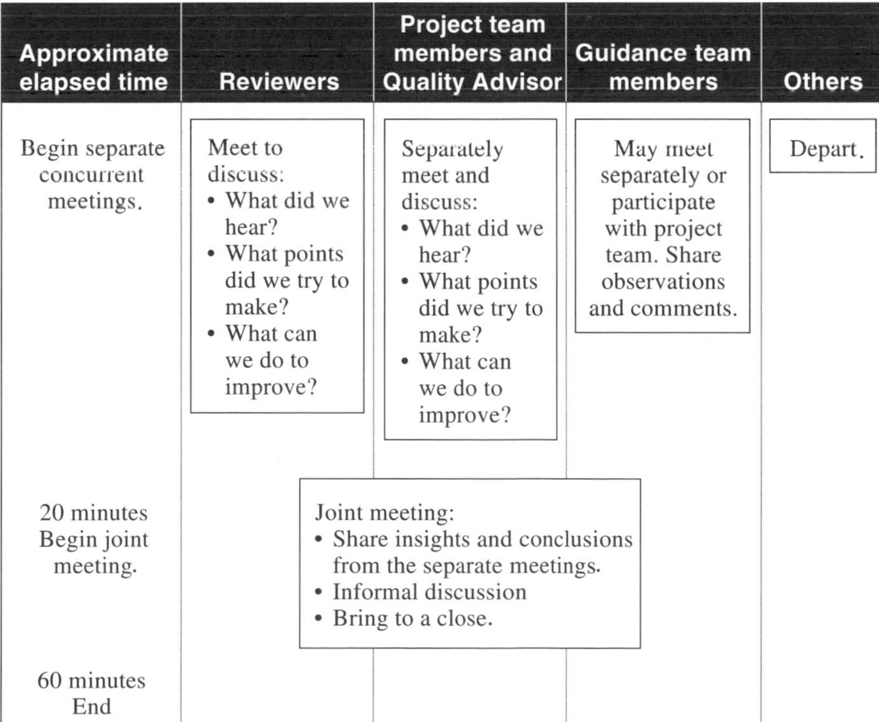

Approximate elapsed time	Reviewers	Project team members and Quality Advisor	Guidance team members	Others
Begin separate concurrent meetings.	Meet to discuss: • What did we hear? • What points did we try to make? • What can we do to improve?	Separately meet and discuss: • What did we hear? • What points did we try to make? • What can we do to improve?	May meet separately or participate with project team. Share observations and comments.	Depart.
20 minutes Begin joint meeting.		Joint meeting: • Share insights and conclusions from the separate meetings. • Informal discussion • Bring to a close.		
60 minutes End				

Figure 6-14. Immediately after the review.

Some notes on the postreview meeting:

- These meetings are intentionally anticlimactic. They tend to be more relaxed and less reserved. Often this second hour is more "real" than the first hour.
- The feedback to both sides is invaluable. Both sides should try to be descriptive in giving feedback and nondefensive in receiving it.
- The joint meeting should be facilitated. Perhaps the quality advisor is in the best position to perform this function.
- After managers, project team leaders, and members have had sufficient experience with reviews, the postreview meeting may cease to be necessary.

Managers as Researchers

What the organization's leaders are doing in this phase is gathering information. This is, in other words, a *research* activity. The plan is a theory and the review is an effort to see whether the theory is proving itself to be valid or whether there must be adjustments to the theory—that is, adjustments to the plan. The managers are engaged, therefore, in several ongoing PDSA cycles and, therefore, several research efforts.

Phase 7. The Organization Learns to Improve and Integrates What Has Been Learned into Future Cycles.

It is not enough to improve. We must know how to design and develop *new* products and services, systems, and processes, not just improve old ones. We must learn to develop the new and improve the old fast enough to maintain an edge in the marketplace. We must learn to develop the new and improve the old fast enough to keep up with the pace of a changing world.

Here we discuss one approach to learning more rapidly. It is not magic, but it is systemic. We must develop *systems* for learning from our experience and integrating what we have learned into the organization's ongoing work. The system is described in Figure 6-15. The PDSA cycle must be a central strategy for everything we do. It is a cycle for learning and integrating new knowledge on a continuous basis.

A Review of Reviews

After several reviews, managers should meet to collate and compare what they have learned in the various reviews.

Affinity diagrams or relationship diagrams may be useful means for taking the various notes, comments, and anecdotal input and sort-

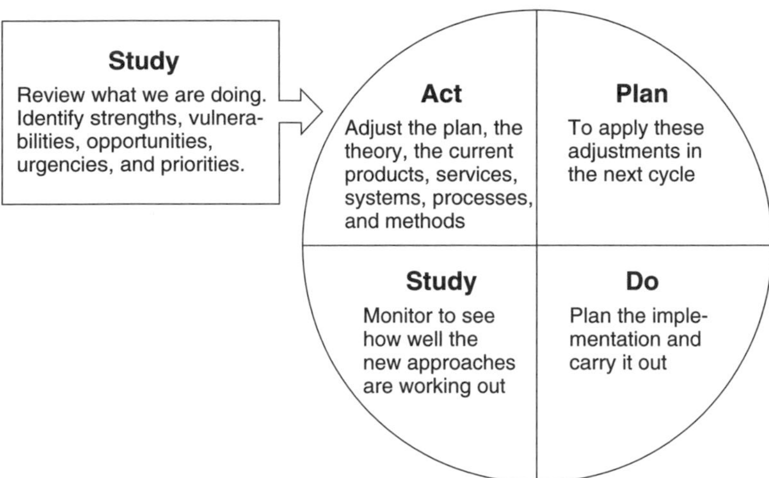

Figure 6-15. Learning from experience and integrating what we have learned.

ing them into some useful form. (See Brassard, 1989.) The purpose of these sessions is:

- To integrate learning into the organization,
- To prepare for next year's plan, and
- To improve on improvement.

CHANGE AND RESISTANCE TO CHANGE

Change is almost always difficult. However carefully you may plan for breakthrough improvement, you are likely to encounter resistance from some quarter. Therefore, we end this chapter with some comments on change.

When people change, why do they change? When people resist change, why do they resist change? The two most popular approaches to change—coercion and rationality—are also the two least effective approaches.

Change Strategy 1: Coercion

This may seem to be effective. The gun at the head or the threat of punishment can produce conformance. But it doesn't produce motivation, only movement. While the coercer may be motivated, the person coerced merely moves: "If we capture their vitals, the rest of them

The Irrationality of Change

People have known the harmfulness of smoking for generations. (My grandparents called cigarettes "coffin nails.") For the last 30 years we have had persuasive data confirming what we had already known to be true. Yet smoking persists, in spite of the reasons, data, and logic against it. The government's approach is to combine rationality (the Surgeon General's reports) with coercion (restrictions on advertising and sales to minors). This approach combines the two least effective approaches to change. These approaches are how parents commonly deal with their kids: lectures and rules. (If you want to increase the likelihood that a child will do something, forbid it!) Whatever our ages, such approaches are more likely to provoke the rebellious child in us.

It is interesting that the tobacco industry's response generally is to trigger our rebellious child. Rather than respond to the science of smoking-induced health hazards, they appeal to our desires to be free of parental-type constraints: "Don't let the Government restrict your freedom."

will follow." But those who use fear to win will have to find a way to coexist with those who lose. Those who lose will use their creativity to find a way to win. Coercion establishes an adversarial relationship that will be almost impossible to eliminate. Coercion leaves in its wake cynicism, grudges, distrust, and demotivation. Change through coercion is, at best, a temporary and fleeting victory. Management through fear and coercion is not a style of leadership. It is the abandonment of leadership, the abdication of leadership. Inducing fear represents not leadership but (in the words of David Couper, the retired chief of police of Madison, Wisconsin), "an excess of testosterone."

Change Strategy 2: Rationality

All change, even that which is coercively imposed, is wrapped in the rhetoric of rationality: "If we capture their intellects, the rest of them will follow." So goes the rationality strategy. Reason and logic may indeed be necessary, more for some than for others. But they are certainly not sufficient to bring about change.

There is an obvious difference between intellectually understanding something to be right or wrong and doing something about it. Explaining why change is important will not make the change happen. We are often disappointed, however, when our efforts to train and educate people do not result in people changing.

Change Strategy 3: The Socialization of Change

Change is generally not a rational process. Why do people change? Let me offer these statements as part of a change theory. *People change because:*

- They become aware of some conditions, factors, or circumstances that make them less content.
- They experience these conditions, factors, or circumstances as occurring outside their current ability to control.
- They become aware that others, whom they respect, are experiencing this discontent and inability to control the events.
- They also become aware that someone or some group whom they respect has proposed a way to deal with this shared experience of discontent and inability to control.
- They become aware of a groundswell of support, especially among people whom they respect, for this new approach.
- They join their respected peers in support of this new approach.

What is described above is not a rational process. Rationality will be used as the process of change unfolds and irrationality can derail the process or at least slow it down. But change does not result from a syllogism. It is seldom logical.

This theory of change suggests that for most people change is a collectively social and somewhat emotional transformation. Even a loner or a socially isolated individual can be affected by the social nature of change. Change is described as a groundswell, a bandwagon. A constituency begins to develop behind the experience of discontent and the agreed-upon approaches. Writers and pundits begin to refer to this constituency as though they were subspecies of the human race: baby boomers, generation X, WASPs, angry white males. The distinction between reality and perception blurs. Self-fulfilling prophecies begin to go to work. Change is a mess! Change becomes much less clean and orderly than the coercion approach or the rationality approach would allow.

Change in an organization is also a process of social transformation. The ideal approach to change is to help people understand the need for change and allow them to participate in planning the response to that need. If you want to encourage resentment and resistance to change, keep people uninformed and uninvolved. (I once heard a seminar presenter extol the virtues of what he called "stealth planning": Don't let people know what is going on until it is too late for them to do anything about it. This says more about his cynicism about people than his knowledge of planning change.)

Step in the change	Approach
• Understand the need	• Rational
• Discuss the need in groups	• Socialization
• Planning the response	• Rational
• Participation in the planning of the response	• Socialization
• Implementing and monitoring the change	• Rational
• Communication and feedback regarding the effectiveness of the change	• Socialization

Figure 6-16. The socialization of change.

As leaders of change, managers or any other change leaders must see themselves as the leaders of a process to sway the hearts of the critical mass. They must seek to create a constituency behind a new idea, building compatibility between the needs, hopes, and misgivings of people and the proposed new idea.

For more on the importance of *participation* in the process of change, see Chapter 10.

Resistance to Change: The Stages of Death

When faced with terminal illness or a near-death experience, we go through some predictable stages. Elisabeth Kübler-Ross (1969) first identified these stages of death. Her work has been confirmed by the research of others. The stages of death:

- Denial: "You have gotten my x-rays mixed up with someone else's."
- Anger: "It's not fair! I deserve better than this!"
- Bargaining: "If I shape up my life, can I survive this?"
- Depression: "I have no control! I don't know what will become of me. I mourn the loss of what once was."
- Acceptance: "I am ready to move on."

When we are faced with some inevitable need for change in our organization, we go through the equivalent stages. I have heard managers offer these forms of denial when they are faced with the need to change their approach, adopting the new philosophy described here:

- It won't work in:

— this culture
— this industry
— this state
— this company
— this plant
— this machine
— this crew
— this year

- Did you people ever have to meet a payroll?
- We're already doing it, have been for years.
- We don't have time. I don't have time.
- This is a good idea, I'll instruct my people to go do it.

I have concluded that these are all variations on a simple statement: "Please God, don't make me have to think about this!" When the need for change is obvious, desperate, and urgent, people are likely to move more swiftly through the stages. Part of the leading of change, however, usually involves patiently helping people through the stages of death. This, of course, becomes more of a challenge when the people in denial are those who should be leading the change.

Regarding any proposed change, there will be a distribution of people concerning their support for or resistance to the change, shown in Figure 6-17 as a bell-shaped distribution. If the change is seen as detrimental to or more beneficial to most people, the curve would be correspondingly skewed to the right or left.

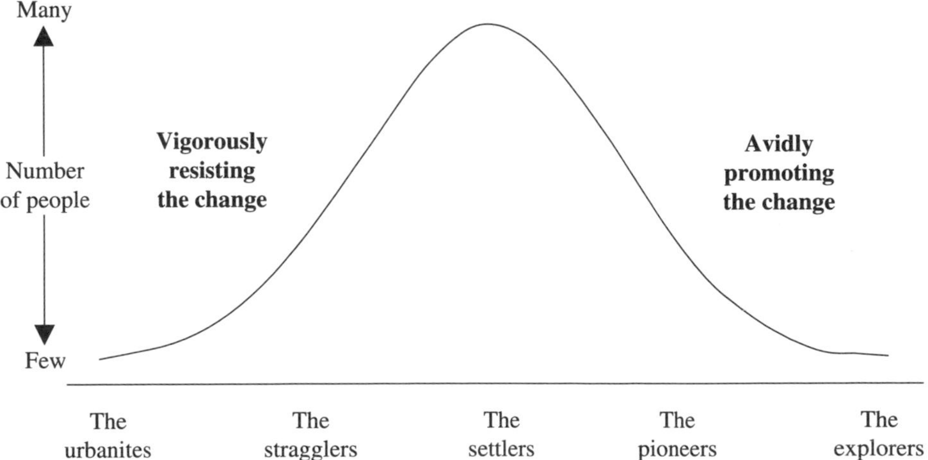

Figure 6-17. The continuum of resistance to change.

At the forefront in favor of change are the explorers. These are the Lewis and Clarks of change, the Chuck Yeagers and Yuri Gargarins, the first consumers of oysters and sushi, those who "boldly go where no one has gone before." In the context of a movement, such as the quality movement, these are the commandos who are so far ahead of the critical mass of people that most people are leery of them. When people say that Deming followers seem like a cult, I suspect that they have been subject to the zealousness of a Quality Commando.

The pioneers are not too far behind the explorers, but are prudent enough to wait and see what happens to the explorers before proceeding. The settlers are more conservative and less risk-taking concerning change. They will embrace something new when its viability has been proven. The stragglers are slow to embrace the change. They need security and predictability and even then may opt for the comfort of the old familiar way. The urbanites will visit the frontier of change only when it is a theme park. They may need to be dragged kicking and screaming into change, or at least exhorted to withhold judgment and let others give it a try.

Individually, we may experience ourselves as moving back and forth on the continuum from one change to another. Many people, however, seem habitually disposed in favor of, or opposed to, all changes.

Planning for change involves different strategies depending on whether the organization's leaders and influential people are pioneers or stragglers.

A Brief Glance at Influence

People have greater or lesser influence over others. They range from the movers and shakers to the moved and shaken. As shown in Figure 6-18, movers and shakers can have influence by virtue of their position in the *formal* organization. These are people who have hierarchical positions and titles of authority. *Informal* influence depends on something else, something often difficult to pin down. These individuals don't necessarily have a position that gives them influence, but they are the people others look to for indications of support or resistance regarding a proposed idea. Such influence may result from personal charisma, longtime experience, widespread respect and trust, intelligence, clarity of vision, persistence, access to information, or access to influential groups or individuals. We could each try to list the attributes of those who have influenced us. The characteristics of the informal movers and shakers might also explain why some members of the hierarchy have more influence than their peers: They may also be leaders at an informal level.

	Moved and shaken	Moderately influential	Movers and shakers
Formal organization	Those in the lower ranks of the hierarchy	Those in the middle ranks	Those in the top levels of the hierarchy
Informal organization	Those in the lower ranks of the hierarchy	No position of importance yet with moderate influence	Those without a high level position but with great influence

Figure 6-18. One's influence in the organization.

The Demography of Change

What is described here is a very political approach to change. It may sound Machiavellian. In fact, it can *be* Machiavellian, though it need not be. I have adapted this from some ideas I learned from Len Hirsch, who was a White House organization development specialist during the Carter administration. (This is not a Democratic approach to change. It is a political approach to change.)

The demography of change accepts without judgment that change is not a rational process. When done with sincerity and benevolence, it is an attempt to create *an agenda for listening*. It will help us think through the distribution of influence and agreement and help us plan whom we will approach and how we will approach them as we seek to build a constituency behind a proposed change.

Figures 6-19 and 6-20 combine the distribution of resistance, as shown in Figure 6-17, and the degrees of influence, as shown in Figure 6-18. Figure 6-19 uses numbers to identify nine different cells or stances regarding change. Figure 6-20 uses the same figures but applies descriptions rather than cell numbers.

Figures 6-19 and 6-20 provide a conceptual framework for analyzing the positioning of people regarding a proposed change. The vertical axis describes the degree of support an individual or group has for the change. The horizontal axis describes the degree of influence the individual or group has.

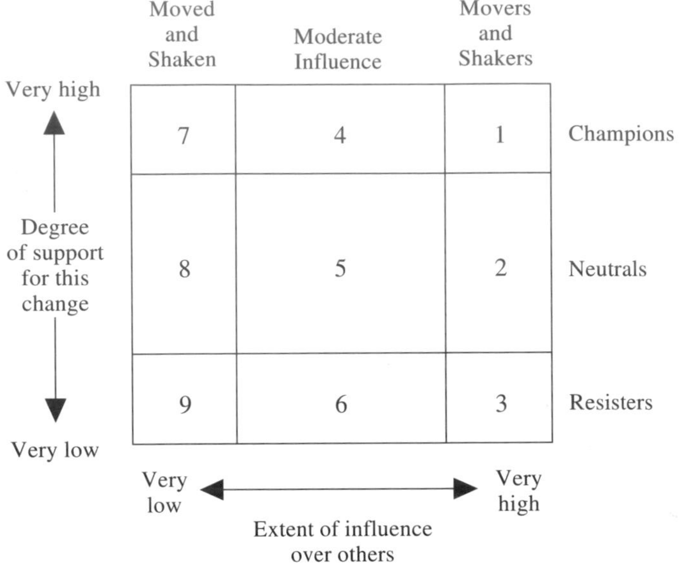

Figure 6-19.

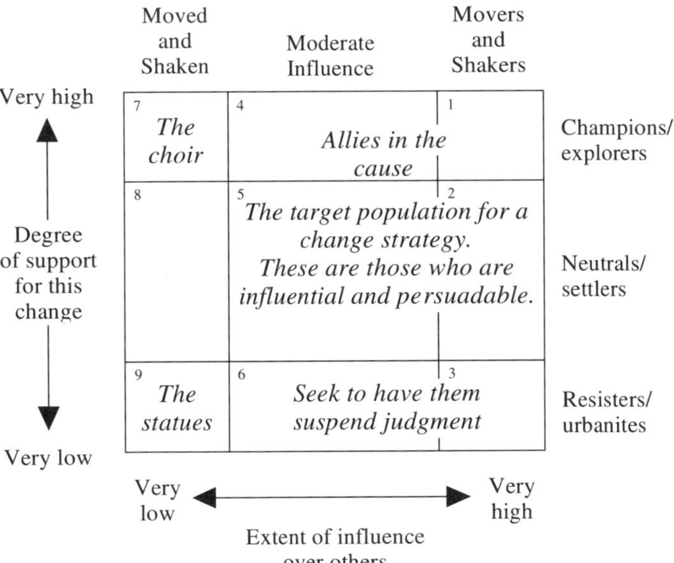

Figure 6-20.

Some Axioms for Change

1. Change would be easy if it weren't for all the people.
2. People don't resist change, they resist *being* changed (Borwick, 1969).
3. Ninety-five percent of all changes have nothing to do with improvement.
4. Change requires knowledge. Improvement requires wisdom (profound knowledge).
5. Changing the outside seldom changes the inside. Changing the structure (organizational chart) doesn't improve the system. Building a new garage doesn't turn a Yugo into a Lexus. Calling the old bosses team leaders doesn't make them that.
6. Some professional disciplines seek to preserve and protect the current status (e.g., corporate lawyers and accountants). Others seek to take the current status and make it look new and improved (marketing). These professions can get in the way of true improvement.

Guidelines for Applying the Demography of Change

- The objective should be to develop a constituency of influential support behind the proposed change.
- There is only so much time available to develop a constituency in support of the change. The demography of change should help you use your time more profitably.
- Without the support of the influential people (formal and informal), you will not create a critical mass.
- The best use of your time is with those who are influential and who are still neutral regarding the proposed change (cells 2 and 5 in Figure 6-19).
- Don't spend a lot of time with those in cells 1 and 4, the influential supporters. It may be comforting to talk to them, but you and they should be approaching the 2's and 5's. Spending time with the 7's is generally not useful. There is no need to preach to the choir.
- Spending time with the 9's is not a high priority. They may be fine people and certainly deserving of respect. Time with them will not have great payoff in terms of building a constituency. Don't, therefore, preach to the statues.

- Resisters with influence are important to approach (3 and 6). Seek to help them move to a more neutral stance or seek to get them to suspend judgment and tolerate an experiment.
- How do you spend time with the 2's, 5's, 3's, and 6's? *Listen* to them.
- Don't seek to *persuade* them; rather, try to *understand* them and their perspectives and concerns.
- Understanding them will allow you to see how (or whether) the proposed change can address their needs.
- Understanding them may help you shape the approaches and priorities.

The demography of change should not be used as a tool of manipulation. Rather, it should be a strategy for understanding and empathy.

SUMMARY

Chapter 5 might have been described as "getting ready for change." It presented the larger-scale, longer-term concepts such as purpose, mission, vision, values, and culture. Chapter 6 has described a more practical approach to systemic change called breakthrough planning. It is the hard-work part of change, requiring clarity, commitment, and persistence. We have also explored other concepts regarding change: how to facilitate successful change and how to deal with resistance to change.

Chapter 7 discusses the need for measurement, an essential dimension of the new philosophy.

CHAPTER SIX ACTIVITIES

1. Describe how you identify and select priorities in your organization.

2. In what respects is your method different from what is described as Breakthrough Improvement?

3. What did you learn from the process by which you developed this year's plan? How will you incorporate what you learned into the process for developing next year's plan?

4. How successful have you been in your pursuit of this year's priorities? How will you include this in the development of next year's priorities?

5. Describe some recent change in your organization.

   A. Was it successful?

   B. How do you know?

   C. Was it an improvement?

   D. How do you know?

REFERENCES

Ackoff, R. 1981. *Creating the corporate future*. New York: John Wiley & Sons.

Bennis, W., Benne, K., and Chin, R. 1985. *The planning of change*. New York: Holt, Rinehart and Winston.

Borwick, I. 1969. Team improvement laboratory. *Personal Journal,* January.

Brassard, M. 1989. *Memory jogger plus*. Methuen, MA: GOAL/QPC.

Heffernan, G., Moran, J., and Nadler, G. 1994. *Breakthrough thinking in total quality management*. Englewood Cliffs, NJ: Prentice Hall.

Kepner, C.H., and Tregoe, B.B. 1981. *The new rational manager*. Princeton, NJ: Princeton Research Press.

Kübler-Ross, E. 1969. *On death and dying*. New York: Macmillan Company.

Nadler, G., and Hibino, S. 1990. *Breakthrough thinking*. Rocklin, CA: Prima Publishing.

Scholtes, P. 1988. *The team handbook*. Madison, WI: Joiner Associates Incorporated.

Wood, G.R., and Munshi, K.F. 1991. Hoshin Kanri: A systematic approach to breakthrough improvement. *Total Quality Management,* 2, 3.

7 KEEPING TRACK: MEASUREMENTS OF IMPROVEMENT, PROGRESS, AND SUCCESS

INTRODUCTION

We measure what is important to us. We spend time almost every day keeping track of things we want to keep track of:

- Some keep their checkbooks balanced.
- Some mark the ever-increasing heights of their children on a wall in the kitchen.
- Some keep track of their own weight, pulse rate, body temperature, blood pressure, triglyceride level, body fat percentage, glucose levels, and ketones. The list could go on and on.
- Some monitor scores on tests and grades on report cards.
- Some simply look in a mirror (for longer or shorter periods of time), checking for necessary adjustments and arriving at self-judgments that may or may not have anything to do with what they see.
- Some focus on mechanically based measures (mpg or rpm, for example).
- Some devour sports statistics: RBIs, ERAs, pass completion percentages. Indeed, for most people, statistics and statisticians are sports terms.
- Some keep track of financial data (Dow Jones averages, currency exchange rates, daily performance of stocks, bonds, or commodities).
- Some look at weather data.

We measure things for two basic reasons:

1. To see how things are going. (Just how hot did it get today?)
2. To predict the future. (What are the chances of it being cooler tomorrow?)

These two uses of data sometimes require different types of data gathering and analysis. Data that help you understand the current situation do not necessarily help you understand the trends and patterns that will help predict the future.

Another refinement of the notion of different types of data is to look at data that describe the *results* you get; for example, how many burnt cookies in a batch. Or you can look at data regarding the *process,* indicators that tell you how well things are going before you ever know what the results will be; for example, the temperature of the oven in which the cookies are baking. To predict the future, you need to understand the process (all the factors that are necessary for good cookies) and you must monitor those key indicators of the process (measures of ingredients, temperature of oven, time of baking, etc.).

If you are someone who begins to clutch when you anticipate the prospect of developing business indicators and measurements, you might find some consolation in knowing that you are already measuring things all the time. Perhaps the difference is that what you measure in the rest of your life is part of your automatic routine (clocks, thermometers, thermostats) and you are monitoring things that are important to you.

SOME BASICS REGARDING DATA

The first thing I had to learn about data is that the word is plural, as in, "Data are often spoken of as though they were singular." Here are some other basics regarding data.

Data are all over the place. There is an abundance of data everywhere.

- Every system, process, or action produces data.
- Data are always there, available, and captureable.
- Most data, however, are not worth capturing. They are seldom useful. Even some data routinely used in our businesses are useless (e.g., tons of product produced yesterday).

It is important, therefore, to determine what data are important to gather.

- If you or your people end up gathering unused and useless data, you will get annoyed and give it up.
- Ask, "If we had these data what would we do with them?" and, "If we didn't have these data, how would (or do) we suffer?"

Start with purpose, customers, safety, and where you suffer pain.

- What indicators will tell you if you are on track, serving your organization's purpose?
- What indicators will tell you if you are routinely serving your customers' needs and delighting them?
- What indicators will help you monitor the conditions that create accidents and injuries?
- What indicators will help you monitor the causes and occurrences of known, chronic problems and breakdowns?

All data vary.

How well or poorly you are doing today, as measured by your indicators, is different from how you did yesterday. Tomorrow it will be different again. In Chapter 2 we briefly addressed the issue of variation and its causes.

When you gather and analyze data on your key indicators, you should take care to do so in a way that allows you to see the range and average of variation and to determine statistically the capacity and predictability of your systems. (For a wonderful reference on this subject, see Wheeler, 1993.)

Types of Data

We might think in terms of the four types of data shown in Figure 7-1. (As you get more deeply into this, you will learn that there are many more. These four are a good start.)

	Opinion data	Observable data
Process data		
Results data		

Figure 7-1. Four types of data.

Opinion Data

Those gathering opinion data don't look to *see* what is real. They ask people what they *think* is real. Those who advocate opinion surveys will argue that facts are feelings and feelings are facts. It is someone's *opinion* that leads him or her to buy a product or vote for a candidate. Therefore, opinions are important.

Observable Data

These data derive from seeing what is there and recording it. Those who advocate using this type of data will argue that because something is assigned a number doesn't mean it is data. Knowing what people believe to be the greatest safety hazards is not as useful or relevant as seeing what safety hazards are the most frequent causes of accidents, the most harmful, etc. People's opinions will only reveal the gap between what is and what is thought to be ... in other words, ignorance.

There is a lag between observable data and opinion data (as shown in Figure 7-2).

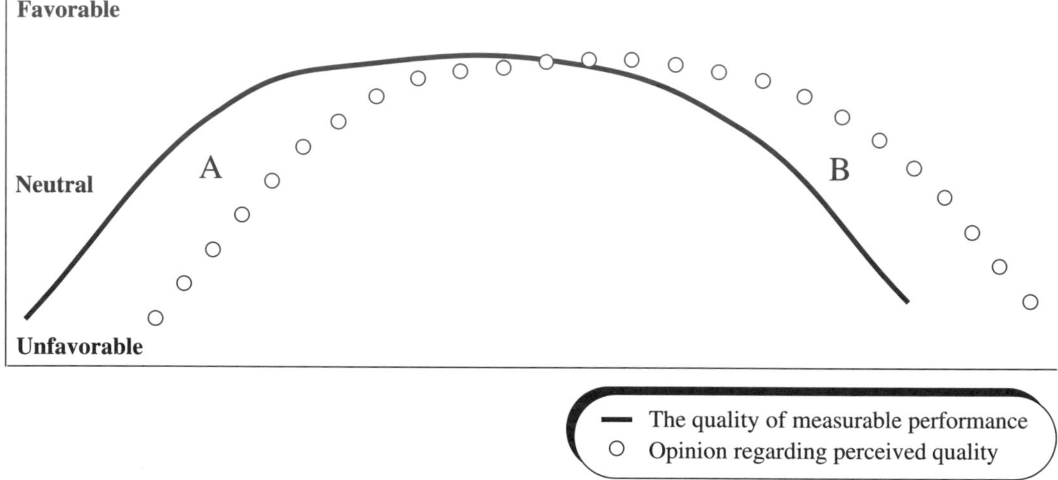

Figure 7-2. The lag between observation and opinion over time.

Some examples of this lag are:

- The actual performance of a company's product versus the customers' perceptions of the company's reputation and performance.
- The public's perception of some problem in society (e.g., crime) and the actual occurrence of that problem.

Comment: One common form of dissemblance (i.e., dishonesty) is to seek to manipulate the perception without a commensurate improvement of quality (trying to perpetuate the B gap: calling something "new" and "improved" when it is neither).

Results Data

The bottom line: After everything has happened, results are what you have. Products manufactured, services delivered, errors, defects, breakdowns, costs—these are all the results of other actions and interactions. You cannot avoid these results. They have already occurred. You can only hope to do better next time.

Process Data

This is a bit of a misnomer because all data are the consequence of some antecedent event. Here, however, we refer to data that are suffi-

What Kind of Food Do Customers Prefer?

One common form of feedback used by restaurants is a response card that invites customers to rate the quality of food on a 3-, 4-, or 5-point scale. The trouble, of course, is that no one knows the difference between one number and another, why someone gave the food a low or high ranking, or what to do with the information.

A restaurant owner could simply keep track of what gets ordered from the menu or what gets selected from the buffet. However, this may be more a measure of how well the dish is described or how good it looks.

The Joban Hawaiian Center in Japan used a clever measure of customer satisfaction: They measured the food returned uneaten, dishes that looked good enough to select off the buffet table, but didn't taste good enough to eat.

This is an example of observable results data. It is too late to change this selection of dishes. But the data may be used to improve future menus.

The Joban Hawaiian Center was the first service organization to win the coveted Deming Prize. They were assisted in this effort by the talented teacher Yukihiro Ando.

ciently early indicators such that we can adjust the process before the undesirable results occur.

Some Guidelines on Data

- Observable data are preferable to opinion data. We will know we have succeeded in making this point when politicians, marketing people, and news reporters understand and agree with us on this.
- Process data are preferable to results data. The further upstream we can observe the key characteristics of the process, the better we can control the process and its output.
- Results data can be used in two ways:
  - — They can tell us how successful we are in our attempts to understand, monitor, and control the process.
  - — They can offer clues about what additional process, improvements, and indicators we need to put in place.
- If opinions are all you can get, then presume you have missed some possible observable indicators and look again for them.
- Opinion data are okay when all we need are opinions. The problems occur when we use opinions as a substitute for real-

ity. "Crime is an increasing problem, according to a survey conducted by...."

- Some problems with opinion surveys and feedback forms are as follows:
  - — It is difficult to formulate unambiguous and unbiased questions.
    - - Will every respondent interpret the question in the same way?
    - - Does the question lead toward or away from particular answers?
  - — They provide a snapshot, not many views at various points over time.
  - — Reactions are influenced by unrelated events.
  - — We cannot assume that those who don't respond are adequately represented by those who do. (Users of mailed surveys usually boast when the response rate is as low as 20 percent.)
  - — The forms seldom have open questions. Instead they have structured categories of response that don't necessarily correspond to the experience of the person responding.
  - — The questions usually betray a culprit-oriented management philosophy. ("Was your waiter or waitress prompt in taking your order?")
  - — Note: Standard market research uses surveys. However, well-done surveys combined with applied research technology can compensate for most of the shortcomings that are characteristic of most surveys.

SOME THINGS TO CONSIDER BEFORE YOU START MEASURING

Start with Purpose

As we continue to emphasize, the purpose is a necessary ingredient to successful measurement.

- If you are going to measure X, first determine what the purpose of X is. Then determine the purpose of the measurement. Example: time cards.

Difficult Data versus Easy Data

When the city of Madison, Wisconsin, did taxpayer surveys in the 1970s, they discovered that the biggest problem in summer was mosquitoes and in winter it was snow. This could have been discovered much less expensively by looking out the window.

- — What do time cards measure? Employees' comings and goings.
- — Why are employee comings and goings being measured?
  - To analyze the system (e.g., to study patterns of lateness)?
  - To feed into another system (e.g., billing)?
  - To control people's behavior (e.g., play "Gotcha!" with tardy employees)?
- Imagine you have the data. What will you do with it? Is there an easier way to get the data?

Who Are the Measurers and Who Are the Measurees?

There are those who do the measuring (plan to take data, take data, analyze and interpret the data) and those whose work is measured. Sometimes measuring is done directly and explicitly (e.g., time cards), sometimes more indirectly and implicitly (breakdowns, waste, customer complaints).

- Who are the measurers and interpreters and why have they been selected to do that?
- How will measuring affect the relationship between the one measuring and the one being measured?
  - — What was the relationship to begin with (trust? respect?), and what is the desired relationship?
  - — There can be a certain paternalism implied in measurement, especially if it is more directly and explicitly examining the work of an individual (tardiness, absence from work, etc.). This is shown in Figure 7-3. (See also Chapter 2 on motivation.)
- To some extent the potential paternalism can be allayed by the style used by the measurer and the degree to which the one being measured is allowed to participate in the measurement process.

Figure 7-3. The implied paternalism of measurement.

Drive out Fear
(Deming's Point 8)

While Deming was very humanitarian in his values, Point 8 did not derive primarily from his feelings for people. Deming was aware of what fear does to data. I have seen him use this picture.

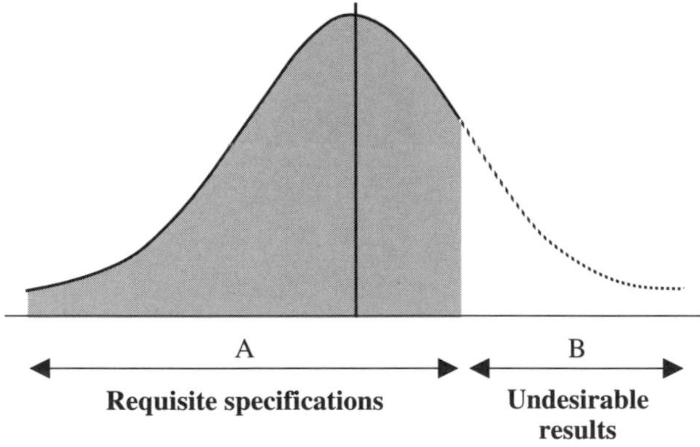

The data from the shop floor indicate that performance, while varied, falls within the requisite specifications (area A). However, the data are aborted, the distribution interrupted by something. What happened to area B, the undesirable results? They were consumed by fear. They were hidden and buried, never reported.

Measurement in an Environment of Fear and Distrust

Where there has been a history of adversarial and paternalistic relationships, measurement will be difficult. It may be necessary to heal the relationship before dealing with measures that may cause the one measured to be suspicious.

Recall what was said about trust in Chapter 2. For you to trust me, you must be confident that I am competent and that I am benevolent toward you. If either perception is lacking, trust is impaired.

One who is distrustful of the measurer will have these questions:

- Are the data legitimate: properly gathered and analyzed, reliable, consistent, accurate?
- Will the data be used against me?
- Is there a built-in bias in the measurement system? Will there be self-fulfilling prophecies (the data confirm what the measurer knew the results would be)?

Measurement and Improvement

Figure 7-4 shows a system of improvement. These are the interdependent components of problems and solutions. Each shapes and influences the others. Each offers opportunities for measurement.

If data are to be used for improvement (rather than to control employees), we should use some systemic view of improvement such as that pictured in Figure 7-4.

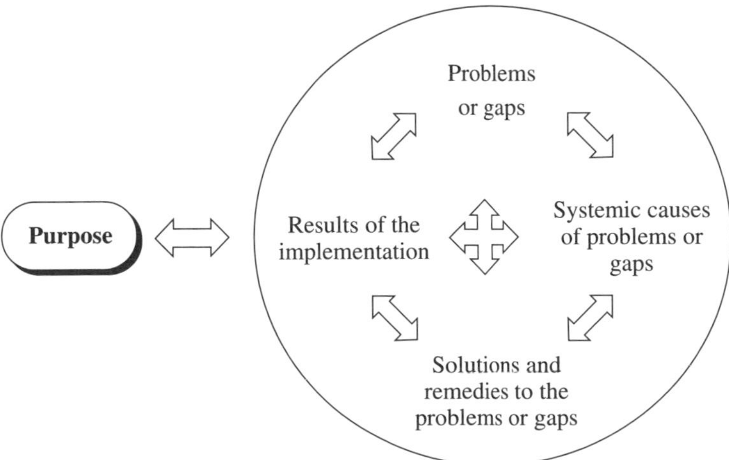

Figure 7-4. A system of improvement.

Some measurements we will need are:

- The nature and patterns of the problems.
- Conditions in the system that cause the problem.
- The solutions or remedies developed and the results of those interventions.
- The relationships between the results obtained, the problems and their causes, the solutions implemented, and the purpose of the organization, system, process, or whatever is under consideration.
- The connections between any of the components of this interactive system of improvement. The data should tell you whether your plan is working and your theories are holding true. An example of a theory: We believe sales are down (problem), and we can improve them by offering incentives to the sales force (solutions). The system described in Figure 7-4 may help identify what to measure (the patterns and trends of sales before and after the incentives). It may also suggest what is missing in your thought process. (What are the causes of the problem?) Similar frameworks of questions will be explored in Chapter 8.

HINTS FOR GETTING STARTED

Step 1. Define the purpose of the data-gathering system as a whole.

- Creating a measurement system will be a lot of work. Why are you subjecting yourself and your people to this?
- How will the whole system be used?
- Who will benefit from the whole system and how will they benefit?
- Pick a network of measures:
  - — Pick a vital few to begin with.
  - — Identify a few results measures and a few process measures.
- Perhaps the SIPOC model will be useful in designing the network of measures (see Chapter 3).
- Identify useful outside resources (e.g., trade associations, consultants).

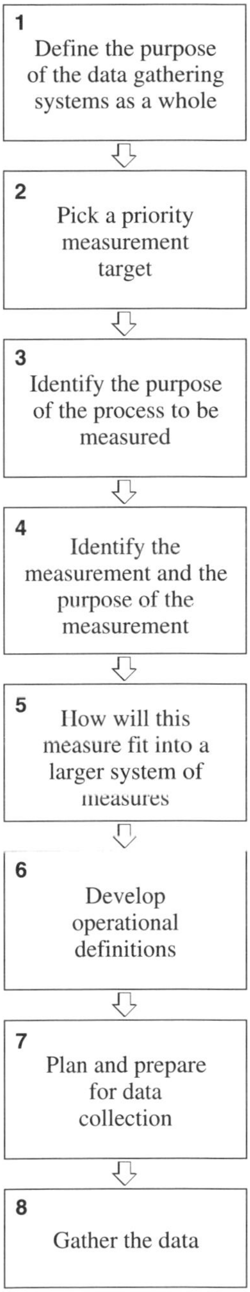

1 Define the purpose of the data gathering systems as a whole

⇩

2 Pick a priority measurement target

⇩

3 Identify the purpose of the process to be measured

⇩

4 Identify the measurement and the purpose of the measurement

⇩

5 How will this measure fit into a larger system of measures

⇩

6 Develop operational definitions

⇩

7 Plan and prepare for data collection

⇩

8 Gather the data

Step 2. Pick a priority measurement target.

- Where will you start?
- Why will you start there? (For example, "The hiring process, because we have not adequately attracted, recruited, and hired sufficient numbers of competent employees into entry-level production floor positions.")

Step 3. Identify the purpose of the process being measured.

For example, to maintain a competent workforce in our production areas by attracting, recruiting, screening, hiring, training, and retaining good employees.

Step 4. Identify the measurement and the purpose of the measurement.

For example, the first measurement may be turnover by frequency and job type. The purpose is to learn how many and how frequently employees in the production areas leave their jobs, the reasons they leave, where they go, and other relevant patterns to such turnover. The data will be used by the HR department to identify needed improvements and to provide a baseline against which to measure our success or progress. Executive managers want to see whether our wages and working conditions are okay.

Imagine you have completed the collecting of data and they are on the table in front of you. What will you want them to tell you? What will you want to learn? What questions do you want answered? Thinking of these in advance will help you design a better measurement system.

Step 5. How will this measurement fit into a larger system of measures?

For example, this measure is part of a larger attempt to examine and improve employee satisfaction. In addition, we have identified employee turnover as one of the key factors that gets in the way of consistently high quality.

Step 6. Develop operational definitions.

What is the operational definition of a "turnover"? The definition should be such that several different people counting the number and frequency of turnovers will be looking for and counting the same thing. When measuring something experienced by the customer, use the customers' definition and method of measurement. (See the sidebar on airline departures.)

You should, through your operational definitions, understand when the process has:

- Changed
- Improved
- Deteriorated
- Completed its task
- Met expectations
- Created disappointment

Step 7. Prepare and plan for data collection.

- Identify the likely patterns of data and design your methods to capture those patterns. This is called stratifying the data.
- Plan how to preserve the integrity of the data.
- Decide the method for gathering the data: Design and test the checklists, control charts, etc.
- What technology will be needed to support this?
- Train the data gatherers.

Step 8. Gather the data.

- Try out your method on a small scale. Work out the flaws.
- Then do it on a larger scale.
- Use continual PDSA.
- When this measurement system is in place, standardize it to assure it continues and then move on to another, starting at Step 1.

A good resource for how to gather good data is *The Team Handbook* (Scholtes, 1988, pp. 2–30 ff. and pp. 5–38 ff.).

What Is an On-Time Departure?

For most airlines, on-time means within 10 minutes of the scheduled departure time, and departure means the separation of the jetway from the airplane. I have seen commercial airplanes conform to this definition by backing away from the gate within the allowed 10-minute window. Then the aircraft paused within several feet of the gate while baggage was loaded onto the plane.

Kevin Jenkins, the president and CEO of Canadian Airlines, announced at an annual quality conference in Alberta in September, 1995 that his people were now measuring on-time departures using "the customers' definition of departure" and "the customers' watch" for telling time. Imagine that!

The Data Gatherers' Hall of Fame: The Intrepid Craighead Brothers

If there is a data gatherers' hall of fame, the Craighead twins, John and Frank Jr., are surely charter members. The Craigheads were participating in a study of hibernation. Part of the operational definition of hibernation, distinguishing it from mere sleep, is body temperature: Hibernating animals have a body temperature 2 or 3 degrees lower than when they are sleeping. Many species merely sleep through the winter without hibernating.

One research project involved an attempt to determine whether grizzly bears hibernated or not. The brothers Craighead took on the challenge. This task involved traveling to Alaska, finding grizzly bears in their caves, and taking their temperatures with a rectal thermometer. A daunting task.

Arriving at the bears' caves, the Craighead brothers discovered a grizzly bear asleep—or hibernating. They, of course, didn't know. Unfortunately, in one of those fateful challenges that only data gatherers could truly appreciate, the grizzly bear was sitting in an upright position. The Craigheads rose to the challenge, fulfilled their duty and took the bear's temperature in the prescribed manner.

Their finding? The bear was not hibernating. It was asleep!

There are several unanswered questions that the connoisseurs of good data are left to ponder:

- How *did* the Craigheads insert the thermometer?
- Was the discovery by the Craigheads that grizzly bears don't hibernate, or was it that their hibernation can be disrupted by the intrusion of a thermometer into their … subconscious?
- What did the brothers do upon discovering that they were in the presence of a grizzly bear that was merely asleep (and whose sleep had been, presumably, disturbed)?
- Finally, why the hell did they volunteer to do this in the first place?

EXAMPLES OF INDICATORS

This section will seem less than stimulating, especially after the adventures of the brothers Craighead. Contained here are lists of indicators that some organizations have found useful. Look for those that may be relevant to your type of work. They are intended to stir your imagination. You cannot simply implant these into your system. You must decide what is important for you and develop your own indicators.

A. **Indicators that seem to be useful to many different types of organizations**

1. ***Customers***

- Number of complaints: patterns and types
- Number or percentage of repeat customers (not a favorable indicator for some professions, e.g., prisons)
- Our performance regarding fulfillment of the basics (Kano model)
- Our performance regarding other key quality characteristics
- Number of customers referred to you by other customers
- Backlog of orders or requests
- Number of orders placed through the Web site

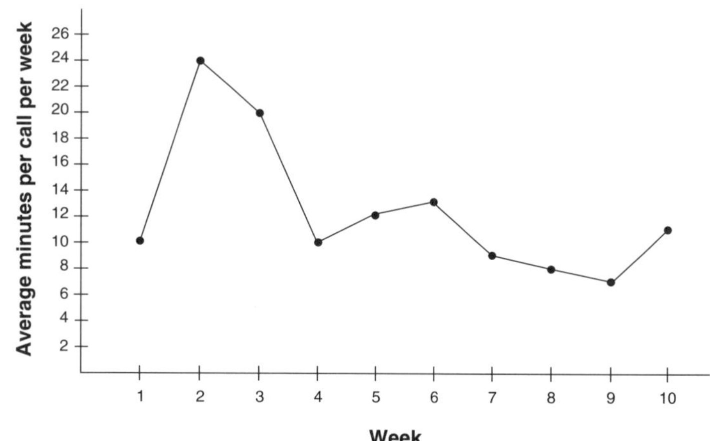

Figure 7-5. Run chart on response time for customer inquiries.

2. ***Employees***

- Turnover percentage
- Reasons for departure, by type
- Number of grievances
- Absence from work, by type
- Number of applicants for vacancies
- Proportion of apparently competent applicants
- Cycle time from the time a position is known to be a coming vacancy, to the time it is filled

What to Do with Customer Complaints

There are two basic types of response when a customer complains. Both are important.

- *Damage control:* Tells the customer that you truly regret that this problem occurred and that you will rectify it.
- *Process or system management:* Improves the process so that this problem will not occur again.

The difference is illustrated in Diagram 7-1.

Diagram 7-1. What to do with a customer complaint.

Customer complains

Damage control: Rectify the immediate problem. Placate the customer.

Enter the information, with other complaints, into an improvement planning process:

- Identify patterns
- Identify priorities
- Institute improvement activities

Satisfy the immediate customer need

- Systems improvement
- Removing the cause of the problem to prevent its recurrence

Two necessary responses when a customer complains

The *process or system improvement* response requires that the systems be in place to capture and record the complaint, to routinely route the information to those who plan for process and system improvement, and to integrate this complaint with others for analysis, planning, and priority setting. As customers we have all had the experience of making a complaint to someone who may be sincerely apologetic, while knowing that our complaint has moved as far into the organization as it is ever going to get. Nothing is in place to help convert our complaint into process improvement. When a complaint from a customer results in some worker being reprimanded, it does twice the harm. It discourages the customers from complaining again and it is a signal that no process will be improved as a result of the complaint.

- Reasons qualified candidates turn down offers
- Hours/quarter spent in education and training
- Number of suggestions
- Proportion of suggestions fulfilled
- Overtime
- Number of accidents, injuries, incidents, close calls

3. ***Operations***
   - Cycle times
     - Order to delivery, by type
     - Breakdown to start up, by type
     - Shutdown to startup
     - Request/question to response/answer, by type
     - Awareness of problem to resolution, by type
   - Frequency and patterns of changes in design or policy
   - Output measures
     - Number of products made per week, shipped per week
     - Number of services delivered
     - Backlog of orders or requests
   - Performance on key process indicators
   - Proportion of process indicators and output measures that are in statistical control

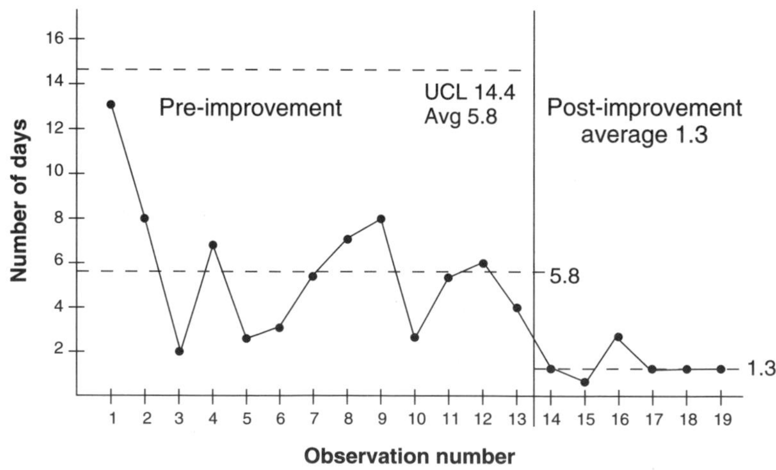

Figure 7-6. Cycle time for book delivery time between library branches.

- Number of processes that are standardized
- Percent of services and deliveries that are on time (customer's definition)
- Amount of waste
  - Proportion of output scrapped, by type
  - Proportion of output reworked, by type
  - Proportion of first pass yield (outputs that succeed "first time through")
  - Proportion of cycle time spent waiting (bottlenecks), by type
  - Frequency and patterns of remedial activities
  - Frequency and patterns of field failures
  - Time elapsed between delivery/installation and the first field failure or user request for assistance
- Amount of work-in-progress (uncompleted and somewhere between order and delivery)
- Inventory
  - Products and support information, by type and by week, month, or quarter
  - Supplies, by type and by week, month, or quarter
  - Materials, by type and by week, month, or quarter
  - Equipment, by type and by week, month, or quarter
  - Back orders, by type of item
  - Range and average of variance of high-volume items
  - Percent over or under estimated need
  - Gaps between recorded inventory and actual count, by type and other patterns
- Equipment breakdown, by type
- Frequency and patterns of maintenance
- Order
  - Length of time to take an order, by type
  - Frequency of order variance and patterns of order intake
  - Frequency of errors, omissions, inaccuracies, by type

4. ***Shipping/delivery***
   - Gap between promised time or date and the actual delivery time or date
   - Cycle time, by type of product or service, deliver/shipper, destination
   - Frequency and patterns of errors, inaccuracies, omissions in delivery
5. ***Budgeting/forecasting***
   - Percent over or under projected costs, by type
   - Percent over or under projected time estimates, by type
   - Percent over or under assessed value, by type
   - Percent over or under projected revenue/income, by type
6. ***Payroll***
   - Time to process, by type of adjustment
   - Timeliness of the submission of information
   - Payroll errors, by type, by cause
7. ***Finances***
   - Volume of sales
   - Earnings, by type
   - Costs
   - Revenues, by type
   - Gross profits, by type
   - Net profits, by type
   - Budget variances

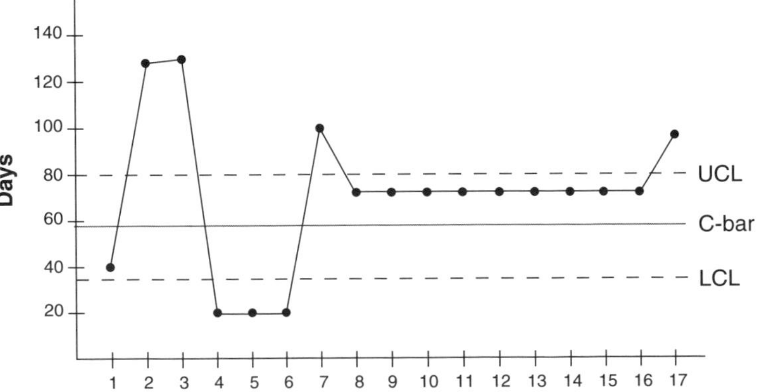

Figure 7-7. Control chart on time to process training reimbursement.

- Cycle time for budgeting process
- Cash flow, actual versus projected
- Cost of money
- Net return on investments, assets

8. ***New product/service development***
   - Time and budget for research and development
   - "Hit rate" for new ideas (proportion of proposals that end up with working products and services)
   - Cycle times, ideas/proposals to working products/services

B. **Additional indicators for specific applications**

1. ***Manufacturing***
   - Frequency and patterns of warranty claims or returns
   - Frequency and patterns of pounds of material disposed or emitted, by type
   - Frequency and type of engineering changes
   - Frequency and type of production changes
   - Scheduled production versus actual production
   - Supplier measures
     — Errors, inaccuracies, and omissions in shipments from suppliers, by type

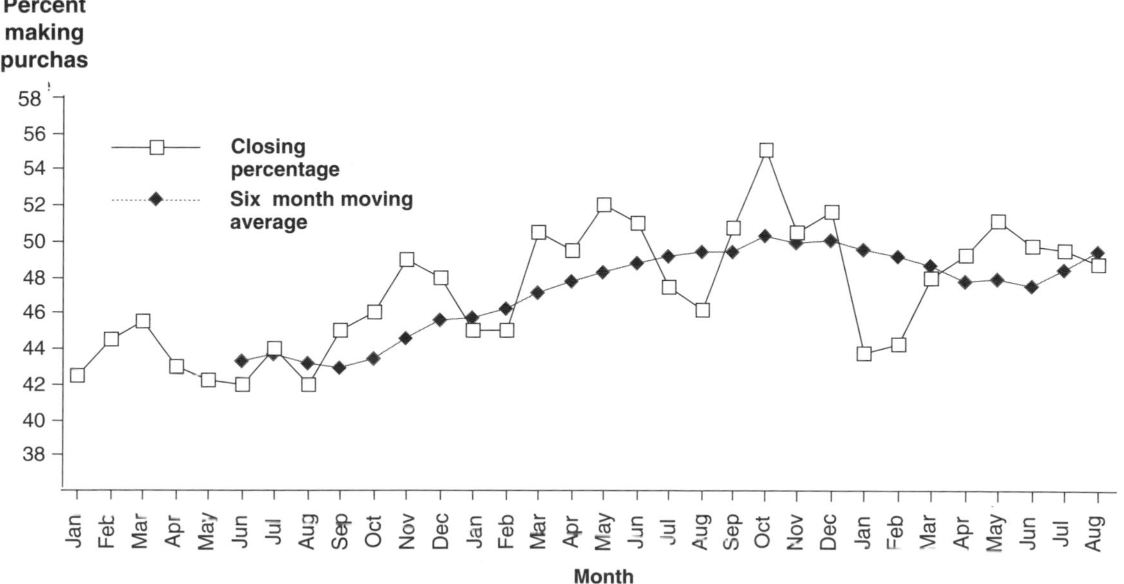

Figure 7-8. Percentage of visitors making a purchase.

   - Patterns of cycle time from when we order until they deliver
   - Conformance to our basics (Kano model) and to our other key quality characteristics
   - Patterns of variation and special causes
   - Actual cost versus promised cost

2. ***Retail***
   - Closings (percent of customers entering the door who purchase something)
   - Sales per square foot
   - Time elapsed between a customer entering the store and finding what he or she wants
   - Patterns of waiting time at cashier
   - Patterns of waiting time for customer on the phone
   - Patterns of waiting for personal service (information, fittings, etc.)
   - Out-of-stock items, by type
   - Requests for items never in stock, by type
   - Fulfillment of basics and other key quality characteristics of the customers
   - Cycle times from our customers' orders to our deliveries to them
   - Cycle times from our order to our suppliers' delivery
3. ***Person-to-person professional services***
   - Frequency and patterns of on-time arrival by clients/patients
   - Patterns, causes, and types of customer waiting time
   - Patterns and types of waiting times for the service provider
   - Time per visit by type of service
   - Time for completed service
   - Frequency and patterns of type of service
   - Time for diagnosis or problem/need identification for type of service
4. ***Billing/invoicing***
   - Cycle time for invoice sent to payment received
   - Dunning: types, patterns, frequency
   - Cycle time for credit clearance

- Frequency and patterns of credit memos and debit memos
- Frequency and patterns of accounts receivable over 60 days

5. ***Banks*** *(see Deming, 1982, pp. 227–238)*
   - Cycle time, loan application to approval
   - Rejection rate, by type: personal loan
   - Rejection rate, by type: commercial loan
   - Frequency and patterns of errors and rejections for machine processed checks
   - Default rate on loans: frequency and pattern
   - Frequency of errors on accounts, by type
   - Errors reported by customers and not picked up in-house (frequency and patterns)
   - Machine downtime
   - Past due accounts, by type
6. ***Health care/hospital***
   - Percentage of patients who have restored various degrees of functionality, by type of illness/injury/procedure
   - Percentage of patients who must be readmitted after discharge
   - Pain experienced, by type of illness/injury/procedure
   - *Laboratory*
     - — Cycle time from receipt of sample/specimen to lab work
     - — Cycle time from lab work to patient's record
     - — Percentage of lab rework, by type
   - *Admissions* (regular or emergency)
     - — Cycle time: how long to admit
     - — Waiting time for patient
     - — Errors/omissions on admissions
   - *Pharmacy/drug administration*
     - — Order to delivery for hospital prescriptions
     - — Incorrect dosage (frequency and patterns)
       - Wrong drug
       - Wrong amount

        - Wrong procedure
        - Errors in recording administration of drug on the patient's record
    - Number and patterns of toxic reactions to drugs
- *Medical records*
    - Percentage of completeness
    - Types of omissions
    - Types of inaccuracies
    - Patterns by type of patient, floor, shift
- Number of surgical procedures, by type
- Percentage of surgical procedures with complications
- Correlation between pre-op diagnosis and post-op diagnosis
- Number of transfusions
- Percentage of reaction to transfusion, by type

This should be a sufficient sampling of indicators to give some sense of how to select what is important and create a system of measurements around these indicators. Remember, you must select and design your own measures. Don't simply copy from another organization.

DATA NEED NOT BE BORING

I want to conclude this chapter with a plug for data. We have all been exposed to data that are, for the most part, stagnant and boring. I hated math in school, hated statistics in grad school, and find most columns of numbers to be a sure cure for consciousness.

I found out later in life that the problem was not so much my inadequacy with things numeric. The problem was that the math and statistics taught to me were boring and the method by which they were taught was even more boring. Data and statistics are too important to be handed over to mathematicians and statisticians. I would rather be taught by someone who loves data but hates the conventional uses of data.

Four Examples of the Imaginative Use of Data

In his book, *The Visual Display of Quantitative Information,* Edward Tufte (1983) gives several examples of how to display data. One of the most moving diagrams is shown in Figure 7-9. It was drawn in 1861 by a French engineer, Charles Joseph Minard.

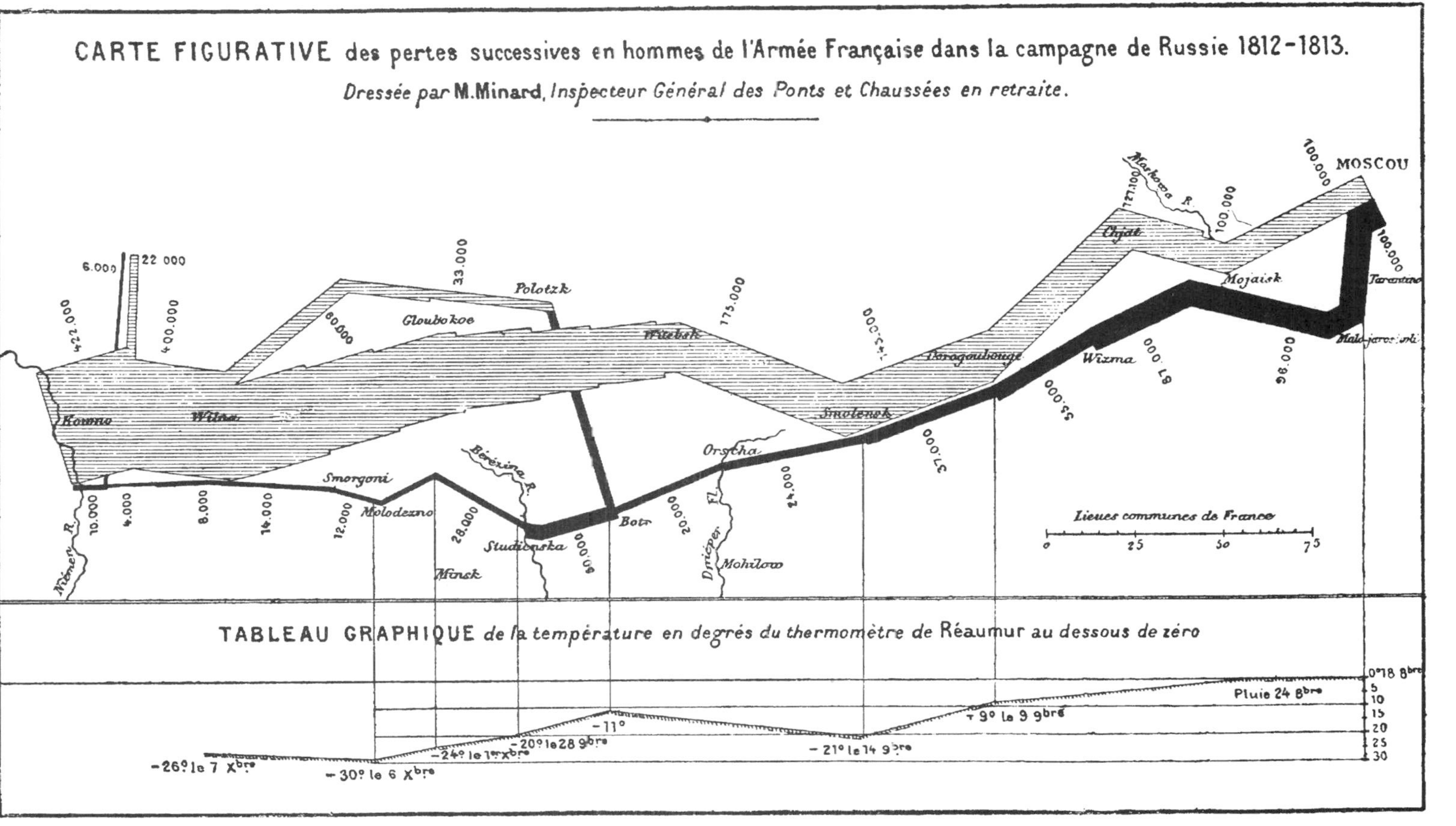

Xbre = December

9bre = November

8bre = October

Figure 7-9. Losses to Napoleon's army during the 1812–1813 Russian Campaign.

Figure 7-9 takes a map running from the Nieman River on the west to Moscow on the east. The forces of Napoleon are shown with an ever-diminishing line, shaded for their eastward movement, black for their retreat back to France.

The width of the line shows the size of the force. They started with an army of about 422,000 troops and ended with only 10,000 survivors. Also displayed across the bottom are the temperatures (from 0° to –30° Centigrade) and the months. (The retreat started in October and ended in December.) When this diagram was shown to the Court of France, they wept.

Two Concentration Diagrams

When taking data, there is a certain type of checklist called a *concentration diagram.* In a concentration diagram you draw a picture of the item you are inspecting (for example, a carton when you are looking for damage, a latex glove when you are looking for punctures, an article of clothing when you are looking for defects, etc.). While inspecting, the data-gatherer simply looks for where the flaw is on the real item and makes a mark on the picture showing where the flaw was located, sometimes including a code to indicate what kind of flaw it is. The cumulative concentration of marks on the drawing will provide useful information regarding frequency and patterns.

The first example is from Ian Hau, who coached a boys' high school soccer team. It is shown in Figure 7-10. (Permission to reprint it has been generously granted by Mr. Hau.)

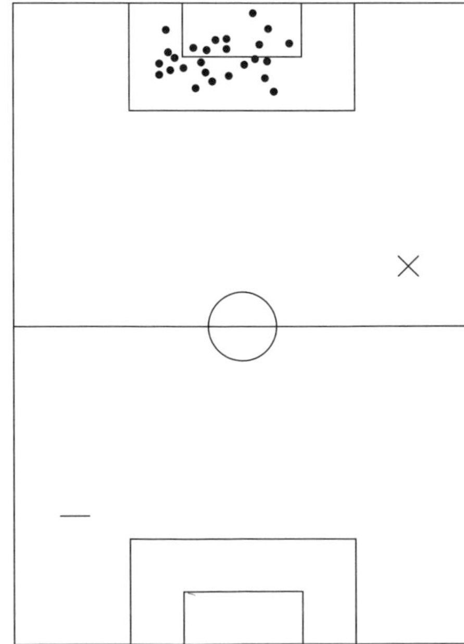

Figure 7-10. From what position on the field does the opposition score its goals?

This diagram allows for a data-based discussion regarding the vulnerabilities of the team's defense and what adjustments to the defense may be considered. According to this diagram, the team seems somewhat more vulnerable to kicks attempted from their goalie's right side and kicked from relatively farther away from the goal.

The third example, also a concentration diagram, comes from the eminent statistician George Box and his colleague Søren Bisgaard (1995), who have graciously given us permission to reprint. This diagram was used to study the patterns of antiaircraft damage to World War II bombers returning to England after their sorties over Germany. It is shown in Figure 7-11.

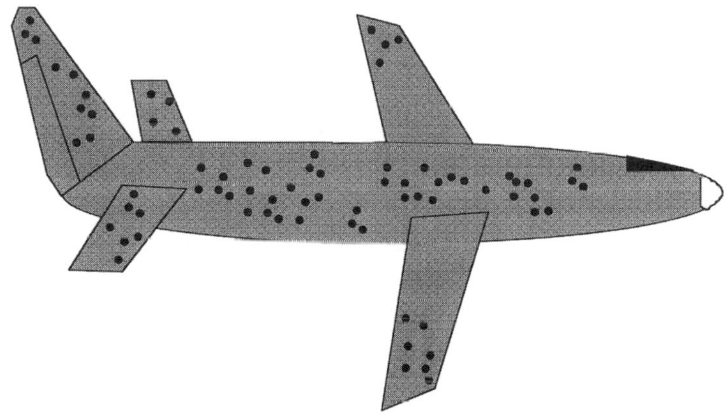

Figure 7-11. Antiaircraft damage to World War II bombers.

The challenge facing those studying this damage: On what parts of the plane should added armor be located? For purposes of minimizing the weight of the plane, added armor must be kept to a minimum. Based on the data shown in Figure 7-11, where would you place the armor? The conclusion of those conducting the study: Reinforce the areas *without* damage. The planes they were studying were, after all, the bombers that *returned* to base.

Finally, an example of a workflow diagram describing the paths of movement in a screen manufacturing operation in an east coast high-tech company is shown in Figure 7-12 (permission to use this diagram has been given by Fred Cox and John Criqui). It shows a diagram of the space and workflow *before* the redesign and *after* the redesign. (Baby Huey is their nickname for a piece of equipment.) As a result of these and other changes, the time required to perform this process was reduced dramatically. No workers were laid off. The company wanted them to stay and make even more improvements.

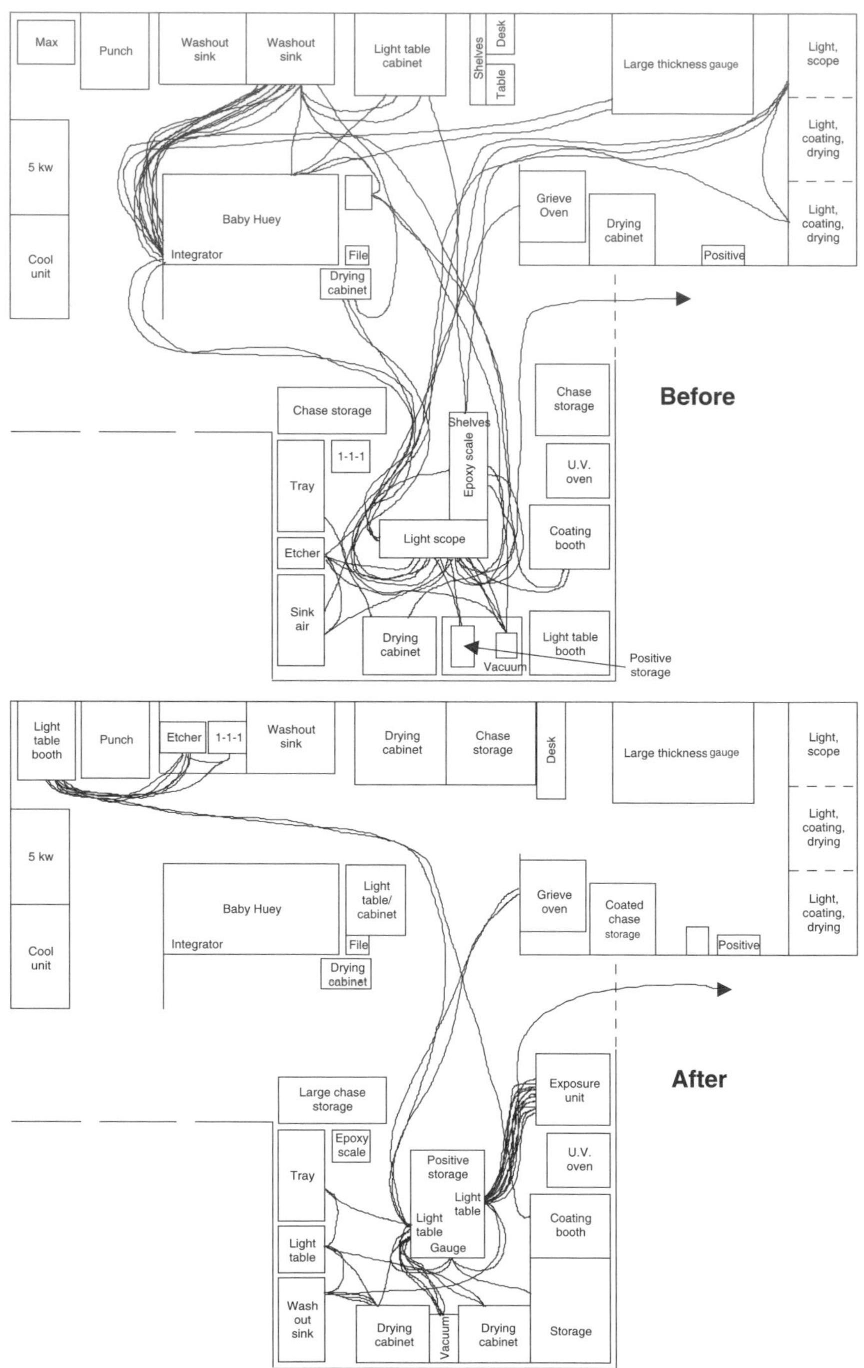

Figure 7-12. A before and after workflow diagram.

SUMMARY

Leaders and managers need to understand systems and must learn to think systemically (Chapters 2 and 3). In order to understand systems we must also understand variation and its causes (Chapter 2). Data are the language of the system: the voice of the system, telling us how it is doing, what it is capable of, and what we can expect from it. It is data that show the variation and the causes of variation. Without systems, data, and a knowledge of variation we cannot lead, manage, or understand the chaos around us.

In this chapter we have explored some approaches to the use of data. If the entirety of what is presented here seems overwhelming, you might keep in mind four notions:

- You are already measuring those things you have considered important to measure.
- What you have seen in this chapter is only a small part of what you might learn to do.
- Start now, start small, and gradually build your capacity to measure.
- Get help from those who are knowledgeable and skilled at what to measure, how to measure, and how to analyze and interpret the data.

CHAPTER SEVEN ACTIVITIES

Discuss the following questions:

1. What are the key indicators (the vital signs) of your organization's work?
   - For now, do not consider financial indicators.
   - Some indicators should be directly related to your organization's purpose and your customers' needs.

2. With what frequency do you monitor each indicator (daily, weekly, monthly)?

3. How do you know that this frequency is sufficient to give you an adequate representation of the organization's performance relative to this indicator? (Ask this for each indicator.)

4. How do you record the data for each indicator?

5. If you do not already do so, begin recording the data for each indicator in *time order,* using the appropriate control chart. (Get someone to help you learn how.)

REFERENCES

Box, G., and Bisgaard, S. 1995. *The efficient generation of knowledge.* A presentation for the Hunter Conference of Quality, sponsored by MAQIN, Madison, WI.

Craighead, F. 1979. *Track of the grizzly.* San Francisco, CA: Sierra Club Books.

Deming, W.E. 1982. *Out of the crisis.* Cambridge, MA: MIT-CAES.

Hau, I. 1991. *Quality improvement for a high school soccer team.* Presented at the Hunter Conference on Quality sponsored by MAQIN, Madison, WI. Mr. Hau is currently the Director of Process Improvement Research and Development for SmithKline and Beecham Pharmaceuticals. Permission obtained from the author.

Hoerl, R.W. 1995. Enhancing the bottom-line impact of statistical methods. *Quality Management Journal,* Summer. In the same issue is a discussion of Hoerl's article by Harry Roberts and George Easton and a rejoinder by Mr. Hoerl.

Kaplan, R.S., and Horton, D.P. 1992. The balanced scorecard—measures that drive performance. *Harvard Business Review,* January–February. (Reprint #92150.)

Orsini, J. 1995. So you want to survey customers. *Ohio Quality Productivity Newsletter,* November.

Provost, L., and Leddick, S. 1993. How to take multiple measures to get a complete picture of organizational performance. *National Productivity Review,* Autumn.

Tufte, E.R. 1983. *The visual display of quantitative information.* Cheshire, CT: Graphics Press.

Wheeler, D.J. 1995. *Advanced topics in statistical process control: The power of Shewhart's charts.* Knoxville, TN: SPC Press, Inc.

Wheeler, D.J. 1993. *Understanding variation: The key to managing chaos.* Knoxville, TN: SPC Press, Inc.

Wheeler, D.J., and Chambers, D.S. 1992. *Understanding statistical process control,* 2nd ed. Knoxville, TN: SPC Press, Inc.

8 LEADING BY ASKING GOOD QUESTIONS

INTRODUCTION

The new approach to organizations requires a new approach to leadership. In Chapter 2 we explored some new competencies needed by twenty-first-century leaders. Here we explore a specific skill: asking good questions.

The reason for emphasizing the asking of questions is directly related to the shift in managerial paradigms presented throughout this book and displayed in Figure 8-1.

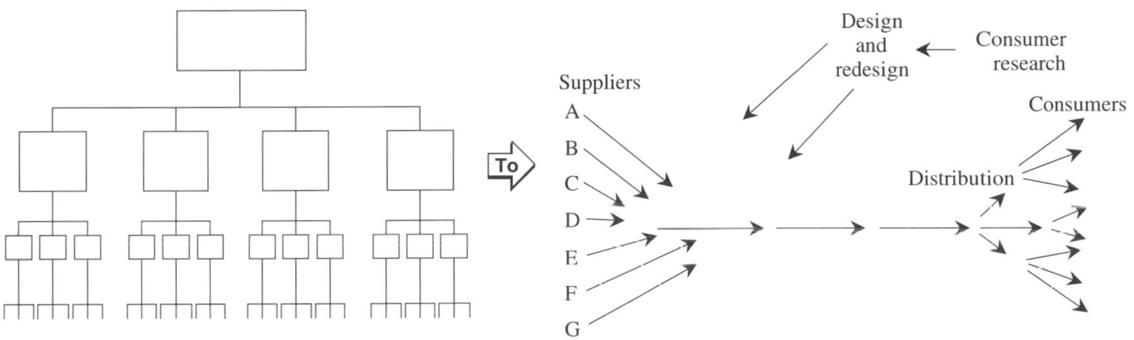

Figure 8-1. The shift in paradigms for leaders, managers, and organizations.

In the old organization we asked "who" questions: "Who is accountable? Who screwed this up?" In the new organization we ask "why" or "how" questions: "Why has this problem occurred? How can we improve the system and eliminate the cause of this problem?" The old managers gave orders or advice and exercised control. The new managers ask questions and promote communication, knowledge, and understanding.

Asking good questions involves more than simply asking good questions. The questions need to be surrounded by collaborative relationships. And the questions should be based on systems thinking and sound strategies for good work. The same question, "What are you doing?" asked by someone I trust will elicit very different responses from the same question asked by someone I fear (see Figure 2-15).

Figure 8-2 shows an example of questions based on a sound organizational strategy. My experience has been that people are more inclined to talk about *activities* (methods) than about *purposes* or *measures of success*. We so easily get wrapped up in *what* we do that we often ignore *why* we are doing it and whether we are succeeding.

In this chapter we will examine other such frameworks or systems of questions. These are *systems* of questions because they lead us to look at an interdependent whole. Purpose, methods, and measures

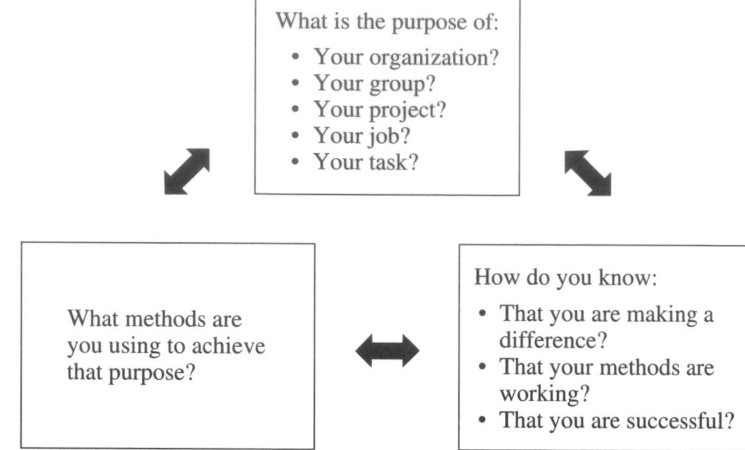

Figure 8-2. A framework of questions based on some fundamental organizational realities.

of success are factors that interact with each other in our everyday lives whether we are raising a family or running a business. Purpose, methods, and measures of success form an interdependent whole and a system of knowledge.

We begin this chapter by exploring some concepts about leadership that are relevant to the challenge of asking good questions. Then we will explore questions and the frameworks within which they fit. We next explore listening and listening skills. Finally, we will step back and review the larger inquiry process, looking at it as a whole.

THE NEW CONCEPT OF LEADERSHIP

In a conversation with Russell Ackoff, I heard him make the following distinction:

- Leaders decide what needs to be done.
- Managers decide how to do those things that leaders have decided must be done.
- Administrators apply the methods designed by managers in pursuit of the purposes selected by leaders.

In real life, things seem to be sloppier than this. But Ackoff's distinction is useful enough. The sloppiness probably occurs when the same person must act sometimes as a leader, sometimes as a manager, and sometimes as an administrator.

It is true to say that Moses did not manage the exodus, he led it. Aaron and Jethro were more like the managers of it. The administrators were undoubtedly there, but administrators generally tend not to be mentioned, at least not in the Bible ... or in *The Wall Street Journal.*

Ackoff (1994, p. 50) has also made a distinction between efficiency and effectiveness. Effectiveness involves doing the right things. This, it would seem, is the purview of leaders. Efficiency involves doing things right, the job of managers and administrators. At some point someone should ask the organization's leaders, "How do you know you are doing the right thing? What indicators tell you so?" But in most organizations, few are courageous enough to ask those questions.

In the old paradigm the answer would most likely have been, "Because I said so!" The new paradigm might require reference to such things as purpose, mission, vision, values, and data on the key indicators (see Chapters 5 and 6). Here, for a moment, we will look at some roles of the new leaders that result in the leaders' needing to ask good questions.

The Leader as Coach Rather Than Director

Not all coaches coach alike. There are autocratic coaches and consultative participative coaches. Here we mean the latter variety, those who seek collaborative relationships with coworkers rather than a command-and-control relationship. Director types will have a harder time learning to ask good questions. They will try to smuggle advice or reprimands into the interchange, still using the grammatical form of a question: "Have you considered doing...?" or "What in the world made you think that was the best way to do...?"

The Leader as Experimenter versus Controller

In Chapter 2, we explored the difference between opinion and fact (Figure 2-6) and theories and application (Figure 2-8). Leaders who understand the differences between hunches, guesses, beliefs, and hypotheses on the one hand and demonstrable truth on the other are more likely to draw their people into inquiry and dialogue. When leaders approach situations as experimenters, they are more likely to say, "What seems to be going on here?" or "How can we find out for sure?" Otherwise the controller in them will make a statement: "This is what is going on here...."

The Leader as Educator versus Advice-Giver

According to Yukihiro Ando, one of Dr. Noriaki Kano's protégés, some of the Japanese teachers of quality believe that when they resort to giving advice they have failed as teachers. They would suggest that the greatest teacher needs only to ask the right questions. The student learns by pursuing the answers. Leaders can develop and educate their employees in a similar way. Directives and advice teach dependence. Questions can lead to independence and greater self-sufficiency.

The Leader as Inquirer or Reviewer versus Inspector

The inspector looks for flaws in someone's work. The inquirer or reviewer, instead, asks questions that help people discover the flaws themselves, as well as the methods and processes of learning and improvement. The inspector says, "This is a mistake!" The inquirer asks, "How will you prevent this problem from occurring?" or "Where in the process did this problem originate? What might you do to track down and eliminate the cause?"

Asking, Listening, Learning, Leading

In an address in Cincinnati in 1994, Congressman Newt Gingrich described what he thought to be a good process for effective leadership: *Ask* and *listen* so that you can *learn* and *lead.* Mr. Gingrich has summarized an important dynamic that is central to the new leadership concept.

ASKING GOOD QUESTIONS

Now we look at some strategies for improvement and the questions that flow from them. We also look at some systems of questions similar to the one shown in Figure 8-2. But first we propose some questions that are almost universally useful.

Seven Basic, All-Purpose Questions

Here I am giving away the trade secrets of the consulting profession. If you can master these seven questions and the questions presented in Figure 8-2, you can charge enormous fees. If you ask the questions with a sincere and innocent look, you can charge even more. As a manager, however, you can master these questions and ask them for free.

1. Why?

When a problem occurs, ask why it occurred. Ask the question, "Why?" as many times as it takes until you get at the systemic cause of the problem. (The Japanese teachers of quality would have you ask "Why?" five times.)

Ask the Question "Why?" Five Times.

This technique, taught us by the Japanese, allows us to pursue the deeper, systemic causes of a problem and correspondingly deeper solutions.

Level of a problem	Corresponding level of improvement
There is a puddle of oil on the shop floor.	Clean up the oil.
Why?	
Because the machine is leaking oil.	
Why?	
Because the gasket is deteriorating.	Replace the gasket.
Why?	
Because we bought gaskets made of inferior material.	Buy better gaskets.
Why?	
Because we got a good deal on them.	
Why?	
Because the purchasing agent gets evaluated on the basis of savings over normal price tags.	Change the policy.

I am grateful to Joop Bokern for this example.

There is no magic in the number five, but if you repeatedly ask "why" you can get past the superficial problem and its immediate cause and look deeper into the systemic causes. The policy that results in leaky gaskets and puddles of oil is undoubtedly contributing to other problems. By solving the deeper systemic cause of the puddle of oil, you can eliminate the causes of multiple problems. Dr. Kano calls this "going an inch wide and a mile deep."

Diagram 8-1.

The person of whom you ask, "Why?" may respond with a "who." "Why? Because George screwed up, that's why!" As a leader, you must disregard the culprit response and look for the systemic "why": "What is there in our system that made it easy for that mistake to occur?"

2. What Is the Purpose?

When someone proposes some new project or doohickey, ask what its purpose is.

> "We are setting up a new team to study a high-performance work culture!"
>
> "Cool! What is its purpose?"

Related to this are the "What will it take ..." questions and "How will you know when it is successful?"

3. What Will It Take to Accomplish This?

This question too should be asked repeatedly when someone describes something he or she would like to accomplish. After asking first about the purpose, help the person or group convert wishes to activities. Dr. Deming's often-used version of this question was, "By what method?"

4. Will the Customers Give a Rat's Tush about This?

Will the outside customer notice or care? How will this proposed effort affect the outside customer? How do you know?

5. What Is Your Premise?

If you are going to impose a new policy on the employees, for example, what is your theory about the policy and the employees? For example, if someone said, "We are going to put all our managers on a three-year contract with measurable performance standards," you might respond, "What, then, are your beliefs about your managers? And what are your assumptions about contracts and measurable standards of performance? On what basis do you hold onto these beliefs and assumptions?"

6. What Data Do You Have?

If you know they have no data, don't rub their noses in it. Instead, ask, "What data might you get?" Dr. Deming's favorite version of this was, "How do you know?" This question is intended to move the answerer from assertions (theory or hunches) to research (see Chapter 2).

7. Where Do Your Data Come from?

A lot of bad data is available out there. How were these data gathered, analyzed, and interpreted? (Just because there are numbers doesn't mean there are data.) How do you assure yourself that the data are valid?

Four Improvement Strategies behind the Questions

Following are four approaches to solving problems. The reason for presenting them here is to provide some frameworks for asking good questions. These will provide a perspective that will help avoid the common management mistakes: asking the wrong question or asking the right question too soon.

Strategy 1. Plan-Do-Study-Act

We have explored the PDSA cycle throughout this book, beginning in Chapter 2. PDSA applies both to large-scale, longer-term, slower turning cycles (e.g., feeding the world) and to small-scale, shorter-term, rapidly turning cycles (e.g., feeding the dog).

When you are seeking to improve a system that is already in place, we recommend beginning with study. In the questions suggested below, we start with study.

Here we introduce an improvement strategy that is an elaboration on the PDSA cycle. It is adapted from an improvement model first developed by Tom Nolan and Ron Moen and published in 1992 by a talented group of consultants, Associates in Process Improvement (API). Their book (Langley, 1996) is a landmark contribution to the philosophy and methodology of improvement. API has given permission for its model to be presented here.

In Diagrams 8.1–8.4 are questions to ask during P, D, S, and A (starting with *study*). These are questions added to the three contained in the API model.

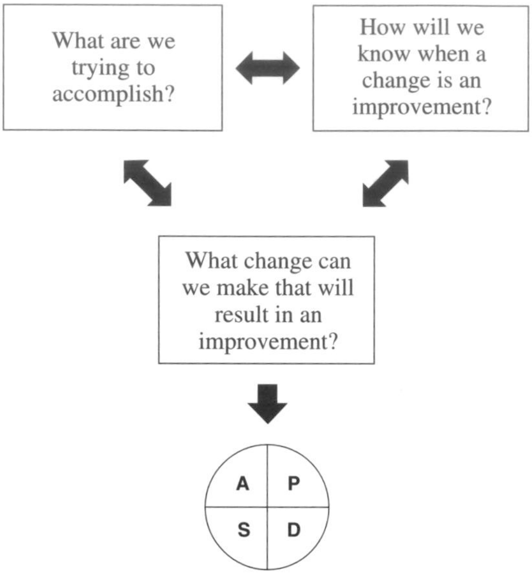

What are we trying to accomplish?

How will we know when a change is an improvement?

What change can we make that will result in an improvement?

A	P
S	D

Figure 8-3. The API improvement model.

Questions to ask	
A. During "study"	1. Why have you selected this process to examine? 2. How well is this process working? 3. What do we hear from customers? • What do they need that they aren't getting? • What are they getting that they don't need? 4. What data can you show me about this process? • Waste? • Errors? • Rework? • Breakdowns? • Cycle times? • Average and range of variation. Is it in control or not?

Diagram 8-2a.

	Questions to ask
B. During "plan"	1. What problems are you seeking to solve? What gaps? What improvements? 2. How will you measure progress? 3. How will you measure success? 4. What solutions or new functions do you expect to begin? 5. How are they related to the problems, needs or gaps? 6. Why are these interventions seen to be better than other possible interventions? 7. What could go wrong with the introduction and use of this new approach? How can these potential problems be avoided, minimized, or responded to if they occur?
C. During "do"	1. What is your plan for: • Testing or piloting this innovation? • Introducing it on a large scale? • Monitoring its progress and success? 2. How easy to follow is your plan for implementation?
D. During "study"	1. What are you monitoring? 2. Why are you monitoring those indicators? 3. How are you using the data? 4. How are you monitoring the use of your plan? 5. What revisions have you needed to make in your plan?
E. During "act"	1. What adjustments have you made to your original intervention? 2. What have you done to standardize the new method? •See the questions regarding standardization.

Diagram 8-2b.

Strategy 2. Standardization

In Chapter 4 we explored standardization, including questions for leaders to ask when something goes wrong. Here we look at four basic stages of standardization and appropriate questions to ask at each stage.

Questions to ask regarding an effort to standardize	
A. Before the standardization effort	1. Why have you chosen to standardize this process rather than some other process? 2. How is the customer affected by the lack of standardization in this process? 3. What characteristics of this process are important to control?
B. While identifying the best-known method (BKM)	1. How will you determine the best-known method (BKM)? 2. Who will be involved? 3. What parts of the process may require gathering and analyzing data in order to determine the BKM? 4. How will you gather the data? 5. How will you analyze the data? 6. What is your plan for implementing the BKM? 7. How will you test or pilot the new BKM? 8. What key process characteristics need to be monitored in this new BKM? 9. How will these indicators be monitored?
C. While implementing the best-known method (BKM)	1. Who will need to be trained? Who will conduct the training? Who will train the trainers? How will the training be scheduled and logistics be managed? 2. How will the BKM be documented and displayed? 3. How will the users of the new method be signaled to start using it?
D. After its implementation	1. What results have you achieved? 2. What do customers say? • Internal customers • External customers 3. What data do you have showing the performance of the key process indicators? 4. What problems remain in the process? 5. What are your next steps?

Diagram 8-3.

Strategy 3. Do It!

"Do it!" is included as an improvement strategy for two reasons. First, people are likely to go ahead and use it anyway. After all, it is probably the most common approach to change. Second, it is not necessarily the worst way to proceed. Since people are likely to go ahead and "Do it!" managers need to be prepared to ask good questions. The major steps of "Do it!" are quite simple, as are the corresponding questions.

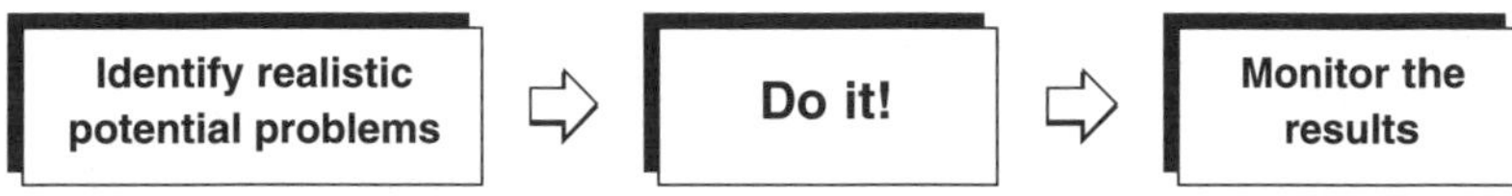

Questions to ask of someone involved in "do it!"	
A. Before doing it	1. What could realistically go wrong? 2. How might that be prevented? 3. What should we monitor to see if the problem is occurring? 4. How might we be prepared to react if it goes wrong?
B. During "do it"	1. What are you doing? 2. Why are you doing it? 3. How do you know this is the right thing to do? 4. What precautions are you taking?
C. After "do it"	1. Are we getting what we wanted? 2. Are we avoiding what we didn't want? 3. Do we need to make any adjustments?

Diagram 8-4.

Strategy 4. The 7-Step Method

The 7-Step Method came to my attention in the late 1980s when I started hearing from people at Hewlett-Packard (especially Tim Fuller) and Florida Power and Light about this very powerful approach to problem solving. I first saw it published in *Statistical Methods for Quality Improvement* by Hitoshi Kume (1985), who describes what he calls the QC Story. Subsequently, Brian Joiner and I put together a rephrasing of the seven steps (Joiner Associates, 1990).

Questions to ask during the 7 Steps	
A. During Step 1: define the project	1. What is the problem or "gap"? 2. Why is it important that this be addressed? 3. How does the problem affect customers? 4. How will progress be measured?
B. During Step 2: look at patterns	1. What graphics do you have to illustrate the problem (e.g., a flowchart of the process)? 2. How was the problem localized to show *what* it was, *where* it occurred, *when* it occurred and *who* it involved? 3. How was the focus of the project narrowed?
C. During Step 3: identify the causes	1. What *potential* causes were identified? 2. How were these causes *verified*? (Also, see "plan" and "do" of PDSA.)
D. During Step 4: plan and implement the remedy	1. What solutions were considered? 2. How were solutions evaluated? 3. How did solutions address the causes of the problem? 4. How carefully were the solutions planned? 5. How was the solution piloted? (Also, see "study" of PDSA.)
E. During Step 5: study the outcomes	1. What before/after data were compared? • In the pilot • In the full implementation plan 2. How completely was the implementation plan followed?
F. During Step 6: standardize the new way	1. How were improvements institutionalized throughout the system? 2. Are there graphic displays and documentation of the new method? (Also, see "standardization" and "act" of PDSA.)
G. During Step 7: decide what to do next	1. What will be worked on next? 2. What was learned as a result of working on this improvement project? 3. How will these lessons be integrated into future improvement efforts?

Diagram 8-5.

The Steps	1 Define the project	2 Look at the patterns	3 Identify the causes	4 Plan and implement the remedy	5 Monitor the outcomes	6 Standardize the new way	7 Decide what to do next
As described by Kume, the *QC Story*	Problem	Observation	Analysis	Action	Check	Standardi-zation	Conclusion
As described by Joiner, the *Joiner 7 Step Method*	Project	Current situation	Cause analysis	Solutions	Results	Standardi-zation	Future plans
Some comments and guidelines	Make sure: • That the purpose of this project is clear • You are ready to do this project • That it is an important undertaking • It is of workable scope • The measures of success are clear • You understand the problem or gap from the customer's point of view	Narrow the focus of this effort by learning: • Where, when, how and with whom it does or doesn't happen • What patterns of variation occur • Which factors have the greatest impact of frequency, re: dissatis-faction, cost, defect delay, breakdown, errors, etc.	• Identify the deeper causes that come from within the system • Identify possible causes and confirm them with data • Ask the question, "why" 5 times • Don't look for "who," no culprit thinking	• Identify alternative interventions to remedy the causes • Make sure the cure is not worse than the disease • Select the best remedy or remedies • Plan how to implement and what to monitor • Take action	• Monitor the use of the plan • Monitor the use of the selected remedy • Monitor the results • Monitor for side-effects and other signals of problems	• Make any necessary adjustments • Document the new process • Train the current employees • Include in training for new employees • Error-proof the new methods • Use visual reminders of the new method	Decide what to do about: • Any remaining problems or causes of problems • Assuring the continued use of the new method • Sharing the learnings with others • Ending the project, not with a whimper, but a bang

Diagram 8-6. The 7-Step Method.

Many companies have their official standardized problem-solving method, often described in seven steps. I haven't seen any that are as thorough as Kume's. Most are short on the use of data and often omit Step 2 in part or entirely. Diagram 8-6 shows the seven steps. The headings at the tops of columns are what I call each step. Below is Kume's phrasing and, below that, Joiner's. The shades of difference are subtle and probably say more about the three of us than about the method itself.

Note: We have already seen the 7-Step Method in Figure 4-24, where it is used to sort out proposed improvements.

When to Use Which Strategy

Each strategy suggests its own questions and its own sequence of questions. Prior to the selection of a strategy we ask a series of questions (a decision tree, Diagram 8-6). These questions will help the project leader select which of the four strategies is most appropriate for the specific effort. These are questions managers may ask when someone proposes a project or an improvement effort.

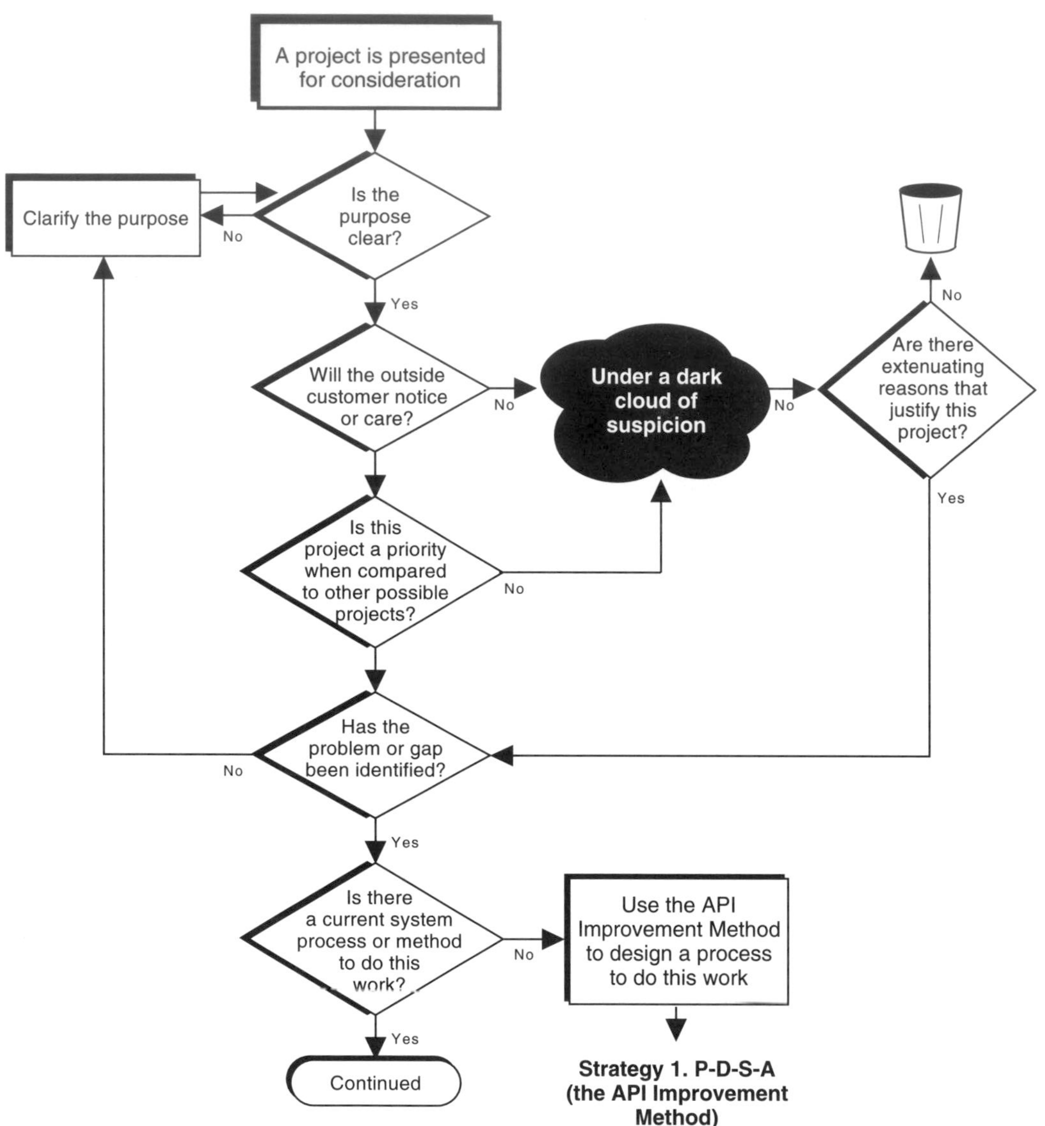
A project is presented for consideration
Is the purpose clear?
Clarify the purpose
No
Yes
Will the outside customer notice or care?
No
Under a dark cloud of suspicion
No
Are there extenuating reasons that justify this project?
No
Yes
Is this project a priority when compared to other possible projects?
No
Has the problem or gap been identified?
No
Yes
Is there a current system process or method to do this work?
No
Use the API Improvement Method to design a process to do this work
Yes
Continued
Strategy 1. P-D-S-A (the API Improvement Method)

Diagram 8-7.

Danger sign: means that at this step there is a risk of self deception

Strategy 2. Standardize the process

Is the process standardized?

No

Yes

Does everyone use the standardized methods?

No

Use the standardized methods

Yes

Does the problem or gap still exist?

No

Yes

Do you know what the remedy is?

No

Yes

Is the known solution simple and low risk?

No

Yes

Prepare for potential problems

Have realistic potential problems been identified and prepared for?

No

Yes

Strategy 3. Do it and monitor results

Strategy 1. PDSA

Strategy 4. The 7 Step Method

Document the new process and bring the project to closure

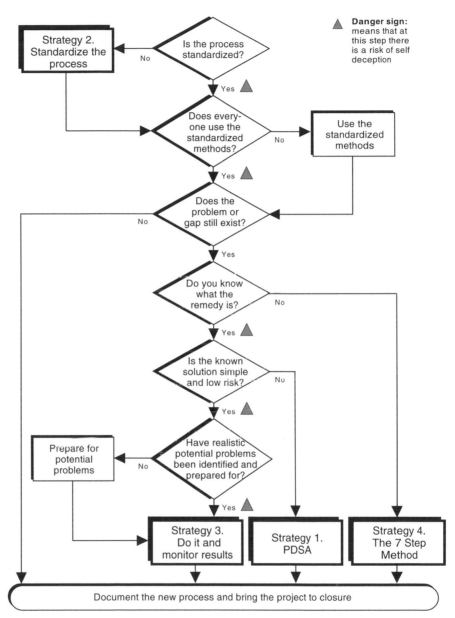

Diagram 8-7. *(Continued)*

Some Frameworks of Questions

By a framework of questions I mean a system or network of interdependent and interactive questions. You can start with any part of the framework and lead to any other part. Often the person with whom you are speaking will begin the conversation with a statement that will lead directly into one or another of these frameworks of questions. You, then, can "dance around" the framework letting the other person's response or your curiosity lead the way. At some point you might move into another framework or bring the session to a close (see "The Inquiry Process," later in this chapter).

We have already looked at one framework of questions in Figure 8-2. What follows will be like that with different frames of reference.

Framework 2: A Basic System of Questions to Use When Meeting with a New Group or Someone Working on a New Project

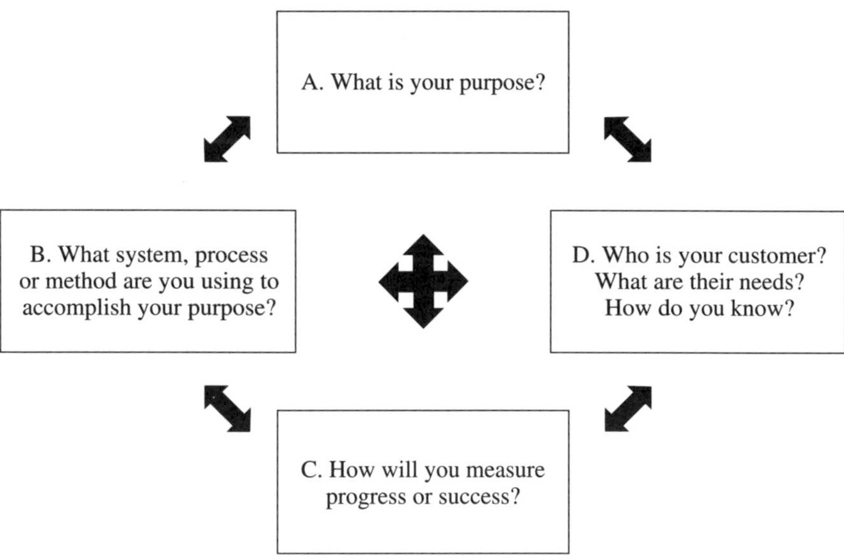

- "Customer" here can possibly refer to an *internal* customer. But any effort should be able to be seen in reference to the *outside* customer.
- Parts of the framework can be combined into sets of two or three or all four. Thus this system creates 15 possible frames of questions. For example, combining A and C: "Explain the connection between your purpose and how you will measure progress or success." Or you may combine A, C, and D: "In what way are the measures used to track the achievement of your purposes consistent with the needs of your customers?"

Framework 3: When Someone or Some Group Is Proposing a Change in a Service

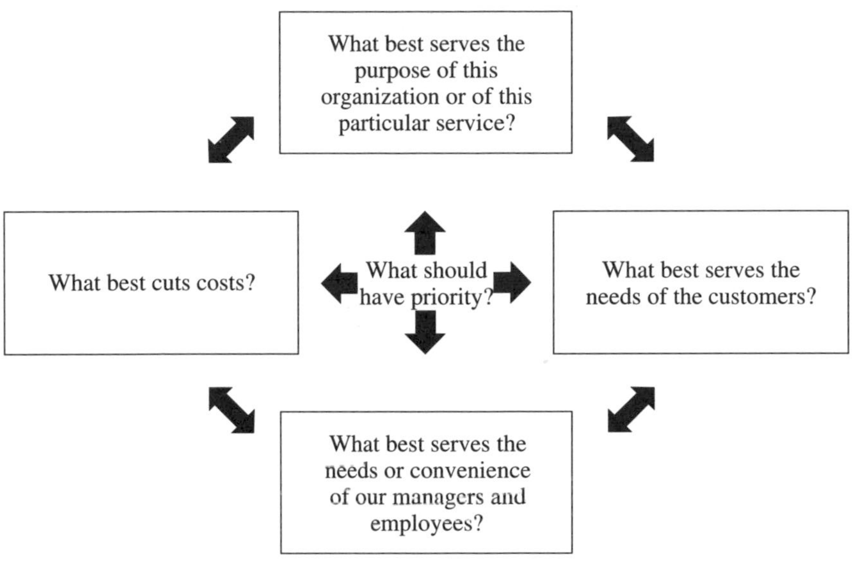

- The questions reflect the reasons usually offered for a proposed change in service.
- Each should be able to be supported by data.
- The question in the center, "What should have priority?" is pivotal. It goes to the organization's basic values.

Framework 4: When Someone Is Proposing a Team or Project

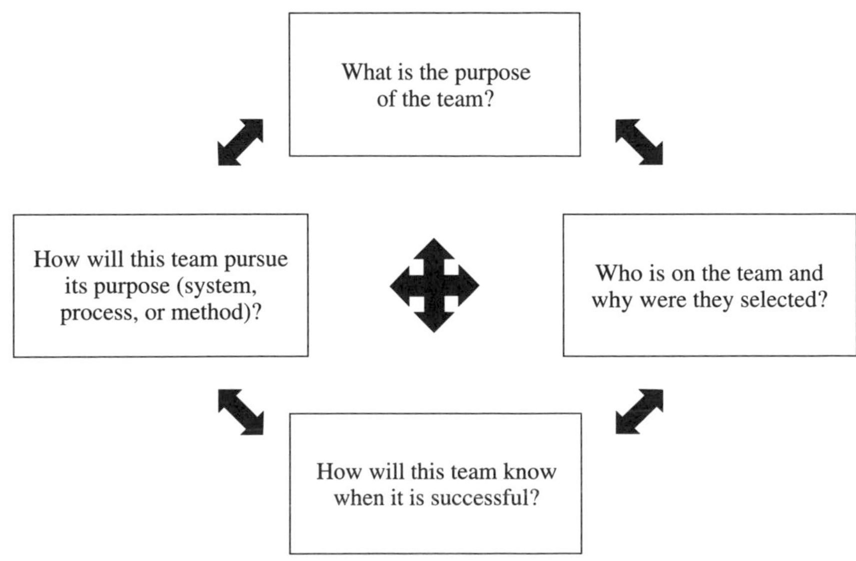

It may be useful to explore the composition of the team and its purpose or its methodology: "Explain the relationship between your team's purpose and the selection of the team's members." Or, "What is the relationship between your team's methods and the selection of members?" See also the discussion questions at the end of Chapter 5.

Framework 5: Questions to Ask of Those Engaged in Problem Solving

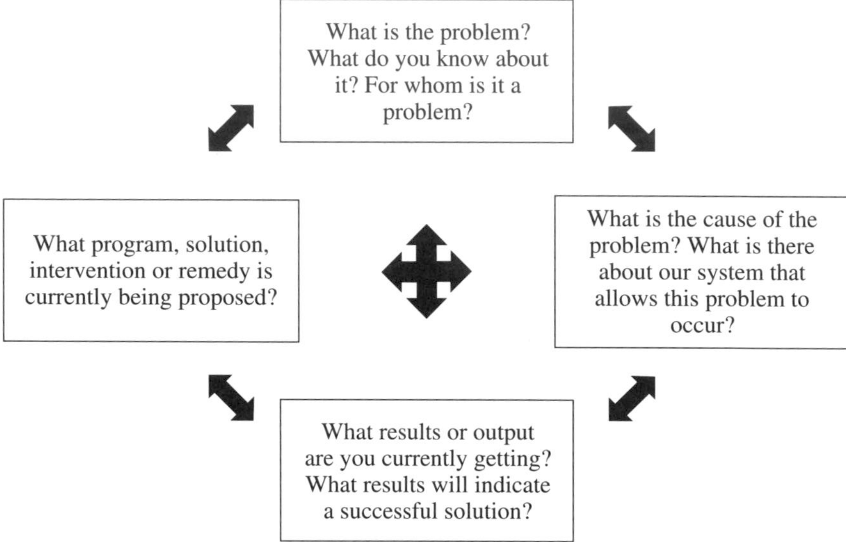

- People tend to jump into solutions without first thinking through the problem or the causes of the problem.
- People sometimes neglect to identify what results their efforts produced or whether their results are related to the original problem, the cause of the problem, or the applied remedy. The connections should be clear.

GOOD LISTENING: WHAT YOU DO AFTER YOU HAVE ASKED A GOOD QUESTION

Listening is not something you do while you await your turn to talk. It is not a passive experience. Listening is an exploration involving both the speaker and the listener. Asking good questions and following them with poor listening is worse than asking no questions at all.

There are many books and courses on listening skills. This technology has been around for 40 years. Dr. Thomas Gordon, the

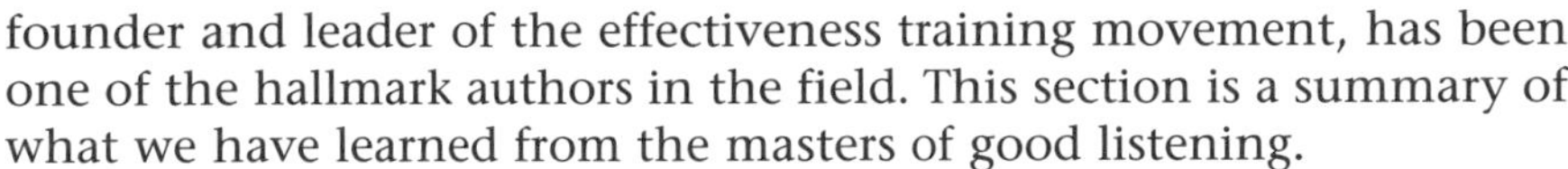

founder and leader of the effectiveness training movement, has been one of the hallmark authors in the field. This section is a summary of what we have learned from the masters of good listening.

The Right Attitude for Good Listening

Good questioning and good listening can be done in a manner that turns them sinister. The words may be neutral and nonjudgmental, but the tone of voice, body language, and other mannerisms send a different message. Don't ask questions when:

- You are angry and want to punish rather than be helpful.
- You are not willing to suspend your judgment or your need to give direct advice.
- You are in a hurry and don't have time to listen to and explore the other's answers.

Good questions have no hint of judgment:

- Judgmental: "The data on your chart don't confirm your conclusions. What made you think you could get your answer from these data?"
- Nonjudgmental: "Help me understand the connection between the data in the chart on page 4 and the conclusions you draw on page 5."

Someone who has been listened to well experiences the following:

- The speaker should feel a deepened understanding of what he or she has been trying to communicate.
- The person should not feel embarrassed or tested. ("Did I give them the answer they wanted?") He or she should feel supported and challenged to continue to study, to dig deeper, to appreciate what is already known and seek to learn more.

A Summary of Good Listening Skills

1. *Attend and be silent.*
   - Maintain eye contact.
   - Use semiverbals ("uh-huh") to let the speaker know that you are there and paying attention.

Virginia Satir's Four Dysfunctional Communication Styles

Virginia Satir (1988) was a pioneer in family systems and family communications. In her book *Peoplemaking*, she identifies four styles of communication, learned in our earliest years, that are not useful when dealing with others: blaming, placating, being superrational, and being irrelevant.

We learn these styles in our families and carry them with us through school and our jobs. Eventually, we teach them to our own children.

Some comments on the four dysfunctional modes:

- None of them is abnormal, nor is using any of them necessarily a sign of deeper personal problems. They just get in the way of helpful interaction.
- Most of us have one or two of these modes that we revert to, especially in times of stress.
- These behaviors serve to keep others at a distance, which may be needed in some circumstances. However, there are more straightforward and less confusing ways to keep distance.
- At the root of each of these self-protective modes of communication is low self-esteem.

1. The blamer

Description	• Looks for a culprit. Seeks to absolve self of fault.
Typical comments	• Who screwed up! • You never do anything right! • Don't blame me for your problems.
Under the surface	• Nobody cares about me. • I am afraid of being found out.
Physical experience	• Tight body. • Ready to spring.

2. The placater

Description	• Tries, first of all, to accommodate everyone's demands. Failing that, the placater apologizes.
Typical comments	• My job is to keep everyone happy. If *they are* happy, *I am* happy. • I keep letting other people down. • I can't seem to do anything right.
Under the surface	• If I keep everyone happy, maybe they will love me.
Physical experience	• Tense stomach.

3. The super-reasoner

Description	• Mostly head, very little heart. Apply rationality and analysis to everything even when such are not what is needed or appropriate.
Typical comments	• Emotionalism gets in the way. I don't care what people feel. • Let's look at this objectively. • People can be so irrational! • Give me a computer and I am content.
Under the surface	• People will respect me for my intellect. • I feel out of control in the presence of emotions.
Physical experience	• Rigid and "dried-up."

4. The irrelevant person

Description	• Deflects attention or diverts attention to something unrelated to the issue at hand. • Doesn't notice what is going on, notices but doesn't understand, or understands but gets distracted.
Typical comments	• The computer crashed? Did you get the other guy's license? • Speaking of travel delays, was the space shuttle able to take off on schedule?
Under the surface	• I want attention, but I am uncomfortable about people getting to know me.
Physical experience	• Off balance, unsteady

2. *Practice* neutral *observation.*

   Neutral observation is not so much a technique as it is a frame of mind. Every statement of the neutral observer embodies this set of values:

   - I will not judge or control.
   - I will not suggest or correct.
   - I will not praise or criticize.
   - I will simply report what I observe.

   Examples from the workplace:

Nonneutral—Nonobservational	**Neutral Observation**
■ "Why in blazes are you doing that?"	■ "I see you're turning that dial to 36.4."
■ "This report is two days late!"	■ "I noticed your report is on my desk."
■ "Haven't you finished that test yet?"	■ "I read in your memo that a test was to take place this week."

3. *Use reflective statements.*

   Use a phrase or fragment of the speaker's story and repeat it.

   Speaker: "… and then the machine broke down and everyone went zonkers!"

   Listener: "Zonkers."

4. *Summarize and check.*

   - Find a break in the speaker's narrative to take what he or she has said and repeat it back in a summary form.
   - Follow the summary with a check question. ("Is this a fair summary of what you said?")

5. *Sort out the speaker's issues.*

   Either along with the summary or as a separate intervention, help the speaker to distinguish between:

   — Problems versus symptoms

   — Problems versus solutions

   — Important few versus trivial many

   — What can be remedied or changed versus what is beyond his or her ability to influence

6. *Find patterns.*

   Find what this issue, described by the speaker, has in common with other experiences in his or her life.

   — "Has something like this ever happened to you before?"

   — "Have you had other issues with this same person?"

7. *Point out obvious gaps.*

   After a while you may notice the conspicuous absence of some element of the narrative that you would have expected.

   "I find it interesting that you have not mentioned your boss so far."

8. *Point out interruptions.*

   Sometimes the speaker will interrupt the continuity of his or her narrative. You might comment on this.

   "I notice that when you started talking about that meeting you quickly changed the subject."

Listening to Abusiveness

I once had a boss who was extremely abusive and ill-tempered, a smart man who was difficult to work with. As a result we did our best to avoid him. It wasn't easy.

Late one afternoon I was in my office trying to finish a project. The boss and I were the only ones still at work, a vulnerable time.

Suddenly the boss stormed into my office, slammed something down on my desk and growled, "What's this?"

A quick scan of the item thrown on my desk convinced me that it had nothing to do with me or my work. So I decided to use a good listening response that I have used before and taught to others.

I said, "You sound like you're angry about that."

To which he responded, "Don't use that workshop s——on me!"

The textbook example of the listening skill did not elicit a textbook response.

The boss, however, did calm down.

9. *Attend to feelings.*
   - Sometimes asking how the speaker feels about the story is useful. Often, however, people will not respond with a feeling (some variation on joy, sadness, anger, or fear), but with a thought. ("I feel I should never have gotten into this mess!")
   - It may be helpful to provide the words to describe the speaker's feelings.

     "I bet you were disappointed when that happened," or "You look angry when you talk about that."
10. *Test for responsibility and follow up.*
    - "What do you plan to do next?"
    - "How will you go about deciding what to do next?"
    - "Do you have a plan? What does it suggest should be the next steps?"

Some final comments on listening skills:

- Keep the focus on what the other person is saying.
- Let the other feel the conversation is his or hers to take in whatever direction he or she wants.
- Don't give advice. It probably won't help. Giving advice more likely meets the needs of your ego than the speaker's needs.

Don't let the speaker draw you into giving advice. Deflect any request for advice back to the speaker: "What advice were you hoping I'd give you?"

- Don't judge. If you can't avoid judgment or you can't suspend judgment, at least avoid the rhetoric of judgment: should, should not, good, bad, right, wrong, etc.
- Don't replace the speaker's story with yours. While a brief reference to a similar experience of yours might help the speaker feel less alone, don't shift the focus of the conversation from the speaker to you.
- Don't try to talk the speaker into or out of feelings. Don't discount the speaker's experience by saying, "Don't feel bad," "It's not so serious," "Things will get better," or, "C'mon, give me a smile." Those interventions are more to help you, the listener, rather than the speaker.
- Don't sympathize. Support the speaker but don't support an inclination toward "poor me." Sympathy tends to reinforce victimhood and inaction. Sometimes people may need a little mothering. Just don't let the speaker indulge in it for long.

THE INQUIRY PROCESS

The inquiry process is described in Figure 8-5. Some comments on the inquiry process:

- Allow yourself to be inelegant when you begin to lead by asking good questions. Let the other person know that you are working at learning a new skill.
- When the session has ended, get feedback from the other person on how you might improve your inquiry skills.
- The other person has likely been conditioned to expect advice and judgment. Make sure the feedback is on your abilities as an inquirer, not on whether the other person would rather have you resume the role of judge and advice giver.

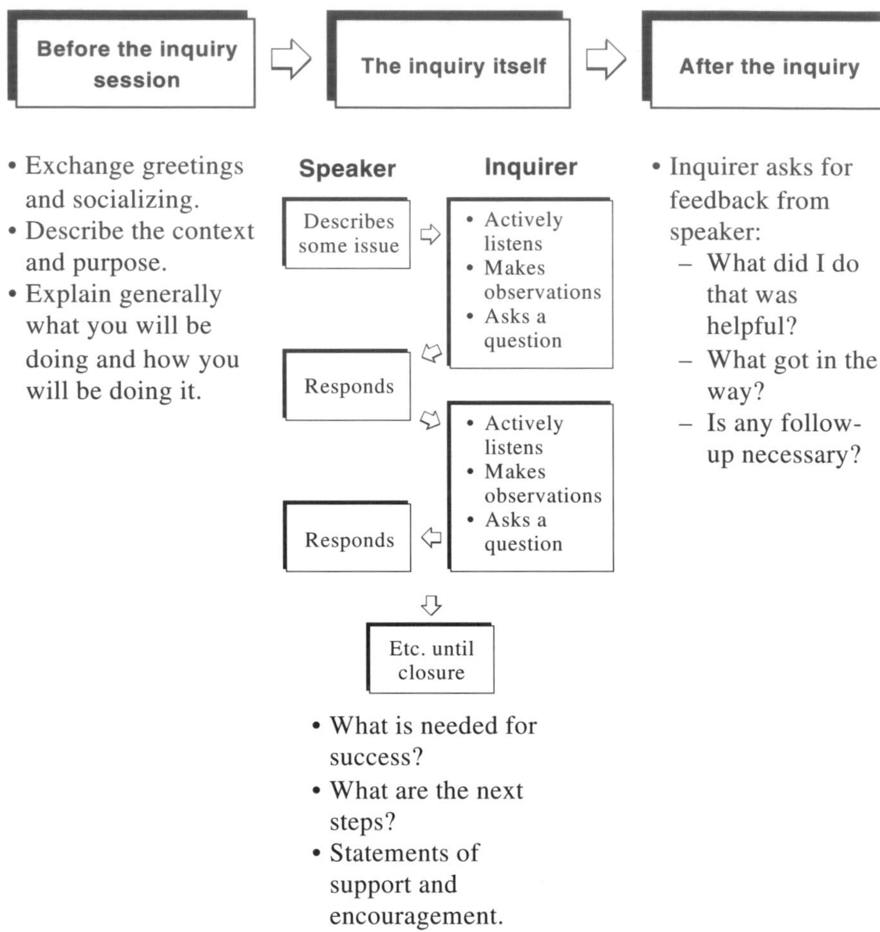

Figure 8-5. The inquiry process.

What to Ask during the Inquiry

Figure 8-6 illustrates most of the directions the inquiry may take. The answer to one question may lead into any of the other areas.

Purpose

- Why are you working on this effort?
- What larger purpose is it part of?
- Why is it important?

Customers

- How does this or how will this affect the outside customer?
- What are their needs with regard to this?

Time

- What is the history of this issue?
- What preceded it?
- What followed its early occurrence?
- What impact is this issue likely to have in the future?

The Speaker

The Inquirer

Data

- What data do you have?
- What key indicators need monitoring?
- What assumptions or theories need to be tested?

Focus–focus–focus

- How can this issue be subdivided into smaller issues?
- What data can help you decide the internal priorities of this issue (Pareto thinking)?

People

- Who else cares?
- Who else should be involved?
- Who can help you?
- Whose expertise is useful in this issue?
- Regarding this effort, where are the:
  - Managers
  - Movers and shakers
  - Coworkers
  - Staff
  - Other important people

Applying the improvement strategies

- Standardization
- Do it!
- PDSA
- 7 Steps

Learning

- What have you learned?
- How can these lessons be taught to others?
- How can learnings be integrated into the organization?

Figure 8-6. What to ask about during inquiry.

SUMMARY

The new approach to leadership requires new concepts, roles, values, and relationships, as well as new methods and skills. Leading by asking good questions is a direct challenge to our old paradigm reflexes and approaches. Asking good questions represents a major new attitude and skill for the leaders of the new century. Asking good questions is something that will take a long time to master. But it is something you can begin practicing right now.

CHAPTER EIGHT ACTIVITY

1. Select two partners, people whom you trust.

2. Agree to meet once a week for one hour.
3. During this hour, practice:
   - Good listening skills
   - Inquiry skills
4. Each 20-minute round consists of the following:
   - *Speaker* gives a brief (2–3 minutes) description of some current issue.
   - *Listener/inquirer* practices listening skills and progresses into inquiry skills.
   - This discussion goes on for 15 minutes.
   - The third person is the *observer/timekeeper.* When he or she stops the discussion after 15 minutes, he or she begins a 5-minute discussion focusing on the listener/inquirer, giving feedback to the listener/inquirer and commenting on what he or she did that helped or that may have gotten in the way. Both the speaker and listener/inquirer participate in this feedback discussion initiated by the observer/timekeeper.
   - When the 5-minute feedback discussion is over, switch roles and do another 20-minute round.
   - It may take a year of weekly practice sessions before you are adept at these skills.

REFERENCES

Bateman, W.L. 1990. *Open to question: The art of reaching and learning by inquiry.* San Francisco: Jossey-Bass.

Gingrich, N. 1994. *Deming's profound knowledge and the renewal of American civilization.* Cincinnati, OH: The Eighth Annual Deming Conference, August 15. Sponsored by OQPF, Piqua, Ohio.

Gordon, T. 1977. *Leader effectiveness training: L.E.T.* New York: Bantam Books.

Joiner Associates. 1990. *The Joiner 7-step method.* Madison, WI: Joiner Associates.

Kerridge, D., and Kerridge, S. 1996. *The zero stage.* Self-published, Old Aberdeen, Scotland. E-mail: dfk@rsc.co.uk.

Kume, H. 1985. *Statistical methods for quality improvement.* Tokyo: The Association for Overseas Technical Scholarship. (Available through: UNIPUB, One Water Street, White Plains, NY 10601, [800] 247-8519.)

Langley, G., Nolan, K., Nolan, T., Norman, C., and Provost, L. 1996. *The improvement guide.* San Francisco: Jossey-Bass.

Nolan, T., and Moen, R. 1987. Process improvement. *Quality Progress,* September.

Satir, V. 1988. *The new peoplemaking.* Palo Alto, CA: Science and Behavior Books, Inc.

Satir, V. 1976. *Making contact.* Millbrae, CA: Celestial Arts.

9 PERFORMANCE WITHOUT APPRAISAL

OK, Smithers, we've got 12 minutes to agree on what was your fault last year.

INTRODUCTION

We are living in a less than humanistic managerial era. Companies use the rhetoric of humanism, but their policies and practices are often based on distrust, paternalism, and a none-too-subtle cynical disregard for their employees.

> In the entrance area of the management training center for a big-3 auto manufacturer I saw a large mural that declared: "Our employees are the most important factor in our success."
>
> Two minutes before I saw this mural, my host informed me that "morale might be down today because yesterday the company announced the elimination of 1200 employees from this area."

When I visit companies I witness many examples of such disparity between the rhetoric and the practice:

- A manufacturer in South Carolina emphasizes teams and teamwork. But it has team members rate and rank each other and discipline their members. It rewards teams for how successfully they compete with other teams in the company. This is an example of the rhetoric of teamwork confounded by the policies and practices of counter-teamwork.
- A bank in Wisconsin has a series of incentives that are meant to urge their loan officers to increase business.
- State legislators all over the country are introducing legislation to hold teachers, principals, and school superintendents accountable for the achievement of students. Student achievement is measured by their scores on standardized tests. If the scores are poor, the teachers' and administrators' jobs are in jeopardy.

Odds and Ends

Continental Airlines came in dead last in on-time performance for June even though it had offered employees everything from cash to pizza to finish first in the Department of Transportation monthly rankings.

—*The Wall Street Journal*
13 August 1995

This is an example of a failure to understand systems and an abysmal lack of profound knowledge (see Chapter 2).

What is behind this patronizing approach to management, this less-than-humanistic era? Behind these managerial practices are some false assumptions and cynical beliefs.

The Assumptions Behind Performance Appraisal

- Evaluation will improve an employee's performance.
- The employee being evaluated has control over the results.
- The employee's individual contribution can be discerned from the contributions of the system and other managers and workers in the system.
- All processes with seemingly identical equipment, materials, training, job descriptions, etc., are, in fact, identical.
- The standards of evaluation are related to factors demonstrably important to the business and its customers.
- The standards are reasonable and achievable.
- Each system in which an employee works is stable and capable of delivering the expected results.
- The evaluation covers performance over the entire cycle of evaluation, not just the period recallable by recent memory.
- All evaluators are consistent with each other.
- Each evaluator is consistent from one employee to the next.

These assumptions are seldom true, though they are commonplace.

The Cynical Beliefs of Conventional Management: Skinner in the Workplace

Current traditional management practice reflects some long-held beliefs about people that have been incorporated into a theory of psychology articulated by B. F. Skinner. Companies and their managers may have never heard of Skinner or his teachings, but their approaches to people still reflect Skinnerian practices. Skinner's teachings have been pervasive in schools and workplaces for most of the last half of the twentieth century.

Essentially, Skinner regards human behavior as a set of responses that can be conditioned. Just as owners of pets train their animals to behave in certain ways with combinations of rewards and punishments, so too must human behavior be formed through such conditioned responses. People are not much different from Pavlov's dogs or the proverbial jackass whose movement is governed by the carrot and the stick. As noted in Chapter 2, the carrot and stick approach is used to move a jackass and, as far as we know, its effectiveness is limited to that species. It is less than flattering when managers try to use on their employees an approach intended for jackasses. (See Levinson, 1973.)

Comments from Dr. W. Edwards Deming

In 1988 Dr. Deming had graciously agreed to write a foreword to The Team Handbook. *Time got short and I had to remind him.*

Meanwhile I had asked him to review my first article on performance appraisal (Scholtes, 1987). The tasks got confused and Dr. Deming wrote a foreword for the article. *Below is his foreword as he wrote it.*

> The fundamental aim of Deming's teachings is to develop a system of management that will ensure pride of workmanship to everybody. In technical terms, the teaching of this aim requires some knowledge of psychology, and some knowledge of variation, with the aim to reduce variation of processes, and to understand something of the interaction of forces, and of operational definitions.
>
> The same aim and theory leads to better understanding of the evils of the so-called merit system or annual appraisal of people. Actually, such ratings are not ratings of people, but are mostly ratings of the system that they work in, and of the interaction of the system with the people that work in it. The fact is that the system that people work in and the interaction with people may account for 90 or 95 percent of performance.
>
> Understanding of common causes of variation and understanding of special causes discloses the fallacy of studies of examples of success. Examples of successful companies repeat the mistake of attributing their success to special causes, outside the system, when actually, success on the one tail of the distribution and failure in the other tail, both come from the same common cause-system. Understanding of variation, common causes, special causes, interaction of forces, and operational definitions should be ingredients of a liberal education.
>
> People that follow the teachings of the underlying theory find that their own lives have changed; likewise their relationships with members of the family and with companions and with associates in business.
>
> Many people are concerned about how to influence others, in particular how to bring about changes in the management of their companies. It is pleasing to note that Mr. Scholtes addresses himself in this book to this important problem on how to accomplish change.

About four years later at a seminar in Washington, D.C., someone in the audience asked Dr. Deming:

> "If we eliminate performance appraisals, as you suggest, what do we do instead?"
> Dr. Deming's reply: "Whatever Peter Scholtes says."

Dr. Deming both paid me an honor and gave me a challenge.

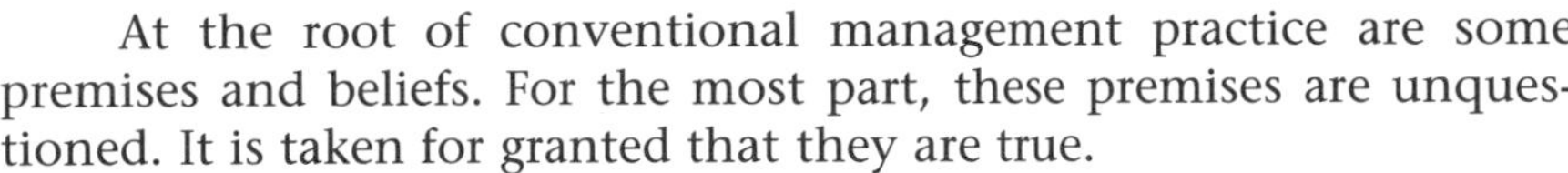

At the root of conventional management practice are some premises and beliefs. For the most part, these premises are unquestioned. It is taken for granted that they are true.

The Unquestioned Premises of Conventional Management

People cannot be trusted.

At least there are a sufficient proportion of untrustworthy people that policies and procedures should be developed on a presumption of distrust. (See the Falk Corporation story later in this chapter.)

People don't want to work or accept responsibility or carry their share of the load.

If you turn your back, they will cease to maintain the illusion of being busy.

People don't want to learn or improve. They want to be left alone.

Any attempt to intervene or help will be rejected or ignored.

People are withholding their best effort and can be induced to do better only through incentives (carrots and sticks) imposed from the outside.

The job of a manager is to motivate his or her people. The way to motivate is to use carrots and sticks.

These unquestioned premises of conventional management (Theory X) would do less harm if they were questioned. The act of identifying these beliefs as assumptions—as premises or theories—and questioning their validity could spark a healthy dialogue. It is the *unspoken* and *assumed* nature of these implied tenets that creates a toxic and perverse environment, a spirit of disrespect that permeates the organization. The message to people is that they are inferior and untrustworthy, even when the official rhetoric speaks of respect for people who are "our most important assets."

Alfie Kohn on B. F. Skinner

In his book *Punished by Rewards*, Alfie Kohn (1993) argues the case against carrots and sticks. Kohn makes several references to Skinner, including an appendix describing a conversation he had with the famous behaviorist. Kohn's comment on Skinner: "B. F. Skinner could be described as a man who conducted most of his experiments on rodents and pigeons and wrote most of his books about people" (p. 6).

Douglas McGregor on Carrots and Sticks

Douglas McGregor's father and grandfather were ministers. They both worked in a homeless shelter, founded by the grandfather, in Detroit during the 1930s depression era. Young Douglas worked in the shelter with his father and grandfather.

As he grew older, Douglas became more and more disturbed by the negative attributions his father ascribed to the unemployed and homeless (that they're shiftless and lazy, etc., much the same as what some say today). The younger McGregor would argue with his father that the poor were no different from others, they were simply down on their luck and the victims of a dismal economy.

Eventually his dispute with his father evolved into McGregor's famous articulation of *Theory X* and *Theory Y* (1960, Chapters 3 and 4).

Theory X assumptions about workers:
The traditional view of direction and control

1. The average human being has an inherent dislike of work and will avoid it if he or she can.
2. Because of this characteristic of dislike of work, most people must be coerced, controlled, directed, or threatened with punishment to get them to put forth adequate effort toward the achievement of organizational objectives.
3. The average human being prefers to be directed, wishes to avoid responsibilities, has relatively little ambition, and wants security above all.

Those who believe the assumptions of Theory X, McGregor teaches, will see carrots and sticks as the only effective way to get things done. Those who use carrots and sticks are implicitly subscribing to Theory X assumptions. Otherwise carrots and sticks would make no sense.

Theory Y assumptions:
The integration of individual and organizational goals

1. The expenditure of physical and mental effort in work is as natural as play or rest.
2. External control and the threat of punishment are not the only means for bringing about effort toward organizational objectives. People will exercise self-direction and self-control in the service of objectives to which they are committed.
3. Commitment to objectives is a function of the rewards associated with their achievement. The most significant of such rewards, the satisfaction of ego and self-actualization needs, can be direct products of effort directed toward organizational objectives.
4. The average human being learns, under proper conditions, not only to accept but to seek responsibility. Avoidance of responsibility and lack of ambition are generally the consequences of experience, not inherent human characteristics.
5. The capacity to exercise a relatively high degree of imagination, ingenuity, and creativity in the solution of organization problems is widely, not narrowly, distributed in the population.
6. Under the conditions of modern industrial life, the intellectual potentialities of the average human being are only partially utilized.

A System of Profound Problems

Problems seldom exist independently of each other. Problems reinforce other problems in a self-perpetuating cycle. Figure 9-1 shows a commonplace system of problems.

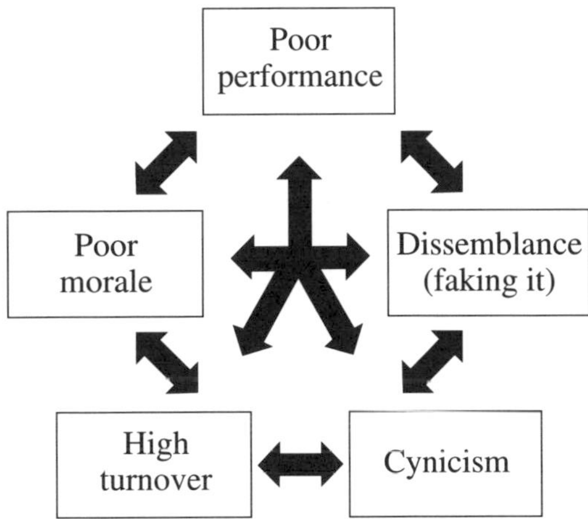

Figure 9-1. A system of problems.

Most problems don't exist in isolation from others. For example:

> A company was experiencing what the CEO considered to be unacceptably high employee turnover (*poor performance, high turnover*). The CEO directed the Vice President of Human Resources to accept the reduction of turnover as a performance goal for the year. The VP of HR knew that turnover was a complex issue, influenced by factors well beyond his ability to control (the economy, pay rates, etc.). He tried to talk his boss out of it, but to no avail. He was angry that his boss was so simplistic and inflexible in his directive (*poor morale, cynicism*). While the VP of HR had little control over turnover, he *could* control the operational definition of turnover. So he changed the definition of turnover from an event that happened relatively more often to one that happened relatively less often (*dissemblance*). The VP of HR, therefore, met his performance goal, although there was no systemic improvement. He created the illusion of progress. (See Petronius Arbiter's quotation on p. 79.)

What Causes a System of Profound Problems?

It is my belief that this system of problems is the result primarily of a system of management policies and programs, as shown in Figure 9-2. My theory: If you practice these management policies and programs you will produce these problems. If you wish to get rid of these problems, you must get rid of these policies and programs.

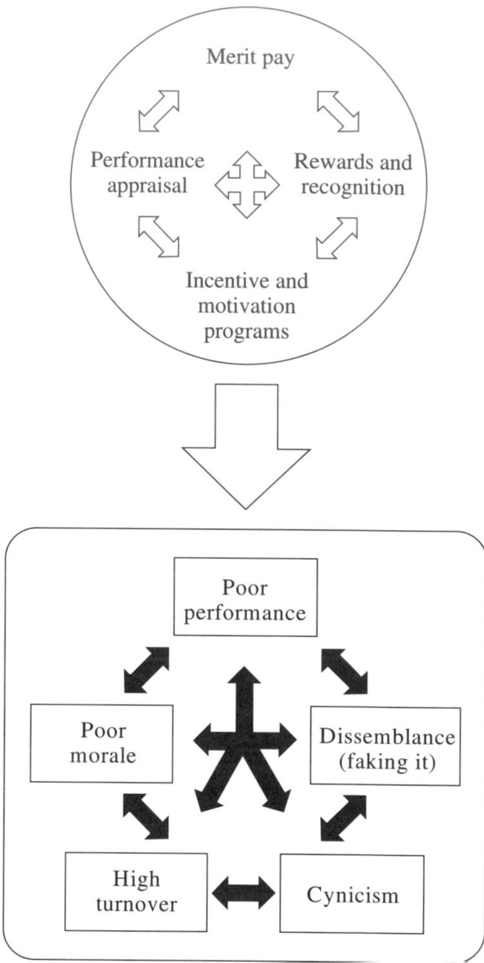

Figure 9-2. A system of management policies leading to a system of problems.

Why Do We Have Such Management Policies and Programs?

This is the heart of the matter! The reason we have devised such policies and programs, creating such a system of problems, has to do with our beliefs and premises about people and work. We come full circle to the points made earlier in this chapter and to the insights of Douglas McGregor: If you distrust your people you will devise programs, policies, and interventions based on that premise. The programs, policies, and interventions become self-fulfilling prophecies: Treat people as untrustworthy and they will act in a way that you may well interpret as untrustworthy. Figure 9-3 shows this self-sustaining system of profound problems.

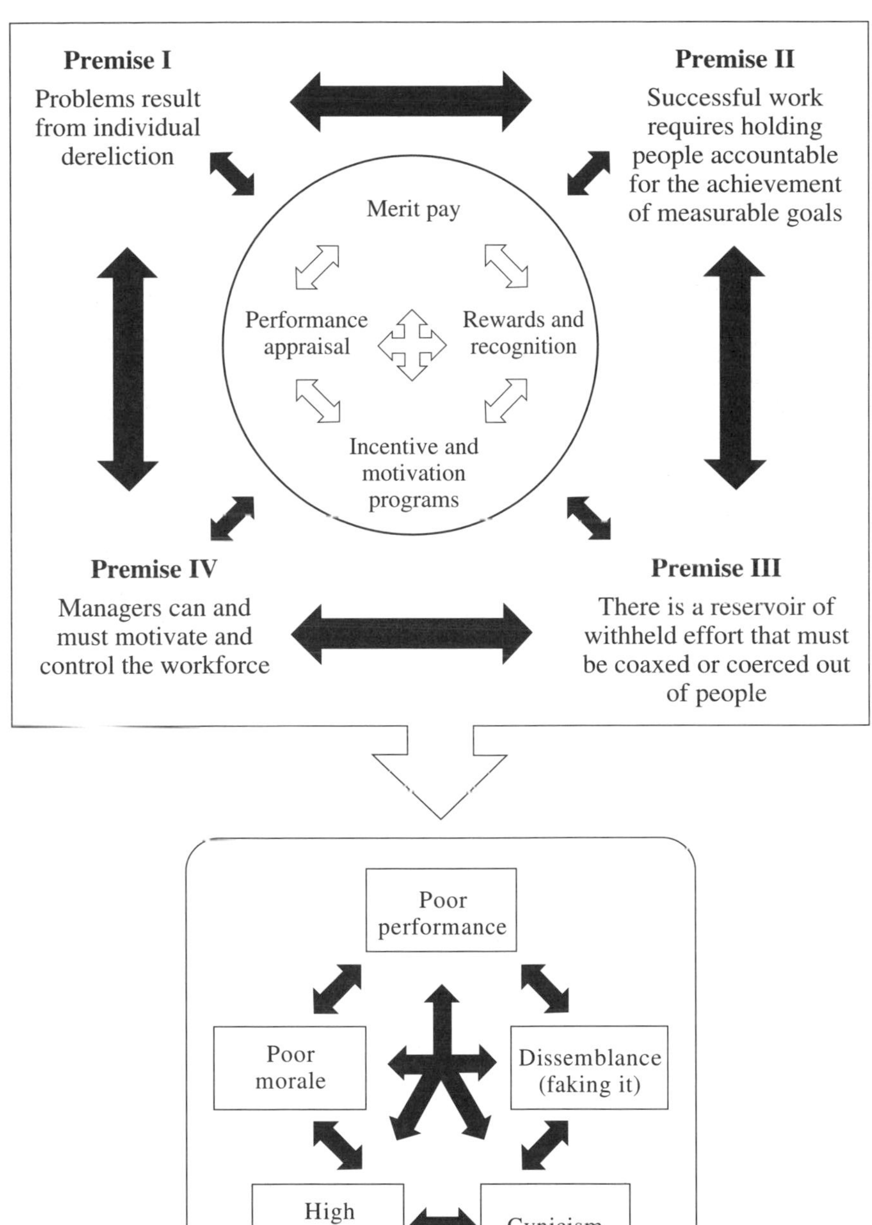

Figure 9-3. The self-sustaining system of profound problems.

The Falk Corporation: Do We Trust Our Employees?

(Adapted from a presentation given by Falk's top managers)

In the mid-1980s, the Milwaukee-based Falk Corporation, a subsidiary of the Sundstrand Corporation, was struggling to understand the philosophy of W. Edwards Deming.

They began to explore the eighth of Dr. Deming's famous 14 Points: Drive out fear. This was a particularly pertinent point for the Falk Corporation because they had experienced a long history of adversarial relationships with their employees. At some point in their discussions, the managers decided to look at the converse of fear. "If there were no fear, what would there be?" Their conclusion: "Trust!"

Then they began to explore the issue of trust: Do we trust our employees? Are our employees trustworthy? How can we develop and maintain a companywide environment that promotes mutual trust and respect?

What is characteristic of a trustworthy employee?

The leaders of Falk decided to try to determine what proportion of their employees were trustworthy. Trust, after all, began with them as managers. They developed two lists of characteristics, one describing a trustworthy employee, another an untrustworthy employee.

THE TRUSTWORTHY EMPLOYEE

- Is a responsible adult
- Wants to contribute and do good work
- Cares about the company—wants it to succeed
- Comes to work every day
- Can be trusted

THE UNTRUSTWORTHY EMPLOYEE

- Given an inch, takes a mile
- Does just what's required
- Feels that it's just another job
- Doesn't really give a damn
- Here today—tomorrow?
- Can't be trusted

Having developed their working definitions of trustworthy and untrustworthy—lists remarkably similar to McGregor's Theory X and Theory Y descriptions—they then attempted to come up with an estimate of how many of their employees resembled the *trustworthy* list and how many the *untrustworthy* list. Their conclusion: *At least 95 percent of our people are trustworthy. Maybe 5 percent of our workforce is untrustworthy.*

The Falk leaders asked whether their policies, practices, and procedures were written for the 5 percent or the 95 percent. Their belief now was that policies written to the 5 percent were not compatible with a commitment to Point 8.

Policies written with trust in mind

The leaders at Falk then initiated a yearlong process of policy revision, education, and training. Here is an example of an old policy based on mistrust and a new policy based on trust.

BEREAVEMENT LEAVE (the old policy)

> *All employees shall receive* time off with pay up to a maximum of three (3) days for working time lost if there is a death in the immediate family.

These days must be within a seven-calendar-day period, the first day of which would be the initial bereavement day paid. However, one of the days must be the day of the funeral. If the funeral falls on a nonscheduled workday (Saturday, Sunday, holiday, during a plant shutdown, or during a period of disability), no loss of pay is involved, therefore bereavement pay will not be made for such days.

Pay will be for eight (8) hours at the employee's day rate plus average premium for the three (3) months prior to the month in which the time off occurred.

A part-time employee's pay will be based on average hours worked in the previous month and will be at the employee's day rate plus average premium.

An employee's immediate family will be considered ... spouse, child, stepchild, mother, father, sister, brother, stepparents, grandparents, and grandchildren of the employee; son-in-law and daughter-in-law; mother, father, sister, brother, and grandparents of the spouse.

Payment will be made by the company upon request by the employee to the personnel department.

The personnel department may require verification of death and relationship of the employee.

BEREAVEMENT LEAVE (the new policy)

If you require time off due to the death of a friend or family member, make arrangements with your supervisor.

What were the results? How did the use of bereavement leave under the new policy contrast with its use under the old policy? The total number of days used for bereavement leave under the new policy was 47 percent of days used under the old policy, less than one-half the previous use of bereavement leave.

The premises hold the practices in place. The practices beget the problems. The premises are untrue and contrary to systemic thinking.

Premise I. Problems result from individual dereliction.

A negligible proportion of an organization's problems—no more than 4 percent according to Deming—can be attributed to the malfeasance of employees. To believe that problems are attributable to worker errors is to elevate a negligible cause of problems to a predominate cause.

Premise II. Successful work requires holding people accountable for the achievement of measurable goals.

Successful work requires having a consistent and reliable set of systems, processes, and methods by which you and your people design, develop, and deliver what the customers need when and how the customers need it. Systems are created, sustained, and improved by insightful and interactive work on the *system,* not by using carrots and sticks. Measurable goals do not improve systems; accountability does not improve systems. *Improving systems* improves systems.

Do people have to be accountable? Of course they do. And they are, almost all the time! The question, therefore, is mostly irrelevant. A better question is: Why do things go wrong even when those doing the work are being accountable and doing their best?

Premise III. There is a reservoir of withheld effort that must be coaxed or coerced out of people.

This is the premise behind incentive pay programs. This is the theory used by Continental Airlines to improve on-time performance (see p. 294). While few managers would admit to this belief about their people, the policies and practices they use give dramatic evidence of this cynical belief. Few managers would say that they themselves need incentives to do a good job. It is others who need to be bribed into giving the extra effort: "*I'm* OK, *you* need incentives!"

Premise IV. Managers can and must motivate and control the workforce.

See the comments on motivation in Chapter 2. Managers must remove the factors that *demotivate* the workforce. They must work together with employees to control and improve the systems, processes, and methods of work. This is less likely to happen in an environment where managers are seeking to control people and blame them for things gone wrong.

When people ask, "If we get rid of performance appraisal, what do we do instead?" my first response is: "Think differently!" Behind this somewhat flippant response is the importance of getting rid of the dysfunctional premises. If managers don't purge these assumptions about the nature of people and work they will not develop true alternative practices, only minor variations on the same theme.

WHAT DO WE MEAN BY PERFORMANCE APPRAISAL?

What, therefore, are we talking about when we discuss performance appraisal, including all the minor variations? Figure 9-4 describes the performance cycle common to most performance appraisal or performance management programs.

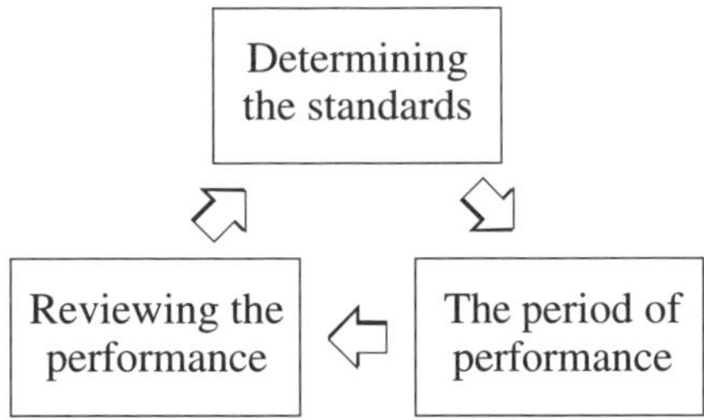

Figure 9-4. The performance cycle.

Determining the Standards

Some variations:

- Using carefully described, measurable definitions of expected accomplishments. (What will be done, by when, with what characteristics and standards, etc.)
- Standards negotiated between the evaluator and evaluatee, imposed by one or the other, or a combination of negotiated and imposed standards.
- No formal separate standards, but general guidelines such as job descriptions or group objectives.
- No standards at all against which to review actual performance, just the prevailing opinions.

The Period of Performance

Some variations:

- Most common: a 12-month cycle
- Next most common: six-month or quarterly cycles
- Rarely more frequent than quarterly

Reviewing the Performance

Some variations:

- Who does the reviewing?
  - — Usually the person's boss
  - — Sometimes the person's peers
  - — Sometimes the bosses, subordinates, peers, internal suppliers, and internal customers (often called 360° evaluation)

- Who is reviewed?
  - — Usually an individual worker is reviewed by his or her boss.
  - — Sometimes an individual is reviewed by his or her peers.
  - — Sometimes a boss is reviewed by his or her subordinates.
  - — Sometimes a group is reviewed by their common boss.
  - — Sometimes a combination of the above applies.
- Does it involve evaluation?
  - — Sometimes the review is an informal discussion with no apparent judgment attached.
  - — Types of judgment or evaluation:
    - - numerical rating
      - 3, 4, 5, etc., a point scale
      - phrases instead of a number rating
      - forced distribution: an imposed bell-shaped distribution of the ratings (see Figure 9-5)

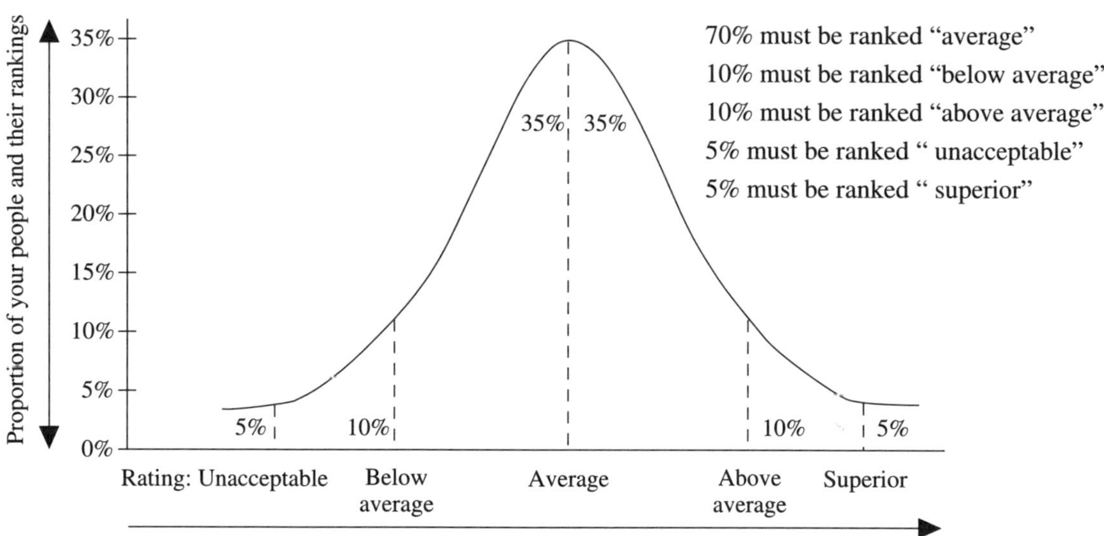

Figure 9-5. An example of forced distribution.

- pass/fail system

Implications of the Review

Some variations:

- No implications: a sort of "for what it's worth" discussion
- Remuneration implications

- Merit pay (salary increase)
- Merit bonus
- Commissions
- Quota or piecework-based pay

- Other implications
  - Determines who is eligible for promotion
  - Determines who is vulnerable to layoffs
  - Preferred treatment (parking places, gifts, trips, etc.)

When I talk of performance review or performance appraisal, I am referring to the basic cycle described in Figure 9-4 and any of the variations described above. The sum total of my comments on "What's wrong with performance appraisal" will apply to the cycle itself and to *all* the variations. What I will be saying is: *There is no good way to do performance appraisal (or performance review). It is inherently the wrong thing to do.*

THE CASE AGAINST PERFORMANCE APPRAISAL

The Three Faults Common to All Variations of Performance Appraisal

1. It doesn't work.

There is no valid research to demonstrate that an organization is better off for having used performance evaluation. There are no long-term benefits to be gained from it that can be confirmed through legitimate research. Most research on performance appraisal consists of opinion polls asking, "Which kind of performance appraisal do you prefer?" These opinion surveys are usually conducted by those predisposed in favor of performance appraisal—consulting companies who teach it, for example. These surveys are usually filled out by HR managers who are, as a group, predisposed in favor of performance appraisal. When biased people ask the opinions of biased people, the results cannot be described as research. If someone wants to claim that performance appraisals are useful, that claim should be based on *real* observable data, not biased opinion data (see Chapter 6).

Are performance appraisals successful? According to one study reported by Timothy Schellhardt in *The Wall Street Journal* (November 19, 1996), over 90 percent of appraisal systems are unsuccessful. I suspect it is far worse.

> Performance appraisal is that occasion when once a year you find out who claims sovereignty over you.
>
> —Peter Block

2. Performance appraisal focuses mostly on individuals, sometimes on groups. Either one is the wrong target.

The false premise here is that improvement occurs one employee or one group of employees at a time. As we have emphasized, most problems, and therefore most opportunities for improvement, are in your systems and processes, not in your individuals and groups. Group evaluation is no better than individual evaluation. Group or individual evaluation conducted four times per year is not an improvement over annual performance appraisal. It is four times worse.

3. Performance appraisal is *judgment,* not *feedback.*

Judgment is a *hierarchical* dynamic. Feedback is a *systems* dynamic. The word feedback is a systems word. In the case of audio-electronics, feedback occurs when sound from the speaker *feeds* into the microphone, creating that horrible electronic sound. It is a loop or circuit of electronic system-based interaction. Organizationally, feedback refers to one part of the system—one stage in the flow of activities and contributions—providing information to a preceding part or stage of the system (see Chapter 4). Here are some major points of emphasis regarding feedback:

- Feedback is systemic, not hierarchical. The hierarchical relationship will almost inevitably turn the nature of the interchange into an act that is, or is perceived to be, judgmental.
- Feedback must be in the form of data, not judgment. Data are often statistical in nature, for example a run chart on the variation in delivery time (see Figure 9-12). Judgment is the explicit or implicit attribution that the other person is right, wrong, good, or bad: "You are late again!"
- The purpose of feedback is the improvement of the process. While the stated intent of performance appraisal may be improvement, the form of it is ratings and judgment. This is less related to improvement and more related to the control of the person being evaluated. Data intended for improvement are data that lead to discovering the patterns of occurrence and the systemic cause of the performance under examination. An act of judgment presumes that the cause is the inadequacy of the person being evaluated, not any systemic origin of poor performance.

Therefore, for any appraisal policy, ask the following:

1. Are there data involved in the exchange, or merely judgment?
2. Is the review from one part of the system to an antecedent part of the system? Or is it from a boss to a subordinate?
3. Is it directly related to improvement of the process or is it related to the accountability of the individuals or groups?

These three questions should help sort out most of the deficiencies of most programs of performance appraisal. The following paragraphs highlight other shortcomings of performance appraisal.

Performance Appraisal and Motivation

Performance appraisal is an example of the reliance on *external* motivation as opposed to *internal* motivation (see Chapter 3). As stated earlier, the problem with external motivation is that:

- It doesn't work (except with simple activities for the short term).
- It affects the relationship between the motivator and the motivatee (patronizing instead of peer-based). It can also affect the relationship between all the individuals being motivated, making them more sibling-like than adult partners.

Again, the very assumption that people *need* to be motivated and that a manager can do it is dubious at best and affects the relationship between the motivator and motivatee.

Performance Appraisal and Teamwork

As depicted in Figure 9-6, the dynamic of performance appraisal is different from the dynamic of teamwork, Figure 9-7.

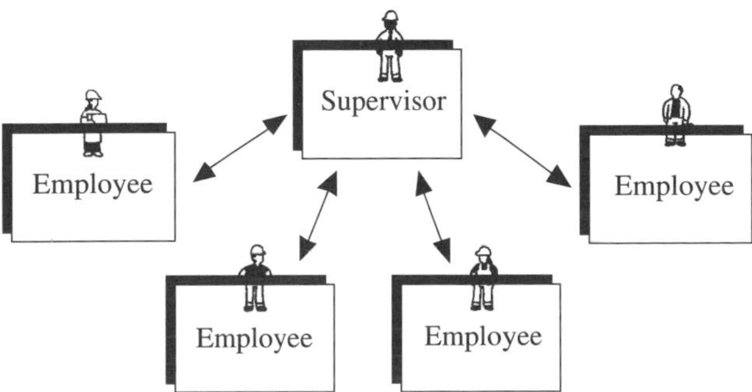

Figure 9-6. The dynamic of performance appraisal.

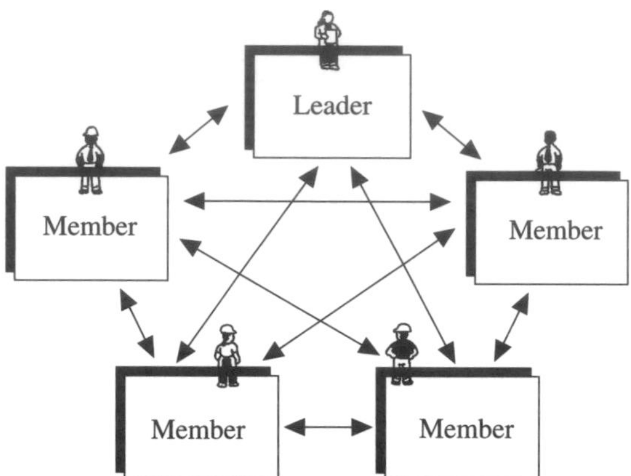

Figure 9-7. The dynamic of teamwork.

Each employee has a separate relationship with his or her supervisor, one that involves performance expectations and review. Each member of a team has a relationship with the team that involves expectations and interdependencies. Sometimes the employee may be forced to choose between what is expected of him or her by the supervisor and what is expected by the team. The conflict may be relatively minor and resolvable (two conflicting events on the schedule) or it may be more substantial (conflicting philosophies, priorities, or methods). Which takes precedence: the team's expectations or the supervisor's? Usually in such cases the team's needs will be displaced and undermined by each team member's obligation to his or her supervisor.

A supervisor, furthermore, is asked to do a nearly impossible act of discernment, when evaluating the performance of one member of a team. Is it possible to take the net output of a team and extract from that the individual contribution of one member? Probably not. Therefore, performance appraisal not only undermines teamwork, it asks the supervisor to pretend that there is no team contribution to an individual's performance.

Performance Appraisal and Systems

In another version of impossible discernment, the supervisor must either pretend there is no system or presume to extract from the net output of the system that which is attributable to the individual employee being evaluated. This is depicted in Figure 9-8.

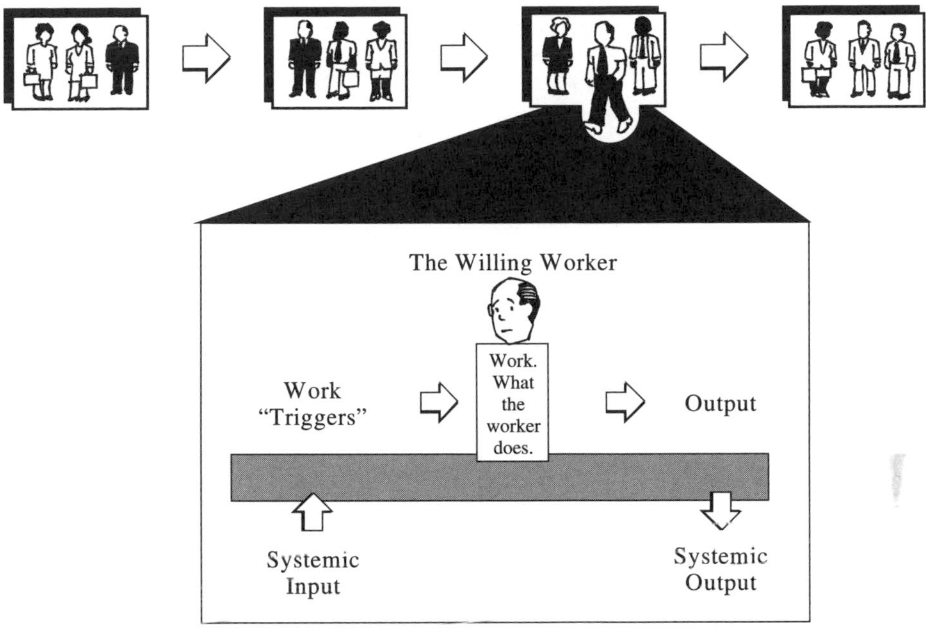

Figure 9-8. The system and performance appraisal.

Whether it is an individual being evaluated or a team, how can a supervisor account for all of the systemic influences that precede the performance of one step in the system? The answer is: The supervisor can't. Yet he or she must pretend to.

Moreover, performance appraisal will undermine the system. When all individuals or groups are seeking to look good, they will tend to optimize their performance regardless of what is best for the system. This is pictured in Figure 9-9.

Performance Appraisal and Variation

As we discussed in Chapter 2, everything varies. We cannot eliminate variation (for example, the amount of time to do a job, the frequency of mistakes and errors, the costs of doing business). But we can reduce variation and eliminate the special causes of variation.

The work of each individual is characterized by variability. For example, the performance of one truck driver, Fred, is shown in Figure 9-10.

Optimize performance	For example	And suffer negative consequences	For example
Here	Biggest television advertising campaign ever	There	No budget left for radio, print or outdoor advertising
Now	Push for highest quarterly sales ever	Then	Next quarter's sales plummet
Short term	Drastically reduce costs	Long term	• Shortages • Breakdowns • Poor quality

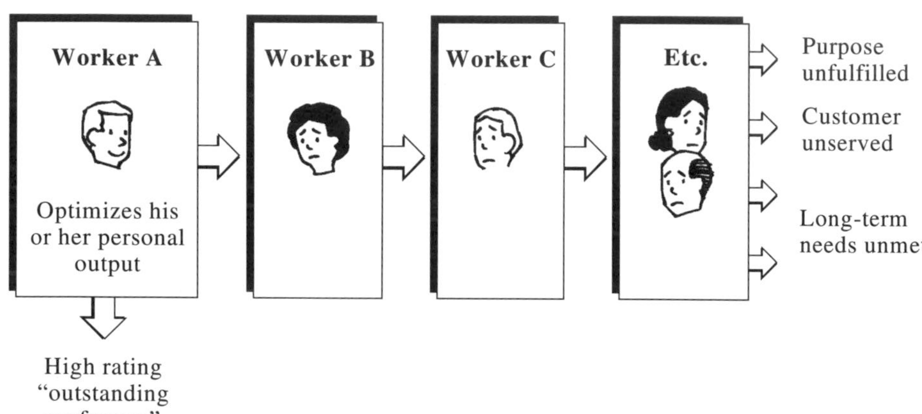

Figure 9-9. Individual optimization versus systems optimization.

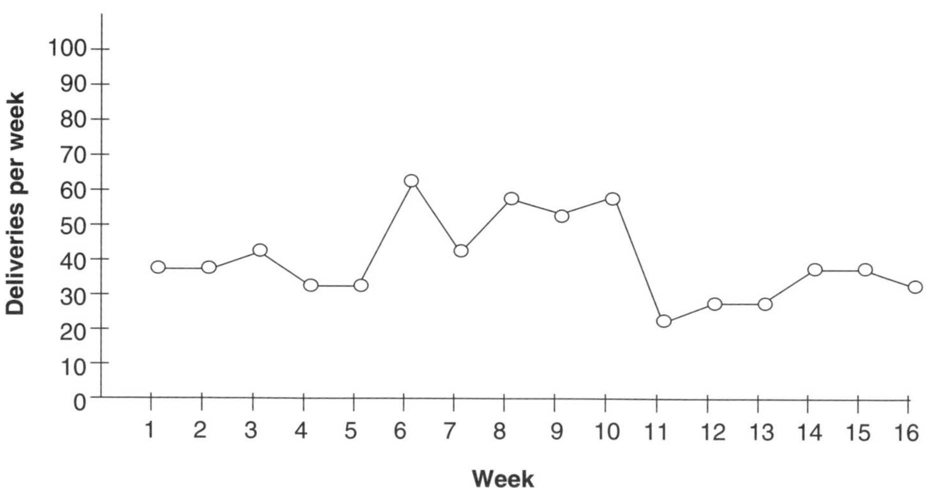

Figure 9-10. Fred's record of weekly deliveries.

Is Fred's performance good or bad? That question is commonly asked. But it is of less importance than the question, How can Fred's performance be improved? One way to answer the "good or bad" question is to contrast Fred's performance with the performance of the two other drivers, Amy and Dave, as shown in Figure 9-11.

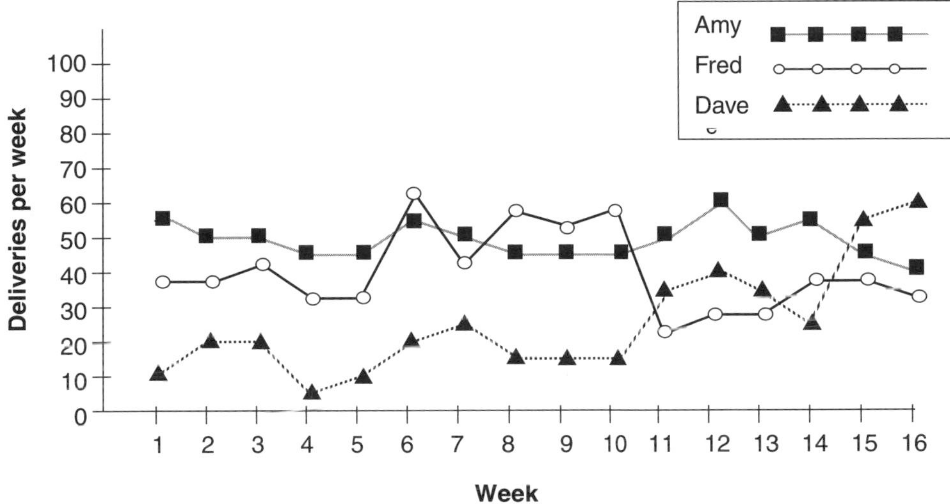

Figure 9-11. Contrasting Fred, Amy, and Dave.

Who is better? Who is worse? If we appraised their performance at week 5 we would have drawn one conclusion, at week 10 another conclusion, and yet a different conclusion at week 16. Which appraisal would be most accurate?

The answer: We don't know. We don't even know if they have the same job (even though they have the same title and maybe even the same job description).

We said earlier that the more important question is, "How can Fred's (or Amy's or Dave's) performance be improved?" The conventional practice is the use of performance-based pay (the proverbial carrot). This would involve paying the drivers on the basis of how many deliveries each made per week.

The repercussions of such a system can be profound and perverse. Some examples are:

- Each driver might compete with the others to get the best, most reliable, largest-capacity truck.
- Each driver might compete for the easiest delivery assignments.

Pass It Down the Line

One east coast manufacturing company had a policy that rewarded teams for defect-free work. The manufacturing process unfolded through several stages, each stage run by a team of workers. Data on the team awards indicated that those teams working in the early stages of the process were virtually defect-free and got more awards. Those in the final stages didn't do so well. Why? It was common practice at each stage, whenever possible, to send defects on to the next stage. "Let them take the hit," as one worker described it.

- Drivers might indulge in creative accounting: trying to get one delivery counted as two or unloading a delivery somewhere nearby where it can be made after hours or on weekends, meanwhile going back to the warehouse to get more jobs.

If the drivers were put in more explicit competition with each other (one merit bonus for the best driver each month), you could expect to see little cooperation, more resentment, and perhaps even subtle sabotage.

Performance appraisal is based on the unconscious premise that *all* performance is a *special cause* attributable to individuals and that there is no variation built right into the system (common cause variation). This is an *unconscious* premise for two reasons:

- Few managers conducting performance appraisal are even aware that there are such things as variation, common causes, and special causes.
- Few managers conducting performance appraisals chart performance data in time order using a run chart or a control chart. Without this kind of data a manager won't know what kind of variation exists or how to deal with it. What managers do, in their ignorance of variation, is likely to *increase* variation. Seeing trends where there are no trends, they will introduce unnecessary interventions into the system. Such tampering will only increase variation.

Performance Appraisal and Continuous Improvement

Approaches to improvement can focus on seeking to improve the system and finding the systemic cause of the problem, or seeking to improve the individual worker and finding the culprit. Performance appraisal encourages a superficial, culprit-oriented approach to problem

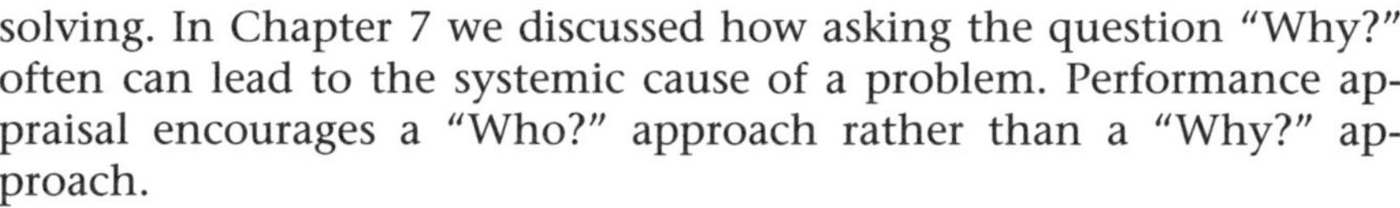

solving. In Chapter 7 we discussed how asking the question "Why?" often can lead to the systemic cause of a problem. Performance appraisal encourages a "Who?" approach rather than a "Why?" approach.

Performance Appraisal and Bias

Our companies use many measurement devices, some of them very sophisticated. We have instruments to measure weight, density, thickness, diameter, PH levels, viscosity, speed, and time. We have instruments that can measure differences in quantity undetectable to the naked eye: instruments of great refinement and exactness.

Except when it comes to measuring human performance.

When it comes to measuring human performance we use the most unrefined, inaccurate, unreliable, and capricious method we could possible devise: one human subjectively reviewing another human. We wouldn't permit the neighborhood butcher to weigh our hamburger with an instrument as inexact as the instruments with which we evaluate the performance of our employees.

Same Label, Different Products

A chemical company received complaints from its customers that their products had too much variation in the contents. The customer would order product X and it would be delivered in a drum labeled product X. But the contents of the drum would vary from one shipment to another.

The cause of the problem?

Different shift supervisors had their own individual recipes for product X. At the beginning of a shift, each supervisor would make his or her own settings and instructions for the making of the product. At the end of the shift, each supervisor would alter the settings and remove the instructions. The result: variation from one shift to the next.

The cause of this behavior?

Supervisors were competing for a bonus awarded to the supervisor whose shift produced the greatest volume of good product. It was not in their personal interest to share their favorite formula for product X with the other supervisors.

It took a major effort and a policy change regarding supervisor bonuses to get these supervisors to agree on a single formula for product X and, therefore, the same contents under the Product X label.

There is inconsistency in the method, criteria, and philosophy of evaluation between one evaluator and another. There is inconsistency in the way a given evaluator evaluates one employee and how he or she evaluates another employee. We are hopelessly subjective and we are not at all objective about our subjectivity.

There are numerous factors affecting favorable or unfavorable bias. Some are universal, some are regional. Here's a partial list:

- Dress style
- Political affiliations
- Military background (or the lack thereof)
- Ethnic origin
- Food preferences
- Educational background
- Age
- Who your family is
- What team you root for
- Hairstyle
- Religious affiliation
- Social affiliations
- What you drive
- How you speak
- Music preferences
- What you do on your own time
- Physical appearance
- What comics you laugh at

None of these are job-related. Almost all of them have some influence on how well accepted and regarded you are and whether performance evaluation will work in your favor or your disfavor.

Performance Appraisal, Relationship, and Morale

When we enter an organization's workforce, we enter a network of relationships. The social structure and interactions of the organization will help us feel more included or more excluded, more valued as a new member or more discounted as an intruder. These relationships are affected by everyone in the organization, not just management. But the leaders have the indispensable role of setting the tone and modeling the behavior. If the leaders are blameful, for example, then it is likely that blamefulness will cascade down and throughout the organization like a rock slide.

The policies and managerial activities put in place can be either divisive or unifying. Leaders can provide challenge and support for the task at hand and the people doing the task, or they can signal indifference to the task and the people. Leadership policies and practices can imply trust of people or distrust of them, loyalty to people or no loyalty to them at all. The leadership and management policies and practices are a pretty good indicator of how the leaders regard their employees in particular and people in general. (See Chapter 10.)

Evaluations and Attractiveness

It has been well documented that if you are physically attractive you will have an advantage over those with ordinary looks. This applies to being hired and promoted, and it applies to getting high marks on a performance appraisal.

Those who are biased toward the physically attractive—and almost everyone is—will be unaware of this discriminatory tendency and, when it is pointed out, will deny it exists.

There appears to be one exception to this attractiveness advantage: Being attractive is a liability for a woman in a management position. This provides women with a perplexing dilemma: Can ordinary-looking women move up the promotional ladder? And can an attractive-looking woman manager get a fair evaluation once she has become a manager?

If there were a truly unbiased, uncapricious performance appraisal program—one that did not reward those who were lucky and pass by those who were unlucky—would we be better off? Half of your people would learn that they are below average. It's a statistical inevitability. Will this help them? Will this improve anything? Some who are classified as below average may resign themselves to their fate. Others will see such classification as clear evidence that managers are hopelessly incompetent. Among your employees you have created some losers and some cynics. And to what end? Maybe some of those classified as below average will decide to redouble their efforts and vow that next year they will either do better or at least appear to do better. They will seek to do this even when it is unlikely that any system has improved. Maybe they will be lucky, appear to do better, and be ranked above average, in which case their below average slot will open up and someone else will fill it.

We all want to work together in a place without discouragement, all on the same side, proud of our work, joyful in our work. Performance appraisal assures that we will never approach such an ideal workplace.

The I-am-not-making-this-up Department

Excerpt from a memo written by a manager, sent to me by one of his people: *"Eighty-five percent of our people are above average. Of the remaining 15 percent, most of them are above average too!"*

The I-am-not-making-this-up Department

No beauties for Kelantan (from the *Star,* Australia, 11 August 1996)

Kuala Lumpur (dpa)—Malaysia's fervently Islamic Kelantan state, ever watchful of possible immoral activities, has added a new directive to its long list of strictures. It will now hire only ugly women at government offices.

The decision will help prevent "unhealthy activities" which may arise in government offices where there are too many pretty women, Kelantan's Chief Minister Nik Abdul Aziz was quoted as saying.

"Since the prettier candidate has already been blessed by God with the gift of beauty, it's only right that we hire the uglier candidate, or else who will?" he added at a village lecture Wednesday night, according to the Malay-language daily Utusan Malaysia.

Perhaps this is Mr. Aziz' way of avoiding the attractiveness advantage during performance appraisals.

OUR FIXATION WITH HEROES AND CULPRITS

Our popular culture seems to reflect a collective assumption that if something wrong is to be made right, it will be because of an outstanding effort by a heroic individual. The system, if thought of at all, is regarded more as the source of the problem than the source of the solution.

Hollywood relies on this perspective. Every generation has had its version of the theme: Things go wrong, the system is either helpless or corrupt, the hero intervenes, and everything is put right. This has been true since Tom Mix and John Wayne and continues with Clint Eastwood, Bruce Willis, Brad Pitt, and a host of others. Let's face it, if the system functioned well the crises would have been prevented, or at least quickly brought under control. And the movie would be over before the first reel and without any special effects. Boring.

Meanwhile our society has created a cult of hero worship. We love to give awards to outstanding performers. America has a proliferation of academy-award-like ceremonies. We have employees of the month and year with photos in the lobby and reserved parking places. Whenever I visit a Holiday Inn, I look for their wall full of employee of the month photos. I have never seen a case in which more than one person is recognized in a given month. Apparently there is a policy of contrived and artificial scarcity. Nor have I ever seen a case in which one employee is employee of the month for more than one month per year. Apparently getting the award carries with it a jinx similar to being on the cover of *Sports Illustrated.* I have never seen an organization that had a photo of the manager of the month hanging in its entrance area (though I have frequently observed reserved parking places for managers). Is this another policy that managers see as needed by "them" but not by "us"? (*I'm OK, you need an employee-of-the-month program.*)

What Is an Outstanding Performer?

First let us deal with some myths. The following are fallacies:

- That it is easy to identify outstanding performance and outstanding performers, be they good or bad.
- That our judgment on this is correct and trustworthy.
- That organizational success should depend on the outstanding performance of its individuals.

A little statistical thinking is in order here.

There is variation in all work. An example:

Figure 9-12 shows the performance of a cross-functional process that includes order entry clerks, assembly workers, and shipping and delivery workers during a one-month period.

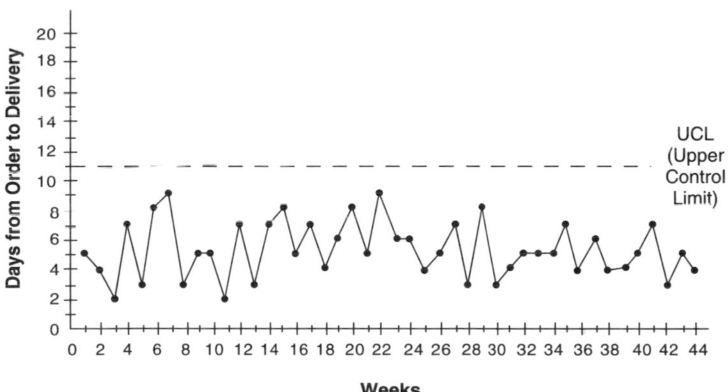

Figure 9-12. Order to delivery cycle (days elapsed) 44 orders; (8 weeks) data.

Analysis of these data will show the following:

- This process appears to be in statistical control. There are no apparent special causes.
- The length of cycle time within this system is predictable within a given average and range of variation. It is predictable because the cycle time is inherent in the system.
- The 2-day delivery time (e.g., in week 11) is presumably better than the 9-day delivery time (week 7), but it is the same system—with its built-in capacity for elapsed time—that produced the results of week 7 and week 11.

- To decrease the time required for this order-to-delivery cycle, the focus must therefore be on the process, not the individual workers who work within the limitations of the process.

Figure 9-13 takes the data in Figure 9-12 and displays it as a histogram. Managers may be unhappy with this performance, because they have pledged delivery in "usually less than five days." This pledge was kept only 17 times in 44 orders. Nevertheless, statistically speaking, there is nothing outstanding, good or bad, in this performance.

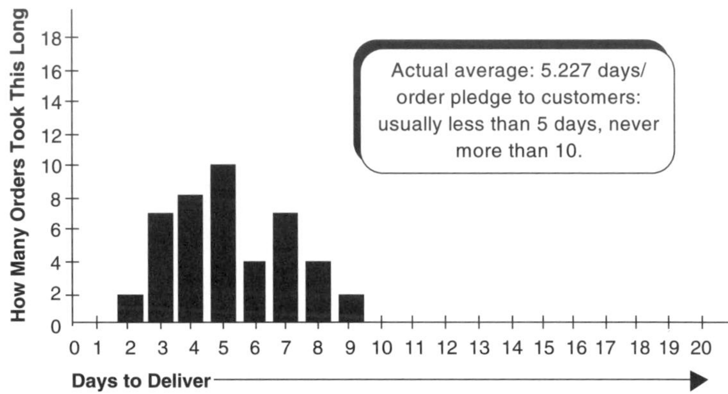

Figure 9-13. Order to delivery in days.

What does *outstanding* mean?

Again, we will use statistical thinking.

Figure 9-14 is similar to Figure 9-12 except for orders 14 and 23. For these orders something extraordinary occurred. Statistical analysis will indicate that the performance in these orders was not predictable and was outside the system's normal variation.

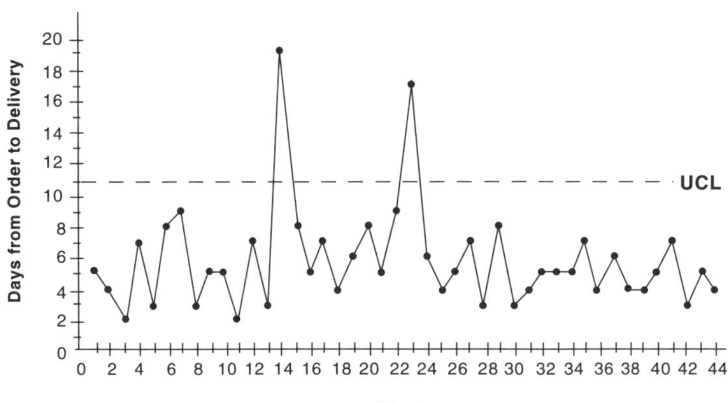

Figure 9-14. Order to delivery cycle (days elapsed) 40 orders; one month's data (with special causes).

Figure 9-15 shows the same data in a histogram rather than a time plot. This also shows the peculiar nature of the two orders from weeks 14 and 23. These two orders are literally outstanding.

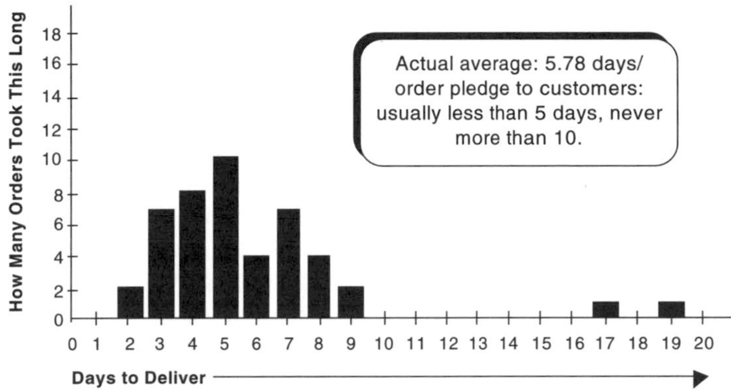

Figure 9-15. Order to delivery in days: with special causes.

Outstanding can be defined psychologically or statistically. Most managers don't use the statistical approach to the word outstanding. In Figure 9-14, there are two orders that took only two days to process. A manager may look at those and say "Outstanding!" This is the psychological sense of outstanding. Statistically, however, the two orders that took two days are not any more outstanding than the 10 orders that took five days or the 3 orders that took nine days to process. These are all from the same process. There are, however, two outstanding events: the delivery that took 17 days and the one that took 19 days. These are, statistically speaking, *special-cause variation* or *outstanding performance.* In this case the performance is, presumably, outstandingly poor.

What is outstanding? Outstanding describes the performance of a system, process, method, or employee that is statistically beyond the predictable range of variation regarding some characteristic. Applied to people, outstanding performance would look like this (Figure 9-16):

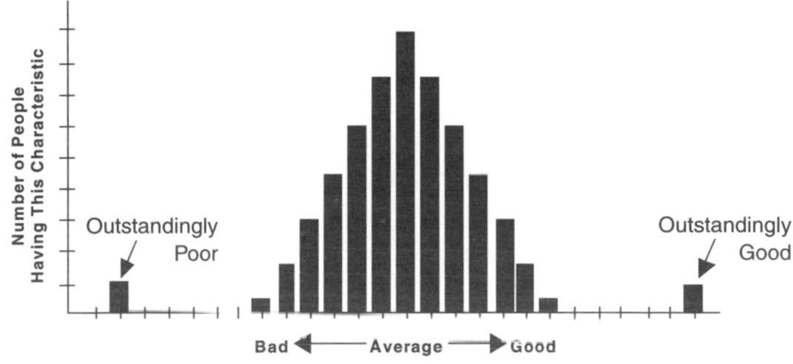

Figure 9-16. The degree of presence of some characteristic (e.g., speed or accuracy).

Looking at outstanding through this perspective we can understand that outstanding is a rare and difficult-to-detect occurrence. Most of what we call outstanding is simply variation built right into our systems and processes. Most of those labeled outstanding are just lucky or unlucky.

Why, then, does performance appraisal occur?

One short answer to this question—why do executives evaluate their employees—is: Because they believe it works. Behind this practice are many assumptions and premises, already discussed in this chapter. The almost unshakable belief of many managers is that they can accurately and objectively identify those employees whose performance is consistently above or below average. They also believe that such performance, in a significant way, contributes to the bottom line, for better (above average performance) or worse (below average). The so-called logic supporting performance appraisal, therefore, goes like this:

- There are good performers and bad performers.
- We can tell the good ones from the bad.
- Good performers make a positive contribution to the net output and prosperity of the company.
- Bad performers are detrimental to the company's performance.
- Performance appraisal serves to clarify an individual's work responsibilities, align the worker with the organization's goals, hold each worker accountable for his or her responsibilities, and motivate them to continuously improve.

This is the logic behind performance appraisal. The alternative logic presented in this chapter is that the *system* is by far a greater determinant of good or bad performance than any individual's work behaviors.

In spite of the logic in favor of performance appraisal and despite the belief of many executives that performance appraisal works, consider these realities:

- As described earlier, 90 percent of managers using performance appraisals describe them as "unsuccessful." (See Timothy Schellhardt's report in *The Wall Street Journal,* November 19, 1996.)
- As we have already suggested, there are no legitimate data to support the effectiveness of performance appraisal.

Once again, why do we do performance appraisal?

- Not because it works. It doesn't.

- Probably because of our unspoken assumptions and beliefs about people, organizations, and the nature of work.
- Underneath it all, I believe, performance appraisal is related to a manager's need to maintain *control,* or at least *the illusion of control.* My observation and theory are summarized here:

> Performance appraisal seems to be most highly regarded by those who are most distant from the everyday work. People in the Gemba are not asking to have their performance appraised, nor are their immediate supervisors. Performance appraisal reflects the needs of some remote executive official or high-level staff person. Headquarters' people want performance appraisal to be imposed throughout the organization because it demonstrates that the executive-level managers and staff are exercising some direction and control over employee performance. Since headquarters and the executive offices are physically removed from real work and real workers, the only forms of motivation and control they have to offer anyone are externally imposed motivation and control, namely performance appraisal.

Outstanding Systems versus Outstanding People

An appropriate question for leaders is: Where in the organization must I exercise control? This will be explored more fully in Chapter 10. However, a few points are emphasized here:

- Leaders should not seek to control the individual employee's job performance. Leaders won't succeed and if they try they are liable to make things worse.
- Leaders have usually sought to control finances. These, indeed, must be in control, but leaders are probably not the right people to do it.
- The same is true of marketing and sales. When leaders get involved they are just as likely to mess things up as to affect them positively.

What do leaders do?

- *Promote systems thinking.* This includes a fixation on the customers and the smooth flow of interdependent activities and events that serve the customers well.
- *Work with all the managers and employees to control the systems, processes, and methods.* Control these and continuously improve them.
- *Seek to create and maintain outstanding systems.* The ideal is: outstanding systems, achieving excellent results, with the ordinary efforts of average people.

Another Tune on the...?

For years I searched for an analogy to describe a change with no improvement. First I would say, "It's a change but not an improvement, like another tune on the accordion." But I discovered to my regret that there were lots of accordion music lovers who took understandable offense at my analogy.

Then I said, "... like another tune on the bagpipe." While there appear to be fewer bagpipe lovers than accordion lovers in America, the bagpipe lovers are more militant in their defense of their favorite instrument.

Finally I found the perfect analogy, "... like another tune on the triangle." The triangle is the perfect analogy for these reasons:

- The triangle has almost no constituency. For instance, there is no national association of triangle players.
- Whatever following the triangle has, it is not composed of militant defenders.
- It is impossible to discern one song on the triangle ("Stars and Stripes Forever") from another ("Happy Birthday to You").

PERFORMANCE WITHOUT CARROTS, STICKS, AND APPRAISAL

As clear as it is to me that performance appraisal is not only useless but harmful, I recognize that getting rid of it is not easy. What are the alternatives to performance appraisal? Let me give two seemingly flippant answers and then one answer that is hard work but has been proven successful.

Change the Way You Think!

This was suggested earlier in this chapter. The point is this: If you retain the same old assumptions, beliefs, and premises about people and work, you are liable to not even see alternatives that are true alternatives. You will merely create variations on the same old theme, three-point scales instead of five-point scales, another tune on the triangle.

This book is dedicated to changing the way you think.

Just Stop Doing It!

If something is demonstrably the wrong thing to do, if it is harmful to you and others, you don't necessarily need an alternative in order to cease doing it. In order to stop beating your head against the wall, you don't need something else to beat your head against.

Performance appraisal is harmful to people and to your organization. For the moment, imagine that tomorrow you decide to get rid of performance appraisal. What chaos will that create? You may be forced to reconsider the way you do some of the following:

- How will we pay people?
- How will we promote people?
- How will we give feedback to people?
- How will we identify training needs?
- How will we fire, downsize, or outplace people?

These questions lead to the third alternative to performance appraisal:

Redesigning Performance Appraisal at Ford: Another Tune on the Triangle

Several years ago Ford Motor Company put together a high-level committee of managers to review their performance appraisal policy and recommend changes. After a year of discussion, the group came to consensus on the following:

1. Change the name from performance appraisal to performance management.
2. Change the nine-point rating scale to a four-point rating scale.
3. The performance process would provide an opportunity for discussion, between a supervisor and his or her employee, on ways to improve the employee's performance. The supervisor was to take on the role of coach.

Over five years later, Ford leaders concluded:

- The revised rating system was not providing useful information.
- The existence of the rating interfered with the coaching.

Dr. Ed Baker, who was with Ford at the time, had these comments on this incident. "These were well-intentioned people and they weren't fools. The moral of this story:

- Don't rush into the redesign of a new policy until you have profound knowledge.
- Consensus arrived at without profound knowledge may relieve your immediate pain, but can have long-term and costly consequences to the organization... and these are the costs that are invisible."

Tailgate Transformation

It was the day of a Green Bay Packers game. The Glenroy Company of Menomonee Falls, Wisconsin, was having a tailgate party in their parking lot prior to the game.

Top management the previous week had held a management retreat. In the course of their retreat the managers decided to review a number of employee policies. Amid the revelry of the tailgate party, therefore, it seemed appropriate to stoke the bonfire with copies of the soon-to-be-outdated copies of the employee policy manuals... all of them! The policies went up in a blaze of glory!

Several weeks later it was time for performance appraisals and for the annual review of salaries for the upcoming fiscal year. Because of the bonfire, they discovered, they had no remaining record regarding pay policies, the methods for determining pay, and the policies regarding performance appraisal.

They started from scratch. They told employees that they were to meet in job classification groups and decide what they would be paid. In every instance the employees were more conservative and tight-fisted than the managers would have been. The wage and salary suggestions of the employees were adjusted upward. As for performance appraisal, they simply dumped it.

The following years were not an unmitigated success. There was lots of chaos and confusion as the company sought to put together a new system of policies and procedures. There was a real test of how much common understanding and consensus had been achieved at the management retreat.

One learning: Transformation by tailgate bonfire is probably not the optimal approach.

Debundling: A Proven, Successful Alternative to Performance Appraisal

Debundling means taking apart all of the various separate services or perceived benefits that one assumes performance appraisal offers an organization. Over the years I have asked clients and seminar audiences, "Why does your company do performance appraisals? What use does it serve?" Here is a list of the frequently cited responses:

- Identifying and responding to outstanding performers
- Creating a basis for pay
- Providing feedback to individual employees
- Giving direction and focus to the workplace
- Identifying career goals
- Identifying education and training needs

- Identifying candidates for promotion
- Identifying candidates for layoff
- Fostering communication between employees and their supervisors
- Creating a paper trail that will serve as a defense against suits for wrongful dismissal or other perceived unfair treatment
- Conforming to regulatory requirements
- Motivating employees

If your organization should undertake debundling, you might undergo the following sequence of discussions:

Step 1. List the various functions benefits and services you hope are derived from your performance appraisal program.

↓

Step 2. Ask of each benefit or service: Is this something important enough to find a way to accomplish?

↓

Step 3. If so… take each benefit or service that is important to accomplish and treat it as a separate function, disconnected from all the others.

↓

Step 4. For each separate benefit or service ask: What is the best way to successfully provide this benefit or service without using performance appraisal?

- What purpose and values must be maintained?
- Which old premises or perspectives must be discarded?
- What actions should be taken?
  - In what sequence?
  - By whom?
  - With what methods?
  - Why?
- What systems or processes are needed to support and maintain these activities?

Some Important Values to Maintain

When debundling these services and designing separate alternative systems, keep the following principles in mind:

- Focus on improving systems, not rewarding or punishing individuals.
- Focus on customer satisfaction, not management satisfaction.
- Don't optimize one part of the system to the detriment of:
  - — the customer,
  - — the purpose of the system, or
  - — the good of the whole system.
- Don't make the cure worse than the disease.
- Don't just play a different tune on the triangle; think outside of the current paradigm.

DEBUNDLING THE SERVICES OF PERFORMANCE APPRAISAL

1. Identifying and Responding to Outstanding Performers

Use *outstanding* in the statistical sense, not in the psychological sense. Statistically, outstanding refers to something occurring outside the current capabilities of the system.

GUIDELINES FOR RESPONDING TO OUTSTANDING PERFORMANCE

Determine for certain that they truly are "outstanding"

As with any special cause, investigate to discover what is behind this occurrence (use data!)

Depending on the explanation behind the outstanding performance, formulate an appropriate response

- Are there data to substantiate "outstanding performance"?
- Are the data plotted over sufficient time to indicate consistent performance at a significantly lower or higher level?
- Is there consensus among the "outstanding performer's" peers (based on observation, not gut reaction or rumors)?

Positive Outstanding

- Better methods that can be taught to others?
- Puts in more hours?
- Wider range of skills?
- More experience?
- More native talent?

Negative Outstanding

- Needs to learn a better method?
- Needs to pick up speed?
- Needs coaching or mentoring for a while?
- Going through a difficult period?
- Lack of basic requisites for the job?

Positive Outstanding

- Teach methods to others
- Change in market value, therefore higher pay
- More latitude in job definition

Negative Outstanding

- Coaching, mentoring, training
- Provide greater structure and more constraints for a while
- Get counseling and support
- Find a more appropriate position
- Outplace (aka fire)

Diagram 9-3.

SHOULD YOU EVER FIRE ANYONE?

Before deciding to fire someone

During the dismissal

After the decision to fire someone

- Make sure he or she is truly a special cause.
- Make sure that your remedial efforts were well chosen, planned, and implemented.
- Make sure there are no other more suitable positions available for him or her in the organization.
- Anticipate problems and responses from others.

- Sensitive and fair treatment for the person being fired
- Adequate communication to others about the event

- Review the systems for recruiting, screening, hiring, training, or promoting people to see how this occurrence might be avoided.
- Reassure the survivors.
- Get feedback from those involved in order to improve the firing process.

Note: Firing someone still leaves you with a systems problem. You must improve the systems by which you recruit, screen, hire, train, and promote people.

Diagram 9-4.

2. Creating a Basis for Pay

Dealing with Some Myths

- A capricious evaluation system will result in a capricious pay system.
- There is absolutely no evidence to support the belief that people work more productively when rewards are tied to performance. There is evidence of the opposite (see Kohn, 1993).
- There are no data to support a predictable relationship between organizational performance and any currently popular executive pay system. Almost all current top management pay is based not on empirical research but on "what sounds about right."

What Is the Purpose of Pay?

- To provide just compensation for work.
- To allow people to sustain themselves in a decent manner with reasonable security.
- To retain qualified employees.

Noncapricious factors on which to base a pay system are listed below:

Market Rate

- People should get paid approximately what they would get paid for doing the same work elsewhere.
- Devise methods to survey the market rate for each position. "What do assistant personnel directors with approximately these same functions and duties get paid elsewhere?"
- You will discover in the market a roughly bell-shaped distribution. You decide where you will pay within that distribution: the 50th percentile? the 80th?
- Adjust pay when there is a substantial disparity between actual pay and market rate.

Tenure or Seniority

- How long the employee has worked for the company.
- How long the employee has worked in the industry.
- How long the employee has worked.
- How old the employee is.

Seniority Pay

The common objection to seniority pay is, "It's rewarding dead wood!" My response is, "Why do you hire dead wood? Or, why do you hire live wood and kill it?"

Tenure and seniority are not necessarily being recommended here as a basis for pay. They are simply presented as nonarbitrary. Seniority implies some recognition that the organization benefits in unmeasurable ways from an employee's experience. In some Japanese companies, seniority is the biggest single factor differentiating employee pay.

Profit Sharing

Employees receive a variable amount each year (or some other increment of time) reflecting the pretax prosperity of the company.

- *Same amount:* Some believe that the size of the profit sharing bonus should be the same for every employee, arguing that the policy should not imply that some people contribute more to the company's prosperity than others. Market share, they suggest, is sufficient differentiation in pay. Profit sharing need not continue that differentiation.
- *Same percent:* Probably the most common form of profit sharing.
- *A seniority factor:* Some allowance for tenure in the share of the profits. Those who promote this suggest that it encourages long-term thinking.

What about Gain Sharing?

Profit sharing is a dispersal of some portion of a company's profits to those whose work created those profits. Employees' fortunes, therefore, rise and fall with the company's. Gain sharing is MBO with a bribe attached.

Gain sharing, therefore, is based on an assumption that some form of motivation or incentive is necessary to get employees to accomplish good work. Gain sharing makes the following assumptions:

- That the goals are achievable and realistic.
- That the goals cannot be achieved using the normal pay system.
- That people need to be and can be motivated.

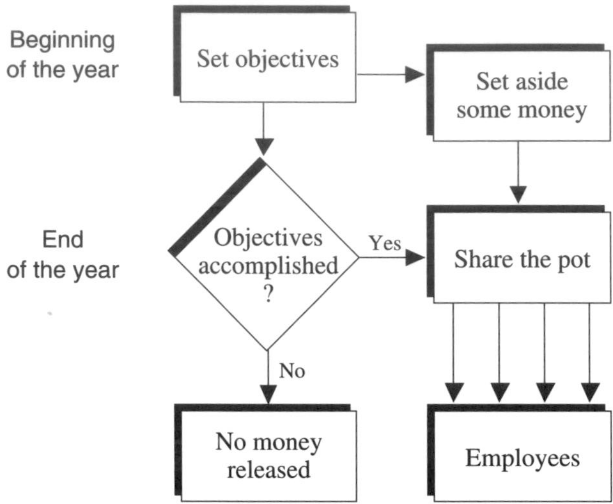

Figure 9-17. Gain sharing.

- That people can be motivated by money.
- That the systems are within the employees' ability to control or improve.

In summary, gain sharing seems to be not much different from the Performance Appraisal/MBO virus. Don't do it.

What about Pay-for-Skill or Pay-for-Knowledge?

The purpose of these is commendable: to encourage people to acquire more flexibility. There are, however, some worrisome elements in these pay-for programs:

- When someone has earned an incremental increase for learning a skill and that skill becomes obsolete (e.g., keypunching or some older word processing programs), what do you do? Drop their pay back? Give them a grace period to learn the new method?
- How do you certify that the employee has learned the new skill? What level of mastery is required? Do you plot data over time to show that a new level of performance is in statistical control?
- Some people work in areas where there is a lot of need for flexible skills. Some work in areas where there is little or no need for flexibility. There may be a matter of luck involved in this approach.

- Won't increased flexibility gradually be recognized as an increase in the market rate?
- How do you ascertain the acquisition of knowledge and some of the more elusive skills (e.g., grace under pressure) without resorting to something perilously similar to performance appraisal?

What about Pay-for-Performance?

There are various P-F-P schemes, the most famous of which is probably Lincoln Electric, where workers get paid on a piecework basis and must do rework on their defective pieces on their own time. Some concerns about these plans are:

- They tend to create internal competition and discourage cooperation.
- They tend to create a sweatshop culture.
- They encourage workers to pass on work that is tolerably mediocre, making your company vulnerable to competition with more consistent, high-quality standards.
- As workers get older and slower, their pay diminishes. Some would say this is okay. It seems to me like an ungracious response to those who have given their prime years to the company. (Do the managers of such companies expect annual automatic reductions in managerial salary after a certain age?)

Some Guidelines Regarding Pay

- Employee compensation should be a completely separate process from the employee feedback system.
- Performance issues are one thing. Pay issues are another. Keep them separate. Don't try to solve performance problems with pay solutions.
- Annual adjustments may include a factor for seniority.
- There should be no merit pay, because it is virtually impossible to differentiate on the basis of merit.
- All employees should benefit from the success of the company through profit sharing.
- The current executive compensation systems in American business cannot be justified on the basis of any reasonable and demonstrable measures of organizational performance. The difference between the highest-paid executive and the lowest-paid hourly worker in an American company is many times more than what it is in Japan or what it was in the United States 20

years ago. CEOs are paid about 187 times more than what the average worker is paid. In the mid-1970s, the ratio was 41 to 1. In Japan the ratio is closer to 10 to 1. (Source: Graef Crystal, University of California, Haas School of Business, reported in *USA Today,* November 17, 1995. See also *Business Ethics,* September–October 1991.)

- Some companies now fix the allowed differential (see *Business Ethics,* September–October 1991). Herman Miller Company fixes their ratio between highest- and lowest-paid people at 20 to 1.
- A compensation system consists of both tangible and intangible items. Tangibles are salary, bonus, fringe benefits, etc. Intangibles are the feelings an employee has of community support, challenge, trust, respect, security, pride in work, and joy in work. Intangibles cannot be bought but may have the greater influence on retaining employees who are attracting offers from other organizations. (See Chapter 10, Healing Workplaces and Learning Workplaces.)
- The greatest sources of motivation are intrinsic. Pay cannot motivate, but pay that is perceived to be unfair can demotivate.

3. Providing Feedback to Individual Employees

There are basically two types of feedback:

A. Performance feedback focused on the system

This has been discussed in some detail in Chapter 4. This feedback is generated either from the outside customers or from one stage in the flow of work to another stage. The purpose of this feedback is to better understand the capabilities and deficiencies of the system in order to improve the system and better serve the outside customer.

While this type of feedback will necessarily involve people handling the data, it does not involve feedback personally descriptive of any individual. "You are late!" is not performance feedback focused on the system. A run chart on the timeliness of deliveries would be systems-oriented feedback. One focuses on an individual's behavior. The other provides a data-based profile of the capabilities of the current system, as shown in Figure 9-18.

Figure 9-18 begins to display data useful in identifying the dimensions and characteristics of the lateness problem. This can lead to other analytical tools (e.g., a control chart) that will indicate whether there is special cause variation or common cause variation (see Chapter 2). Other forms of study would contrast types of projects or other factors that may show unique patterns of variation in the data.

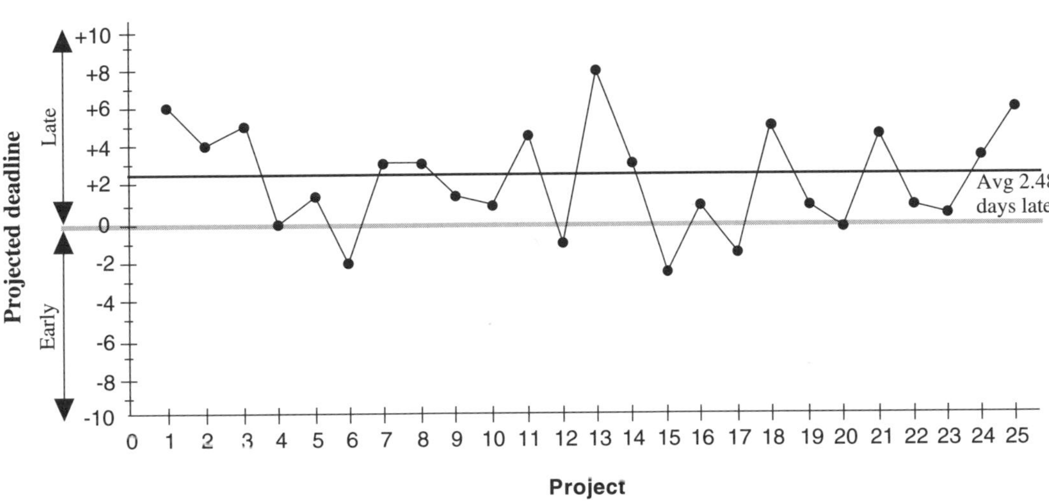

Figure 9-18. A run chart showing the timeliness capability of the current system.

Systems feedback may indeed originate from a single individual and be shared with an individual. This is inevitable when some stages in the process are conducted by one person. But the nature of what is observed, documented, and shared is focused on the *process,* not on the person. Moreover, the presumption is that any deficiency lies in the process, not the worker.

B. Personal feedback focused on the individual

This is the kind of feedback that becomes most problematic. There will inevitably be times when someone with whom you work does something that annoys you. The person may be your boss, your subordinate, or your peer. Their annoying behavior may be more or less work-related, or not at all related to their work. Do you give the annoying person feedback? If so, when and how?

Here are some guidelines:

- Don't give feedback when you are angry.
- Don't give feedback when the other person isn't ready for it.
- When the issue is a matter of personal characteristics and not job-related, the person who would receive the feedback should have control. He or she gets to decide:
  — Whether or not he or she wants feedback.
  — If so, regarding what kinds of issues. He or she decides what subjects are not to be feedback items.
  — From whom he or she is willing to receive feedback.

Marshall Industries

Robert Rodin is the CEO and president of Marshall Industries, a distributor of Industrial Electronics. Their 100 or so suppliers of electronics include Texas Instruments, IBM, Hitachi, Sony, Toshiba, and AMP. Their 30,000 customers include IBM, Apple, Hewlett-Packard, Motorola, Xerox, GE, and many other well-known electronics-based firms. Marshall's sales are over $1 billion and they are among the top three or four industrial electronics distributors.

Prior to 1990, Rodin reports, Marshall had performance evaluation, rating, and publicly displayed ranking of people, management by objectives, sales promotions, quotas, incentives, contests—all of the gimmicks typical in a sales dominated company.

Then Mr. Rodin started reading about Dr. Edwards Deming and went to a four-day Deming seminar. Also at this time he met one of Dr. Deming's closest associates, Dr. Nida Backaitis. Mr. Rodin, with Dr. Backaitis' help, began to rethink their policies and practices. To quote Rodin:

> The fundamental and scary change that we made over a series of years was to take every one of our individual departments off their own MBO, off their own incentive programs, and out of the commission environment. We put every single person, all 1360 at Marshall Industries, solely on salary and profit sharing. Everybody in the system is entirely aligned with customers and suppliers, who are the constituents we must focus on to keep our company alive.
>
> The amazing thing was that, on the day we took all of management (a thousand people who had been preparing for the change for one year) off the old system, we immediately received new levels of cooperation.

Marshall Industries also eliminated all promotions and contests. The top managers went out to Marshall's suppliers and persuaded them to discontinue their incentives to Marshall's sales force.

The bottom line. What was the business result of this dramatic charge? During this time, sales went from $530 million to $1 billion. Earnings doubled. Turnover went down by more than 50 percent. Stock rose from 17½ to 59½ and has since split. The bottom line is not all that has improved. Again, Robert Rodin:

> More importantly, intangibles are up: customer satisfaction, morale, teamwork, efficiency, productivity, consistency, and relationships.

The Marshall Industries story is told in *Beyond the Sounds of Silence* (Rodin and Backaitis, 1995).

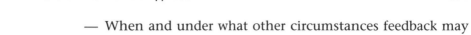

— When and under what other circumstances feedback may occur.

- One format for giving feedback that has been found useful is the "I" statement:

"When you ________________________________,
Describe the behavior that you observe in the other. No labels. No judgments.

I feel ________________________________
One or two words that describe a *feeling*.

because ________________________________."
Explain as well as you can why you react this way.

This formula allows the feedback giver to be descriptive without being prescriptive. One person is not saying the other must change. He or she is simply describing the effect of not changing. The feedback giver is not attributing motives to the other, but is simply describing what he or she sees or hears.

For more on feedback, see *The Team Handbook* (Scholtes, 1988).

Some may find the guidelines above overly restrictive. The guidelines are based on the following premises:

- The purpose of personal feedback is to be helpful to the person receiving the feedback.
- The helpfulness of the feedback is dependent on how ready the person is to receive the feedback.
- Anything else is serving the needs of the giver of feedback, not the receiver.

One final guideline on personal feedback:

- Look on personal feedback not as a simple event but as part of the larger system of relationships within work groups. The readiness for feedback can be the result of a carefully fostered environment of trust and candor, a nonthreatening set of relationships. Combine this supportive environment with some built-in routines that create an opportunity for feedback and some ground rules for giving feedback and receiving feedback, and you can create a work group that is both supportive and challenging, as shown in Figure 9-19.

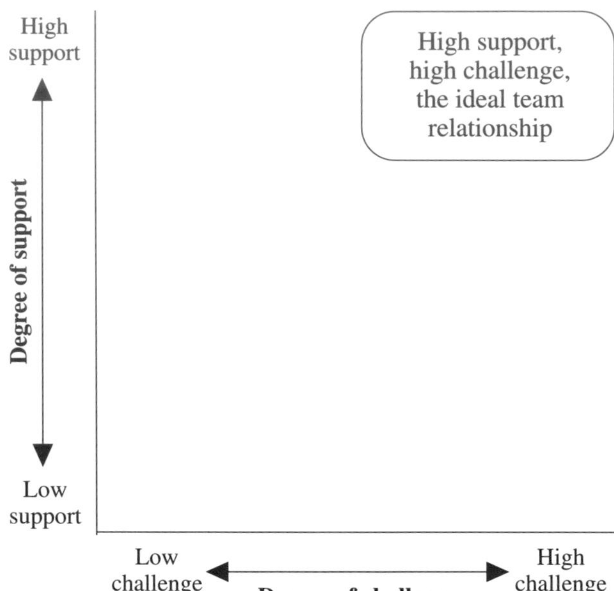

Figure 9-19. Challenge and support (adapted from Blake and Mouton's *Managerial Grid*).

4. Giving Direction and Focus to the Workforce

Performance appraisal is a woefully inadequate means to give direction and focus to either individuals or groups of employees.

Imagine your organization using the direction-setting systems introduced in Chapter 2 and described in detail in Chapters 5 and 6. Imagine also that the vast majority of your operations, processes, and tasks are standardized. Imagine that instead of vague job descriptions, people's jobs are largely standardized and described in the form of flowcharts. Imagine that your workplace follows the guidelines for standardization described in Chapter 4.

With all these in place, you have clearly established direction and focus. Performance appraisal can add nothing more of any value. Without what is described in Chapters 4, 5, and 6 your organization is unlikely to have any clear direction and focus, and performance appraisal can still add nothing of value. The time spent on performance appraisal would be far better spent giving your workforce a true sense of direction and focus. (See Figure 9-20.)

The Big Picture

- Mission
- Vision
- Values
- Philosophy
- Data on the key indicators
- Long-term goals and plans
- Mid-term goals and plans

Daily Work

- Standardized processes
- Everyday efforts to find better methods for daily work
- Feedback loops built into daily work
- Use of P-D-S-A on the job

Annual Priorities

- Organization-wide annual improvement plan and network of breakthrough improvement activities
- Department and local-site annual improvement plans and networks of improvement activities

Figure 9-20. The worker has direction and focus.

5. Identifying Career Goals

Dealing with Some Myths

- It is seldom necessary for a supervisor to get involved in helping employees sort out their career needs.
- Career counseling and career development are specialized services. Most supervisors have neither the time nor the ability to provide these services, except at a rudimentary level.

Guidelines

Managers and supervisors can provide moral support, at a personal level, for an employee's career ambitions. But what employees need are systems of (A) career counseling, (B) career ladders, and (C) education assistance.

A. Career Counseling

- Career-mindedness is a personal need. Most people go through stages when ambition and advancement are prominent in their thinking. At other times in their lives, they aren't ready to think about career. Therefore, assistance in career planning should be a service available at the option of the employee.
- General Motors Powertrain division, for example, has a career development module available for use by employees. This replaces a more or less required conversation on career goals between supervisor and subordinate as part of the annual performance review.

GM Powertrain

In the early 80s, Dr. Deming started a series of regular consulting visits to the Powertrain Division of General Motors. During the same time, GM began sponsoring four-day seminars led by Dr. Deming and held in Detroit for its employees. In the mid-1980s GM Powertrain began to debundle its old performance appraisal program. Their new development program was to be based on two very nonconventional premises about people:

1. People want to do their best.
2. People want to be in control of their own development.

The new development program consisted of modules: aggregates of materials and services available to employees. Some of the modules were:

1. *The feedback module (this refers to personal feedback)*
    - It is controlled by the employee.
    - Employee controls timing, frequency, and design of the feedback.
    - It is voluntary.
    - Employee decides who will give him or her the feedback.
    - Feedback is given directly to employee, not conveyed through a manager.
2. *The development module*
    - Helps the employee become knowledgeable about the formal and informal systems in the company that are available for personal development
3. *The "what interests you" module*
    - Helps employees explore what they like to do and find ways to develop their current jobs to fit those preferences

The development program was developed by a 12-member panel, people who were the customers of Powertrain's Human Resources department. Some other key points:

GM recognized a need for a diversity of approaches:

- Individual's needs for feedback and development are variable.
- The employee can opt in or out of the development process.

Important features of the development process:

- It doesn't involve MBO.
- It is not a method for business plan deployment.
- It is not a performance identification vehicle.
- It is a process involving self-knowledge.
- The employee identifies where he or she is and where he or she wants to go.

Key values:

- Let people assess themselves.
- The supervisor is not the exclusive source of feedback.
- The employee has control.

This information is adapted from videotaped interviews by Mary Jenkins and Chris Oster of the GM Powertrain HR department. Mary is now a private consultant.

- Consider providing access to a professional career counselor for those employees interested in exploring career options.

B. Career Ladders

- For careers within your own organization, create career ladders showing the steps of possible progression from entry-level, nonprofessional positions to advanced, professional-level positions. For example, show the movement from receptionist or filing clerk to partner in a law office.
- Career ladders should be based on meaningful increments of accomplishment, building greater skills, flexibility, or qualification to do the work.
- Steps in the career ladder should be measurable. Accrediting documents from licensing or certification organizations may be necessary requirements but don't necessarily demonstrate applied capability. A better measure may be shown in a time-ordered plot of some key process indicator or key quality characteristic. These data can demonstrate ongoing capability, not just the completion of training activities.
- Along with the career ladder, describe the education, training, or work experience necessary to help move from one position to another.
- Be careful not to promise what cannot be delivered. Don't imply that people are entitled to a position if they complete the requirements. Don't elevate expectations, especially if your organization is becoming flatter.
- Respect the freedom and choices that individuals make for themselves. There is nothing inherently better or worse about choosing to climb the ladder or choosing to stay on the rung where you are.
- Figure 9-21 is an example of a career ladder in the Assessor's Office of the City of Madison. It begins with entry-level positions in the clerical, technical, and professional areas and describes the steps to management positions. This information is provided to all new employees as part of their orientation. One employee, over several years, progressed from "Clerk Typist I," an entry-level clerical position, to "Deputy Assessor," the second highest position in the agency.
- You can only state the current system and the current requirements for progressing through the system. Be sure people understand that the systems and requirements will certainly change. Flexibility will be important. Keeping people informed is important.

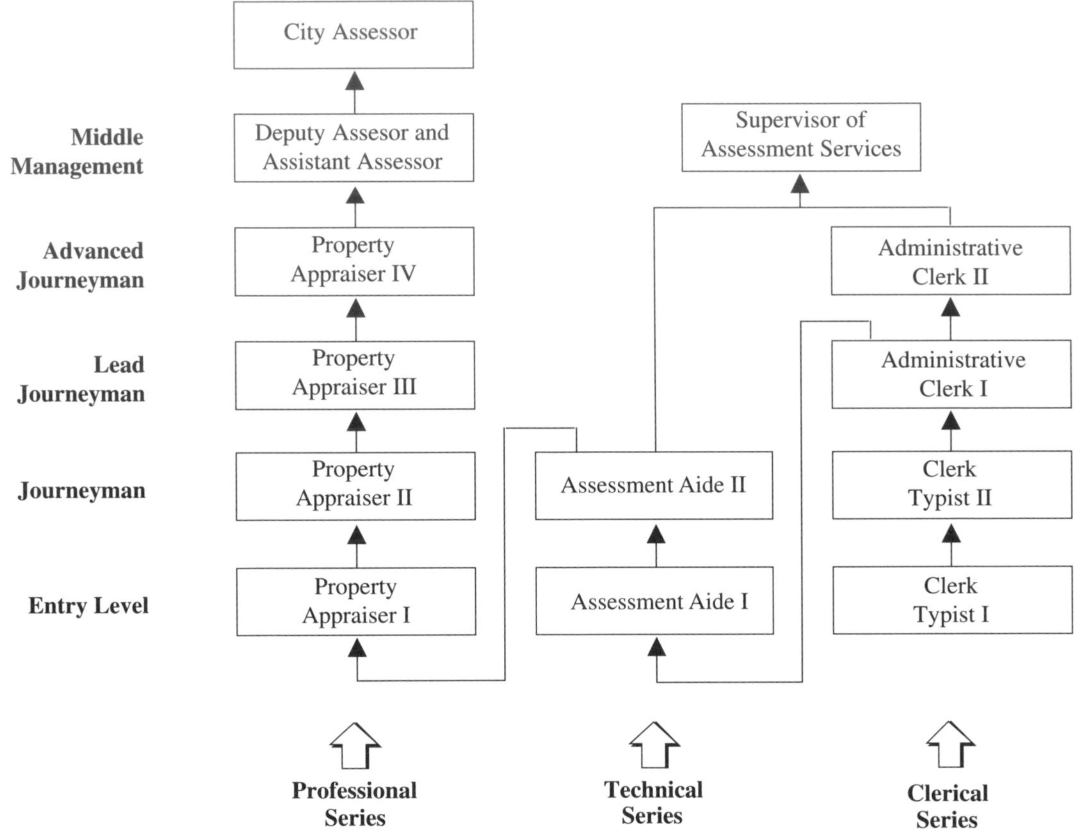

Figure 9-21. The career ladder for the City of Madison, Wisconsin, Assessor's Office.

- As useful and important as career ladders can be, organizations are, and should be, getting flatter. There is a greater need to redefine leadership in a flat organization. A flat organization will affect the culture, the definition of career progression, and therefore, the use of career ladders. (See Chapter 10.)

C. Education Assistance

Many companies have programs for tuition reimbursement. Some comments on such programs:

- A company needs to decide the degree of departure from company-related functional education it will subsidize. Will a law firm pay for someone to learn to be a cosmetologist? There is one school of thought that believes that any and all educational directions are valuable. The nature of creativity is such that perspectives gained in studying one area are often used to discover insights in another, unrelated area. Deming seemed

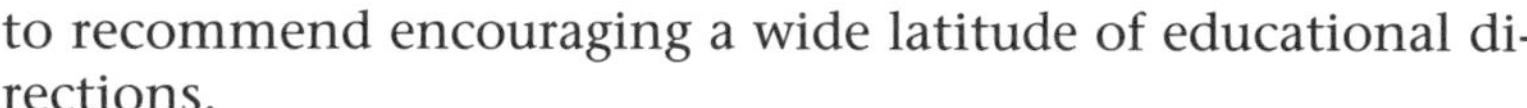

to recommend encouraging a wide latitude of educational directions.

- In some companies, tuition reimbursement depends on the employee achieving a certain grade in the course. This only reinforces another organization's dysfunctional performance appraisal system. The important issues have to do with learning and development, not credentials and report cards.
- It is important to foster lifelong learning. The motivation for continuous learning must come from inside each of us. The organization cannot motivate an employee to learn, but it can nurture and support and avoid annihilating an employee's internal motivation to learn. It can try to make it as easy as possible for an employee to act on that motivation.

6. Identifying Education and Training Needs

Education versus Training

While there is clearly a difference between these two—Deming has a separate point for each—these notes do not focus on that distinction. There are some things that are clearly education (e.g., statistical thinking: understanding variation and its causes) and some that are clearly training (e.g., how to calculate the control limits on an $\overline{X}$ R chart). There is also a gray area: things that are a little bit of both and could tilt one way or the other with very little change in how the presenter or instructor approaches the subject.

The context in which to think about this debundled service is: How do we identify the needs people have to learn something new, whether it is education or training that is needed?

Dealing with Some Myths

- Attributing a problem to an individual employee's lack of training is too often a convenient avoidance of data-based problem solving. Training directors agree that problems classified as training needs are often some other need that cannot be addressed through training. We have already discussed the peril of attributing to the individual worker problems that are inherent in the system. (See the guidelines for Responding to Outstanding Performers.) Here we risk making two mistakes: taking a systems problem and attributing it to the individual worker, and declaring the problem a training need when it may have nothing to do with training.
- Education and training can become an addiction. When something goes wrong, we get a training fix. It takes time to organize and implement the training fix and time to see if the

training worked. But meanwhile, the attention of management has moved on to other things that are, in turn, declared training needs and given their training fix.

- If the purpose of the education and training is career development for the individual employee, there are more effective and more informal ways to pursue this goal. Look at guidelines for "Identifying Career Goals" (pp. 339-343).
- Other than for an individual new employee, most needs for training, and the most important needs for training, are systemic. Systemic training is training focused on across-the-board teaching of some new, better method that has been discovered through careful study. These better methods cover a wide range of work: production methods, administrative methods, product or service design, delivery methods, managerial or staff operations methods.
- Systems-based training is seldom focused on an individual employee's need. Systemic training is a collective need whereby whole groups of people need to learn the new method.

Guidelines

Use the following systems as resources for identifying training and education needs.

- Studies of the existing systems and processes that show inadequacies that can be corrected with training in a new method.
- Organization priorities that require new capabilities and skills necessary to lead and operate new systems and processes.
- New mission, vision, philosophy, or values that require a concerted education and training effort to help people understand why the shift is occurring, how and when it will happen, and what new approaches and capabilities will be required of them.

Individually focused training should occur:

- When there is a special cause, supported by data that indicate:
  - This person's performance is uniquely inadequate.
  - The source of the inadequacy is a training issue (see "Outstanding Performers").
- When it is focused on the individual's career development plans (see "Identifying Career Goals").
- When it is part of an effort to create more flexibility in the workforce and give each employee a wider diversity of skills. This may often involve a work group and not just an individual.

Measuring the Success of Training

- Evaluation forms at the end of a training session are useless and usually become a form of performance appraisal (for example, "Rate this seminar on a five-point scale").
- Feedback forms at the end of a session can be a useful way of getting information for the purpose of improving the logistics (time, place, temperature control, food, service, etc.) and the teaching *methods* ("Were the instructions for the activities clear?").
- The success of training is best measured at the time and place where the capabilities acquired through the training and education are applied by the student.
- For most manual skills, the most effective measure of success is a control chart. (See Figure 9-22.)

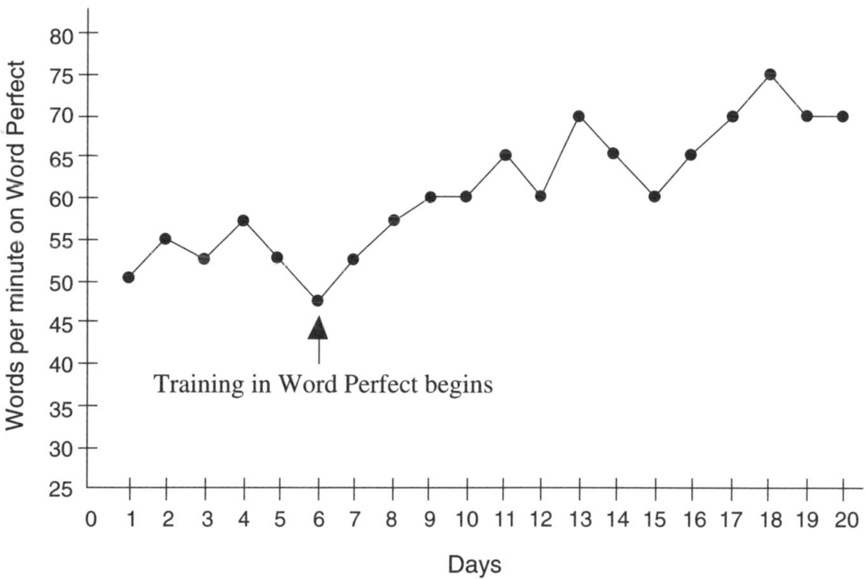

Figure 9-22. Measuring the success of training.

7. Identifying Candidates for Promotion

Dealing with Some Myths

- Past performance is not a predictor of future performance.
- Even if performance appraisal were a reliable and valid measurement system (and it is *not*), it can only tell you about success in the current job. This would be useful only for those few job elements that may *also* be part of the new job. Even then the person may be very different when performing those same activities in a new system and environment.

Some Guidelines for Promotion Systems

Succession systems

- Promotions are part of a slow-cycling system. The need for promotions can be anticipated, most from one to five years in advance.
- Succession planning is an acknowledgment that vacancies will occur and that the organization needs a strong bench—people ready to move into vacancies.
- The recurring processes that are part of a job should be clearly documented. So should the systems-based feedback processes established for those recurring tasks. When the job becomes vacant, then, the transition between leaders can be accomplished more smoothly.
- Succession planning includes creating opportunities for employees to experience leadership: the challenges of planning, coordinating, decision making, problem solving, monitoring, dealing with people, etc.
- Ad hoc leadership opportunities groom employees to be future leaders. These opportunities should not be tests, but challenging experiences surrounded by support. The future leaders should be helped to succeed.
- The organization provides these opportunities and defines the needed skills. The individuals choose to learn the skills needed to qualify for the opportunity. (See "Identifying Career Goals.")
- When a vacancy is about to occur, there is an opportunity for a study step: review and perhaps redefine the position, using input from customers and those who report to whoever will occupy this position.
- Some jobs require high degrees of creativity, art, and genius (e.g., certain types of research, programming, design, or performance skills). Special policies may need to be developed for such positions because these are harder to document.

Assessment Centers

An assessment center is a series of activities designed specifically to simulate the major functions and dynamics of a position. When a vacancy is anticipated in that position, the various candidates participate in the assessment center activities where they get a sense of their own abilities and capacities for the demands of the soon to-be-vacant position. This creates some opportunity to learn and an opportunity for self-screening. Usually there is a panel of observers who monitor the participants and make notes that can be used for feedback both to the candidates and to those who must make a choice for filling the vacant position.

Some General Comments

- We are usually haphazard and superficial in our selection and promotion processes. It is as though we take solace in our ability to discard the errors resulting from our flawed promotion process. We would be better off, and so would those whom we promote, if we were meticulous and painstaking in our promotion processes. The time and money we invest in a careful promotion process—succession systems, assessment centers, etc.—will more than pay for itself in the long term.
- Our organizations will become flatter. Even fewer opportunities for hierarchical advancement will become available. Our challenge will be to satisfy people's desire to become leaders with fewer hierarchical positions into which people may advance.
- Ultimately, when it comes down to selecting one candidate to promote from among a group of people applying for a job, it will involve an act of judgment. While the element of personal judgment is inescapable, what we are trying to do is remove subjectivity and luck as much as possible from the decision-making process.
- Often performance appraisal is used to reduce the number of candidates for a job when the pool of potential candidates is huge. For example, in the military there may be a global list of promotable service personnel. In such cases, it may be necessary to redesign the system to decentralize the selection process. The suggestions provided here about succession planning and assessment centers might apply, but on a more localized selection process.

8. Identifying Candidates for Layoff

In the box on page 162 there are questions regarding downsizing that may be considered here.

Dealing with Some Myths

- A capricious performance appraisal system will result in a capricious system for laying people off.
- When we examine why companies decide to lay off large numbers of personnel, one or more of the following reasons appear to explain the need for layoffs:
  — A drop in the economy.
  — A change in the market.

— Inability to remain competitive on quality, cost, or delivery compared to the products and services offered by others.
— Poor business decisions by managers (e.g., IBM's need to lay people off when their mainframe strategy proved to be uncompetitive).
— Unexpected substantial financial losses (e.g., recalls, lawsuits).
— Cessation of funding due to change in policy (e.g., closing military bases).
— Cycles of business fads: a seasonably fashionable exercise in downsizing. (This seems to be quite prevalent, though of course no CEO would acknowledge laying employees off because it was the current management fad.)

Those who are laid off have no control over these phenomena. What is particularly pathological about using performance appraisal as a basis for deciding who gets laid off is that it shifts the burden for the layoff from management (who has some control over many of the factors listed above) and blames the worker for his or her own layoff. This represents nothing short of a cruel perversion of leadership. It is management at its insensitive worst.

Guidelines

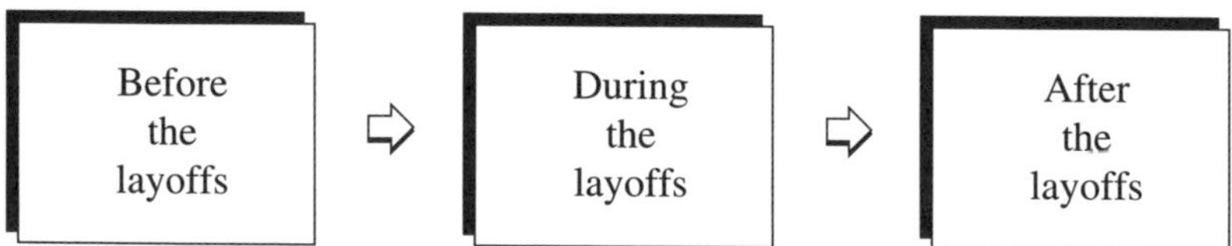

Before the layoffs	During the layoffs	After the layoffs
• Intensive planning and review of the business • Honest communication throughout the time of the business review • Incremental cost-cutting measures if the need is temporary	• Honest communication throughout the time of laying off • "Stripping" a subsystem if the need is permanent	• Check—PDSA (see below) • Be sensitive to the needs and fears of the "survivors" • Honest communication

Figure 9-23. Guidelines for layoffs.

Before the layoffs

Before any layoffs are made, consider a sequence of cost-cutting measures throughout the company (ensuring that customers will not be hurt by such measures). For example:

- Furloughs for temporary and probationary employees
- Reduced dividends to stockholders
- Reduced salaries for top managers
- Cutback in hours for staff jobs
- Cutback in hours for all employees consistent with maintaining plant or service delivery functions

During the layoff

An approach to downsizing that respects the integrity of the system is what may be called *stripping a subsystem.* Your organization is a system consisting of subsystems for developing and delivering various products or services. During a time of downsizing, there are two basic choices:

- Thinning the ranks of the organization, expecting those who survive the layoff to regroup and provide the same output with fewer workers.
- Stripping a subsystem: removing a line of work—a product or service—and laying off those whose work revolved around the discontinued work.

There are problems with thinning the ranks. These are:

- How do you select who gets laid off without indulging in something like performance appraisal?
- When management thins the ranks but expects the same amount of output with fewer people, this is presumably based on one or more of the following beliefs:
  - — People weren't working very hard anyway.
  - — We have a specific plan for breakthrough improvements in efficiency and productivity.
  - — It won't really matter if our quality slips a little.
- Thinning results in hurting the systems. There is the short-term displacement of the regular workforce. Long-term harm may result from chronic understaffing or overloading of the workforce.

Stripping the subsystem

- See Figure 9-24.
- Look at your systems.
- Select products or services that will be eliminated.
- Strip that flow of work and the workforce attached to it.

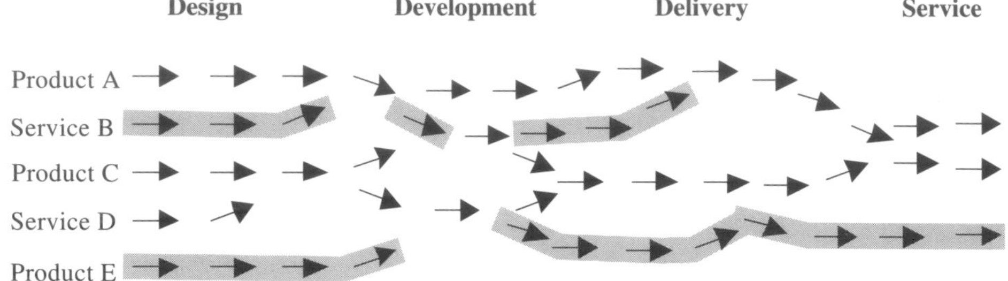

Figure 9-24. Stripping a subsystem to eliminate the interactive steps of various processes. The shaded areas represent lines to be eliminated and people to be laid off.

When stripping a subsystem:

- Select the systems carefully, considering the history and projected future for this market.
- Communicate with the customers of the services or products to be eliminated. Help them identify alternatives.

The underlying principle here is to undertake the downsizing while serving the customers and respecting the integrity of the systems and, at the same time, treating those who are laid off with sensitivity and respect.

The best approach to layoffs is prevention. Get rid of short-term, results-oriented, old-paradigm management. Pursue the principles of quality enunciated by Deming and Ishikawa. This will go a long way toward reducing the need for layoffs.

When all is said and done, layoffs, sometimes in massive numbers, may be inevitable and sometimes with short notice. In the end, there are no good ways to lay people off, just better ways or worse ways. Using performance appraisal is the worst way.

9. Fostering Communication between Employees and Their Supervisors

Dealing with Some Myths

- You don't need performance appraisal to communicate. In fact, performance appraisals are ordinarily so stilted and anxiety-ridden that they are the worst possible situation for communication.
- Performance appraisal ordinarily consists of two conferences totaling approximately two hours of meeting time per year. If this represents the main vehicle for communication between boss and subordinate, there is a *much* bigger problem.

Some Guidelines for Supervisor–Employee Communications

- Two major obstacles to communication are attitude and style. Managers need to learn to make nonjudgmental observations or ask neutral questions. When managers blame, attack, or patronize, they guarantee that communication won't take place. Managers need to learn active listening skills and to teach others how to listen (see Chapter 8). (For a good resource, see *Leader Effectiveness Training: The No-Lose Way to Release the Productive Potential of People* [Gordon, Thomas. NY: Bantam Books, 1977].)
- Regular, well-run team meetings are an indispensable form of communication. Most managers' meeting skills are primitive. Gordon's book is a good resource, as is *The Team Handbook* (Scholtes, 1988).
- Management by Wandering Around (MBWA) or Management by Settin' Around (MBSA) are in contrast to the open door policy, a timeworn management cliché. With the open door, an employee may feel invited to approach the manager's office, but must have a sufficient reason for walking through the open door.

  With MBWA or MBSA, on the other hand, the employee needs no reason because the boss is in the employee's workspace. At first, MBWA will be awkward. No one will know exactly how to do it or what to expect. Eventually, however, it should become more routine and conversation should occur casually. The nuance added by MBSA is that the boss lingers a while, observing what it's like to perform a job, engaging in longer conversations.

Focus Groups and Social Gatherings

Two other important ways through which to foster communication are focus groups and social gatherings. Focus groups are carefully planned and facilitated meetings with employees, getting input and feedback from them on specific selected topics.

Social gatherings include both planned and serendipitous informal get-togethers to create more diversity in the relationship. Many managers have a cycle of breakfasts or lunches with their people. My favorite small company president had a barber's chair next to his office and gave free haircuts to his staff (see p. 118).

Summary

Communication is a matter of mentality and method. The methods should be multiple and varied. But the methods won't work if the manager seeking communication inspires fear and is patronizing. (See the sidebar APOP later in this chapter.)

10. Creating a Paper Trail That Will Serve as a Defense against Suits for Wrongful Dismissal or Other Perceived Unfair Treatment

Dealing with Some Myths

- Performance appraisal is an illusion of objectivity. The illusion is easily undone in court.
- Some attorneys who defend their companies from wrongful dismissal charges have said privately that for every case they win with performance appraisal records, they lose three or four because of those records.
- An attorney who specializes in representing individuals who claim unfair treatment has said he would rather bring suit against companies that use performance appraisal records in their defense. He claims it is a virtual certainty that he will find inconsistency and irrationality in such records.

Some Guidelines for Protecting against Lawsuits

- Work on the environment of distrust in which employees conclude they are treated unfairly, or in which communications are not straightforward. Work where decisions are seen as inaccessible and arbitrary. Using data and logic, plan for slower turning cycles for such activities as promotion and layoffs, rather than making impetuous, quick decisions.
- People are resentful when they feel that they weren't given a fair opportunity to be considered or that the best candidate was passed over. People resent even the appearance of favoritism or capriciousness in the promotion process.
- Claims of unfair treatment are usually leveled at the point when one person is promoted. But the problem occurs and can only be resolved long before the promotion, in the succession planning stage.
- Perhaps you might use performance appraisal—written standards of expected work—as a temporary intervention with an employee whose work is outstandingly poor (see "Outstanding Performers"). Performance appraisal thus becomes like a brace on a weakened member, not a brace where there is no need for artificial support. The documentation of performance appraisal may then be used to demonstrate an extraordinary effort to remove any possible ambiguity regarding short-term expectations for a specific employee whose work performance is troublesome.

11. Conforming to Regulatory Requirements

Dealing with Some Myths

Those under regulatory requirements frequently suffer from two illusions:

- That the regulatory agency will never change ("You can't fight City Hall!").
- That there is no flexibility in the modes of compliance.

Neither of these is usually true.

Guidelines for Dealing with Regulatory Requirements

- Those regulatory agencies that require performance appraisal are suppliers. They supply policy. In this case, they are supplying a dysfunctional policy. Get together with others whom the supplier regulates and help the supplier to supply a more workable policy.
- Work with the regulator to allow your organization to be an exception or an experiment.
- Study the regulation to discover what is the minimum required to remain in conformance with the policy. Do the literal minimum and do not volunteer a millimeter more than that.
- Thus having satisfied the *letter* of the regulation, study the *spirit* of the regulation. Ordinarily those who require performance appraisal have good reasons for such a policy. They expect some good to occur or some evil to be avoided. Find ways to accomplish these intentions in a better way without performance appraisal. This is simply applying the concept of *debundling* to the needs of the regulator.

12. Motivating Employees

Following is a summary of points made elsewhere in this book. (See Chapters 2, 5, and 8, and the Introduction to this chapter.)

Dealing with Some Myths

- It is a management conceit to believe that one can motivate others. Managers can demotivate, but not motivate (Herzberg).
- The carrot and stick approach was developed for use with jackasses, and its legitimate use is limited to that species.

APOP

Parkview Medical Center is located in Pueblo, Colorado. In 1989 the former president of Parkview proposed that the hospital learn a new approach to quality based on the teachings of Dr. Deming. Subsequently, a team was formed to develop a new approach to performance appraisal.

Like all hospitals, Parkview needed to be licensed by an accrediting agency. JCAHO, the Joint Committee on Accrediting Hospital Organizations, had the authority to grant or withhold a license. The Joint Commission, as a regulatory body, required performance appraisals of its licensees. The team within Parkview was aware of this requirement from JCAHO. What the letter of the requirement demanded was an annual meeting between bosses and subordinates and a paper-trail record of that meeting.

The Parkview team also recalled that Dr. Deming suggested that, at least once per year, each leader should sit down and spend significant time with each employee reporting to him or her.

The Parkview team thus devised what they at first jokingly called the APOP process. APOP was an acronym for "annual piece of paper." The name stuck. The APOP was literally an agenda for an annual discussion. As each discussion item was completed, the item would be checked off. When all the items were covered the supervisor and subordinate would each sign the agenda sheet and the APOP would be put in the files, ready for inspection by a JCAHO inspector.

The piece of paper may have reflected the demands of JCAHO, but the content and process reflected the needs and values of the leaders of Parkview. It is a nonjudgmental, informal, and informative conversation. Supervisors received a lot of training in how to approach and conduct this kind of dialogue. The results?

- Leaders and employees alike prefer APOP much more than the previous rating and ranking procedure.
- APOP has become the focal point of a leadership training process.
- APOP and its methods represent how communication now routinely takes place.

The APOP approach emphasizes active listening and problem-solving skills. It incorporates an attitude of mutual trust and respect. Nothing patronizing. Simply peers working things out together.

The APOP agenda in a check-off form

1. Review the job description with the employee and make any changes or adjustments:
   - To assure that the major processes are still the same
   - To provide an opportunity for the employee to think in terms of processes and how those processes support the mission and vision of the Center
2. What barriers to pride of work is the employee experiencing?
   - This is the the heart of APOP.
   - Managers use open-ended questions and are coached on possible responses to any barriers that may be raised.
3. Process improvement.
   - Discuss past and current efforts.
   - Provide an opportunity for the employee to boast.
   - If useful, use it as an opportunity to coach and identify training needs.
4. Identify learning needs and learning objectives.
   - Try to have a learning plan in place.
5. Anything else.

This information is adapted from a videotaped interview of Dorothy Gill of the Parkview Medical Center.

- People start out motivated. It is legitimate to discover what happened to that original, intrinsic motivation.
- To believe that pay motivates is to believe, quite cynically, that people reserve a certain amount of effort to be left unused until it is bribed out of them.
- Imagine that beginning next Monday, you will be paid twice what you are now paid. Will you work any more effectively? (No, though you may be happier ... for a while.)

Some Guidelines Regarding Motivation

- If employees are unmotivated, investigate what happened or is happening to demotivate them.
  - — Are the demotivators personal or on-the-job?
  - — Are they transitory? Chronic?
  - — If they are personal, what can the organization do to help the employee through this rough time?
  - — If there are on-the-job demotivators, what are they and what can the company do about them?

DISMANTLING PERFORMANCE APPRAISAL: DECISION TREES

The decision trees described in this section are based on the path several companies have followed when seeking to dismantle performance appraisal. What is described here, therefore, is real, not speculative. It is a composite. Several different companies contributed to this, each focusing on issues more uniquely relevant to it. All the various organizations, however, struggled with many of these questions.

Therefore, if the leaders of your company plan to embark on this effort, you will probably need to adapt this format to your own needs. Some suggestions:

1. Do not too easily skip an item that seems at first to be irrelevant. Struggle with it a little. Make sure you are skipping the item because it is irrelevant, not simply because it is controversial.
2. It is a good idea to have an outside party act as a facilitator for these sessions, a neutral third party with some skills in group process. An outsider can help you discuss the undiscussables. (For a discussion of the undiscussables, see Ryan & Oestreich, 1991.)

Peterbilt Wisconsin

Peterbilt is a well-known brand of heavy-duty trucks. Peterbilt Wisconsin doesn't make the trucks, but sells, repairs, services, finances, and leases them. The company also does body work and sells parts and used trucks. It operates out of several locations in Wisconsin and Illinois.

In 1992, with the assistance of Britt Hall, a consultant and a faculty member at Waukesha County Technical College, Peterbilt Wisconsin started on its effort to transform itself, applying Dr. Deming's philosophy. Since 1992 Peterbilt Wisconsin has taken on such practices as these, all of them unconventional by trucking industry standards:

- Stopping the use of performance appraisal
- Moving away from commissions and devising a new compensation policy not based on merit pay, quotas, or incentives
- Issuing financial statements in the form of a control chart, displaying variation and allowing the determination of common cause or special cause variation

Peterbilt Wisconsin had the added challenge of trying to help the old conventional policies evolve in an organization that was geographically dispersed, with each separate organization having its own history and traditions. This required a longer, more difficult consensus-building process—evolutionary rather than revolutionary.

The decision-tree process described on these pages was based partly on the process used by Peterbilt's leaders.

3. Take each item seriously. Agree in advance that once a decision is made there is no going back. Treat each question as a bridge to cross. There must be consensus on the answer. No one may be left on the other side. Once the bridge is crossed—once the question is answered—burn the bridge.
4. One of the jobs of the facilitator is to make sure that there is true consensus. Everyone must understand the question, the answer agreed upon, and the implications of the answer.

I. Starting Questions

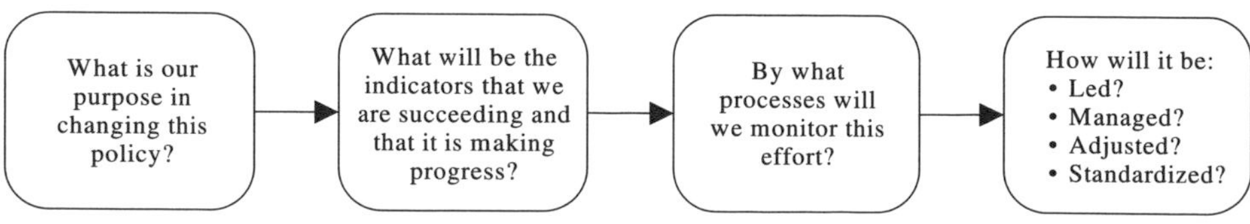

II. Reconsidering Performance Appraisal and Pay

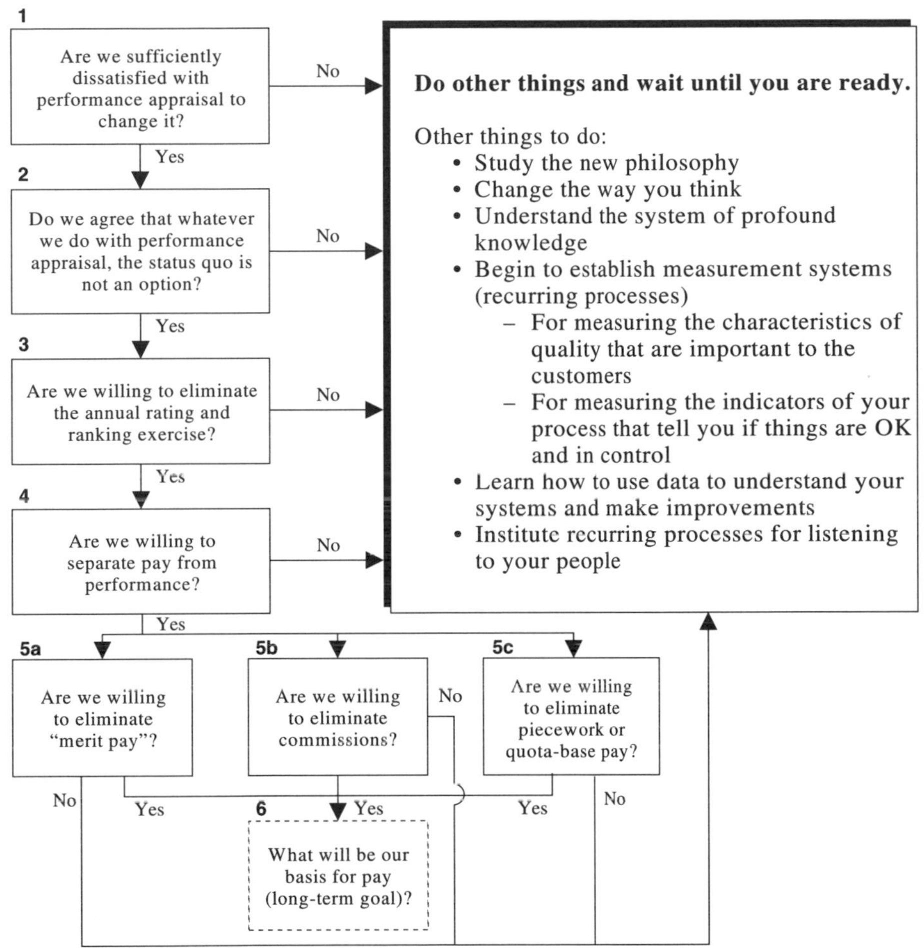
1
Are we sufficiently dissatisfied with performance appraisal to change it?
No
Yes
2
Do we agree that whatever we do with performance appraisal, the status quo is not an option?
No
Yes
3
Are we willing to eliminate the annual rating and ranking exercise?
No
Yes
4
Are we willing to separate pay from performance?
No
Yes
5a
Are we willing to eliminate "merit pay"?
5b
Are we willing to eliminate commissions?
5c
Are we willing to eliminate piecework or quota-base pay?
No
Yes
No
Yes
Yes
No
6
What will be our basis for pay (long-term goal)?
Do other things and wait until you are ready.
Other things to do:
• Study the new philosophy
• Change the way you think
• Understand the system of profound knowledge
• Begin to establish measurement systems (recurring processes)
– For measuring the characteristics of quality that are important to the customers
– For measuring the indicators of your process that tell you if things are OK and in control
• Learn how to use data to understand your systems and make improvements
• Institute recurring processes for listening to your people

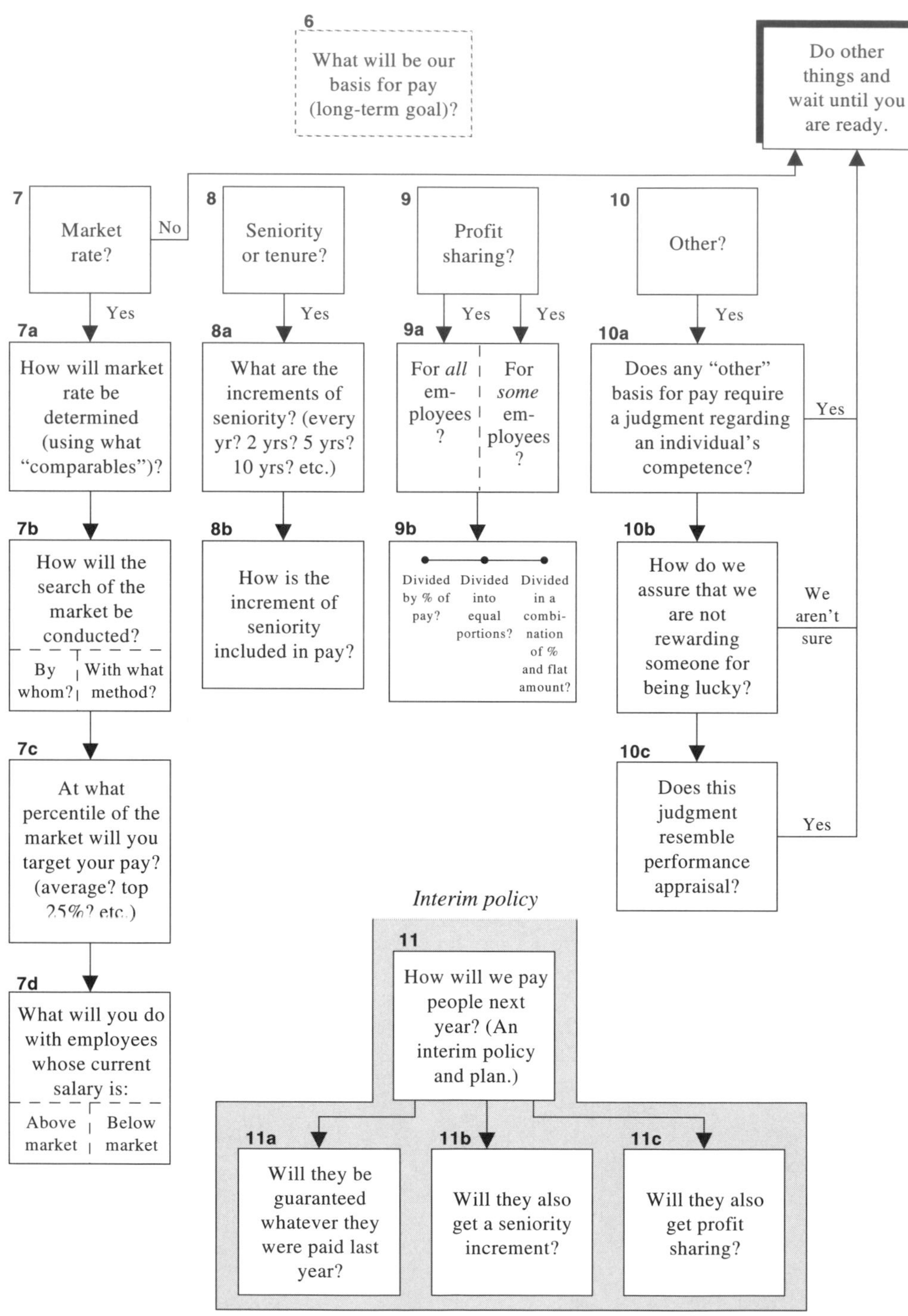
6
What will be our basis for pay (long-term goal)?
Do other things and wait until you are ready.
7
Market rate?
No
8
Seniority or tenure?
9
Profit sharing?
10
Other?
Yes
Yes
Yes
Yes
Yes
7a
How will market rate be determined (using what "comparables")?
8a
What are the increments of seniority? (every yr? 2 yrs? 5 yrs? 10 yrs? etc.)
9a
For all employees?
For some employees?
10a
Does any "other" basis for pay require a judgment regarding an individual's competence?
Yes
7b
How will the search of the market be conducted?
By whom?
With what method?
8b
How is the increment of seniority included in pay?
9b
Divided by % of pay?
Divided into equal portions?
Divided in a combination of % and flat amount?
10b
How do we assure that we are not rewarding someone for being lucky?
We aren't sure
7c
At what percentile of the market will you target your pay? (average? top 25%? etc.)
10c
Does this judgment resemble performance appraisal?
Yes
Interim policy
7d
What will you do with employees whose current salary is:
Above market
Below market
11
How will we pay people next year? (An interim policy and plan.)
11a
Will they be guaranteed whatever they were paid last year?
11b
Will they also get a seniority increment?
11c
Will they also get profit sharing?

III. Reconsidering Formal, Structured Annual Meetings between a Manager and Those Individuals Who Report to Him or Her

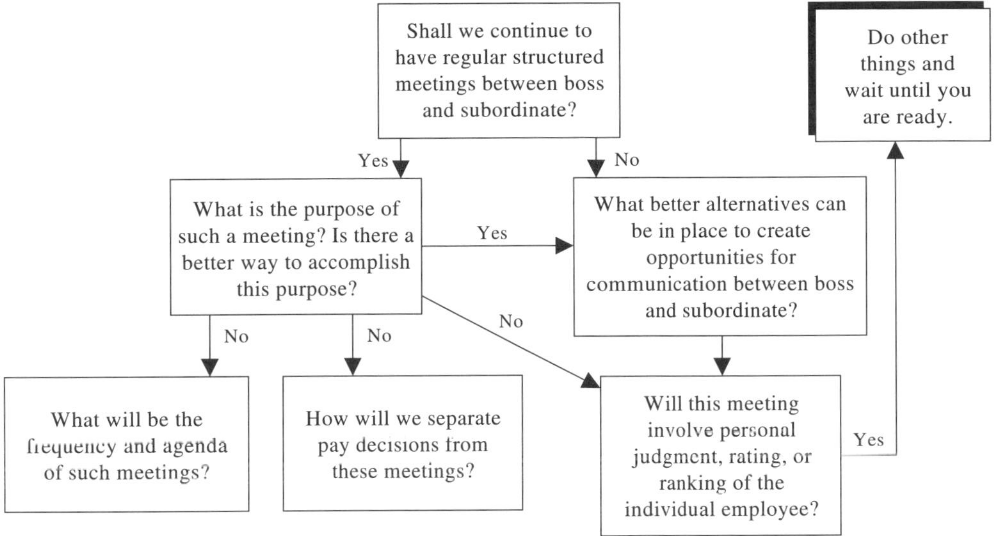

SUMMARY

Western management has co-conspired to accept the practice of performance appraisal (aka performance evaluation, performance review, or performance management) as a useful exercise. Corporate headquarters, regulatory agencies, elected officials, HR managers, and CEOs have enacted policies that require others to practice performance appraisal even when those others upon whom they impose performance appraisal disagree with the practice. A large proportion of managers and employees dislike performance appraisal (see *The Wall Street Journal* article of November 19, 1996 by Timothy Schellhardt). More than 90 percent of appraisal systems are unsuccessful. Yet managers are required to continue practicing this unsuccessful policy.

A common belief among CEOs and HR practitioners is that performance appraisal is a good thing to do, we just have to design the right way to do it. There is a large, thriving industry among consultants who are willing to teach managers the "right way" to do performance appraisal. We change the name from performance evaluation to performance management or from performance appraisal to coaching and counseling. We change the rating scale from five points to three points or from four points to four descriptive phrases. We introduce 360° evaluation and other fads. They are all variations on the same theme, a different tune played on the same old triangle.

What I have proposed in this chapter is that there is no right way to do performance appraisal. Performance appraisal is inherently the wrong thing to do. It is derived from the most inhumane instincts of people and it hurts both those who are evaluated and, in the long run, those who evaluate. It provides no demonstrable benefit to the organization or its customers.

Those who would insist on practicing performance appraisal must accept the burden of proving that, first, it does no harm and, second, it makes a demonstrable, conclusive, positive contribution.

CHAPTER NINE ACTIVITIES

Discuss the following questions with your management group.

1. The following is a story, in its entirety, from *The Wall Street Journal*.

Odds and Ends

Continental Airlines came in dead last in the on-time performance for June even though it had offered employees everything from cash to pizza to finish first in the Department of Transportation monthly rankings.

The Wall Street Journal
August 18, 1995

What assumptions does Continental make?

Below is a story from Gannett News Service, dated November 10, 1996.

On-time competition: TWA won't be waiting for anyone anymore

GANNETT NEWS SERVICE

The next time you need to catch a connecting flight on TWA, better hope you're not late.

TWA is one of several major airlines trying to climb higher in the Department of Transportation's monthly ranking of on-time flights. To do that, TWA is no longer holding connecting flights for passengers on other TWA flights that are behind schedule. It wants 85 percent of its flights to arrive on time.

"Except for the last flights in the evening, we will not hold planes for connections," TWA spokesman John McDonald says.

TWA is already seeing improvement. In September, 75.6 percent of its flights arrived on time, compared with an average of 66 percent last summer. TWA says it will reward every employee with a $65 check for each month TWA makes the top five in the DOT's ranking. Employees will get $100 if it's No. 1.

TWA's incentive plan is modeled on one Continental Airlines launched in 1995 that helped it move from last to a consistent place among the top five.

What others are doing:

- United Airlines is boarding 5 minutes earlier. Passengers get 30 minutes to board narrow-body planes and 40 minutes for wide-bodies. United says the change, which began Oct. 1, has already cut delays 15 percent.

United also plans to link on-time performance to bonuses for 600 mid- to high-level executives; it's adding more mechanics to cut down on mechanical delays, and it's set aside two jets, a 757 and 737, as spares to bring its total spare jets up to nine.

- Delta Air Lines now boards coach passengers in the back rows ahead of those in the front rows. And it no longer makes a special boarding announcement for disabled and elderly passengers. Instead, gate agents identify people that need help and assist those who ask. Delta also is strictly enforcing boarding procedures.

"We were too nice and didn't enforce boarding rules. It was chaos with everyone trying to get on at once," Delta spokesman Bill Berry says. Delta's goal: to break into the top five in the DOT's ranking.

- Alaska Airlines, which saw only 50.9 percent of its flights arrive on time in August, has sped up its boarding procedures. It's boarding passengers in rows of five instead of 10 or more.

2. What observations do you have about TWA's approach?

3. What about United's approach?

4. What about Delta's approach?

5. What about Alaska's approach?

6. Why do companies such as these resort to incentives in order to bring about improvement?

7. What are the reasons why incentives may not be a good approach?

8. Deming has said:
   - "Everyone is doing his best."
   - "We're being ruined by best efforts."

   What does he mean?

9. What are the differences between the following?

   A. Performance evaluation

   B. Performance appraisal

   C. Performance review

   D. Performance management

   E. Performance feedback

   Are they different tunes on the same triangle? Explain why or why not.

10. How do employees get feedback if not through performance evaluation?

Policy checklist

Use this checklist to review your performance appraisal policy or any other employee policy. The purpose is to stimulate a discussion, not arrive at a number.

1. This policy seems to focus more on:

								Not Applicable
Improving or controlling individual behavior	1	2	3	4	5	6	Improving or controlling the system and processes	☐

2. This policy is consistent with:

Short-term thinking, quick rewards	1	2	3	4	5	6	Long-term thinking, slow, steady growth and survival	☐

3. This policy focuses on:

Better results regardless of methods	1	2	3	4	5	6	Better methods to achieve results	☐

4. This policy seeks to:

Only satisfy needs internal to the organization	1	2	3	4	5	6	Satisfy the external customer	☐

5. This policy aims at:

Motivating individuals	1	2	3	4	5	6	Removing those conditions which demotivate people	☐

6. This policy is based on the premise of:

								Not Applicable
Protecting the organization from untrustworthy employees	1	2	3	4	5	6	Treating all employees with trust and respect	☐

7. This policy has rewards or gives recognition which:

Gives credit to a few (or one) for the entire result	1	2	3	4	5	6	Gives everyone a share in the credit	☐

8. This policy—explicitly or implicitly—encourages:

A perspective of personal and individual performance	1	2	3	4	5	6	A perspective of team and system performance	☐

Weaknesses of the policy:	Strengths of the policy:

REFERENCES

Blake, R., and Mouton, J. 1964. *The managerial grid.* Houston: Gulf Publishing.

Blinder, A.S., ed. 1990. *Paying for productivity.* Washington, DC: The Brookings Institute.

Brennan, E.J. 1989. *Performance management.* Englewood Cliffs, NJ: Prentice Hall.

Cardy, R.L., and Carson, K.R. 1996. Total quality and the abandonment of performance appraisal: Taking a good thing too far? *Journal of Quality Management,* I, 2.

Clemmer, J. 1995. *Pathways to performance.* Rocklin, CA: Prima Publishing.

Daniels, A. 1989. *Performance management.* Tucker, GA: Performance Management Publications.

Eisenberger, R., and Cameron, J. 1996. Detrimental effects of reward: Reality or myth. *American Psychologist,* 31, 11.

Gabor, A. 1990. *The man who discovered quality.* New York: Times Books.

Gibbs, M. 1990. An economic approach to process in pay and performance appraisals. *Harvard Business School,* Working Paper 91-051. (Contact: Professor Michael Gibbs, Harvard Business School, Humphrey 2nd Floor, Soldiers Field, Boston, MA 02163.)

Gilbert, G.R., and Nelson, A. 1989. The pacer share demonstration project: Implications for organizational management and performance evaluation. *Public Personnel Management,* 18, 2.

Graves, S.B. 1992. Compensation systems and other human resources policies to promote quality and productivity improvement. *International Productivity Journal,* SGA Report 91-4, 13.

Haller, H., and Whittaker, B.J. 1987. *Barriers to change: Does the performance appraisal system serve a logical purpose?* Cleveland: Statistical Studies Incorporated. (Contact: SSI Management, Attn.: Carol Haller, 24803 Detroit Road, Cleveland, OH 44145, [216] 871-6597, Fax: [216] 871-1182.)

Heilman, M., and Guzzo, R. *The perceived cause of work success as a mediator of sex discrimination in organizations.* Greensboro, NC: The Center for Creative Leadership.

Herzberg, F. 1987. One more time: How do you motivate employees? *Harvard Business Review,* September–October, 109–120.

Hitchcock, D. 1990. Performance management for teams—a better way. *Journal for Quality and Participation,* September.

Hopkins, B., and Mawhinney, T. 1992. *Pay for performance.* New York: Hawthorn Press.

Huber, V. 1989. Comparison of the effects of specific and general performance standards on performance appraisal decisions. *Decision Science,* 20: 545–557.

Kane, J., and Freeman, K. 1987. MBO and performance appraisal: A mixture that's not a solution. *Personnel,* Part 1, 1986 (pp. 26-36), Part 2 (pp. 26-32).

Kohn A. 1993. *Punished by rewards.* Boston: Houghton Mifflin.

Kohn, A. 1986. *No contest.* Boston: Houghton Mifflin.

Kohn, A., Nelson, B., Scholtes, P., and Hudetz, F. 1994–95. Do employee rewards and recognition programs work? *Small Business Forum,* Winter.

Levinson, H. 1973. *The great jackass fallacy.* Cambridge, MA: Harvard University Press.

McLean, G., Damme, S., and Swanson, R. 1990. *Performance appraisal: Perspectives on a quality management approach.* Alexandria, VA: American Society for Training and Development.

Merisalo, L. 1994. Glenroy hits a few bumps along the road to quality. *The Milwaukee Sentinel,* April 4.

Orsini, J.N. 1987. Bonuses: What is the impact? *National Productivity Review,* Spring, 180–184.

Purcell, D., Hall, B., and Scholtes, P. 1996. Peterbilt: A study of debundling. A presentation at OQPF's 9th Annual Deming Conference.

Rodin, R., and Backaitis, N. 1995. *Beyond the sounds of silence.* El Monte, CA: Marshall Industries. (Order from: Marshall Industries, 9320 Telstar Avenue, El Monte, CA 91731 [818] 307-6004, e-mail: robrodin@001.marshall.com.)

Ryan, K., and Oestreich, D. 1991. *Driving fear out of the workplace.* San Francisco: Jossey-Bass.

Scherkenbach, W.W. 1993. *The Deming route to quality and productivity.* Milwaukee: Quality Press.

Scherkenbach, W.W. 1985. Performance appraisal and quality: Ford's new philosophy. *Quality Progress,* April.

Scholtes, P.R. 1994–1995. Reward and incentive programs are ineffective—even harmful. *Small Business Forum,* Winter. (Available from Scholtes Seminars and Consulting.)

Scholtes, P.R. 1994a. Alternatives to performance appraisal: Twelve guidelines for "debundled" policies. (Available from Scholtes Seminars and Consulting.)

Scholtes, P.R. 1994b. Performance appraisal: Obsolete and harmful. *Electronic Buyer's News,* November. (Available from Scholtes Seminars and Consulting.)

Scholtes, P.R. 1994c. Performance without appraisal. (Available from Scholtes Seminars and Consulting.)

Scholtes, P.R. 1993. Total quality or performance appraisal: Choose one. *National Productivity Review,* Summer, 349–363. (Available from Joiner Associates, Inc., P.O. Box 5445, Madison, WI 53705 [800] 689-8326.)

Scholtes, P.R. 1987. An elaboration on Deming's teachings on performance appraisal. (To order contact: Joiner Associates Inc., PO Box 5445, Madison, WI 53705 [800] 669-8326.)

Walton, M. 1990. *Deming management at work.* New York: Putnam.

Whitney, J. 1994. *The trust factor.* New York: McGraw-Hill.

10 LEADERSHIP INTO THE NEXT MILLENNIUM

INTRODUCTION: WHAT IS LEADERSHIP?

Over the past 35 or so years, I have read hundreds of books and articles about leadership and written a few myself. Even more useful to me and my learning about leadership, I have known and worked with over a thousand leaders.

Some of the leaders I have observed and known were wonderful: respectful of their people, knowledgeable about their business, dedicated to their customers, and men and women who conveyed a clear sense of direction and focus. These leaders have been a joy to work with.

And then there are the others. They might be described as dismal. What separates these two ends of the continuum? What distinguishes the wonderful from the dismal? Based mostly on my experience, I believe the following characteristics make the difference.

Creating and Communicating Meaning

Wonderful leaders leave no doubt in their people's minds about what it is important to do. Everyone knows why the organization exists, what it does, where it is headed, and what the important things are to do *now.*

Dismal leaders are aimless and, therefore, so are their people. Dismal leaders then blame the people for their aimlessness.

Dismal

The word *dismal* comes from two Latin words meaning *bad day.* Dismal leaders are leaders who create bad days for their people.

External Focus

Wonderful leaders look for purpose *outside* of their organizations. They are committed to customers. For them the organization exists in order to serve customers, not stockholders, not boards, not policy makers—customers. It is the customers who get to decide whether the organization is doing well or poorly. Wonderful leaders develop a workforce committed to the outside: to pleasing the customers. The dismal leader looks inwardly: internal self-aggrandizing measures, bottom lines, and MBOs. Employees of the dismal are also surrounded by measures that encourage them to compare themselves to each other and compete with each other. Dismal managers want their employees to compete with each other in order to please management.

Genuine Caring about People

Wonderful managers are drawn to people, enjoy the diversity that people represent, care about people, and want to know their stories.

Dismal managers tend to see people as an untrustworthy nuisance or a threat, a necessary expedient and an expendable commodity. Two dismal managers are the unredeemed Ebenezer Scrooge and the unrepentant Chainsaw Dunlap.

Awareness of the Larger Context

Wonderful leaders understand, and help their people understand, the larger contexts within which they work. This is *systems* thinking. They have developed a finely tuned sense of cross-purposes, of one system or one part of the system at odds with another. Wonderful leaders have an instinct for alignment and synchronicity. While they understand ambiguity and know how to lead their organization through it, wonderful leaders don't try to turn ambiguity into a virtue.

For dismal leaders, chaos is commonplace. Work is viewed one isolated event at a time. Cross purposes abound. A sense of context doesn't exist. Parts of the organization are pitted against each other. Individuals compete for scarce rewards. Fellow employees are adversaries.

Clear, Honest Communication

Wonderful leaders tell the truth to their people, their customers, their suppliers, their stockholders, and others who care about the organization. The spin doctors and hype masters are not given access to the leader's communications. Wonderful leaders speak plainly.

Chainsaw Dunlap

When Albert Dunlap is hired as the CEO of a troubled company, the stock goes up and morale plummets. Dunlap, whose sobriquet is "Chainsaw," was hired by Scott Paper Company. Dunlap proceeded to sell off subsidiaries of Scott, shut down operations that he deemed unimprovable, lay off 11,000 employees, and sell what was left to Kimberly Clark. There is no more Scott Paper. Dunlap, in a fit of hyperbole, boasted that "Scott Paper Company never had a better year." Dunlap, of course was remunerated generously for his grave-digging approach to what he called "turning the company around." He moved on from Scott to Sunbeam Electric, where stockholders were delighted and employees updated their resumes.

Speaking Plainly ... about Gemba?

On the one hand, you are urged to speak plainly. On the other hand, a chapter of this book talks about Gemba and elsewhere you can read about common cause and special cause variation. Why are these any more acceptable than empowerment or high-performance? Here is my rationale:

- I use unconventional terms when I think it is important to draw attention to the concept. For me there is a difference between hype and specific differentiation.
- I use unconventional words when there is content and substance behind them. Behind common and special cause is a well-established, specific explanation of something real (i.e., variation). Behind empowerment and accountability is mostly meaningless, empty babble.

Dismal leaders' messages can't be trusted. They exaggerate the good news, cover up the bad news, and indulge in double talk and management babble. They use empty phrases like empower, reengineering, high-performance, accountability, and self-directed. Dismal leaders sound like a Dilbert cartoon.

What Is Leadership?

There is no formula for leadership. Leadership consists of more than the approaches, capabilities, and attributes talked about in books such as this.

Leadership is the presence and spirit of the individual who leads and the relationship created with those who are led. Good leadership accommodates the needs and values of those who need to be led. Good leadership takes into account the skills and capabilities of those with whom the leader shares leadership. Good leadership adapts to the purpose and future needs of the organization. Leadership is an art, an inner journey, a network of relationships, a mastery of methods, and much, much more. And because we cannot expect any single heroic individual to possess all these traits, leadership, ultimately, must be a system.

LEADERS OF SYSTEMS

The leader of the next decade, and probably the next century and millennium as well, must understand systems and let the awareness of systems inform every plan and decision.

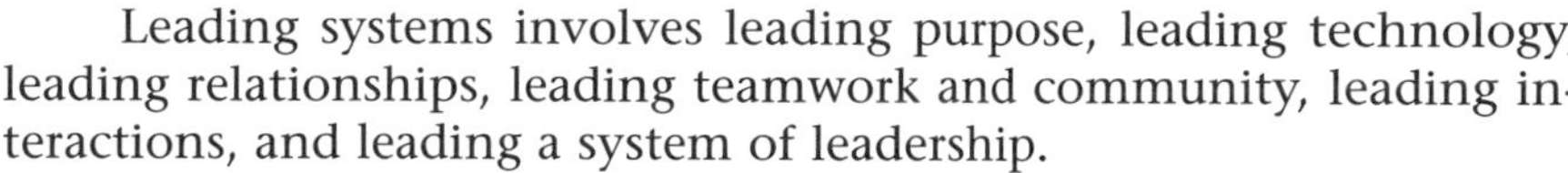

Leading systems involves leading purpose, leading technology, leading relationships, leading teamwork and community, leading interactions, and leading a system of leadership.

Leading Purpose

Organizations have a continuous need for a sense of purpose and vision. Caught up in the daily absurdities, we need to be reminded of why we are out here doing what we are doing. We need a means of determining whether what we are doing as individuals has any relevance to the greater good. This is a quintessential leadership role, to give people a reason to persist and a direction toward which to persist.

Leading Technology

By *technology* we are referring to the expertise necessary to run the business and keep current on innovations that will change the way work is done. This is not just equipment technology or computer technology, but the whole range of knowledge and know-how that we collectively need to acquire in order to survive and thrive.

It is obviously impossible for individual leaders to gain all this new knowledge, know-how, and technological skill. Leaders lead the establishing and maintaining of systems that keep the organization as a whole knowledgeable of current and upcoming technology, and capable in its use. A leader needs to know which technology he or she personally needs to master, and which information he or she personally needs to understand.

Leading Relationships, Teamwork, and Community

An organization is a social entity. Look back on your years in school. The important moments were not limited to the processes of learning the subject matter. Equally important were the friendships, learning how to relate to others. Similarly, there is more to the workplace than work. Socialization in the workplace can be treated as taboo, as a detriment to work. We have known for a long time that human interaction improves *work life,* making the job a source of support and healing. But interaction also improves *work,* quality, and productivity.

When given a clear purpose and proper methods, teams of people will work together in pursuit of something that they could not attain individually.

Leaders need to believe in the benefits of human interaction, socialization, and teamwork. The company or organization would be better off if it were like a community: a community with a shared purpose and vision, with collaborative efforts, a commonwealth of learning. Leaders can promote this and relate to people in ways that support such values. Leaders can do immeasurable good in creating an atmosphere of pride and joy in the workplace. They can also do immeasurable harm by being indifferent, cynical, and negative toward their people.

Leading Interactions

There are not only human and social interactions in the enterprise. There are also organizational interactions. We discussed earlier the interactive and interdependent flow of work as it moves from one activity, step, process, phase, or subsystem to another (Chapter 3). Everyone in your organization is engaged in work that is affected by the work of others and in turn affects the work of others. Leaders must insist that the barriers be torn down and that collaborative, interdependent relationships be developed and maintained. How a leader meets with people, assigns activities, approaches planning, and engages people in solving problems can either reinforce the isolation between them or create healthy collaboration.

Leading a System of Leadership

The word leadership usually conjures up pictures of individuals in positions of authority: the hierarchical view of leadership. But leadership is also a system and a process. Leading takes place in many different ways. *It is the job of the leader to see to it that leading occurs.* It is probably more important for the leader to do this than to lead by himself or herself. In fact, it is the only way that leaders can successfully accomplish all the functions of leadership discussed in this chapter. Leaders set up an organizational environment and systems of support in which various people at various times are free to take on leadership functions and run with them.

A Flat Organizational System

I am not referring here to flatness by fiat whereby an executive declares, "Let there be flatness" and removes layers of the hierarchy. Flatness must be earned the hard way. When your organization has virtually eliminated waste and created efficient, smooth, uncluttered flows of work, you can then create flatness. Many middle managers are for the most part expediters or troubleshooters: the scrapers of burnt toast. These positions will become unnecessary as a result of your hard work.

The flat organization creates a human problem in your organization: the *flat-organization dilemma*. You have employees who want to be promoted, to take on a position of leadership and make a better salary. Yet you have created fewer positions into which these people can be promoted. If a *flat-organization system* is not created, these people will go to less efficient organizations where they can make more money by being promoted into positions that your organization no longer needs.

The flat-organization system needs to address pay issues by allowing people salary increases without promotion in the hierarchy. The flat-organization system needs to deal with leadership issues by providing people with opportunities to take leadership without being promoted in the hierarchy.

A more fluid sense of leadership, ad hoc assignments, rotating leadership teams, allowing people to pick up a function and run with it: These are perhaps the characteristics of flat-organization systems.

In a flat organization I see a greater role for some seniority-based pay—a notion that seems repugnant to many contemporary managers. "If we pay according to seniority," they object, "we will be rewarding dead wood." Don't reward anyone, give just remuneration. Don't confuse performance issues with pay issues.

In Japan, seniority is a major factor in determining pay for many companies. They seem to be doing okay. However the issue of pay is decided, a flat organization will require us to rethink leadership with systems-oriented approaches.

THE FOOTPRINTS OF LEADERSHIP

The concept of leadership as a system allows us a second perspective on leadership. Before, we concluded that leadership is what leaders do. We can now also conclude that where leadership functions take place, there we will find leaders. We can learn leadership by studying leaders. We can also identify that there are leaders by finding their footprints in the organization, looking for leaders where leadership occurs. Therefore, see how the following occur in your organization, and then infer where and who the leaders are.

Where Meaning Is Created, Leadership Occurs

Through their actions or questions, people can reduce ambiguity and create clear focus. Where in your organization does meaning, purpose, vision, and focus get developed and articulated? The need for meaning is continuous and must occur at all levels and apply to the larger-scale, longer-term purposes as well as those of narrower scope and more immediate concern. Who are the meaning-givers, the ambiguity-removers, the articulators of direction and focus?

Where Systems Are Developed, Leadership Occurs

There is a need to identify the sequence, the points of interaction and interdependence, and the larger contexts of work. There is a need to align the effort so that no part is working at cross-purposes with another part or with the whole. This need applies to huge organizational efforts as well as small tasks. Where the interactive flow is developed, described, and improved, leadership occurs.

Where Relationships Are Formed and Sustained, Leadership Occurs

Who is building the bridges between previously disparate, perhaps even adversarial, groups? Who is creating channels of communication and connectedness? Who is doing the hard daily work of building trust? Who promotes everyday civilities and politeness? Who sees the isolated individuals and includes them? Who helps the organization see the value of diversity and the pathology of exclusivity and harassment? Who creates community at work? These are also your leaders.

Where Technology Is Current, Leadership Occurs

The technology may address electronics, mechanics, learning, communication, the methodology of improvement, or any new knowledge or know-how. When and where your organization is kept current on such developments, leadership is occurring.

All these leadership functions and those who perform them will benefit if these efforts are not haphazard but the output of well-designed, smoothly functioning systems. The spontaneous and serendipitous activities can continue. A system, however, will incorporate the methods and gains into the everyday routines of the organization.

A KIND WORD ABOUT LEADERS

The settling of the American West seems to have been a defining moment in our culture and tradition. Courageous people and their leaders left what was familiar and predictable and went forward into the unexpected, facing adversity and peril.

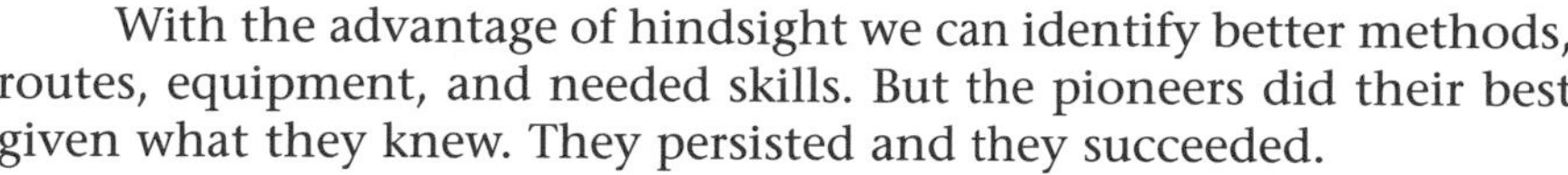

With the advantage of hindsight we can identify better methods, routes, equipment, and needed skills. But the pioneers did their best given what they knew. They persisted and they succeeded.

After All, We Have Been Successful

Much the same can be said of the American manager. We have the benefit of hindsight, gained mostly by learning from the experience of our predecessors. For all we see about management that we wish were better, and there is much, we must acknowledge that Western management during the past 150 years has been spectacularly successful.

In this book we are presenting what we consider to be a profoundly different and dramatically better approach to leadership. But the old way wasn't all that bad. This may explain why changing is so difficult for so many. There is not all that much wrong with the old way, except that 50 years ago a better way came along.

Today's Leaders Must Move against Contrary Tides

There is much at work in our world that makes it hard for today's leaders to adopt this new philosophy. There is little to make it easy.

This transformation is a challenge all by itself, but today's executives must deal with Wall Street analysts, financial institutions, shareholders, government regulators, suppliers, and even customers who by and large don't understand this new philosophy or care about it.

When the value of stock is driven by short-term profits, it is very difficult for top executives to promote long-term thinking. The top executives, therefore, and those who work with short-term-thinking outsiders, must work within both sets of beliefs. They are truly standing at transformation's threshold and they must be functional in both philosophies, a monumental challenge.

Leaders Lead the Dancing When the Band Is from Neptune

We know how to dance the old dance. We all grew up in traditional organizations with conventional leader and role models. Now the music has changed. We don't know the new steps and there are no footprints on the floor.

Learning to Dance at Ford

On February 10, 1982, Donald Petersen, CEO of Ford Motor Company, addressed Ford's most senior executives with these words.

> ...As I was thinking about this meeting, it struck me strongly that you are the ones who are going to decide whether we are really successful in making a dramatic change in how we do business. You are the ones ... . *It can be very difficult to make significant changes,* especially when you have been in the habit of doing things differently for decades, and especially when *the very success that brought you to the positions you now hold was rooted in doing some things, frankly, the wrong way. It is going to be hard for you to accept that—that you were promoted for the wrong reasons a time or two. [Italics mine. (PRS)]*
>
> I seriously suggest that you give that some heartfelt thought as to whether you really understand what we are talking about. I had the experience in January at our Management Review, that most people in the room thought I was talking about something so elementary that we, of course, already do it in the Ford Motor Company. They could not understand why I was talking about it. It left me with the sense that many of us still do not understand what we are really trying to change. So I urge you to ask yourselves, do you really understand what it is we are trying to change....
>
> Cited in Scherkenbach (1986).

The most sincere, earnest, knowledgeable leader will have a tough time with this new philosophy and these new methods. Those who follow must be patient, slow to judge and quick to forgive. The dance is new and those who lead will inevitably step on the toes of those who are led.

So the old way wasn't all that bad and the new way is difficult to master. The generation that understandably takes pride in their capabilities and accomplishments, the talent and hard work that got them where they are, must now come to grips with the need to change how they lead. They got to the top and a message arrived saying: *Much of what you know and do is outdated. Welcome to leadership!*

Today's leaders deserve all the support we can give them. Even then, the job is overwhelming.

HEALING WORKPLACES AND LEARNING WORKPLACES

At one point in my life I had to choose between one of two careers: (1) to specialize in being a psychology-oriented therapist and counselor and (2) the one I chose—to specialize in organization development. The primary basis for my decision was this: When people were experiencing tough times in their lives most of them continued to go to their jobs every day. I observed that their experience at work was, for some, a source of healing and, for others, a source of the problem. Some found that doing work that they were proud of and that benefited others combined with a network of supportive colleagues was more therapeutic than anything I could offer in one hour a week of counseling. Others would leave my counseling session and return to a workplace where there was so little support and so much stress, where they felt so little pride in their work, that the benefit of the therapy session was vitiated by the craziness of the job.

I decided that the better opportunity was to help people through difficult times by helping to create workplaces that provide help and healing.

Add to this the notion introduced by Dr. Deming and developed by writers such as Peter Senge that we can have a workplace where the worker doesn't just check most of his or her real and satisfying life at the door, picking it up on the way out. Now we can imagine a workplace where people can live their lives as people, not as mere functionaries and valued assets. Let us, therefore, briefly look at crazymaking, healing, and learning, and how leaders can lead healing and learning.

Crazymakers in the Workplace

These are eight commonplace, dehumanizing realities in our organizations, management interventions that create dissonance and disintegration in the community of workers.

1. Policies that force competition around a contrived scarcity.

- Performance appraisal with forced ranking
- Merit pay
- Employee of the Month (year, decade, century, or millennium)

2. Policies of distrust and disloyalty

- For example, Falk Gear's old bereavement policy concluded with, "You may be required by the personnel department to furnish proof of death and proof of relationship" (see Chapter 9).
- Disloyalty to the employee demonstrated by downsizing (see Chapter 5).

3. Dysfunctional systems combined with a culprit mentality

- See Figure 10-1 for a picture of this crazymaker.

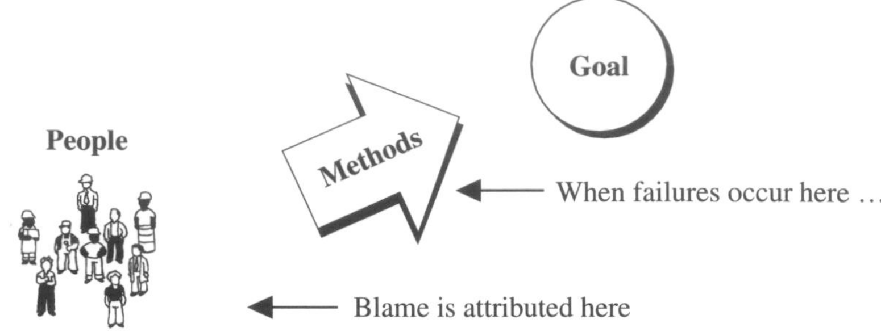

Figure 10-1. Blaming individuals for dysfunctional systems.

4. Paternalistic relationships

Parent figure		*Child figure*
■ Domineering	Expecting	■ Subordinate
■ Judging	others to be:	■ Apologetic
■ Controlling		■ Compliant
■ Blaming		■ Acquiescent
■ Giving motivation		■ Needing motivation
■ Empowering		■ Needing empowerment
■ See Chapters 2 and 9.		

5. Narcissism, arrogance, and greed

- "We are the definition of what is good to do. If it is any good, we invented it. If we didn't invent it, it isn't any good."
- We (management) are wiser than:
  — The employees
  — Other departments
  — The customers
  — The clients, patients, recipients of services
  — The competition
  — The community around us

> In management, the first concern of the company is the happiness of the people connected with it. If the people do not feel happy and cannot be made happy, that company does not deserve to exist.
> —Kaoru Ishikawa (1981)

- Profit (or cost reduction) is the most important measure of success.
- Ultimately our only meaningful purpose is to satisfy the needs of those who own or manage the organization.
- Business is part dog eat dog and part honor among thieves.
- See "Skeuomorph" on page 132.

6. *Employees as objects of utility*
   - Employees are an expense and we should seek to reduce our dependence on them. They are commodities, interchangeable parts that we should discard and replace when they show signs of wear.
   - No opportunity to grow and improve.

7. *Pathological loyalty: teamwork gone bad*
   - Groupthink: unquestioned allegiance to the group's process and output.
   - The word *teamwork* is used interchangeably with conformity or anonymity.
   - Suspicion of personal effort, solo performance, or individual attention.
   - Unnecessarily rigid conformity to a norm (standardization gone bad).
   - See "Bureaucracy" in Chapter 4.

8. *Lean and mean-ism*
   - Calibrating the staffing level to accommodate workload at its lowest level of variation. Any increased level of work is overload (see Figure 10-2).

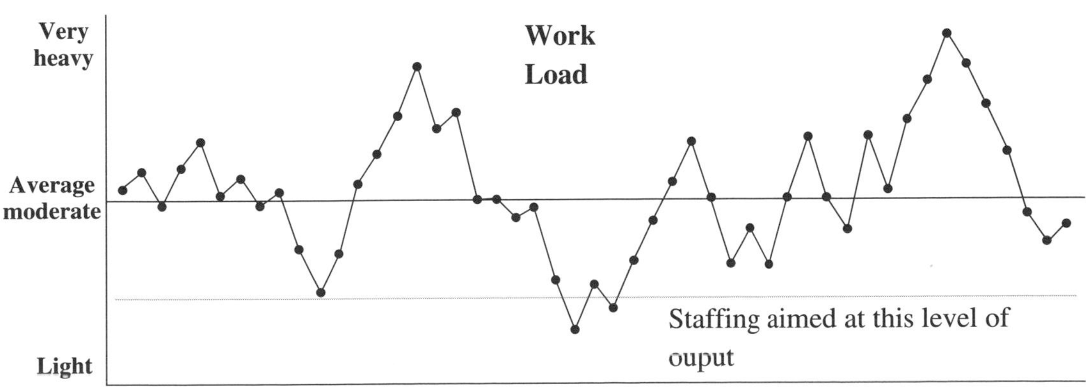

Figure 10-3. Lean and mean turned anorexic and vicious.

- No breathing space or discretionary time for education, training, team building, improvement efforts, or backing away from the everyday absurdity to get a fresh perspective.
- No tolerance for activities not directly involved in production.
- See "Questions for Downsizers" in Chapter 5.

Healing and Learning in the Workplace

These are the policies, practices, and environmental factors that make the workplace a healing place.

1. *Clear, constant, ennobling purpose*

   - Individuals and groups throughout the organization work cooperatively toward common, elevating goals.
   - The primary measures of success such as customer delight are altruistic.
   - See Chapters 2 and 5.

2. *Opportunities to learn and grow*

   - Learning is an articulated expectation and is part of the cycle of everyday work life.
   - Lifelong learning is modeled by the top leaders and promoted throughout the workforce.
   - There are time and money available to sustain continuous learning.
   - See Chapter 3.

3. *Continuous improvement of the methods and processes*

   - When things go wrong, we work together to find the systemic inadequacies and systemic remedies.
   - Throughout the organization we learn to master the methodology of improvement.
   - See Chapters 2 and 6.

4. *Mutual respect and trust*

   - People in the organization are regarded and treated as equals: trustworthy adults, each with different experience, skills, and other resources.
   - People are treated respectfully: noticed, greeted, listened to, and invited to participate.

- No empty, humanistic-sounding slogans, but genuine caring for people. People are valued as people, not assets or functionaries.
- See Chapters 2 and 10.

5. Frequent communication and access to information

- The organization hums with communication.
- People are told the truth and have points of access for asking questions, checking out rumors, and finding out what is going on from trustworthy sources.
- Communication is accomplished through various media: electronic, print, video, and face-to-face.
- Communications are not packaged messages carefully designed by spin doctors.
- See Chapters 2, 4, and 10.

6. A sense of community

- The experience of the people in the organization is an experience of community. The organization is a place where a person is known and cared about by others and where he or she knows and cares about others.
- As in any community, people maintain their individuality and sense of personal boundaries and thresholds of need: no compulsory joy, no obligatory holding hands and singing "Kumbaya," no frowning on those who won't go bowling with the group. Rather, there is individual choice within an environment of support.
- Community is less a matter of big, planned events and more a matter of treating each other well every day.
- Community is a reflection of the values lived and promoted by the people at the top of the organization.

7. Participation

Healthy participation has two aspects: There is the benefit of the participation itself and then the need for clarity about what participation is.

Managers can seem to promote participation, a good thing, and drive people crazy by being unclear or inconsistent about exactly what participation is.

- THE VALUE OF SPECIFIC PARTICIPATION. When people are allowed to participate in decision making, generally:
  - — The decision will be a better decision.

Kurt Lewin and Participation

Kurt Lewin (1890–1947) was a graduate student in the United States at a time when his homeland, Germany, was overrun by Hitler's Nazis. His family and friends back home became victims of the Holocaust. Some of the perpetrators or at least passive supporters of the Holocaust were people he knew in his youth. Lewin was faced with the horror of his family being killed by his former acquaintances.

Lewin pioneered the field of organization development. Among his teachings, perhaps reflecting his struggle with his family's tragedy, were these:

- We are likely to modify our own behavior when we participate in problem analysis and solution.
- We are more likely to carry out those decisions that we help to make.
- Groups provide a force and power to work beyond what the sum of individual efforts can produce.
- Groups can involve themselves in Action Research, a process by which they can take action and study what they do so that they can learn from and improve their own efforts. (See Weisbord, 1987, p. 89.)

— There will be less resistance to the proposed change.

— Those who implement the change will be better able to carry it out.

— See Chapter 6 on the socialization of change.

- THE VALUE OF PARTICIPATION IN GENERAL. When people aren't allowed to participate, they get hurt. To put it another way, the hurting of people invariably occurs through a process that excluded those people from participating. We are living in a world of hurt, a business climate in which people have been hurt by decisions made without their involvement. The importance of involvement applies to work, to communities, and to nations.
- CLEAR EXPECTATIONS AND PARTICIPATION

  There are various stages that may lend themselves to participation:

  a. Identifying the problem, issue, need, or opportunity.

  b. Examining the situation to determining the various factors and causes at work.

c. Identifying the goal or purpose of the effort: What are we trying to accomplish?

d. Identifying the indicators of progress, success, or completion: How will we know that our effort is making a positive contribution?

e. Designing the process or method by which the problem, issue, need, or opportunity will be addressed.

f. Planning the effort.

g. Implementing the effort.

h. Monitoring the effort (study of the plan–do–study–act cycle).

i. Making adjustments based on what was learned in the study phase.

j. Standardizing or institutionalizing the new way.

Participation in any of the stages of development—those listed above or any others—is not a matter of absolutes: You participate or you don't. Participation is a relative concept.

Tannenbaum and Schmidt (1968) in the 1960s identified a continuum of management control that is pictured in Figure 10-4.

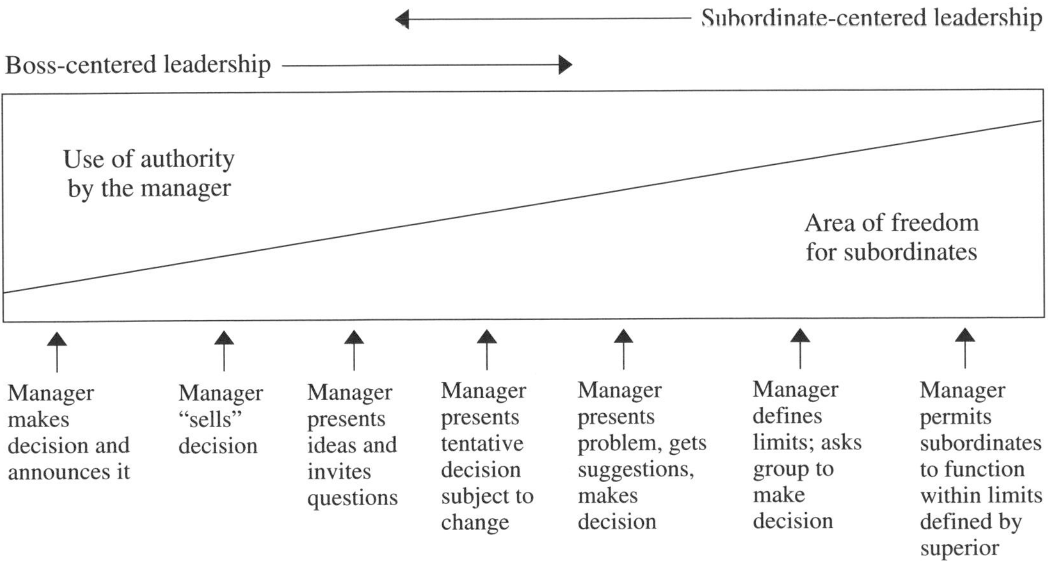

Figure 10-4. Continuum of leadership behavior.

Roland Coates and Liz Freeman have taken this model by Tannenbaum and Schmidt and developed it into an integrated and comprehensive approach to teamwork and consensus building. I have learned much from them and recommend them as superb teachers. (To contact them, write Liz Freeman and Roland Coates, 410 Ashby Road, New Ipswich, NH 03071.)

You will notice that Tannenbaum and Schmidt's figure has a diagonal line that does not quite touch either corner. This is to indicate that there is no absolute authority for managers or absolute freedom for subordinates.

Problems arise with participation when the subordinates have unspoken expectations regarding their participation that are more expansive than the unspoken expectations of the authority who has set participation in motion. Ambiguity is the greatest enemy of participation. Clarity is an important ingredient for successful participation. People are liable to resent more the unkept promise of participation than being left out of the decision altogether.

8. The healing leader

The healing leader can be characterized by the following:

- He or she tells the truth.
- He or she can be counted on to be consistently benevolent toward the workforce.
- He or she can be counted on to be competent in his or her job. See Figures 2-15 and 10-5.

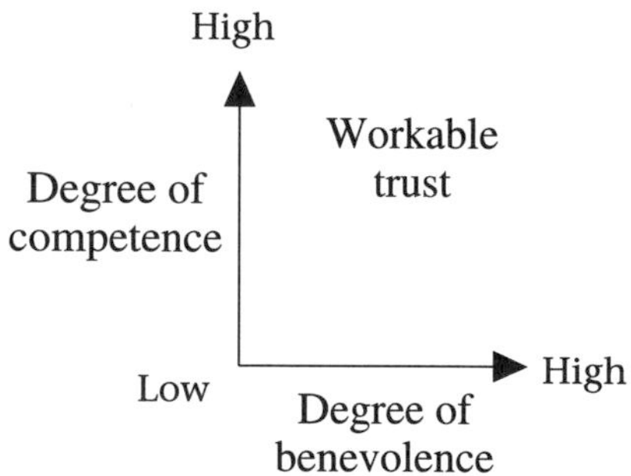

Figure 10-5. Workable trust of the healing leader.

- He or she listens to people's stories.
- He or she engages in entry conversation (civilities and chitchat and other forms of letting people know that they count).

- He or she seeks systemic causes to problems, not culprits.
- He or she leads continual improvement: Things keep getting better.
- He or she keeps everyone focused on the constant and elevating purpose and the importance of serving the outside customer.
- He or she promotes participation and is clear about what kind of participation is needed and expected on any given issue.

HOW TO CONVERT YOUR BOSS

Most of the people reading this book are not top executives. This is fortunate because if only top executives read this book we wouldn't sell very many.

What can those buried in the lower ranks do to influence those at the higher ranks? We offer several suggestions here. Realistically, however, we should be clear about a few things.

- Converting the boss is a long shot. You may not be in a position to have influence and those in such a position are probably not working from the same agenda you are.
- You may succeed at doing marvelous things, but until you win the hearts and minds of the people at the top, you will not have had significant impact on your organization. In such cases, the best that may happen is that you personally will benefit from what you learn and bring it with you to your next job.

What to do if you are not a muckety-muck?

Listening

Recall what we said in Chapter 8 about listening: It is not a passive activity but an active pursuit of understanding what the other is trying to say. Before approaching any official leaders, see their world from their point of view: their priorities, their sleep-disrupting worries, their visions for the future, what creates satisfaction, and what drives them crazy. This will affect how you understand the changes you want to propose and how you approach introducing any new ideas.

Learning to Say "Uh-huh"

Bill Burke was vice president of sales for Sunbeam Electric in the 1960s and is a noted management consultant in Vero Beach, Florida. Bill teaches salespeople a skill that he considers the salesperson's most powerful weapon: say "uh-huh" and be quiet. "It will increase your sales by 65 percent," he says with his tongue only partially in his cheek. "If you say 'uh-huh' with a stupid look on your face, you will increase your sales by 90 percent!" Bill's point is that the process of selling is less an act of persuasion and more an act of listening, understanding, and relationship building.

When you have little control and want to introduce change, listen to those who are movers and shakers. (See "The Demography of Change" in Chapter 6.)

Success

Nothing captures the attention of the movers and shakers more than success. Nothing lends more credibility to the message-bearer than success. From the viewpoint of the top executive, success will be defined in terms of what you have done that has helped the business, providing better service to the customer at a lower cost.

During my various careers, I worked for two organizations at which the work I did was worthwhile from my point of view, but not of much value in the minds of my bosses. That was the equivalent of an artist achieving aesthetic success without commercial success, or a politician espousing what he or she considers wonderful positions yet losing the elections. My pride of work was growing but my credibility was diminishing. (Fortunately this period of my career ended, and I have been able to achieve both pride and sufficient commercial success to keep me satisfied.)

Therefore, using upper management's definition of success, you must create achievements that are satisfying to you, are appreciated by the customers, and meet the priority needs of the movers and shakers. If you are successful you will begin to develop a willingness on management's part to consider new approaches. Without these successes, your credibility is vacant and your ability to influence is nil.

Community

In Chapter 6 we discussed the socialization of change, saying that to plan for change is partly to develop a constituency of supporters for the change. This also applies to converting your boss. There are people who directly or indirectly affect whether your boss is in favor of a change, opposed to it, or indifferent to it.

Sometimes bosses might be inclined to try a new method but are talked out of it by colleagues or others who report to them. Therefore, your effort to convert your boss to any of these new approaches will require converting others who might have influence over your boss. Knowing your boss involves knowing whose opinions he or she respects. Your boss, for example, may trust his or her secretary's sense of what changes the clerical staff will accept or resist. The boss may rely on the warehouse manager to represent the feelings of the hourly workers. These influential others are some of the people you need to get to know, understand, listen to, and say "uh-huh."

Persistence

Being persistent without being a pest is an important part of converting your boss. I know one employee who collected a lot of what he referred to as "one-pagers" and "elevator comments" that he had ready for opportune moments. He was ready for any appropriate moment when he could say something or hand out something to those he was trying to convert. He tried to do this in a non-preachy but persistent way, providing examples or information from either outside the organization or within. He also had an available collection of resources—books, articles, videotapes—that he could offer to anyone who wanted to learn more.

Learning from the Martial Arts and The Art of War

The difference between Western and Eastern approaches to combat provides an apt metaphor for converting your boss. I first learned this from Andy Bryner and Dawna Markova (1996, pp. 100–109). Football's line of scrimmage is symbolic of the Western approach to combat: nose-to-nose, smash-mouthed, head-on collisions. Nothing subtle. It is my power against yours and may the toughest player win. (The current tendencies of stunts and deception are almost un-American.) In the East the strategy is, instead of opposing your adversaries' force, to use their own power against them. When your opponent rushes toward you, step aside and move with your opponent, letting his or her momentum carry you both. Then gradually turn your opponent and his or her force and momentum toward the direction you wish to go. It is more a process of working *with,* rather than working *against.* Opposing your boss is foolish, just as it is foolish for a smaller person to engage in head-to-head combat with a larger person. Don't seek to control the person. Seek to influence the flow of energy.

In the 2000-year-old classic *The Art of War,* Sun-Tzu (1989) teaches how the art of prevailing in conflict is less the result of one's strength and more the result of one's planning and preparation. "Information is your best friend," he tells us. Sun-Tzu would advise the subordinate that the success of his attempt to convert the boss should be assured before the effort is ever engaged. The conversion should seem to the boss to be his or her own idea.

Eastern philosophy, therefore, would encourage the longer-term, indirect approach to changing another's mind, an approach that is, nonetheless, well-planned and persistent.

The Onion Patch Strategy

Here we describe some guidelines that are extensions of the onion patch strategy first presented in *The Team Handbook* (Scholtes, 1988). The phrase *onion patch* is borrowed from an absolutely dreadful 1950s song titled "I'm a Lonely Little Petunia in an Onion Patch." These guidelines, therefore, suggest what you can do when you're a lonely little low-ranking, cubicle-inhabiting, systems-thinking petunia trying to introduce the new philosophy of leadership to those rooted in the onion patch of an obsolete managerial philosophy. (The analogy is exhausting all by itself.)

Guidelines for the Onion Patch

1. *Learn everything you can.* At the very least it may be useful in your next job.
2. *Identify the area over which you have influence.* Even if it is small, you can make things happen there.
3. *Identify some priorities.* Select some improvement efforts that:
   - Help the outside customers.
   - Help the Gemba (see Chapter 4).
   - Impress your boss' boss. ("Hey Dithers, that was a terrific project you had Bumstead working on!")
   - Will prove to be dramatically successful. (Don't pick a loser.)
4. *Recruit allies.* The more people of influence you have who are interested in what you do and who support your effort, the more likely you will be to succeed (see "Demography of Change," Chapter 6).
5. *Have data.* Use data to indicate the validity of your approaches. Use data to describe the current situation and to measure progress. By implication, anyone who disagrees with you should do so on the basis of better data.

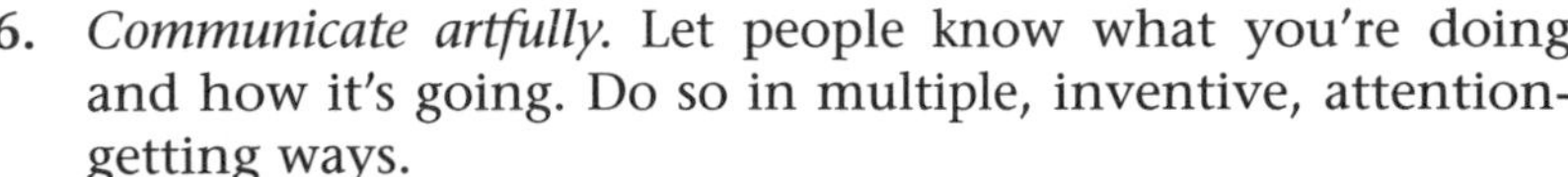

6. *Communicate artfully.* Let people know what you're doing and how it's going. Do so in multiple, inventive, attention-getting ways.
7. *Don't argue with those who disagree.* Don't even seek to persuade those who resist. Be clear about what you want to do and move ahead as far as you can as rapidly as you can. Your success will attract a following.

THE 47 HABITS OF PRETTY GOOD LEADERS

Here is a summary of the advice this book offers to leaders. The list of items is admittedly long. This is in keeping with one overriding guideline for leaders:

> Leaders must avoid simplistic answers to complex issues. They must seek the "simplicity on the other side of complexity" (Oliver Wendell Holmes).

1. *These are the new competencies of leadership:*
   - Systems thinking (Chapter 3)
   - Understanding the variability of work (Chapter 2)
   - Understanding how we learn, develop, and improve (Chapter 2)
   - Understanding people (Chapters 2, 8, and 9)
   - Understanding the interactions between systems, variability, learning, and human behavior (Chapter 2)
   - Giving vision, meaning, direction, and focus to the organization (Chapters 2, 5, 6, and 10)
2. As they learn the new way, leaders must be patient with themselves and others, persistent, and humble, and allow themselves and others to be inelegant. (Chapter 1)
3. Regarding this new approach, we are moving from unconscious incompetence through conscious incompetence, the most difficult transition of all. This may take three years or more to achieve. Then we may move into conscious competence and on into unconscious competence. This cycle will go on forever. (Chapter 1)
4. Leaders need to understand the organization *systemically:* clearly understanding the purpose of any undertaking, then understanding the interactions and interdependencies between the parts that result either in the achievement or in the failure to achieve that purpose. All *output,* desired or

undesired, is the net result of the system and its interactions (not the people and their inadequacy). (Chapter 2)

5. Everything is part of a larger system. For leaders to understand what is going on, they must understand the larger system of which any effort is part and with which it interacts. (Chapter 2)
6. Changing the system will change what people do. Changing what people do will not change the system. (Chapter 2)
7. All the teamed-up, accountable, empowered, incentivized, motivated, and paid-for-performance people you can muster cannot compensate for a dysfunctional system. (Chapter 2)
8. Leaders must understand variation and the difference between common cause variation and special cause variation. (Chapter 2) Leaders who do not understand variation will:
   - See trends where there are no trends.
   - Miss trends where there *are* trends.
   - Attribute problems to individuals who have no control.
   - Give credit to people who are simply lucky.
   - Fail to understand past performance.
   - Be unable to predict future performance.
   - Not understand their systems or how to improve them.
9. Leaders need to instinctively use the Plan–Do–Study–Act cycle, seeing themselves less as directors and controllers and more as the leaders of learning and experimentation. (Chapter 2)
10. Leaders need to understand the difference between necessary and unnecessary change as well as the difference between change and improvement. Leaders must know what is needed to assure that any proposed change will be an improvement. Change requires knowledge. Improvement requires profound knowledge. (Chapters 2 and 5)
11. Leaders need to understand motivation, the difference between intrinsic and extrinsic motivation, that they cannot motivate, and that their attempts to do so will probably make things worse. Leaders need to understand that they can, however, *de*motivate people. (Chapters 2 and 9)
12. Leaders need to understand the importance of participation and the involvement of people when solving problems and planning change. Participation results in better decisions, solutions, and improvements. Excluding people and stealthful

or coercive approaches to change do great harm to the organization and its people. (Chapters 2 and 10)

13. Leaders may well seek to discover what their organization's culture is, keeping in mind that they are the people least likely to understand it. (Chapter 5)
14. Without personal, face-to-face relationships there is no leadership. Leaders create and foster networks of personal relationships within the organization and between the organization and those on the outside. (Chapters 2, 9, and 10)
15. Leaders must go an inch wide and a mile deep and lead the organization in this focused approach. The organization must focus its efforts so that it does a few things thoroughly rather than many things inadequately. (Chapters 2 and 5)
16. Leaders develop clarity and consistency regarding the organization's purpose, continually reminding the workforce of that purpose. (Chapter 3)
17. Leaders need to understand the purpose of the organization in terms of the capabilities acquired by the customer as a result of interacting with it. (Chapter 3)
18. Leaders need a customer-in perspective, helping the whole organization define a good job from the customer's perspective. (Chapter 3)
19. Feedback is the mother's milk of improvement. Leaders need to establish ongoing feedback loops from the customer to the organization. Within the organization, leaders need to promote the establishment and maintenance of ongoing systems and process-based feedback loops. (Chapters 3, 4, and 9)
20. Leaders need a strong sense of Gemba (the work flow going directly toward the outside customer), understanding this as the important daily customer-oriented work, to which leaders give priority and support. (Chapters 3 and 4)
21. Leaders need to promote the standardization of recurring processes and an understanding of how each person's standardized processes of work fit with other processes and within the larger systems. (Chapter 4)
22. Leaders need to understand the difference between simplistic approaches to standardization such as ISO 9000 and a more systemically based, holistic, and integrated approach to standardization, an approach that is part of a larger philosophy and context. (Chapter 4)

23. Leaders need to use and promote the use of flowcharts that help to display how the systems and processes unfold and how the work of one individual or group fits into a larger flow of work. (Chapter 4)
24. Leaders need to lead the removal of internal barriers, breaking them down and creating interactive systems and processes based on collaboration, cooperation, and interdependence. (Chapter 4)
25. Leaders must not succumb to the latest fashions and fads. (Chapter 5)
26. Leaders need the ability to lead the planning and action necessary for breakthrough improvement and large systems change. (Chapter 6)
27. Leaders must lead the creation of purpose, mission, vision, and values, statements that are unique rather than generic, statements that are from the heart, not empty exercises in wordsmithing. (Chapter 5)
28. Leaders need to lead the establishment of systems and processes for routinely collecting and analyzing critical data, the vital signs that indicate the organization's well-being, needs, and opportunities. (Chapters 6 and 7)
29. Leaders must believe strongly that planning consists not only in identifying goals and priorities but also in specifying the methods and activities necessary and sufficient to successfully achieve those goals and priorities. (Chapter 6)
30. Leaders need to lead not only the *planning* process—the establishment of priorities and the methods needed to accomplish them—but also the *review* process. Leaders visit those engaged in the improvement efforts to ask good questions and offer challenge and support. (Chapters 6 and 8)
31. Leaders need to understand and appreciate the importance of clear, workable operational definitions, specifically defining characteristics from the customer's point of view. (Chapter 7)
32. Leaders need a reflex for smart measurement, not simplistic, conventional, and unuseful measurement. People throughout the organization must know *what* to measure, *how* to measure it, *why* it is important to measure it, *how to interpret* the data, and *how to react* to whatever the data indicate. (Chapter 7)
33. Leaders need to see themselves (Chapter 8):
    - More as coaches and less as directors.
    - More as experimenters and less as controllers.

- More as educators and less as advice-givers.
- More as inquirers and less as inspectors.

34. Leaders need to appreciate the importance of good questions and develop an instinct for asking good questions. (Chapter 8)
35. Leaders must know what good listening is and how to practice it. (Chapter 8)
36. Leaders too often use the rhetoric of humanism and combine it with inhumane actions. Leaders need to see this disparity and make their actions consistent with their words. (Chapter 9)
37. Leaders need to examine the assumptions behind their organizations' policies, for example, the implicit belief that employees cannot be trusted. What is implicit and unspoken must be called into question. (Chapter 9)
38. Leaders need to understand the inherently demeaning nature of incentives or carrot and stick approaches. (Chapter 9)
39. Leaders who desire to solve problems of employee performance or morale need to see those problems as part of a larger, self-perpetuating system of problems. (Chapter 9)
40. Similarly, leaders need to understand that behind any self-perpetuating system of performance and morale problems are unspoken and false assumptions about the nature of people and work. (Chapter 9)
41. Some of the common, and false, assumptions leaders have about workers and work are (Chapter 9):
    - Problems, for the most part, result from individual dereliction.
    - Successful work requires holding people accountable for the achievement of measurable goals.
    - There is a reservoir of withheld effort that must be coaxed or coerced out of people.
    - The leader's job is to motivate and control the workforce.
42. Leaders need to understand that there is no good way to do performance appraisal. It is inherently the wrong thing to do. Leaders need to know what is wrong with performance appraisal and what to do instead. (Chapter 9)
43. Rather than seeking control of their people, leaders must work with their people to gain control of the systems and processes. Rather than dysfunctional systems that require the heroic efforts of outstanding people, leaders should

seek the creation and maintenance of outstanding systems and processes that continuously succeed with the ordinary efforts of average people. (Chapter 9)

44. At the heart of many conventional management policies is a desire on the part of some leaders to maintain control, or the illusion of control, over people. Leaders need to learn whether this is true of them and learn what can be gained from the control of the work, not the workers. (Chapter 9)

45. Leaders need to understand that in order to develop an alternative to performance appraisal they must change the way they think. (Chapter 9)

46. Leadership is not just a position. It's a process. The responsibility of those in the *position* of leadership is to see to it that the *process* of leadership occurs. (Chapter 10)

47. A workplace can be a place of healing or a place where crazymaking takes place. A leader's job is to create an environment that is healing. (Chapter 10)

CHAPTER TEN ACTIVITIES

Discuss these questions in your group.

Questions on leadership

1. Disregarding anything you've read or been taught about leadership, what are the characteristics of excellent leaders with whom you have directly worked and whose leadership you have directly observed?

2. How does your experience with excellent leaders differ from the ideas presented in this book?

3. What in blazes are the following individuals talking about?
   - Douglas McGregor said, "Every managerial act rests on theory."
   - Deming said, "All theories are right in some world."
   - George Box said, "All theories are wrong but some are useful."
   - Deming said, "Management is prediction."

The crazymaking versus healing workplace continuum

Have people describe your organization using the crazymaking versus healing workplace continuum. Look at the varying patterns of response (e.g., those at the top versus those at the bottom).

Instructions: Place an X on this continuum corresponding to the overall placement of the organization in the crazymaking—healing sets of attributes.
Zone 1: Strong crazymaking
Zone 2: Moderate crazymaking
Zone 3: Moderate healing
Zone 4: Strong healing

Note: Don't place your X on any borderlines.

When you have marked the continuum, compare your placement of the X with that of the others in your group. Discuss the differing experiences and perceptions.

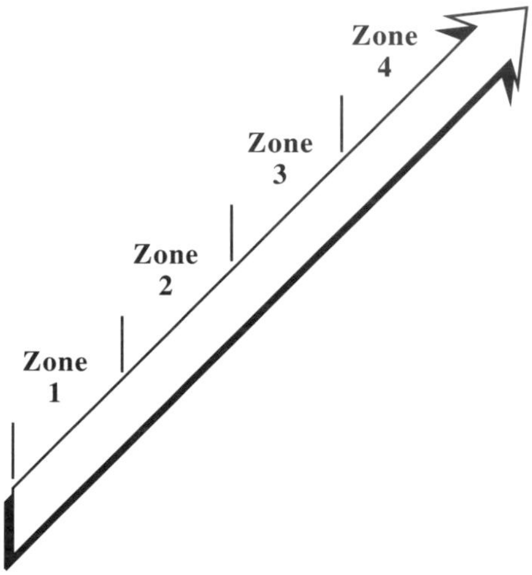

Healing workplace

- Clear, constant, ennobling purpose
- Opportunities to learn and grow
- Continuous improvement of the methods and processes
- Mutual respect and trust
- Communication which is frequent and open
- Workers valued as people
- A sense of close-knit community

Zone 4

Zone 3

Zone 2

Zone 1

Crazymaking workplace

- Unclarity of purpose
- Inconstancy of purpose
- Culprit mentality
- Workers valued for utility
- Distrust
- Distance, divisiveness
- Paternalism
- Work not worth doing
- Little communication

Questions about business

1. What is the purpose of *a* business?

2. What is the purpose of *business*?

3. Albert Dunlap:
   - Was appointed CEO of Scott Paper (he is now CEO of Sunbeam).
   - Shut down several plants and facilities, laying off nearly 11,000 people.
   - Sold off several individual parts of Scott.
   - What was left was purchased by Kimberly-Clark.
   - Scott's return on investment was never better. "It was Scott's best year," said Dunlap.
   - Describes himself as a "turnaround artist."

   What can you infer to be Dunlap's beliefs about business, customers, employees, and stockholders?

Questions about yourself

1. What attracts you to leadership or management?

2. What do you hope to be doing 10 years from now?

3. What legacy would you like to leave behind?

The traits-of-leaders exercise

Below are 28 pairs of statements, each describing a characteristic of a leader. For each pair select that statement—A or B—which you believe is the most important of those two traits.

When you have completed selecting from each of the 28 pairs of characteristics, use the scoring key to identify which traits you selected with what frequency. Discuss your results with others who have done the exercise.

Pick one of each of the paired statements, selecting which characteristic of the two you believe is most important for a leader.

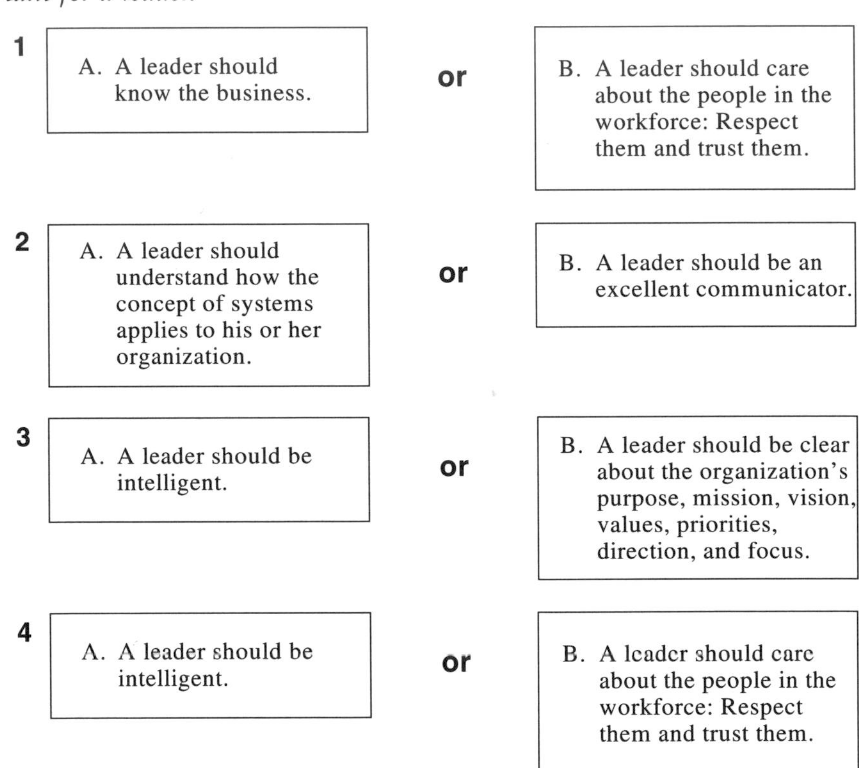

1	A. A leader should know the business.	or	B. A leader should care about the people in the workforce: Respect them and trust them.
2	A. A leader should understand how the concept of systems applies to his or her organization.	or	B. A leader should be an excellent communicator.
3	A. A leader should be intelligent.	or	B. A leader should be clear about the organization's purpose, mission, vision, values, priorities, direction, and focus.
4	A. A leader should be intelligent.	or	B. A leader should care about the people in the workforce: Respect them and trust them.

5	A. A leader should be committed to serving customers.	or	B. A leader should be an excellent communicator.
6	A. A leader should know the business.	or	B. A leader should be committed to creating shareholder gain.
7	A. A leader should be intelligent.	or	B. A leader should understand how the concept of systems applies to his or her organization.
8	A. A leader should be committed to serving customers.	or	B. A leader should be committed to creating shareholder gain.
9	A. A leader should know the business.	or	B. A leader should be clear about the organization's purpose, mission, vision, values, priorities, direction, and focus.
10	A. A leader should be an excellent communicator.	or	B. A leader should be committed to creating shareholder gain.
11	A. A leader should be committed to serving customers.	or	B. A leader should understand how the concept of systems applies to his or her organization.
12	A. A leader should be intelligent.	or	B. A leader should know the business.
13	A. A leader should care about the people in the workforce: Respect them and trust them.	or	B. A leader should understand how the concept of systems applies to his or her organization.

14	A. A leader should be clear about the organization's purpose, mission, vision, values, priorities, direction, and focus.	or	B. A leader should be committed to creating shareholder gain.
15	A. A leader should understand how the concept of systems applies to his or her organization.	or	B. A leader should be clear about the organization's purpose, mission, vision, values, priorities, direction, and focus.
16	A. A leader should care about the people in the workforce: Respect them and trust them.	or	B. A leader should be an excellent communicator.
17	A. A leader should know the business.	or	B. A leader should understand how the concept of systems applies to his or her organization.
18	A. A leader should be intelligent.	or	B. A leader should be committed to serving customers.
19	A. A leader should know the business.	or	B. A leader should be an excellent communicator.
20	A. A leader should be intelligent.	or	B. A leader should be an excellent communicator.
21	A. A leader should be intelligent.	or	B. A leader should be committed to creating shareholder gain.
22	A. A leader should care about the people in the workforce: Respect them and trust them.	or	B. A leader should be committed to serving customers.

23	A. A leader should be committed to serving customers.	or	B. A leader should be clear about the organization's purpose, mission, vision, values, priorities, direction, and focus.
24	A. A leader should care about the people in the workforce: Respect them and trust them.	or	B. A leader should be committed to creating shareholder gain.
25	A. A leader should be an excellent communicator.	or	B. A leader should be clear about the organization's purpose, mission, vision, values, priorities, direction, and focus.
26	A. A leader should know the business.	or	B. A leader should be committed to serving customers.
27	A. A leader should understand how the concept of systems applies to his or her organization.	or	B. A leader should be committed to creating shareholder gain.
28	A. A leader should care about the people in the workforce: Respect them and trust them.	or	B. A leader should be clear about the organization's purpose, mission, vision, values, priorities, direction, and focus.

Scoring key

	Leadership traits							
Circle A or B depending on your choice	1 Intelligent	2 Know the business	3 Care about the people	4 Committed to serving customers	5 Understand systems	6 Excellent communi-cator	7 Clear about purpose and direction	8 Committed to share-holder gain
Pair 1		A	B					
2					A	B		
3	A						B	
4	A		B					
5				A		B		
6		A						B
7	A				B			
8				A				B
9		A					B	
10						A		B
11				A	B			
12	A	B						
13			A		B			
14							A	B
15					A		B	
16			A			B		
17		A			B			
18	A			B				
19		A				B		
20	A					B		
21	A							B
22			A	B				
23				A			B	
24			A					B
25						A	B	
26		A		B				
27					A			B
28			A				B	
Totals (maximum of 7 points)								

REFERENCES

Adams, S. 1996. *The Dilbert principle.* New York: Harper Business.

Anderson, T.D. 1992. *Transforming leadership.* Amherst, MA: HRD Press.

Argyris, C. 1964. *Integrating the individual and the organization.* New York: John Wiley & Sons.

Belasco, J., and Stayer, R. 1993. *Flight of the buffalo.* New York: Warner Books.

Bennis, W. 1989. *On becoming a leader.* Reading, MA: Addison Wesley.

Block, P. 1987. *The empowered manager.* San Francisco: Jossey Bass.

Brown, D. 1995. *Technimanagement.* Englewood Cliffs, NJ: Prentice Hall.

Bryner, A., and Markova, D. 1996. *An unused intelligence.* Berkeley, CA: Conari Press.

Byham, W.C. 1989. *Zapp!* Pittsburgh, PA: Developmental Dimensions International Press.

Delavigne, K.T., and Robertson, J.D. 1994. *Deming's profound changes.* Englewood Cliffs, NJ: Prentice Hall.

DePree, M. 1992. *Leadership jazz.* New York: Doubleday Currency.

DePree, M. 1987. *Leadership is an art.* New York: Doubleday.

Dobyns, L., and Crawford-Mason, C. 1994. *Thinking about quality.* New York: Random House.

Drucker, P.F. 1966. *The effective executive.* New York: Harper & Row.

Egan, G. 1988. *Change agent skills.* San Diego, CA: University Associates.

Gluckman, P., and Reynolds-Roone, D. 1993. *Everyday heroes of the quality movement.* Knoxville, TN: SPC Press.

Goldratt, E.M. 1990. *The theory of constraints.* Croton-On-Hudson, NY: North River Press.

Greenleaf, R. 1977. *Servant leadership: A journey in the nature of legitimate power and greatness.* Paulist Press.

Hesselbein, F., Goldsmith, M., and Beckhard, R., eds. 1996. *The leader of the future: New visions, strategies, and practices for the next era.* San Francisco: Jossey-Bass Publishers.

Ikezawa, T. 1993. *Effective TQC.* Tokyo: PHP Institute.

Johnson, B. 1992. *Polarity management.* Amherst, MA: HRD Press.

Lane, T., and Green, A. 1994. *The way of quality.* Austin, TX: Dialogos Press.

Lareau, W. 1991. *American Samurai.* New York: Warner Books.

Lundin, W., and Lundin, K. 1993. *The healing manager.* San Francisco: Berrett-Koehler.

Maslow, A.H. 1965. *Eupsychian management.* Homewood, IL: Richard Irwin, Inc. and The Dorsey Press.

Maynard, H.B., and Mehrtens, S. 1993. *The fourth wave: Business in the twenty-first century.* Berrett-Koehler Publishers.

Ozaki, R. 1991. *Human capitalism.* New York: Penguin Books.

Rehfeld, J. 1994. *Alchemy of a leader.* New York: John Wiley & Sons.

Roberts, H., and Sergesketter, B. 1993. *Quality is personal.* New York: The Free Press.

Sashkin, M., and Kiser, K. 1991. *Total quality management.* Seabrook, MD:

Ducochon Press.

Scherkenbach, W.W. 1986. *The Deming route to quality and productivity.* Washington, DC: Ceepress Books.

Scholtes, P. 1997. Management is prediction and Competition in the organization: A house divided. (Available from Scholtes Seminars and Consulting.)

Semler, R. 1993. *Maverick.* New York: Warner Books.

Spears, L. 1995. *Reflections on leadership: How Robert K. Greenleaf's theory of servant-leadership influenced today's top management thinkers.* New York: John Wiley & Sons.

Sun-Tzu. *The art of war* (translated by Thomas Cleary). 1989. Boston: Shambala Publications.

Tannenbaum, R., and Schmidt, W. 1973. How to choose a leadership pattern. (Reprint #73311.) *Harvard Business Review,* May–June.

Tannenbaum, R., and Schmidt, W. 1968. *How to choose a leadership pattern: Organizational behavior and the practice of management.* Glenview, IL: Scott, Foresman & Co.

Walton, M. 1986. *The Deming management method.* Putnam, NY: Peregee.

Wheatley, M.J. 1992. *Leadership and the new science.* San Francisco: Barrett Koehler.

Wright, L., and Syme, M. 1996. *Corporate abuse.* Toronto: Key Porter Books.

Index

About the Author

Peter R. Scholtes is an internationally known author, lecturer, and consultant. From 1987 through 1993, he was an instructor sharing the platform with Dr. W. Edwards Deming. Mr. Scholtes' postgraduate education and early professional experience were in Organizational Development. He was one of the first to combine this discipline with the teachings of Dr. Deming.

Mr. Scholtes has consulted with more than 20 companies during the past 13 years, helping managers to apply the principles and methods of Quality, looking at work with the perspective of systems, statistical thinking, and teamwork.

Mr. Scholtes is the author of *The Team Handbook* that has sold nearly 800,000 copies. He has written award-winning articles on several Quality-related topics, especially with Dr. Deming's encouragement, on the controversial topic of performance appraisal: What's wrong with it and what to do instead. He is featured on over 12 videotaped presentations, and has been a keynote speaker at many international conferences in such places as London, Sydney, Moscow, and Rio de Janeiro. In March of 1995, *Quality Digest* recognized Mr. Scholtes as one of the 50 Quality leaders of this decade.